Leo Rosten's Giant Book of Laughter

A carnival of stories, anecdotes, true tales, and jokes: about Irishmen, Scotsmen, Englishmen, Jews; Frenchmen, Hispanics, Greeks; gurus and cuties and *kibitzers;* drunkards, shnorrers, lunatics, lords; doctors and brokers, scoundrels and shlemiels; geniuses, charlatans, psychiatrists, waiters; plus a gallimaufry of doggerel, limericks, boo-boos, graffiti, and typos and outlandish signs—a wayward treasury, collected and embroidered throughout a lifetime of delight.

Leo Rosten's Giant Book of Laughter

Bonanza Books
New York

The author wishes to acknowledge the following for their kind permission to reprint excerpts from their published materials in this book:

The JOYS OF YIDDISH, copyright ©1968 by Leo Rosten; THE 3:10 TO ANYWHERE, copyright ©1976 by Leo Rosten; and PASSIONS AND PREJUDICES, copyright ©1978 by Leo Rosten. All books written by Leo Rosten. All rights reserved. Used by permission of McGraw-Hill Book Company.

CAPTAIN NEWMAN, M.D. by Leo Rosten, copyright ©1958, 1961 by Leo Rosten. All rights reserved. Reprinted by arrangement with Bantam Books, Inc.

LEFT-HANDED DICTIONARY by Leonard L. Levinson, copyright ©1963 by Leonard L. Levinson. All rights reserved. Used by permission of Macmillan & Co.

HOORAY FOR YIDDISH! by Leo Rosten, copyright ©1982 by Leo Rosten. All rights reserved. Used by permission of Simon & Schuster, Inc.

Author's Note

The provenance of jokes, limericks, doggerel, puns, and wisecracks is notoriously difficult, and often quite impossible, to establish with any degree of confidence, much less accuracy. I have credited the originators of such material wherever possible.

Some uncredited items may be found, in their substance, if not in their wording, in such anthologies as THE READER'S DIGEST TREASURY OF WIT AND HUMOR (1958) or THE ENCYCLOPEDIA OF MODERN AMERICAN HUMOR by Bennett Cerf (1954), both vast collections which, at times, credit different people with the same items and sometimes credit no one at all. Therefore, I hereby offer an omnibus thanks and acknowledgment to the Reader's Digest Association and to Doubleday & Company, publishers of these respective anthologies.

This 1989 edition is published by Bonanza Books,
distributed by Crown Publishers, Inc.,
225 Park Avenue South, New York, New York 10003,
by arrangement with Crown Publishers, Inc.

Printed and Bound in the United States of America

Book design by Jacques Chazaud

Library of Congress Cataloging-in-Publication Data

Rosten, Leo Calvin, 1908–
Leo Rosten's giant book of laughter.
Reprint. Originally published: New York : Crown, c1985.
1. American wit and humor.   I. Title.
PN6162.R658   1989   818'.5202   88-35331
ISBN 0-517-67727-X
h g f e d c b

To
my wife,

ZIMI,

who makes it all possible

Contents

Leo Rosten's Giant Book of Laughter

"The real secret of communication? That's easy.
It's honesty. Absolute, irresistible honesty . . .
Once you learn to fake that,
you'll make a fortune."*

*The same is true of Actors (page 20).

Preface

The Strategy of Humor

"Humor is the affectionate communication of insight." I wrote this definition almost thirty years ago. It did not, so far as I know, cause wild cheering in the streets. I quote it now because I cannot improve upon it.

I also said that humor is "the chanciest of literary forms. It is surely not accidental that there are a thousand novelists, essayists, poets, journalists for one humorist."*

The first exposure of a child to formal humor (as distinguished from funny happenings) usually comes in the form of a riddle, such as: "What's black and white and red all over?" *My* first riddle, as fresh in my mind as when I heard it so many decades ago, was propounded by my father: "What is it that hangs on the wall, is green, wet—and whistles?"

I knit my brow and thought and thought. "I give up."

"A herring," said my father.

"A *herring?!*" I echoed. "A herring doesn't hang on the wall!"

"So hang it there."

"B-but a herring isn't *green!*" I protested.

"So paint it."

"B-but a herring isn't *wet!*"

"If it's just painted, it's still wet."

"But—" I summoned all my outrage, "—a *herring—does—not—whistle!*"

"Right," smiled my father. "I just put that in to make it hard."

The joke, in every culture, is the swiftest, surest trigger of laughter. A joke is a very short short-story, carefully structured, a very brief narrative designed to reach a comedic climax through skillful cues, deliberate miscues, and sudden surprise.

To *write* a joke is much more difficult than to tell one. Just consider the arsenal of props available to you when you tell a story: the calculated pause, the ironic inflection, the ingenuous smile, the warning frown, the accented adjective, the changes in pace—in accelerated rhythm or decelerated momentum. All of these devices serve to cue and control your listeners:

*Preface to *The Return of H*Y*M*A*N K*A*P*L*A*N*, 1959.

gestures, nods, smiles, cunning chuckles, grunts or murmurs, the gasp of affected astonishment, the moan of pretended dismay.

None of these is available to the writer of a joke. Each must be replaced by silent and nonvisual devices, devices that are far more subtle, and require far rarer skill, than the mimicry deployed by the raconteur. I, for one, find telling a story (or joke) child's play compared with writing one, for complex and frustrating road blocks impede the course of written narration. Yet the central stratagems of both forms are similar; both must use camouflage with creative cunning. What this entails is the disguising of purpose, the distribution of tantalizing but misleading "leads," the planting of totally deceptive expectations. All of these elements must combine to explode in the surprise of that laughter Hobbes called "sudden glory."

Consider the multitude of questions that surround so apparently routine a matter as where to place the mundane "he said." Suppose I intend to use the line "I do not think I'm ready for that." The wholly neutral expository phrase "he said" conveys varying overtones according to where I place it in the sentence:

> "I," he said, "do not think I'm ready for that."
> "I do not think," he said, "I'm ready for that."
> "I do not think I," he said, "am ready for that."
> "I do not think I'm ready," he said, "for that."
> "I do not think I'm ready for," he said, "that."
> "I do not think I'm ready for that," he said.

Suppose I am not satisfied with the flat "said" and search for a more evocative verb. Consider the tapestry of connotations, moods, implications I can weave by using "frowned . . . glared . . . chuckled . . . scoffed . . . murmured . . . laughed . . . blurted . . . gasped . . . shouted . . . groaned . . . pleaded . . . (etcetera)." Each verb injects an entirely different meaning (from amusement to menace to propitiation) into the line.

Ring Lardner made a gorgeous contribution to comedic technique when he coined the astonishing " 'Shut up!' he explained." You can manipulate readers' responses with similar incongruities:

> "The man is dead as a door-knob!" he hinted.
> "It's exactly five o'clock," she wondered.
> "Put down that ax!" he murmured.
> "I'm going to pull this trigger and blow your goddam brains out!" he implied.

A word of warning. Dangers attend the obvious overexcitation of prose. Dramatic verbs, if not used with rigorous restraint, may call the attention of the reader to the device, which can convert a smile into a sneer. Ernest Hemingway, of course, almost never used a synonym for "said," making the dialogue stand by itself, unaided by expository glosses. That two whole pages of unidentified dialogue might send many readers back to serialize the speakers, so to speak, in order to discover who was saying what and who was answering whom, did not seem to bother Hemingway in the least; it only confused his readers.

Because of all these mischievous ingredients, the tales in the pages that follow are of different length; they require different scaffolding and individual pacing. Some of my entries are only one or two lines long, since their humor is enhanced by the most unadorned telling; others are set in the form of unembroidered dialogue; still others take a whole page; and some I have extended beyond that, with a multitude of "delaying" detail, to build up to a payoff that becomes all the more risible because it is so long deferred.

The first true joke I ever heard still seems to me a marvel of technique:

> Three cross-eyed prisoners stood before a cross-eyed judge. He glared at the first prisoner. "What's your name?"
> "Eli Krantz," said the second prisoner.
> "I wasn't talking to you!" snapped the judge.
> "I didn't *say* anything!" cried the third prisoner.*

Perhaps the best way to drive home my point is through illustration. Consider the following ways of ruining the same joke:

Version 1

> Two friends, Nelly Jenkins and Marie Duval, who had been to high school together in New Rochelle, from which they both came, happened to run into each other in New York, on Park Avenue, one very hot summer day in July.
> "Why, Nelly Jenkins!" cried Marie. "Imagine meeting you here!"
> Nelly Jenkins laughed, "Long time no see."
> "You can say *that* again," replied Marie Duval.
> "What's new?" asked Nelly.
> "What's new," replied Marie, with a mischievous glance, "is that I have just come from Dr. Herman Sorenson's office—"
> "Dr. Herman Sorenson, the gyne*co*logist?!" exclaimed Nelly knowingly.
> "That is right," confirmed Marie.
> "I suppose you went to Dr. Sorenson for your annual checkup?" suggested Nelly in a friendly, although familiar, manner.
> "Oh, no," chuckled Marie. "I had my *regular* complete medical examination last December—"
> "But this is July," observed Nelly, "and that's not a year from last December—"
> "I *know*," affirmed Marie, "but you see, it just so happens that I got *pregnant* last February—"

*This joke, like several others in this Preface, appears later in the text in different forms.

"Pregnant?!" echoed Nelly, in astonishment, "Oh, my. That *is* a true surprise. What wonderful news! Marie, that's absolutely fantastic! I can't say that I actually envy you—my *God,* the number of diapers alone, and the heat rashes, and the orthodontist's bills—!"

"I know. What you say is certainly all true," agreed Marie seriously. "But—Nelly, can you keep a secret? A very important secret?!"

"Just you try me!" challenged Nelly.

Breathlessly, Marie confided: "Dr. Sorenson said—*I may be carrying triplets!*"

"Triplets!" gasped Nelly. "Why, Marie Duval, that is fan*tas*tic! I never before knew *any*one who has had triplets! Do you?"

"Oh, no," huffed Marie. "I *heard*—but that was years ago—that Sally Norton's cousin, Eileen, who lives in Ohio, had triplets . . ."

"I don't know Sally Norton," Nelly disclosed.

"Well, I only *heard* she did. . . . In fact, triplets are very *unusual,* the doctor told me," added Marie.

"I can imagine!" chuckled Nelly.

"In fact," gloated Marie, "he said that triplets happen once every—*three million times!*"

"My *God!*" shouted Nelly. "Marie—"

(Punch line appears below)

Version 2

Two women met on Fifth Avenue. "Guess what," hinted the first.

"I give up," retorted the second.

"I am pregnant."

"Preg . . . Golly! Gosh! Gee whiz—that's wonderful!" ventured the first woman. "Congratulations!"

"Thank you. And what's even more remarkable," smiled the pregnant female, "is that my obstetrician tells me there is a good chance that I will have—triplets!"

"Trip . . . oh, my *God!*" gasped the second woman. "You must be beside yourself—but there I go, carrying on. How *do* you feel about having triplets?"

"I'm still knocked for a loop," confessed the mother-to-be. "Do you realize, according to my obstetrician, the statistical odds on having triplets are one in—*three million!*"

"Lands sakes alive! Tell me—"

(Punch line appears below)

Version 3

Two women met in the Bronx. "Hello, Sara," said the first. "Say—you've gotten pretty fat! Or are you pregnant?"

"I certainly am, Cora!"

"Congratulations! That's actually wonderful!"

"What is even more wonderful," said the mother-to-be, "is that I—it looks like I'm going to have triplets!"

"Triplets!" gasped Cora.

"That's what my obstetrician told me!" said the mother-to-be. "Do you realize that, according to the statistics, the odds on having triplets are one in three million!"

"Lands sakes alive! Tell me, dear—"

(Punch line appears in version 4)

Version 4

ELLEN: "I'm going to have triplets!"

BLANCHE: "Congratulations!"

ELLEN: "My doctor tells me that triplets happen once every three million times!"

BLANCHE: "My *God*, Ellen! When did you find the time to do the housework?"

The same point must be made about aphorisms, epigrams, and one-liners.

1. He has such dreadful luck that he burns a cigarette hole in the jacket of a suit which has an extra pair of trousers.

2. He's the kind of *shlemiel* who buys a suit with two pairs of pants—and burns a hole in the jacket.

1. Human beings say "Let bygones be bygones," but they don't really mean it.

2. No one ever forgets where he buried the hatchet.

1. Sex is very enjoyable, but humorless.

2. Sex is the most fun you can have without laughing.

Consider the universe of wit and impact that separates the following:

Version 1 A bore is a person who when he leaves a party in a living room makes the room feel that instead of containing one less person it feels like it contains one more.

Version 2 A bore is someone who, upon leaving a room, makes you feel that someone *fascinating* just walked in.

Version 1   A diplomat sends a woman a telegram that reads "Happy Birthday"—but not "Happy Fifty-second Birthday."

Version 2   A diplomat never forgets a woman's birthday, and never remembers her age.

The funny story is a matchless teaching device. (The rabbis of old, in the
Talmud, instruct a teacher always to begin a lesson with something amusing.) What better way is there to convey the commanding influence of
"context," say, than in the marvelous anecdote about the artist and the
model he is painting in the nude (page 38)? What more vivid way is there
of describing paranoia than with the tale of the man who complains to the
psychiatrist that for reasons he simply cannot understand people regard him
as crazy (page 407)? What more crushing example of a "put-down" do you
know than the one about the *mohel*'s retort to the Englishman who wants
his watch fixed (page 435)? What neater example of the Freudian slip can
you concoct than the telegram on page 203?

The japeries that ignite *my* most grateful laughter are those which are
built upon so conventional and matter-of-fact a framework that their climax
is completely unexpected:

"Stella, is it true that you're going to have a baby?"
"Absolutely."
"How wonderful! Are you hoping for a boy or a girl?"

Intercession: How many thousands of times has any of us, during a lifetime,
heard this question asked of a mother or father? But until now has any of us
heard this delicious reply:

"Certainly."

It grieves me to inform you that most joke books are just not funny; and
very few are very funny. Most collections intended to provoke laughter are
simply tiresome. Often, they are in bad taste. Nearly always, they display an
irritating ineptitude applied to exhausted jocularities. Most joke books are
abominably *written*.

Humor can be crippled by the tiniest insufficiency—or excess. The
rhythm ("timing") of a joke or anecdote dictates its effectiveness. A joke
must tantalize without annoying; where the prolonging of narrative tension
is demanded, a joke must "pad" without boring; it must defer without
frustrating; it must reward the reader (or listener) with a crowning climax
that is exact, immediate, and absolutely clear. The punch line of any joke is
designed to ignite the cord, carefully prepared, that explodes the bomb of
laughter; and that laughter offers the reward of catharsis: a joyous revela-

tion that justifies all the ploys deployed to maximize the power of a sudden, always surprising climax.

I hope you are not foolish enough to consider humor insignificant and dismiss jokes as "trivia." The laughter of a people can be as illuminating as its patterns of pride, guilt, and shame. I think humor is an isotope that locates the values of a culture. The japery of a nation runs up and down the scale of its scorn and its admiration, its approval or contempt.

Any collection of ethnic jokes is, perforce, a parade of its heroes, patsies, wise men, clowns. The particular genius, or inherent limitations, of any group beholden to the same preferences and taboos is as much revealed by a sampling of its humor as by a sampling of its IQs, indeed more so, I submit, since the IQ protocol tests only a certain kind of intelligence; it reveals nothing about humor, judgment, affability. God preserve us from those who have no sense of humor, for they are the scourges of humankind.

Now, before we set forth on our revels, permit me to remind you of the admirable words of A. P. Herbert:

> Don't stop me if you've heard this one before. There is no reason why a joke should not be appreciated more than once. Imagine how little good music there would be if, for example, a conductor refused to play Beethoven's Fifth Symphony on the ground that his audience might have heard it before.

Accents

Perhaps because I was raised within a sea of exotic accents, in a neighborhood surrounded by Poles, Irishmen, Germans, Bohemians, Ukrainians, Italians, Greeks, I was enchanted early on by the surprising consequences of English as spoken by the foreign-born—especially English as transformed by Jews from Russia, Poland, Lithuania, Latvia, Hungary, Romania, Austria, Germany, Egypt, Palestine. . . . Accents added a mischievous dimension—of color and humor—to our noble tongue. I still think dialect is one of the most endearing aspects of human communication.

L. R.

A belle from Alabama, visiting Philadelphia, went into a large stationery store and said, "Ah'd like to buy some rotten pepper, pu-leeze."
The clerk said, "We don't sell pepper, ma'am. Try the supermarket."
"Thank y'all." The belle started out.
"Eh—miss!" called the clerk. "Can you tell me why you want *rotten* pepper?"
"Why shaw," smiled the southern peach. "It's fo' rotten letters—t' m' folks in Mobile."

Wu Chan owned a laundry next to the New Acropolis, where Nick Matsoutas was the chef. Matsoutas, it so happened, made superb spareribs and fried rice—which is what Wu ordered every day. And every day Nick Matsoutas heaved with laughter as Wu said, "Spallibs—and flied lice, prease."
"Why you always raugh?" asked Wu one day.
"Because of the way you pronounce 'spareribs' and 'fried rice,' you crazy Chinaman. Why don't you hire some American kid to teach you how to pronounce English?!"
A month later, Wu entered the New Acropolis. In a firm, confident tone, he declaimed, "One order of spareribs, please, with fried rice."
Nick's jaw dropped. "I can't believe it! What did you say?"
"You heard *exactly* what I said," sneered Wu, "you rousy, clazy Gleek!"

Scene: New Orleans

"Like mah new frock, Melanie?"

"Oh, *yis*, Ah do."

"Sho' nuff?"

"It sho' does!"

Abe Tarshow was returning to Manhattan for a visit. In Penn Station, an old friend, Myron Kishner, greeted him: "Abe! For goodness *sake!* Where in the world have you been?"

"Hollo, Myron! Mine goodness, it's nice to see you."

"Abe, you look like a million! Tanned, trim, no fat—"

"It's this new life. For a year now, me and my Sonya been living in the country."

"In the *country?*" Myron Kishner clucked several times. "I never would of taken you for a country type, Abe."

"Me nider."

"Tell me, was the adjustment hard?"

"At foist, we were lonesome. But now, we got a whole bunch friends. . . ."

"But what about the work? All the chores? Day in, day out, doesn't a house in the country just wear you out?"

"True, true," sighed Abe. "It *was* hard. Then everyt'ing changed—as soon as I got mineself a paramour."

"You? Abe?" Myron giggled. "A *paramour?*"

"Absolutely."

"But, Abe . . . does Sonya know?"

"Uf cawss she knows!"

"And Abe—I don't mean to stick my nose in—but doesn't Sonya *mind?*"

"Mind?" Abe echoed. "Why should she care *how* I cut the grass?"

WELSH ROMANCE

Lloyd Llowell llooked at Llana llonginglly. "Llana, I llove you!"

"I llove you, Lloyd."

"I'd llike to kiss you!" Lloyd bllurted.

"Oh. Llets!"

Sllowlly, their llips met.

It was their first kiss—and their llast, because Lloyd was drafted the next morning. He was killled in an artilllery drilll on Llong Islland.

Old Zeke Lumpkin and his wife were sitting on the porch of their old home, on the edge of the Pumpkin Patch cemetery, rocking back and forth in their chairs. The moonlight bathed the scene in silver.

"Yeah, maw," sighed Zeke, "it's been a long life—and, everythin' considered—a purty good one . . ."

"I sure like settin' here with you, Zeke," sighed his wife. "Lookin' out
over the old cemetery . . . where our own two daughters are layin'. . . ."

"Yup," said Zeke. "Sometimes I wish they wuz dead."

❧

To Mr. Solomon Duvno, who was in the hospital after an operation,
came Ellis Twersky, secretary of their synagogue. "Sol," said Ellis, "I am
bringing you the good vishes from our board—that you should get vell soon,
comm back to the congregation, and live to be a hondred and tan years
old—at least!"

"Oh, that's nice," said Duvno. "Vary nice."

"*Nice?* Listen, Sol. That vasn't just a simple 'get-better and goom-bye'
from the board; it vas an official *rasolution*—"

"My!"

"—pessed by a vote of fourtin to saven!"

❧

José Castanado, newly arrived in London, eagerly got on the bus, raced
up the stairs to the upper deck—and within a moment hurtled down the
stairs, ashen.

The conductor said, "Is anything wrong, sir?"

"Ees no driver up zere!" cried Castanado.

❧

Scene: Toodle's Club, Mayfair, London

"Chadwick, old boy," said Lord Effingham, "may I have a word with
you?"

"Of course, old man," said Chadwick.

"Chadwick, old bean, I *do* hate to embarrass you, but I'm shaw you'll
understand . . ."

"My dear Lord Effingham, fire away."

The tenth earl cleared his throat. "Well, then . . . I *say*, Chadwick . . . did
you sleep with my wife last night?"

"Not a wink, old sock. Not a wink!"

Effingham beamed, "Awfully decent of you, old chap. *Aw*fully decent."

❧

The Reverend Selkirk from Aberdeen was visiting the Holy Land. He was
especially moved by the Wailing Wall, where a long line of men, draped in
prayer shawls, holding small prayer books, were swaying back and forth,
murmuring their ancient prayers. Then the Reverend Selkirk noticed a man

far from all the praying ones, standing alone before the wall. He had no prayer shawl, no prayer book; he was not swaying back and forth. Indeed, he was not praying at all, it seemed; he stood erect and made gestures. . . .

The Reverend Selkirk walked over. "*Shalom*, friend. I dinna mean to be intrudin' . . . D'ye come here often, then?"

The figure turned. "*A* very day! Two o'clock, exactly, I am in this same place—for toity-vun years awready!"

"Och, mon! Therty-one years, is it? And how long d'ya pray?"

"Pray?" the Jew echoed. "Who prays? I'm not praying. I talk to God, blessed be His name. I esk His advice."

"Ay . . ." The reverend hesitated. "I'm nae wantin' to pry, friend, but—what type o' advice?"

"All types. What should Israel do about Jordan? Who I should vote for? How I can convince my wife we should move to a smaller apartment? Should I let our daughter marry that no-good Shmuel Yavno?"

"My! . . . An' what does the good Lord tell you?"

"Ha!" the Jew snorted. "Nothing! In toity-vun years—not vun void! . . . Mister, it's like talking to a *vall!*"

Two Texans met in a hotel lobby in Fort Worth.

"Hiya, Mert."

"Hiya, Arkey."

"Ha y' folks?"

"Maghty fine, maghty fine. . . . Your'n?"

"Couldn't be better. . . . Say, Mert, Ah hear you hit another lalapalooza of a gusher . . ."

"Yup."

"And I hear y' got y'self a spankin' new hobby."

"Right. Ah jist got tard of them vintage auto*mo*biles."

"What ez y'r new fancy?"

"Oh, Ah collect miniatures."

"Minitcheers? Ha come you ever fell into a funny pastime like that?"

"Well, Arky, it began with my buyin' l'il ole Rhode Island . . ."

Pedro, walking his dog, met Jaime, who was walking his. "Eh, Jaime," said Pedro, "that ees some *beau*'ful chihuahua!"

Jaime grinned. "*Gracias.* I got heem for my wife."

Sighed Pedro, "I weesh I could make a deal lika that."

They were snuggled in a corner of the Inverloch Pub, Glasgow, were Fergus and Lorna, and Fergus whispered, "Lorna . . . oh, bonnie, bonnie lass. . . . Drinkin' brings out all yorr beauty. . . ."

"But Fergus," said Lorna, "I ha' nae been drinkin'. . . ."
"Ay, Lorna—but Oy have."

"Operator? Collect call, please. Huh? My name? Frank Zyblinczki. . . .
Spell it? 'Z-y-b-l-' What? *First* letter? I give it to you so you don't make
mistake. 'A-b-c-d-e-f-g-h-i-j-k-l-m-n-o-p-q-r-s-t-u-v-w-x-y-z. Z.' Did you
heard that? . . . Hello? Operator, where *are* you?"

Scene: Pullman Sleeping Car
Time: Morning

PASSENGER:	Porter! Porter!
PORTER:	Yas, suh?
PASSENGER:	Look at the shoes you returned to me!
PORTER:	Ain't they shined good?
PASSENGER:	One shoe is black, the other's brown!
PORTER:	Ain't that somethin', boss? Thass the *second* time this morn-in' thass happened!

Stockholm: Borggren Department Store
Time: 5:55 P.M.

Throughout the store, on every floor, the ringing of a bell is heard.

VOICE (*over loudspeaker*):	Five minutes to closing. . . . All shoppers, please note: store closes at six.
GUARD (*at door*):	Olie. Hey, Olie.
SECOND GUARD:	Ay?
FIRST GUARD:	Olie, it's no good.
SECOND GUARD:	What's no good?
FIRST GUARD:	Bell. Ring, ring, ring. Every night the same. And still, every night, *some* dummy is the last one out.

The learned Viennese healer, Dr. Leopold Lochmacher, said to his patient, "Mrs. Rhinebeck, zis terror you feel about lightning and t'under. . . .
Zese are natural phenomena. Zey are not directed against *you*. Ze next time
zere is a bad storm, and you begin to shake and shiver, do—do like *I* do."

"What," quavered Mrs. Rhinebeck, "do you do, doctor?"

"Ze moment I detect a storm, I crawl unter ze bed, put pillows over ze
ears, and cry until zat goddam trauma goes avay!"

"James P. Jordan," said the job applicant.

"Age?" asked Mrs. Flournoy.

"Forty-two."

"Mr. Jordan," asked Mrs. Flournoy, "do you—drink?"

"Me? Never."

"Do you smoke?"

"No, ma'am!"

"And what is the general state of your health?"

"I've not been one day in bed in all of my years. You might say I am blessed by the Lord with perfect health."

Mrs. Flournoy leaned back in her chair. "Well, Mr. Jordan, you have *spotless* qualifications. Speaking frankly, and in complete confidence, can you think of any—blemishes on your record?"

"In complete confidence, ma'am?"

"Of course."

James P. Jordan leaned forward and whispered, "The naked truth is—I just *love* to lie."

THE MAN WHO COULD SPEAK
EIGHT FISH DIALECTS

Scene: Gluckstern's Supreme Seafood

The waiter, a veteran fish-server of thirty years' standing, served "To-day's Special" with a flourish to a meek little man, a customer new to the piscatorial fare for which Gluckstern's Supreme was famed. "So enjoy," said the waiter, starting off—when he stopped short; for the meek little man had leaned over the plate, close to the flounder, and was whispering! To the fish!

The waiter exclaimed, "Mister—!"

But the diner held up a silencing hand, now turned his *ear* close to the flounder, listened, nodded, turned to whisper something to the fish again, then listened again. . . .

The waiter could contain himself no longer. "*Mister!* Vhat are you *do*ing?!"

"I am talking mit de fish."

"You talk to *fish?!*"

"Soitinly. I know eight fish dialects. I talk Flonder, Carp, Selmon, Pike, Vhitefish—"

"B-but what do you talk to them *about?*" the waiter goggled.

The little man said, "Vell, take dis little flonder. Ven you put him in front of me, I leaned over and said, nice, polite, 'Hollo dere, little flonder. How do you feel?' He said, 'So-so.' So I esked, 'Fisheleh, vhere do you come from?'

So he said, 'Peconic Bay.' So I esked, '*Nu*, how is everyt'ing in Peconic's Bay?' So he looked me straight in the eye, cold, and said, 'How should *I* know? It's been *years* since I vas dere!' "

Sandy Straith beheld his friend, Fergus Fitch, rushing down the street, heaving and panting and mopping his brow. "Fergus, Fergus!" sang out Sandy. "Is th' world coomin' t' end, mon? Y're as red as fire an' drippin' o' sweat!"

"Aye," gasped Fergus. "All morning I am roonin' this way—"

"Bu' *why*, mon?"

"B'cause I been tryin' t' get *somethin'* for th' wife!"

Sandy shook his head in sympathy. "Hoot, mon. C'd y' nae get *one* offer?!"

Mr. Fortescue, tossing and turning in an upper berth, could not get to sleep because, from the berth below, came a woman's mournful muttering. "*Oy* . . . am I toisty. . . . *Oy* . . . am I toisty. . . ."

On and on went the lament, until Mr. Fortescue got out, crawled down the ladder, padded the length of the Pullman car, filled two paper cups with water, brought them back, and handed them through the curtains to the passenger in the lower berth. "Madam, here. Water!"

"God bless you, mister! Thank you . . ."

Fortescue crawled back into his berth. He was on the very edge of somnolence when, from below, came the suspiration: "*Oy* . . . vas I toisty. . . ."

The professor of philosophy, riding the Amtrak to Boston, asked the Pullman porter, "How long have you been working on the railroad?"

"Oh," the porter sighed, "gettin' on t' fo-ty years, Ah reckon."

"Tell me, have you found, as some people say, that the rich usually give measly tips, and the poor are much more generous?"

The porter took a moment before answering, "Thass true, suh. On account de rich folk don't want *no*body to know they'se rich, an' de po' folk don't want nobody to know they'se po'."

At dinner, Señor Tilliera, a visitor from Brazil, said, "My wife ees a wonderful woman. We are very, very hoppy, except for thees one thing: we hav no children." He sighed. "My wife ees—unbearable."

Tilliera saw the others glance at each other and hastened to correct himself. "What I mean: she ees inconceivable." And when *this* brought amused exchanges, he exclaimed, "Ah, no, no! My wife ees impregnable!"

"Yumpin Yiminy!" exclaimed Thors. "That Bjorn—he has some memory!"

"Eh?"

"Like blotter!"

"That is good."

"Why 'good'?"

"Blotter soak up everything!"

"Aye, Osvald: backvard!"

At a meeting of the Parent-Teacher Association in Rego Park, the chairperson, Mrs. Leona Potenik, said, "—And now we come to the most important part of our meeting: the suggestion, from the board of trustees, that the salaries of our teachers should be adjusted entirely on a merit basis. Not length of service, age, degrees in education. Only merit. . . . Who would like to lead off the discussion?"

Up stood Mrs. Rabinov.

"Yes, Mrs. Rabinov?"

"Vat I have to say is straight, plain, and simple," said Mrs. Rabinov. "Salary shouldn't matter if teachers are single *or* merit. Treat them just the same."

Moke Scrogg's battered, fenderless, overladen jalopy, bearing Oklahoma license plates, chugged up the George Washington Bridge. At the toll gate, Moke said to the attendant, "Howdy."

"A dollar and a quarter," said the attendant.

Moke pushed back his weather-beaten hat, took the match from between his lips, and said, "Giss Ah'll take et."

Little Italy: New York

Dr. Parelli examined Mr. Mavocci's complete record—cardiogram, pulse rate, X-rays, blood count. . . . "Mavocci, you no *seek.* But is not so good you *condition!*"

"What I should do?" anxiously asked Mavocci.

"What you hava to do is changa—changa whola way life. Ata you age, no more smoke, no more drink, no *dissiparsi* with the woman. . . . If you do alla thees—will be besta t'ing in world for you!"

Luca Mavocci had turned paler and paler. And when Dr. Parelli finished his disheartening litany, Mavocci croaked, "*Dottore* . . . what is *nexta* best t'ing in world?"

On a bench on the shore of a large lake in Pennsylvania, two old Germans, Oskar Grossheim and Heinrich Sundermann, were sitting, staring at a motorboat speeding across the blue water with a beautiful girl, in a bathing suit, speeding close behind on her water skis.

After watching this for some time, the motorboat skimming around the perimeter of the lake, then crossing and crisscrossing back and forth, Sundermann rose. "*Ach*, Oskar!" He wrinkled his nose in disgust. "Ve may already leaf zis zpot."

"Vas is it? Vhy?"

"Vhy?" repeated Heinrich. "I tell you vhy, Oskar: zere is no more use to vaiting; zat girl vill never ketch him!"

Abner Gormitsky, having made a good deal of money in his leather works, was considering his wife's suggestion that they move from Central Park West to one of the tonier parts of Long Island. "—and Abner, if we do that, I think we ought to change our name . . ."

After some weeks, the Abner Gormitskys became the Alexander Gormans, and they bought a fine mansion in Oyster Bay and furnished it with antiques. Their friendliness made friends for them easily, and their hospitality was so gracious, their cuisine so excellent, that the Gormans soon shone on the social scene. Indeed, they were invited to become members of the emphatically non-Jewish St. Andrew's Country Club.

The trustees gave a huge welcoming dinner at the club for the newly elected St. Andrewians; four couples: the Townsend Fillmores, the Clyde Watson-Setons, the Harley Hammonds, and the Alexander Gormans.

And there, at the head table, the liveried servant serving Mrs. Gorman spilled an entire bowl of St. Germain soup in her lap.

"*Oy!*" cried Mrs. Gorman—but swiftly added, "—whatever *that* means!"

"Now what, Mrs. Gallagher, can I do t' help you in y're woes?" said Father O'Grady. "I came the minute I heerd y' was ailin'. . . ."

"Ailin', is it, father?" sighed Mrs. Gallagher. "Sure an' it's terrible *sufferin'*, I am."

"Did y' thin go to hospital?"

"No—"

"See Dr. Brannigan?"

"Tomorrow, maybe—unless, the saints be praised, I'm recoverin'. . . ."

"From *what*, dear Mrs. Gallagher? Pray tell me. . . ."

"It's burnin' up with pain, I am—in me head, father! A headache—God presairve me—such as I never before did have. And my back—full of hot needles, it is. Even worse, as Saint Joseph is me patron, than my pore, pore stomach. And my eyesight! Father O'Grady—'tis not fit for a blind bat, it isn't. Why, me sight is scarce better than m' hearin', which, to tell the bare truth of it, is almost entirely gone. Plus—my feet! Oh, father, my arches—flat as pancakes they are—not to mention the bunions . . ." On and on and on went Mrs. Gallagher, barely pausing for breath, until, after ten uninterrupted minutes, she suddenly stopped, sat erect, and broke into a wide smile. "Father O'Grady, sure and a miracle from heaven has struck me! Me fearful headache, that terrible monster of a headache that began all the sorrows—the headache has disappeared!"

"No, no, Mrs. Gallagher," sighed Father O'Grady, "it has not. Now *I* have it."

Scene: Grocery Store

"Are you the owner here?" asked Mrs. Pozener.

"I am the owner here," said Mrs. Kadinsky.

"So—eh—how much is this"—Mrs. Pozener pointed to a plump pickle in a tray on the counter—"pickle here?"

"That pickle is a nickel," said Mrs. Kadinsky.

"A *nickel* for this pickle?" Mrs. Pozener sniffed. She pointed to another, smaller pickle. "So—how much is that pickeleh?"

"That pickeleh," said Mrs. Kadinsky, "is a nickeleh."

MRS. ORLANDO: Hey, Carlotta! What you do? Almost I no reco'nizin' you! You grow seex inches ina one week? Or—eh!—you wearin' a weeg?!

MRS. SALAZAR: *Sí.*

MRS. ORLANDO: Imagine! Nobody could guess.

On Purim eve, finding himself in Tokyo on business, Mr. Rubinoff asked the Japanese hotel clerk: "Excuse me. Would you happen to know if there is a synagogue—here—in Tokyo?"

"Synagogue?" replied the clerk. "Ah, so. *Is* synagogue. Reave hotel—ralk down street two brocks, turn reft—banzai!—is synagogue."

So Mr. Rubinoff left the hotel, walked two blocks, turned left, and there—lo and behold! a Star of David was on a door, and under it a small sign:

CONSERVATIVE SYNAGOGUE
Michio Myako, Rabbi

Mr. Rubinoff entered. It was indeed a synagogue. The rabbi, the cantor, all the worshipers were Japanese. The Purim services had begun, and Mr. Rubinoff happily joined in.

When the services were over, he went up to the rabbi and said, "Rabbi, I am from America. I just want to tell you how happy I was to be here tonight."

The Japanese rabbi beamed. "Is honor! . . . But excuse, prease; you a Jew?"

"Certainly."

"That's funny," said the rabbi. "You don't rook Jewish."

Scene: Yorkville, New York City

Dr. Schapentaur adjusted his head-mirror, turned off the overhead light, and directed the beam of a small flashlight into the left eye of Christian Jorgen . . . then into the right eye. . . . "Herr Yorgen," said the doctor, "I see nozzing wrong. . . . How long you said you are seeing green spots in front your eyes?"

"Six-saven monz, Herr Doktor."

"Did you go to ophthalmologist?"

"No, doktor."

"Optometrist?"

"Alzo no."

"Vell, Herr Yorgen, haf you seen any ozer doktor?"

"No. Only zose green spots."

"Mrs. Smolinsky," said the doctor earnestly, removing the stethoscope from his ears, "when did you last have a complete physical examination?"

"Must be . . . let's see . . ." Mrs. Smolinsky screwed up one eye "so long ago, I dun't even remember."

"A year ago, five years ago?" the doctor insisted.

"Could be fife . . ."

"Mrs. Smolinsky, how many doctors have treated you—"

"Not vun!" exclaimed Mrs. Smolinsky. "I alvays pay!"

"Well now, Mrs. MacLiammor, are y' feelin' fit?"

"Oh, no, doctor. It's not feelin' fit, I am."

"Are ye thin sufferin' pains, Mrs. MacLiammor?"

"No pains neither, doctor. I just ain't t'right, I'm not."

"Well, do ye have a tech o' melancholia?"

"Melan—" Mrs. MacLiammor stopped. "T' be tellin' ye the truth, Dr. Cohalen, if I was feelin' that good—would I be here now?"

See also **English Language, Freudian Slips, Goldwyniana, Jews, Just Jokes, Languages: Pitfalls**

Actors

ACTING

The most important thing in acting, the one crucial factor is *honesty.* Absolute honesty . . . Once you learn to fake that, it's a cinch.

John Wayne demonstrating facial isometrics, based on the technique of Calvin Coolidge.

HARVARD LAMPOON

ACTOR

The eternal triangle: an actor, his wife, and himself.

A well-known actor met a friend on Sunset Boulevard. "Larry! How wonderful to run into you! Did you hear about the sensation my latest film is causing? Such reviews I've never seen in all my years on stage and screen. One critic said I'm sure to get an Oscar. Two directors said my performance will rank with—but forgive me, Larry. Here I go on rattling all about myself, and not a *word* about you. . . . Tell me, Larry, how did *you* like the film?"

An actor of more than ordinary vanity asked a friend, "I sometimes wonder if my fans—you know how they admire my pictures—will still love me after my career—well, begins to go downhill?"

"Of *course* they do," said the friend.

Modesty: The artifice of actors, similar to passion in a call girl.

JACKIE GLEASON

See also **Hollywood, Reviews of Note**

Adam and Eve

Eve (to Adam): After we eat the apple, Adam, we're going to do *what*?!

"No doubt about it, *tovarich*. No doubt at all: Adam and Eve were Communists."

"Who said such a thing? Not Marx. Not Lenin."

"Adam and Eve *had* to be Communists!"

"Why?"

"They didn't have shoes, they didn't have clothes, they ate nothing but one apple—"

"So, food was scarce."

"—and they thought they were in Paradise!"

Eve (to Adam): What do you mean, the boys don't look like you?!

RED BUTTONS

Adam and Eve had many advantages, but the principal one was that they escaped teething.

MARK TWAIN

Advertisements

Note: Anyone who reads advertisements as a hobby, as my wife does, is certain to get an interesting (albeit curious) view of the economy, professions, unemployment, and any number of other matters. Here are some dandy examples.

AUTOMATIC BLANKET
Ensure sound sleep with one of our
authorized dealers.

BED FOR SALE
Four-poster, over 100 years old.
Perfect for antique lover.

Send no money. You will be bilked later.

FINE FURNITURE
At sensible prices. Antique, Colonial,
and Temporary.

TO ALL OUR PATRONS
This week, the Saturday matinee will be
held on Tuesday instead of Thursday.

Testimonial in advertisement

"I used your soap two years ago and have not used another since then."

NOTICE

GNANASAMUNTHAMURTHI NAICHER intends to change his name to Gnanasamunthamurthi Moodley, reports the government *Gazette* in Durban (India).

"You can fool some of the people all the time, and all the people some of the time, but you can't fool all the people all the time." That is the idea on which our business has been built up.

Rev. Jarvis has spoken in the largest Baptist churches in America. To miss hearing him will be the chance of a lifetime!

Expert Stenographer

Wants work at home. Anything awful considered.

GIVE US YOUR DIRTY CLOTHES
Ladies! If you drive by our new launderette and drop off your clothes, you will receive very swift attention!

"Do you think advertising gets results fast?"
"You bet I do."
"Can you prove that?"
"Sure. On a Tuesday, one of my clients advertised for a night watchman. That night his safe was blown open."

ROOM WANTED

Young, sentimental, loving male. Loves to play. Wants Room and Board with loving female. Cannot pay rent, but offers true love, constant company, and 24-hour protection. Will serve as escort to and from classes if desired. Will keep you warm all night long. Allows you complete freedom to date others. Call EG 4-6627.

DO NOT CALL unless you are truly interested in giving a home to this adorable puppy.

URGENTLY WANTED:
BY MACHINE TOOL FACTORY.
Male parts handlers.
Box 132

"Bathing suit, 50% off" turns out to be topless, and "Simple, Elegant Coat-hanger" turns out to be a nail.

DAVID FROST and ANTONY JAY

Virginia Beach
Comfortable apartments. Short walk
to beach. Daily or Weekly. Attractive germs.

WHITLEY ACADEMY
In beautiful Vermont. Coeducational.
Special openings for boys.

The strike committee met in a bra near the factory, a locale which created more drinking than discussion.

Ad in Variety

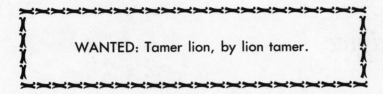

WANTED: Tamer lion, by lion tamer.

LIFE AND DEATH MATTER
Important Notice: If you are one of the hundreds
of parachuting enthusiasts who bought our course
entitled *Easy Sky Diving in One Fell Swoop,*
please make the following correction:
On page 8, line 7, change "state zip code"
to "pull rip cord."

See also Applications, Bloopers, Conversations I Cannot Forget, Graffiti, Headlines That Haunt Me, Movie Marquees, News Items That Haunt Me, Signs

Advice

When a man comes to me for advice, I find out the kind of advice he wants, and give it to him.

JOSH BILLINGS

THE SIX COMMANDMENTS OF SATCHEL PAIGE

1. Avoid fried food, which angers the blood.
2. When your stomach disputes you, lay down and pacify it with cool thoughts.
3. Go light on the vices, like carryin'-on at night in Society, 'cause the social ramble ain't restful.
4. Avoid running at all times.
5. Keep your juices flowin' by janglin' gently as you move around.
6. Never look back: something might be gainin' on you.

The only thing to do with good advice is pass it on; it is never of any use to oneself.

OSCAR WILDE

Always do right; this will gratify some people and astonish the rest.

MARK TWAIN

Never buy something you don't want merely because it is expensive.

OSCAR WILDE

One raw, rainy night, a desperate man was about to jump into the East River—when Patrolman Mylan O'Shaughnessy ran toward him. "Don't! No! Stop!"

"Stay back!" cried the man. "Stay *back!*"

"Okay, okay," said O'Shaughnessy. "But why—*why*, just tell me—should a foyne-lookin' man like you aim on takin' his own life?!"

"I don't want to live! My wife has betrayed me with my best friend! My son is in prison! My business is bankrupt—"

"Oh, man, it's a sad, sad tale you tell," said Patrolman O'Shaughnessy.

"It's true! Every word!"

O'Shaughnessy nodded. "But look at it a different way, now. Supposin' you jump—down, down, a good twelve feet it is into that dark, cold water. I—in duty-bound—must jump in after you. That I'll do, man. But—I *can't swim!* Think of that! I have a mother, my dear wife Rosie, an infant pair o' darlin' twins . . . And I would drown, *drown*. Sir, would you want such a terrible deed on your conscience? Robbin' a mother of her son, a wife of her husband, a darlin' pair of baby twins of their lovin' father?! . . . I cannot believe you would be so *selfish*, sir. No, no . . . Pray, put the very thought out of your mind. Go home. Things will look brighter. And if they don't, man, well, in the peace and comfort of your own home, hang yourself."

Gretchen Plattenring, a sturdy, pleasant Swiss maiden, had been taking flute lessons since she was a child. Her idol was the celebrated flautist Pierre Bronteaux.

When the great Bronteaux arrived in Zurich for a series of concerts, Gretchen summoned up enough nerve to write him.

```
Dear Maestro:

    Ever since I am small girl, you are my
idol. I hear your every recording. I dream
of also playing flute for you—and receiv-
ing honest opinion. That will mean whole
world to me!
    To answer, please—by phone 72-60, or to
mail address below.

                    Your admirer
                    Gretchen Plattenring
                    Flat D
                    196 Zwingli Strasse
```

To Gretchen's surprise and delight, the phone rang the next morning. "Here is Klaus Umglick, Maestro Bronteaux's secretary. Please you come to Hotel Hofburg, eleven o'clock, Suite three twenty-two, bringing flute, music, *und so weiter*."

Promptly at eleven, an excited Gretchen knocked on the door of Suite 322. Pierre Bronteaux's secretary admitted her. "I am Klaus Umglick. Now, Fraulein Plattenring, you must go into next chamber. Maestro awaits you. He is sitting by window. His eyes are closed. Do not talk to him, as he does not wish any distracting. He is already concentrating—entirely—on you . . ."

"Herr Umglick," said Gretchen nervously, "I should maybe *tell* which composition I play?"

"No, no," sneered Umglick. "The maestro know *every* composition for flute. You yust go in, bow, put sheet music on stand near piano—and play."

Gretchen Plattenring entered. It was a fine room with an imposing chandelier, a grand piano—and, at the high French window, seated in a huge wing chair, facing her, his chin low, his eyes closed, was none other than Pierre Bronteaux.

Gretchen bowed her homage, put her music on the stand next to the piano, placed her flute to her lips, and began to play. . . . She played from Mozart's *Magic Flute* and from Debussy's *Afternoon of a Faun*. After each selection, she paused, glancing toward the large wing chair. But the maestro simply nodded and waved a finger, as if to say, "Next piece . . ."

Gretchen played from Chopin and Boccerini.

Pierre Bronteaux sat expressionless.

Gretchen played pieces from Vivaldi and Stamitz. Still Bronteaux made no reaction.

Finally, Gretchen blurted, "Maestro, shall I play more?"

The maestro opened his eyes. "No, *merci*."

Gretchen hesitated. "What is your opinion? For my future—what I should do next?"

Pierre Bronteaux said, "Get married."

An unmarried southern belle asked her mother, "But, mama, what can I give Charles? He simply has *every*thing!"

Mother smiled, "Encouragement, my dear. Just give him encouragement."

See also **Criticism, Fan Mail, Graffiti, Ingenuity, Kibitzers, Old Saws Sharpened, Sarcasm, Signs**

Answering Machines

When the recording machine at one executive's office went on the fritz, his secretaries answered the phone:

> "Hello. This is four-one-two, two, five, nine, two. Our answering machine is out of order. This is a real person talking."

❧

The man on the phone cried desperately, "What do you mean 'This is a recording?' *You* phoned me!"

❧

When George Minter dialed Essex 8-6433 he heard, "This is a recording. Essex-eight, six, four, three, three is not a working number. You have dialed the wrong recording."

❧

The chief executive of an international corporation so hated being disturbed at his home, fifty miles from the city, that he talked this message into his answering machine, "This is Brentwood-six, nine, nine, oh, seven. If that is the number you wanted, leave your name and number. If Brentwood-six, nine, nine, oh, seven is not the number you dialed, hang up, try again, and don't be so goddam stupid!"

See also **Computers**

Anthropology

The mother of the famous anthropologist Clara Raskin was visiting her new apartment, which was full of primitive wooden carvings from Central Africa. "So, are all these little statues you brought back from your expedition, dollink?"

"That's right, mama."

"And—eh—this thing on the mantel—what is it?"

"It's used in the tribe's fertility dances. It's—a phallic symbol."

Mrs. Raskin sighed. "Dollink . . . I hate to tell you what it looks like."

The anthropologist in the very remote village, a thousand miles up the jungles of the Amazon, was part of the circle of natives sitting around the fire, drinking the native grog that was passed around in a gourd. He felt something brush his side. He turned. To his indescribable astonishment, taking a place on the ground right next to him was a man, only one foot tall, dressed in a colorful military uniform.

The chieftain called to the anthropologist, "Meet General Hercule Martinez of the Mexican Army. . . . General, tell our visitor about the time you called our witch-doctor a goddam faker."

See also **Cannibals, Can You Believe It?**

Anti-Semitism

Mrs. Chauncey Ashley III telephoned the headquarters of the infantry base near Great Oaks, her ancestral home. "This is Mrs. Chauncey Ashley the Third, and with Thanksgiving coming up, I thought it would be nice for us to have ten of your fine enlisted men share our family feast."

"That's very kind of you, Mrs. Ashley."

"There's only one thing—I'm sure you understand: my husband and I prefer not to have any Jews . . ."

"Madam, I *quite* understand."

When her front doorbell rang on Thanksgiving Day, Mrs. Ashley, dressed to the nines, hurried to the door herself. She flung it open. "*Welc*ome to Great—" She stopped, aghast.

Under the great portico stood ten smiling black soldiers.

"Omigod," gasped Mrs. Ashley. "There has been a terrible mistake!"

The black sergeant said, "Oh no, ma'am. Captain Finkelstein *never* makes a mistake."

When Herr Doktor Oskar Dorfman, associate professor of brain surgery in the University of Vienna's medical school, was denied promotion to a full professorship, a colleague confided to him: "I was present when we discussed the promotion. You must never repeat what I shall tell you, Oskar— but you were turned down because—well, because you are a Jew."

Doktor Dorfman nodded glumly. "I suspected as much. . . . Who got the professorship?"

"No one yet, Oskar. A special committee, headed by Wolfgang Bloeringen, is searching for the right man."

That night, after considerable thought, Dorfman sat down and wrote the following letter:

> Dear Prof. Wolfgang Bloeringen:
>
> Permit me to make a hearty recommendation for the vacant chair in Brain Surgery at the University: Rudolf Heffelklinger.
> I have known Herr Heffelklinger for seventeen years and can testify that he is remarkably conscientious in the perform-

```
ance of his duties, and exceptionally effi-
cient in how he performs them. Furthermore,
he does not drink, works extremely hard, and
is happy with a relatively modest salary.
     Herr Heffelklinger, I should add, is not
an M.D. But he meets your primary quali-
fications for the Professorship in Brain
Surgery; he is not a Jew.

                       Faithfully yours,
                       Oskar Dorfman, M.D.


P.S. Herr Heffelklinger can be reached at
1726 Kaiserstrasse, the same building in
which I have lived for the past seventeen
years. He is the janitor.
```

Scene: Berlin, 1936

A Jew, crossing the street, accidentally bumped into a burly Storm Trooper.

"*Schweinhunt!*" snapped the Nazi.

"Goldberg," bowed the Jew.

Yorki Brastonyovich, commissar of education in Novgorod, came to the elderly rabbi, one of the few Jews left in the region, and said, "It is well known that you Jews employ a special form of reasoning, called Talmudic, which explains your cleverness. I want you to teach it to me."

"Ah, Comrade Commissar," the old rabbi sighed. "I fear you are too old for that."

"Nonsense! Why?"

"Well, when a Jewish boy wishes to study Talmud—we first give him an examination. It consists of three questions. Those lads who answer the questions correctly are admitted to the study of Talmud; those who can't, are not."

Yorki Brastonyovich glowered: "Give me the exam!"

The old rabbi shrugged. "The first question in the exam is: Two men fall down a chimney. One emerges filthy, covered with soot; the other emerges clean. Which one of them washes?"

"The dirty one, of course," sneered Brastonyovich.

"Wrong, commissar. The clean one washes."

"The *clean* one washes?" Brastonyovich was all astonishment. "Why?"

"As soon as the two men emerge from the chimney," explained the rabbi, "they look at each other, no? The dirty one, looking at the clean one, says to himself, 'Remarkable! To fall down a chimney and come out clean!' But the *clean* one, looking at the dirty one, says to himself, 'We certainly got filthy coming down that chimney!' So *he,* the clean one, washes. . . ."

"Ah," said Brastonyovich. "*Very* clever! . . . Now let's have the second question."

"The second question," sighed the rabbi, "is this: Two men fall down a chimney. One emerges filthy, covered with soot; the other emerges clean. Which—"

"That's the same question!" exclaimed Brastonyovich.

"No, no, commissar, please. This is an entirely different question."

"Very well," glowered Brastonyovich. "You won't fool me. The one who's *clean* washes!"

"N-no," sighed the rabbi.

"But you just told me—"

"That was an entirely different problem, commissar. In this one, the *dirty* man washes. Look: the two men look at each other. The one who is clean sees the dirty one and says, 'My! How dirty *I* must be!' But then he looks at his own hands. He sees that he is *not* dirty. . . . But the dirty man, on the other hand, looks at the clean man and says, 'Can it be?! To fall down a chimney and emerge so clean?' So *he* looks at *his* hands, and he sees that *he* is filthy. So it is he, the dirty one, who washes. . . ."

"Clever, Jew," muttered the commissar. "Very clever. . . . Now the third question?"

"Ah, the third question." The rabbi hesitated. "The third question is the hardest of all."

"Ask it! Ask it! You will not fool me again!"

"Very well." The rabbi stroked his beard. "Question three: Two men fall down a chimney. One emerges clean, the other—"

"But that's the same question!" cried Brastonyovich.

"No, no, commissar. The *words* may be the same—but the problem is entirely new. . . . Which man washes?"

"The dirty one!" snapped Brastonyovich.

"Wrong," murmured the rabbi.

"The clean one!"

"I'm sorry," said the rabbi. "Wrong again. . . ."

"Then what is the right answer?" seethed Brastonyovich.

"The right answer," said the rabbi, "is that this is a cuckoo examination! How can two men fall down the same chimney and one come out dirty and the other come out clean? . . . Anyone who doesn't see that at once will, I'm afraid, never be able to understand Talmud."

Gerhart Kleinschmitt did not like Jews. He also did not like Frenchmen, Italians, Englishmen, and Puerto Ricans. He especially did not like Frenchmen, Italians, Englishmen, and Puerto Ricans if they were Jews, too.

When the Norman Pivniks moved next door to Gerhart Kleinschmitt, in Hammond, Indiana, he was not happy. He made snide remarks to Mr. Pivnik, obscene phone calls to Mrs. Pivnik, and declared their little puppy a public menace.

One night, when the Pivniks were away, Kleinschmitt pried the little tin oblong (a *mezuzah*) off their front doorjamb and hurried home. He slid the cover off the *mezuzah*. Inside there might be dire evidence of some conspiratorial group. Fingers trembling with excitement, Gerhart Kleinschmitt opened a tiny scroll—on which was printed:

**HELP! HELP! We are prisoners in
Gerhart Kleinschmitt's *mezuzah* factory.**

In Leningrad, two KGB agents saw old Boris Glatkoff on a park bench—reading a book.

The first KGB agent asked, "What is that book you are reading?"

"A book about grammar," said Glatkoff. "Hebrew grammar."

The second KGB agent sneered, "Why bother, Jew? We'll never let you go to Israel."

"Well," sighed Boris, "I think that in Heaven, they speak Hebrew."

"What makes you think you'll get to Heaven? Suppose you go to Hell?"

Boris shrugged. "I already know Russian. . . ."

See also **Behind the Iron Curtain, Communism, Jews, Russia**

Aplomb

Mendel Kissenbaum, age seventy-three, assembled his three children and said, "Dear children, I want to make an announcement to you. The life of a widower is very, very sad. It is ten years since your dear mother passed away. I want my remaining few years go be a *little* happier. So—well, I have decided to get married. To a very fine girl, a good cook—"

" '*Girl?*' " echoed Mendel's son Morton.

"Papa, did you say '*girl*'?" asked Mendel's son Ira.

"That's right."

"*Papa!*" cried Mendel's daughter, Miriam. "How old is this girl?"

"Nineteen."

The room shook with the exclamations of astonishment and outrage.

"Papa, you are seventy-three!"

"It's a scandal, a *scandal!*"

"Papa," cried Miriam, "how can you even *think* of such a thing?! Aren't you *ashamed?*"

Mendel Kissenbaum cleared his throat. "Why should I be ashamed? Children! Take hold of yourselves. After all, when I married your mother she was not even eighteen!"

Arthur Rampolovski, the internationally known concert pianist, was in his apartment on Central Park West, rehearsing furiously for his concert that night. He had issued strict instructions to his wife and Beulah, the maid: Under no circumstances was he to be interrupted; he would see no callers, answer no phone calls, refuse all interviewers until the following day. . . .

The phone rang. Beulah swiftly lifted the receiver. In a low voice she murmured, "This ez th' Rampolovski raisedence."

"Hello," came an agitated voice. "Here is Mrs. Czernov! Mrs. Valdmir Czernov! It is emorgency! I *must* talk to maestro! At once!"

"M'z Czernov," said Beulah, "the maystrow ain't here."

"What? *What* you say?" the woman demanded.

"Ah sayd, the maystrow ain't *in*."

"And who are you?"

"Ah'm Beulah, the maid."

At this point Rampolovski struck a loud, soaring arpeggio.

"Look here, you maid!" the indignant caller snapped. "I can hear the maestro playing. In foct, he is playing Tchaikovsky's First Concerto —"

"Oh, no, ma'am," cried Beulah. "No, that ain't maystrow. Thess me—jest dustin' the keys!"

Scene: China Sea
Aboard H.M.S. Plantagenet

Midshipman Stacy, the Communications Clerk, knocked on the cabin door, on which a sign read:

MEETING IN PROGRESS
NO UNAUTHORIZED PERSONNEL

Hilary Staunton-Quade
Captain

A buzz of earnest voices came from the cabin.
Midshipman Stacy rapped louder.
A disapproving lieutenant opened the door. "*Do* you not read English?"
"Yes, *suh*," the midshipman faltered. "But this m-message just came through, from the C.O.C., Fleet Maneuvers. 'Urgent!' For Captain Staunton-Quade."
"Enter."
There were a dozen men around the table, poring over a huge map.
Stacy snapped to attention before Captain Staunton-Quade, saluted smartly, and barked, "C-compliments of Leftenant Noland, suh! Urgent cable from C.O.C., Fleet Maneuvers!"
Captain Staunton-Quade scarcely looked up, so intent was he in perusing the naval chart. "Read it . . ."
"B-but, suh—"
"Just *read* it—aloud," the captain repeated.
Stacy cleared his throat:

> <u>To</u>: Captain, H.M.S. *Plantagenet*
> <u>From</u>: Commander in Chief, Fleet Maneuvers
> Your last three successive movements are
> without a doubt the most stupid, futile,
> transparent tactical follies I have
> witnessed in forty—one years at sea.
>   C.O.C.

A hush had fallen upon the assembled brass and braid.
Captain Staunton-Quade drew erect, placed a monocle over his right eye, and said, "Midshipman, take that cable back to Leftenant Noland—and have it decoded."

The contracting firm of Brodie and Kahane Ltd., in Manchester, made a bid for the digging of the "Chunnel," a tunnel under the English Channel, in the international bidding for that prestigious contract. To the astonishment and delight of Meyer Brodie and Monroe Kahane, their bid was the lowest of all the offers from around the world.

All Manchester buzzed with the news. Congratulatory messages deluged Brodie and Kahane—by phone, telegram, cable. But Carter Chittering, an engineer friend of Brodie, took him to one side and said, "Meyer, old man, what on earth made you and Monroe put in a bid for a tunnel *under water* twenty-five miles long?!"

"What's the big deal?" grinned Brodie. "Monroe and I have built warehouses, bridges, roads—"

"But this is different, Meyer. I happen to know. Ask any expert in hydraulics—and he'll swear on a stack of Bibles that the tunnel is one of the most complicated engineering undertakings—"

"Bah. Lookahere, Carter. Me and my crews will start excavating from Dover; and Monroe and his crews will start digging from Calais. We both dig and dig—until we meet."

"Good Lord! That's precisely the point, man!" exclaimed the engineer. "One of the hardest, most nettlesome problems in all of engineering is precision in plotting underground directions. For you to start digging in England and your partner in France—and have those tunnels meet—*exactly*. That's a job to baffle the finest technicians!"

"Calm yourself, Carter. Just push your thinking ahead one step. Suppose the two tunnels do *not* meet? No tragedy."

"*What?* Have you taken leave of your senses? The two tunnels will come out at different places!"

"In that case," said Brodie, "our clients will get two tunnels for the price of one."

See also **Can You Believe It?, Chutzpa, Diplomacy/Diplomats, Put-downs, Squelches, Stratagems, Texans**

Appearances

Only shallow people do not judge by appearances.

OSCAR WILDE

"Father Bryan, Father Bryan!"

"Yes, Mrs. McGillicuddy?"

"I do believe me poor daughter's husband—Davey O'Shea—has been unfaithful to her!"

"Faith, an' that would be a terrible thing, Mrs. McGillicuddy!" said Father Bryan. "Are ye sure o' that?"

"Well," huffed Mrs. McGillicuddy, "just you look at their baby, father. Does he bear the faintest resemblance to Davey?!"

She has a winning smile, but a losing face.

BOB HOPE

Paris: Latin Quarter

Michelle Fauver, a pretty painting model, skipped up the stairs to the studio of Jacques Benoit, for whom she was posing in the nude. She entered the atelier with a bright, *"Bon jour,* M'sieur Benoit."

"Bon jour, Michelle," he sighed. "No, no, *cheri,* don't undress. I'm not feeling up to snuff this morning. I don't feel like working. Sit down. Let's have some coffee. We'll get back to the painting tomorrow."

They were having coffee, chatting about inconsequential matters, when Benoit suddenly froze. Footsteps were heard coming up the stairs. The painter listened, slammed down his cup, and said, "My wife! Michelle, quick—take off your clothes!"

A captain of the U.S. Cavalry, riding through a small town in Oklahoma, drew up his horse in astonishment, for on the side of a barn he saw about a hundred different chalked bull's-eye circles—and in the center of each was a bullet hole! The captain stopped the first passer-by. "Who is the marksman in this place? Look at all those bull's-eyes!"

The passer-by sighed, "That's old Tim Decker's boy. He's a mite peculiar. . . ."

"I don't care what he is," said the captain. "The cavalry needs anyone who can shoot that well!"

"Ah," said the pedestrian. "You don't understand, cap'n. Y'see, first little Timmy shoots—*then* he draws them circles."

"Listen, Cutler, how is it that you're not married?"

Cutler shrugged. "Every time I meet a girl who would make a good wife, a nice home, even cook like my mother . . ."

"Yes?"

"She looks like my father."

It was Mr. Kreyber's first trip to Israel. And after a few days, passing an optometrist's office, he dropped in. "Doc," he said, "I'm having trouble reading, ever since I got here. Maybe it's the climate, maybe an allergy, maybe I need stronger reading glasses."

The optometrist said, "Let's see what we can do." He asked Mr. Kreyber to sit on a stool before a large optical chart. "Now, sir, just read the letters on the bottom line."

"Those tiny, *teeny* letters?!"

"Yes, if you can. Try."

Mr. Kreyber squinted hard. "Nope, I can't."

"Then try the next line up. The letters are larger."

Mr. Kreyber stared, narrowed his eyes, and shook his head. "Sorry . . . no . . ."

"Then try the top line. The letters are quite large."

Again Kreyber stared, squinted, and shook his head.

The optometrist frowned. "Listen, mister. Do you realize you're almost *blind!*"

"Me? No, no, doc," said Mr. Kreyber earnestly. "I just never learned to read Hebrew."

See also **Accents, Can You Believe It?, Evidence, Hanky-panky, News Items That Haunt Me**

Applications

Note: What is true of Advertisements *(supra)* is also true of job applications. Personnel *mavens* have encountered the following:

Name: Hortense Dressler
Sex: Not yet

❧

Denomination preference: I prefer "Jimmy."

❧

Marital status: Eligible.

❧

Reasons for wanting to become a teacher: June, July, August.

❧

Person to notify in case of accident:

Doctor, ambulance, or anyone nearby.

❧

Beneficiary: Melba Farwell.
Relationship to you: Very nice.

❧

Accident report

Condition of driver of other vehicle: Poor.

❧

How many people in department, broken down by sex:

Drinking is more of a problem with us.

❧

Insurance policy application

> **Beneficiary**: Alice P. Moody.
> **Relationship to you**: Miserable.

"Your job application, Miss Cooley, looks quite good—but may I ask one question? You say your reason for leaving your last job was: sickness."

"Yes, sir."

"Was the sickness serious, Miss Cooley?"

The pretty young girl thought for a moment. "I never asked him."

"*Him?*"

"My boss said he just got good and sick of me."

Name:	Violet Andrews
Address:	832 Eustace Way
Date of Birth:	Feb. 7, 1959
Weight:	6 pounds, 10 ounces
Height:	20 inches
Color of hair:	None

Name:	Rinaldo Piaccelli
Address:	166 Mulberry St.
Length of residence:	29 feet

See also **Advertisements, Can You Believe It?, Graffiti, Signs**

Arabs

The sheik in his diaphanous kaffiyeh and embroidered slippers came into the women's dress department of I. Magnin's posh emporium in Beverly Hills. The saleswoman asked, "May I help you, sir?"

He waved regally. "I wish to inspect your garments."

"Certainly, sir." She escorted the glittering figure down aisles and aisles of clothes racks, chattering away.

Finally, the oil prince stopped. "Ah, *this* style I like. Very fetching . . . I'll take this lot."

" 'Lot?' " echoed the saleswoman. "Sir, there are seventy to eighty dresses in this particular style—"

"Very good. Deliver them to this address." He handed the bewildered clerk his card.

"But, sir—these dresses are different sizes!"

The sheik said, "So are the ladies."

Art

Sign in antique shop

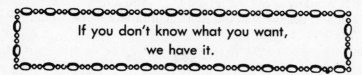

If you don't know what you want,
we have it.

Sign on music store

Bach at 2
(Offenbach sooner.)

Button worn by a Greenwich Village English major

MARCEL PROUST

IS A

YENTA

There once was a sculptor named Phidias,
Whose judgment in art was invidious,
He carved Aphrodite
Without hint of a nightie,
Which outraged the ultra-fastidious.

Norwich Neo-Ultra-Abstract Gallery
175 Pine Street
Cleveland, Ohio

Dear Sir or Madman:

An avant-garde art gallery in Kensington, London, was having a showing of the latest Ultra-Abstract-Anti-Representational paintings of Zoltan Ferrucci.

An American tourist from Texas sauntered about the gallery, then stopped before a small, oblong, white panel, in the center of which was a tilted black prong. The Texan lady studied this *objet d'art* for a while, then signaled to the gallery owner. "I find myself interested in this one. . . . *Very* provocative. I may buy it, for my husband."

"Madam—"

"Very *orig*inal. What does the artist call it?"

"The artist doesn't call it anything—"

"Ah, these geniuses. How they *hate* ordinary names. . . ."

"Madam—"

"What would *you* call it?" asked the Texan lady.

"I, madam, believe that the most appropriate name would be: 'Light switch.' "

Mr. and Mrs. Emmanuel Nudelman, taking a fiftieth-wedding-anniversary trip to Paris, went to the Louvre. Past all the masterpieces they slowly sauntered, marveling at the display of genius. "Look, Manny," said Mrs. Nudelman, stopping in front of a huge Renaissance painting called *The Child in the Manger*.

"Colors . . . beautiful," said Mrs. Nudelman. "Although dark, still very rich . . ."

"True," said Mr. Nudelman.

"You know what the scene is about, Manny? What it shows?"

"Certainly I know what the scene shows, Stella."

"So why are you standing there with such a puzzled expression?"

"I have on a puzzled expression, because I can't figure the whole thing out!"

"What's to figure out?" asked Mrs. Nudelman.

"What's to figure out, Stella, is this: here is a family living in a *stable*, with animals, the floor is *dirt*, covered with straw, and the little baby is naked . . ."

"So?"

"*So*, how could they afford to have their picture painted?!"

Scene: Loft Gallery, Greenwich Village

Sir Bennet Cranfield and his wife, Gladys, were in the Post-Constructionist section of the gallery. They had stopped before a huge painting, a chaos of dark smudges and blotchy writhings. There were no discernible shapes, no possible forms.

After several moments of earnest appraisal, Sir Bennet turned to his wife. "My dear, what on *earth* does this nonsense purport to be?"

Lady Cranfield stepped closer to the canvas and bent over its nameplate. "It is called *Anguish in Yellow Mud*. . . . But I *don't* see any yellow at all, Bennet. Do you?"

"Not a speck of yellow. Though it certainly *does* resemble mud."

Lady Cranfield sighed, "I do hate to be old-fashioned, darling, or not approving of new and possibly quite original work . . ."

"Oh, yes, my pet. My position to a T."

"Yet—this *is* simply atrocious, darling. Why, *why* do they hang this sort of rubbish?"

Sir Bennet stroked his mustache. "Perhaps they couldn't lay their hands on the painter."

Arno Kunudsen, having made a fortune in toothpicks, began to buy *objets d'art* for his mansion in Oslo. He went off to the galleries of Berlin, Paris, New York. . . . When he returned to Oslo, it was with four large paintings, all by the same artist, the ultra-abstract-reductionist Arkady Jakolski.

Kunudsen held a reception to show off his treasures. The paintings were hung in successive rooms: the parlor, the library, the conservatory, the salon. Arno Kunudsen shepherded his guests from one room to the other: "This the artist calls *Night Journey.* . . . Here, ya, is Jakolski's *Summer Storm.* . . . Here, yoost look: *Flaming Horse by Sea.* . . ."

The only thing puzzling about the great Jakolski's canvases was their titles—each canvas was simple enough: a large white surface, completely blank—save for a dot of blue. For *Night Journey,* the dot was in the upper right-hand corner. For *Summer Storm,* the blue dot was in the lower right-hand corner. *Flaming Horse by Sea* consisted of a dot in the upper left-hand corner. . . .

"Now, Arkady Jakolski's latest composition!" Kunudsen ushered his guests into the salon. "Yoost admire . . ." On a long wall hung a long oblong canvas, twice the size of the other three, and all white; but this painting contained *two* blue dots, in the exact center. "Jakolski's masterpiece!" exclaimed Kunudsen. "*Soul Reborn!* . . . Ay? So eloquent . . . composition . . . Jan Islak, tell me. What you feel?"

Jan Islak cocked his head to one side, narrowed his eyes, then murmured, "Arno, ay wonder . . . is it not too *busy?*"

Laurence Alford had his easel set up in Regents Park, London, and was painting a sylvan scene. Over his shoulder two cockneys, Howie and Harry, mufflers around their throats, were gravely watching.

After a while, Alford rested. "Well, now," he said to his observers. "I should like your opinion, please. You, sir?"

"Blimey!" said Howie. "Right bloody wonderful, Oy says. What about you, 'arry?"

"Loikwise," said Harry. "Guv'nor, how long'd you 'ave t' study t' do somep'n loike this?"

"To tell you the truth, sir, I never studied painting at all," smiled Alford.

"Then," said Howie, "it'd 'ave t' be somep'n you—you inherited. Roight?"

"N-not necessarily," said Alford. "Take a fine painter like Tintoretto. Did you ever hear of Tintoretto's father?"

"Can't say as Oy 'ave."

"Or Tintoretto's mother?"

"Naw."

"Well there you are!" beamed Alford.

The two Cockneys looked at each other, then Howie said, "T' tell you th' bloody truth, guv, we ain't never 'eard o' Tintoresky neither."

POP ART, SHMOP ART, LEAVE ME ALONE!

Dear Lefty:

Well, pal, I just *have* to tell you what has transpired, even altho you won't hardly believe it. I might not believe it myself if I did not see it with my own 2 eyes and ears.

Well, last Saturday I am strolling up Madison Av. with a new chick, Marcia, this blond I am soffening up for the finals. When what do I spot in a window of an art gallary but—a red Garbage Pail! Full of blue Custard, with 100 popsikles stuck in the custard. Across the Pail in pukey purple letters is 1 word—*BEING!* And across the *custard* is a Fish-net, and there (honest!) our good old U.S. FLAG is planted! And across our Stars & Strips is pasted the word *NOTHINGNESS.*

I do not have to inform you I am fit to be tide, but Marcia is regarding this cockamamy mish-mosh with aw and even rapture, and she asks me, "What do you think of this artist?"

"I wish him a speedy recovery."

"He is trying to make a statement about our times!" she xplains.

"The statement is that he can blow bubbles in his head without first inserting soap."

"This artist has a Committment!" she cries.

"They should parole him," say I.

She narrows her 2 orbs. "You have no feeling for Pop Art!"

"Pop Art?" I ecko. "Why, baby, you suprise me. Pop Art is Out to anyone who is In."

"O, then you prefer *Op* art?" she lights up.

"Op Art is as dead as Calvin Cooledge," I toss her.

"Then what school *do* you espouse?"

In a casual manner, I snow her: "Mop Art."

"Mop Art?" she gasps. "What is that?"

"That is where you paint with a Mop made of chicken-fethers dipped in Yogurt."

Lefty, a look of pain from some old and crooshal ailment crosses her features. "Let us go in," she strangles.

So we go into this joint, which is jumping with people and I see right away is Very Chic. A place is Very Chic when the broads are very skinny and the mens legs are held together by tight pants instead of skin. And Lefty, the noise in this Tempel of Culture—well, you never *heard* such a gaggel of babbel and giggel. On account of all the kooks are trying to prove they are xcstatic Art Lovers in the Avon Gard, acting like connosewers as they plop phrases like "Kinnetic Action" and "Vibrant Validity" and "Fluid Drive."

And what is creating these fancy labels? The stuff hanging on the walls—which would not pass an Insanity Test by Casey Stengel.

Take a picture which is actualy a chunk of Burlap dripping oatmeal. It is named *Farewell to Brer Rabbi*.

Another is a big, empty, white Square—with a cornflake in the mid-dle!—and is called *Cerebral Cereal*.

And where is Marcia?! Standing with her mouth open, admiring a STOP sign. I mean a real STOP sign, Lefty, that was probly lifted from some needy intersexion. Only this is not *just* a STOP sign. Parish the thought! *This* STOP sign has a lace Brassier draped above the letter "S"—and from the middle of the letter "O" a red flannel Tongue is hanging down!

"How re-freshing," Marcia is cooing.

"I was a bottle baby myself," I crack.

"So spontan-eous!" throbs Marcia.

"It stinks on ice!" says a voice from a nearby broad who is xtremely well stacked. This tomato is holding a Martini glass, with one eye to match, and she has a knockout of a bazoom as she grabs me, xclaiming, "My name is Iona Fliegelsheeser!"

"It's not your fault," I say.

"You are a *scream*," she screams.

"Observe *A Soul in Torment*," cries Marcia.

"All I see is a bunch of straight lines," I crack.

"But are they not *xciting?*" snaps Marcia.

"Sure," I say, "if you are a ruler."

Now Marcia hands me a look you can cut into ice cubes. So I croon, "Now there is *my* favorite." and I point to a yellow-&-blue arrow wich reads: MEN'S ROOM.

Well, Lefty, that about raps it up.

I have given Marcia back to the Bronx, her being too dam dum for my tastes. I am now making time with Iona Fliegelsheeser who I will escort to Madison Square Garden tonight to enjoy the Knicks playing the Boston Celtics. Iona does not give me a ringing in the ears, between BEING and NOTHINGNESS.

Hoping you are the same,

Your old pal,
Vern

PS.—Did you hear the one about the guy who got his wife a job with a near-sited Knife-thrower?? Ha, Ha, Ha, Ha.

L. R.

Astronauts

In the debriefing of one of the first astronauts to return to Andrews Field from outer space, a psychologist asked, "Can you tell us what was the very last thing that went through your mind just before liftoff?"

"You bet," said the hero. "What kept running through my mind was the thought: Every goddam part of this vehicle was supplied by the lowest bidder."

"Hey, grampa! You're alvays so cynical. Did you hear that we put a man on the moon!"

"Sure, sure."

"Grampa, that feat cost ten billion dollars!"

Grampa cocked his head to one side. "Including *meals?*"

"And on my sixty-fourth orbit," said the astronaut, "I made another prayer."

"*Another?*"

"Well, from that spot it's just a local call."

MRS. DONALD: An' did y' hear the Yanks sent
                  a mon t' the moon?!

MRS. MCGREGOR: Like Ay always say: them
                  that hos money, travel.

Autos

Sign on back of ten-wheel truck

> Watch my rear—not hers.

🖎

On auto-repair shop

> May we have the next dents?

🖎

On a trailer

> Reluctant Draggin'

🖎

In auto junkyard

> Rust in Peace

🖎

On used-car lot

> Fine used cars—in first-crash condition

🖎

In auto-maintenance handbook

This adjustment should not be made by owner but should be done at one of our service stations, since it can only be done by special fools.

🖎

Sign on a five-minute car wash

> Grime Doesn't Pay!

On tow truck

24-hour service.
We are always on our tows.

Bachelors

A man who tries to avoid the issue.

❧

A man who comes to work each morning from a different direction.

SHOLEM ALEICHEM

Unlanded gentry.

OGDEN NASH

❧

A man who has no children to speak of.

A man who is crazy to get married—and realizes it.

Bachelors are usually broad-minded: in fact, they don't think of much else.

A bachelor never met a woman he couldn't live without.

❧

He seems too good to be true—and isn't.

LOUIS SAFIAN

❧

Hilary Follard, a very shy Englishman, was taking a cruise on the S.S. *Frontenac.* At the table next to his, he noticed an extremely attractive American woman. . . . The orchestra began to play a popular tune, and from different parts of the dining salon, couples drifted onto the floor.

The Englishman glanced toward the American woman yearningly, but she was absorbed in her food. Follard's waiter leaned over him. "And your entrée, sir?"

Follard said, "I *say,* I wonder if—well, could you could do me a *very* great favor? . . . Do you see that charming lady? Well, could you be a good chap"—he slipped a pound note into the waiter's palm—"and ask her—for the next dance?"

The waiter said, "Anything to oblige, sir."

Follard watched out of the corner of his eye. He saw the waiter go to the table, bow, and whisper to the American woman. She smiled, nodded, and rose. They glided onto the floor together.

In County Sligo

"Teddy, m'boy, do y' realize y're approachin' the fortieth year o' your birth and y're still a bachelor?"

"Ay, realize it I do."

"But Teddy—in all them years, did y' not *once* think of tyin' the connubial knot?"

"Ay, many toymes," said Teddy. "An' that's why I stayed single."

See also **Hanky-panky, Just Jokes, Shadchens**

Banks

AT THE BANK

GIRL: Please give me change for this one-hundred-dollar bill.
TELLER: Of course—oh-oh. Miss, this is a fake one-hundred-dollar bill.
GIRL: Omi*god!* I've been raped.

A Texas billionaire made out a check for a huge sum of money. It bounced. Stamped on the check was:

INSUFFICIENT FUNDS

—under which was written:

Ours, not yours.

Sign on president's desk

**In this bank, "No" is
a complete sentence.**

STROM: I'm phoning to ask if you got the check I sent you.
BIRKETT: Twice.
STROM: Twice?
BIRKETT: Once from you and once from the bank.

The Chase Manhattan Bank's memorable advertising campaign is built around the slogan:

YOU HAVE A FRIEND AT CHASE MANHATTAN!

'Tis said that a sign in the window of the nearby Bank of Israel reads:

—BUT HERE YOU HAVE RELATIVES!

"Hello. Is this Mrs. Patterson?"

"Yes."

"This is Mr. Crowley, your bank manager. Mrs. Patterson, I'm afraid I must call your attention to the fact that your account is considerably overdrawn!"

"Oh, dear. How much am I overdrawn?"

"The exact amount is $4,336.74."

"Well, Mr. Crowley, don't you worry about it. I'll sit right down and make out a check."

TV announcer in Biloxi, Mississippi

. . . So save a part of your paycheck each week. Come into Fidelity Bank. Save for the good things in life: a home, a new car, a trip, a broad.

Bank of Powhatan
Powhatan, N.Y.
September 26

A. D. Rogers
112 E. 47 St.
New York, N.Y.

Dear Sir:

I have been examining your account, notably the sizable loans you have made since January 4. You are now overdrawn $3,874 as well.

May I suggest that we go back to the very pleasant relationship that existed between us before January 4—in which *you* banked with *us*.

Yours,

L. O. Morton
President

See also Business

Barbers

Sign in window of hair salon

FOUR BARBERS
Constant Discussion

To the fetching manicurist in the Ritz Barber Shop, Sheldon Caster, a compulsive skirt-chaser, smiled, "When do you quit work?"

"Seven o'clock."

"Well, how about you and me having dinner? . . ."

"Sir, I'm married."

Caster shrugged. "Maybe your husband won't be home early. . . . Why not phone? Ask him."

"Ask him yourself. He's just stropping his razor to give you a shave."

Scene: Palermo Tonsorial Parlor

Marcello, the snappy barber, whipped the white cover around the new customer and asked, "Okay, *commendatore,* a haircut, eh?"

"*No,*" said the stranger icily. "Ia joost come in for a estimate!"

In a barbershop

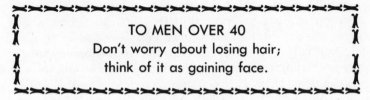

TO MEN OVER 40
Don't worry about losing hair;
think of it as gaining face.

Sign in barber's window

During vacation of owner, a competent
hair-stylist will be here.

Baseball

THE GENIUS OF YOGI BERRA

Lawrence Peter Berra, the short, squat, beetle-browed, waddle-gaited, jug-eared, drum-chested, short-legged, long-armed, solemn-faced non-pareil of baseball, is enshrined in the temple of that sport as a giant, even though he played for the Yankees.

When Mr. Berra first took baseball's vows, as a catcher, his somewhat freakish figure made him the instant target of mockery, raspberries, and other energetic sounds of disesteem, not excluding variations of the Bronx cheer, aimed at him from the dugouts of his opponents. His adversaries accompanied their verbal fusillade by Darwinian suggestions anent his ancestry, which slander they illustrated by scratching their armpits, grimacing like baboons, placing their tongues under their upper lips to magnify their simian derivations, all the while affecting to swing from branches while uttering cryptic cries.

To these unfriendly salutations, which were based on perfectly sound principles of primitive warfare, Lawrence "Yogi" Berra responded with noble forbearance and increasing proficiency—whether crouched behind the plate or standing at it. He became the best damn catcher in baseball, a fixture on the coveted All Star squads, and a slugger who made fear endemic among pitchers in the American League. Mr. Berra set no fewer than eighteen separate World Series records. He set a high-water mark for consecutive games caught without an error (148). He whacked 358 home runs. He also got more hits (71) and drove in more runs (39) than any player in a World Series. One can only stand reverent before such prodigality.

In addition to his other exceptional talents, Mr. Berra was a rarity encountered, among professionals, once in a generation: He was a phenomenal "bad-ball" hitter. This means that he would not only "bite at" balls flung so remote from the strike zone that most batters would sneer at them: Mr. Berra clobbered them. He luxuriated in very low, very high, very wide, or very close pitches that no batter in his right mind would attempt to hit. I do not mean to imply that Mr. Berra was of unsound mentality; I mean that once the man was permitted to lift his bat, his subsequent capacity to hit any ball within his vicinity, however wild or "safe" the pitcher of that ball considered it to be, was of an order of excellence not seen since the days of Shoeless Joe Jackson.

On one memorable occasion, Mr. Berra came to bat in the twilight of the ninth inning, with two out for the Yankees and the Chicago White Sox two fat runs ahead. With the count 2–2 against him, Mr. Berra suddenly seemed to confuse baseball with golf, for he dropped his bat like a driving iron and, brushing the ground, smote a veritable ankle-duster into the distant bleachers. This scored three runs and cruelly snatched victory from the Chicago team in a game the Yankees clearly deserved to lose. When the understandably embittered losing pitcher was asked for his expert opinion on the best way of getting Yogi out, that White Sock morosely replied: "With a pistol."

But I salute Mr. Berra in these pages not for his sparkling achievements on the diamond, but for his astonishing originality as a linguist. Even Jacques Barzun would not deny how greatly the redoubtable Berra has enriched our tongue with his altogether new, breathtakingly fresh, and immensely creative use of ordinary words which he borrowed, as it were, from English. I quote examples, each in a separate branch of knowledge:

Education: "You can observe a lot by watching."

The Fourth Dimension (upon arriving five minutes late, instead of his usual half hour, for a radio interview): "I guess this is the earliest I've ever been late."

Restaurants: "*No* one goes to that place anymore. It's too crowded."

Logic: "How can that pitcher stay in the majors, considering the stuff he keeps striking me out with?"

Endings: "A game isn't over until it's over."

The Future of Fiction (to his roommate, a summer second baseman and winter medical student, who spent hour after hour, when the Yankees were on the road, studying his anatomy textbook, which he finally finished): "How'd it come out?"

Etiquette (opening his acceptance speech on "Yogi Berra Day" in St. Louis, his hometown): "I just want to thank everyone who made this day necessary."

What can one say of such versatility? These days, when I think back on the golden era Yogi Berra adorned, I think of Byron—his immortal lines slightly adapted for the purposes of my paean:

> The isles of Greece, the isles of Greece!
> Where burning Berra swat and sung,
> Where grew the arts of war and peace,
> Where Mantle rose, and Musial sprung!
> Eternal summer gilds them yet,
> And none, except their sun, is set.

from my *People I Have Loved, Known or Admired*

❧

Opera in English makes about as much sense as baseball in Italian.

H. L. MENCKEN

❧

Going to bed with a woman the night before a game never hurt a ballplayer. It's staying up all night looking for one that does them in.

CASEY STENGEL

❧

O, RARE BABE HERMAN

One of my special heroes is Floyd ("Babe") Herman, outfielder for the much-mourned Brooklyn Dodgers, whose inspired confusions on the baseball diamond forever enriched my memories.

Mr. Herman holds records to this day for achievement in categories no one had the foresight to establish: Getting Entangled with Own Feet; Running Bases in Wrong Direction; Trying to Catch Fly Balls with Head, Elbow, or Shoulder.

Mr. Herman was surely the most *involved,* to say nothing of self-involved, outfielder our national game has yet produced. Malacologists tell me that he surpassed the octopus, which has eight arms and legs, in what he could do with only four. This is not meant as a compliment, mind you; it is a comment on Mr. Herman's habits as a fielder, in which capacity his mishaps verged on the spooky.

The moment Mr. Herman set forth in pursuit of a ball that had been hit into his neighborhood—whether to catch it, stop it, retrieve it, or just slow it down—the ball went crazy. Buffs with 20–20 vision have sworn by their mother's memory that line-drives headed right for Mr. Herman's station would take abrupt detours or even fight their way back out of his glove. Some students of the game claim that Mr. Herman was haunted—and the baseballs knew it, hence fled from him whenever batted within his ectoplasmic *gestalt.* I cannot agree with this. Haunting had nothing to do with it.

My theory is that there was something in Mr. Herman's molecular mass that physicists have only recently identified: anti-matter. His nuclear singularity was such that baseballs were *repelled,* not attracted, once they entered Mr. Herman's gravitational field. This astonishing reversal of the behavior of matter understandably confused Mr. Herman. He misjudged, dropped, fumbled, or lost balls with such frequency that unkind observers claimed that the man was a somnambulist or was trying out for a part in a circus. Whenever he committed a *faux pas,* rabid Dodger fans would wail that Mr. Herman's fingers were made of butter. Others cried that his brain was made of lard. Extremists charged that his feet were coated with glue.

Sometimes the inflamed fanatics would shift the zone to which they addressed their calumnies, accusing Mr. Herman of possessing an inordinately fat head, rubber tibia, or a cerebellum composed of mush. The unkindest of all, I think, were the spectators who shouted questions about which team Mr. Herman was playing for.

What was even more humiliating to Mr. Herman than dropping, bobbling, or altogether losing baseballs was the places the balls landed *after* Mr. Herman had done so: the spheroids showed a propensity for striking him on the knee, ear, elbow, or forehead. Whenever this occurred, the enraged sages in the bleachers would switch from aspersions on Mr. Herman's biochemistry to slander of his ancestry. One must have had a heart of stone not to sympathize with his plight; the emotions of an outfielder hit on the head by a fly ball are akin to those of a ballerina whose tutu drops to her knees in mid-jeté.

Mr. Herman always denied that baseballs actually struck his body after evading his glove. To hear him explain why his fielding went awry was to hear a master of creative alibi. But his efforts to correct his public image collapsed when one reporter inquired: "Well, how about your getting hit by a pop fly, *today*—right on your shoulder?"

Mr. Herman considered this thoughtfully before replying, "On the shoulders don't count."

Mr. Herman also complained about the report that he carried lighted cigars in his pockets. I do not know how often Mr. Herman carried a lighted cigar in his pocket, but at least once, concluding a *tête-à-tête* with a sportswriter, he reached inside his coat pocket, removed a cigar, and proceeded to smoke it. Since he did not light the cigar and since smoke was clearly seen to issue from it, I think we may conclude that Mr. Herman *had* placed a lighted stogy in his pocket.

Ring Lardner, the Rochefoucauld of baseball, once anathematized a baseball player thusly. "Although he isn't a very good fielder, he isn't a very good hitter, either." That, I am happy to tell you, could not be said about Babe Herman. He was a dandy hitter! In fact, it was only his hitting that kept him in there fielding—if that is what we may call his daily debate with ground balls.

But even where hitting was concerned, the malevolent fates placed monkeys on Herman's back. His excellent hitting was often nullified by his heretical base running, in which he carried originality to extremes. Herman is the only man in history who twice invalidated home runs by the subsequent peculiarity of his movements, suddenly reversing the direction in which he was running, reversing, that is, the conventional or legal course traversed by runners who desire to increase their team's score. Once, Babe was on base when a teammate walloped a home run over the wall, and Babe whirled around and ran *toward* the teammate, whom he then passed. Strategists of the game call this Herman's Paradox. It has never been solved.

Babe also once negated his own homer. I know this sounds impossible, but it is true. He accomplished it by swatting the ball far out of sight and running around the bases in the legal, counterclockwise pattern. The only trouble this time was that he overtook and passed two teammates who happened to be on bases ahead of him. This negated three runs and made men delirious for weeks.

Mr. Herman also once doubled into a double play. Of *course* that sounds like a contradiction in terms, but it isn't. In fact, had there not been one man out for Brooklyn at the time, the Babe would have doubled into a *triple* play. The details of this historic achievement should be memorized by every schoolboy.

Mr. Herman came up to bat with the bases loaded and, as was his wont, dispatched a high drive into deep right field. The Dodgers on first and second hesitated near their bases, naturally, before streaking ahead, in order to make sure that Herman's drive would not be caught; and it was while they were hesitating, in the manner approved by every authority on the game, that the Babe ran right past the man on first, head down, eyes glazed, intoxicated by team spirit and premonitions of glory. Herman's illegal passing so electrified his friend on first, and so paralyzed his colleague on second, that all three players reached *third* base at the same time.

This trailblazing *contretemps* caused the long-suffering manager of the club, "Uncle" Wilbert Robinson, to announce: "That is the first time the men in this club have gotten together on anything."

I feel for him.

from my *People I Have Loved, Known or Admired*

Behind the Iron Curtain

Stasya Korjagov, honored for his exceptional productivity as a coal miner, was rewarded by his Communist Party local with a free tour, in a group of twenty-four Heroes of Soviet Labor. To his friends, Korjagov promised he would send picture postcards from each country the group visited.

Here are the postcards Stasya Korjagov sent:

From Warsaw

> Greetings from Free Poland.

From East Germany

> Greetings from Free Germany.

From Prague

> Greetings from Free Czechoslovakia.

Then there was a hiatus—not a word for eighteen days. At last came a postcard, postmarked Vienna, with this message:

> At last!
> > Free Stasya!

Yuri Pridlykev, the last Jewish engineer in the Kiev office of the Soviet Commissariat of Electrical Energy, had been ordered to move to a minor post in the faraway, godforsaken Siberian outpost of Stredna-Kolymsk. His parents, in tears, were watching him pack. "I'll write every day," said Yuri.

"But the censorship," wailed his mother. "They'll watch every word. They'll open every letter. Yissel," she said to her husband, "you must make a secret code—"

"No, no, codes are dangerous. Yuri, I have an idea. Anything you write in black or blue ink, we'll know is true. But anything you put in red ink, we'll know is nonsense!"

A month passed; then from Stredna-Kolymsk came a long letter—all in blue ink!

```
Dear Mama and Papa,

    I can't tell you how happy I am here in
this workers' paradise! We are treated like
kings. I live in a fine apartment—and the
local butcher has meat every single day!
There are many concerts, theater, movies—
all free. And there is not one tiny bit of
anti-Semitism!

                    Your loving son,
                    Yuri


P.S. Now that I think about it, there's only
one little thing you can't find in Stredna-
Kolymsk: red ink.
```

When the Commissar of Education was visiting a model elementary school in Albania, he patted an honor student on the head and asked, "Who is your father, young comrade?"

"My father is Karl Marx."

"And who is your mother?"

"My mother is the Communist Party."

"*Very* good. And when you grow up, what do you most want to be?"

"An orphan."

In Budapest, two strangers stood admiring a beautiful new automobile that was parked on Embassy Row. "What automobile!" said the first man. "How refined. How magnificent. Historic triumph for Communist engineering!"

The second man growled, "It not Soviet car! It Cadillac. *American* car! Don't you know American car when you see one?"

"Sure. . . . But I don't know you. . . ."

"Madam Director," said Heinrich Klopstock, to the manager of the Engels Stocking and Underwear Works in East Berlin, "can I please leave an hour early tonight?"

"Why?" froze the manager.

"Because I am part of the delegation going to the State Opera tonight, Madam Director."

"All right. . . . But stop calling me Madam Director! I am not French. I am not a Madam. I have no patience with decadent, bourgeois hypocrisies. . . ."

"Certainly, I agree!" said Klopstock.

"And which opera is playing tonight?"
Klopstock cleared his throat. "Comrade Butterfly."

The Communist journal *Izvestia* recently announced an important change in editorial policy.

NOTICE
TO ALL READERS

It is rumored, by certain comrades who have been deceived by filthy capitalist-imperialist propaganda, that legitimate complaints from loyal members of the proletariat are not being published in the democratic Communist press. We intend to squelch these false, baseless rumors once and for all. Starting immediately, we are instituting a

WORKERS' COMPLAINTS COLUMN

It will appear three times a week. We will print the unedited letters of workers with a legitimate grievance—about their pay, conditions of labor, their supervisors.
Send in your Letter of Complaint now!
Important: Be sure to sign your letters. Print address and next of kin.

Lev Bryshkov stood before the three judges in Uzbek.
"—And your punishment is ten years of hard labor in Siberia! Have you anything to say?"
Lev cleared his throat. "Comrade Judges, *tovarichchi*. The United States is a terrible, decadent, capitalist country. It savagely exploits the proletariat. Hunger, unemployment, racism defile every corner of that reactionary land. Is that not right?"
"Right!" The three judges assented as one.
"Then why not, Comrade Judges, send me there?"

The teacher of the senior class led the familiar catechism: "Why do we revere Marx and Lenin?"
"Because they dared bring the truth to the oppressed proletariat of the world," chanted the students.
"Why do we love the glorious leaders of the Communist Party?"
"Because they ended our peoples' exploitation by vicious capitalists!"
"And why do we hate the imperialist forces of NATO and America?"
"Because they have not liberated us!"

The flabbergasted instructor shouted, "Who said that?"
From two dozen mouths came the instant: "*He* did! *He* did!"

Pravda: The Russian paper that runs contests for political jokes, first prize being thirty years.

IRVING R. LEVINE

At a meeting of Local 46 of the Communist Party in Lodz, Poland, a worker rose and demanded, "Comrade Chairman, for five years the Central Executive Committee has promised us more meat, more butter, more flour, more milk. For five *years,* comrade. So why have we not gotten one ounce more meat, butter, flour, or milk?!"

There was a spontaneous burst of applause.

"That is good, important question," said the chairman, "which I will answer at next open meeting. What is your name, Comrade Worker?"

"Kranpofski. Georgi Kranpofski."

At the next open meeting, the chairman of Local 46 had scarcely announced the agenda when a noisy ruckus broke out at the back of the hall.

"Quiet, order!" sang out the chairman. "I know what you want and I will tell you what happened to more meat, butter, flour, and milk. Right?"

"No!" thundered the caucus. "We want know what happened to Comrade Kranpofski."

Medical circles are abuzz with the news from Warsaw: Dr. Jaczi Gredzinczki just announced he has performed history's first successful transplant of an appendix.

In East Germany, a Russian soldier and a German boy were fishing on opposite sides of a broad river. The boy kept yanking fish after fish out of the water on the west side; but after an hour, the Russian had not made one catch on the east bank. He finally flung his pole down and shouted to the boy: "What the hell goes on here? I can't get a single bite, and *you* pull out fish after fish! What's your secret?"

"No secret," said the boy.

"Nonsense! What bait are you using?"

"Worms."

"I'm using worms too. What sort of hook are you using, German?"

"Exactly the same hook as you."

"Then— it's the pole! What kind of pole—"

"My pole is just like yours."

The Russian fumed, "There has to be an explanation!" He aimed his rifle at the boy. "Now—tell me or I'll blow your head off!"

The boy said, "Don't get excited. Please. I catch all these fish because on this side of the river the fish aren't afraid to open their mouths."

Mrs. Czernik marched into the leading toy store in Poznan. "My son is having a birthday tomorrow. I want to buy him a fine bicycle."

"We have no bicycles," said the manager.

"*What?* A big toy store without bicycles?"

"We have only *tri*cycles," said the manager.

"Tricycles are for little boys. My son is twelve years old! You expect him to ride a tricycle?"

"Psst." The manager beckoned Mrs. Czernik to one side. "Buy the tricycle, and don't worry. Before the week's over, one wheel is absolutely sure to drop off."

An English tourist came out to the best hotel in Warsaw and looked about for a taxi. None was to be seen. He walked several blocks and saw a cab, parked at the curb. The Englishman said, in accented Russian, "Driver, are you free?"

"No. I'm Polish."

See also **Communism, Russia, Stratagems**

Birth Control

In Prague: Canceled Czechs.

❧

Copulation without fertilization.

❧

Copulation without population.

❧

The new bride, Maggie Sheehan, returned from her ten-day honeymoon, hurried to her doctor in Belfast, considerably upset. " 'Tis them pills y' did give me, doctor. . . . For—for the birth control. They jist ain't *aworkin'* royt!"

"Not workin', is it?" the doctor frowned. "But Maggie Sheehan, ye've not been married two weeks! Sure, an' ye cannot tell if they be workin'."

" 'Tis sure, Oy am. Sure as snuff."

"But that is not *pos*sible, lass!"

"Doctor, Oy been usin' them pills ivery night, an' many a time durin' the day—but the damn fool things keep afallin' out!"

❧

The doctors and nurses at the maternity ward of Cedars of Lebanon Hospital could not get over the just-born Cargill baby: he was grinning broadly. All day and all night, little Cargill's pudgy face was split in a grin that reached from one ear to the other.

A nurse found out why: noticing that the baby kept his left fist firmly closed, she pried it open. What little Cargill was clutching was—the pill.

Bloopers: Radio and TV

Here, collected with profound gratitude down many years, are some choice boo-boos, boners, malapropisms, and spoonerisms cheerfully committed on American, Canadian, and British radio/television programs.

L. R.

"Good evening, ladies and gentlemen of the audio radiance."

"—and when the Queen arrives you will hear a twenty-one sun galoot."

"And now—the president of the United States: Hoobert Heever."

"We take you now to Rome, where we will hear the Christmas greeting from His Holiness, Pipe Poess the Fifth."

"It is a privilege to present to you now the distinguished Virgin of Governor's Island."

"You have been listening to a message by our Honorable Minister of Wealth and Hellfire."

"I am very happy to speak to you over this nationwide hick-up."

"The first thing the doctor has to do when a baby is born is he has to cut the biblical cord."

"Mr. Plummer won a ten-pound turkey at Saturday's shurkey toot."

"Don't fail to miss tomorrow's double-header."

✌

"—this company is America's largest producer of alceminum, magnoosium, and stole."

✌

"—and at Fonseca's Pharmacy you can be sure of having your prescriptions filled with scare and kill."

✌

"Why not drop in on your nearest A and Poo Feed Store?"

✌

Radio M.C., introducing Walter Pidgeon: "Mr. Privilege, this is indeed a pigeon."

✌

"—And when you're hot and thirsty, men, there's just nothing like a glass of cold Buppert's Reer!"

✌

"—and once again, it's smope-piking time."

✌

"This news roundup has come to you through the wild-word facilities of the Appociated Sess."

See also **Boo-Boos, Freudian Slips, Goldwyniana, Malaprops, Old Saws Sharpened, Typos**

Boasts

Al ("Alkali") Crawford, a Texan, driving down a great flat desert in Israel, spied a tiny house in the distance, with a neat picket fence. An old man, wearing a skullcap, was leaning on the fence.

Alkali stopped in front of him. "Ha there . . ."

"Hollo."

"You speak English, friend?"

"Oh, sure."

Alkali put out his hand. They shook hands. Then Alkali said, "You own this little house?"

"Yes."

"Man, what in the world do you *do* way out here to hell an' gone?"

"Oh, I raise up chickens."

"Mmh. And how large is your property?"

"Well, " said the Israeli, "in front, it's a good eighty fitt—and in back, must be a hundred, a hundred and ten, at *least*."

Alkali grinned. "Well, sir, I'm not aimin' to brag, but you just might be innerested to know that back home, on *my* ranch, I get up and after breakfast I get in m' car, around nine A.M., and I start to drive—and I drive and drive and drive, and I don't reach the end of m' property until six o'clock that night!"

"Tchk, tchk!" sighed the Israeli. "I once owned a car like that."

Strom Germond, a loyal son of Texas, was visiting Washington, D.C. At a dinner in his honor, Strom boasted of the wonders of his beloved state—and of his own riches. "Now, I know some of you folk will find this hard to believe, but it jest happens I have *five hundred* head of the finest St. Gertrudis cattle!"

Another Texan spoke up. "Oh, come off'n it there, Strom. I know heaps of Texans own five hundred head of cattle!"

Germond Drew himself up in *hauteur*. "In their *freezer?*"

ROTH: People say you always act like such a wise guy, Goldfarb. As if you knew everything!

GOLDFARB: Not *every*thing. But it happens I know a lot, so people are jealous.

ROTH: You know anything about—tennis?

GOLDFARB: Why shouldn't I know about something as simple as tennis? What makes you ask?

ROTH: Because my boy Sheldon has begun to take lessons from a pro.

GOLDFARB: For what position?

The Erwin Schlangers, just returned from a Marco Polo All-Expense Tour around the world, were regaling their friends in Milwaukee with tales of their travel. "China?" Erwin replied to one question. "*Far*. Also crowded. And we never got any of that great food they serve big shots."

"India?" Gerta Schlanger answered someone. "You could *die* from seeing such poverty, misery, sickness—and those crazy *cows* dumping on the sidewalks. . . ."

On and on came the questions, and the candid answers of the voyagers.

"Venice? Okay if you like water instead of streets."

"So, Madrid? You seen one bullfight you seen them all."

"Paris? Mi*god* is that town expensive! And the traffic is so noisy you can't hardly sleep."

"In Rome," said Mr. Schlanger, "you can't cross a street. Those drivers are *mur*derers. And the whole town smells . . . gasoline fumes, bus fumes, garbage . . . But still, it was a high spot—on account of, as Gerta will tell you, we had an audience with—the pope!"

"Hey!" "Wow!" "That must of been some thrill! . . ." "Tell me, Gerta, what was your impression?"

"*Him,*" said Gerta Schlanger, "I liked. *Her,* I didn't."

Mrs. Quincy Stoneham, a boastful Bostonian dowager, visiting Israel, cornered a young Israeli soldier and asked, "Have you ever been to the United States, sonny?"

"No, ma'am."

"Do you want to visit us?"

"Oh, yes."

"Well, I can hardly blame you," smiled Mrs. Stoneham. "After all, there's no place in the world like America. I'm not trying to put down your little country, sonny; but when you've been born and raised in the U.S.A.! Why, just think of the great men in our history . . . Washington, Franklin, Jefferson, and from my own part of the country John Adams, Paul Revere! . . ."

"Paul Revere?"

"Oh, yes. One of our greatest heroes—"

"But lady, isn't he the one who ran for help?"

See also **Kibitzers, Put-downs, Squelches, Texans**

Boo-boos

1. A verbal mistake: a *faux pas*.
2. An embarrassing error.
3. A blunder.
4. (Originally) Accidental loss of bowel contents by a baby or child.

This euphemism rocketed to public attention around 1949–1950 as a trademark of the comedian Jerry Lewis in nightclub and television skits with his then-partner Dean Martin.

Boo-boo began as a parent's/nurse's code word (like B.M.) for a child's "accident" in diapers or panties. It was, because expressive and amusing, inevitably taken up by children.

Boo-boo became popular among radio and television performers for it was a funny sounding, indispensable label for any *faux pas:*

"In front of the whole class? What a *boo-boo!*"

"If I don't get to a men's room fast, will I make a *boo-boo!*"

Among Gentiles in the Bronx and other boroughs, the tympanic *boom-boom* served as the genteelism for "bowel movement."

from my *Hooray for Yiddish!*

❧

The bride was wearing a gorgeous old lace gown that fell to the floor as she came down the aisle.

❧

Despite the many delays, the game began promptly 35 minutes late.

❧

We note with regret that Mr. Jordan is recovering after his serious accident.

❧

Mr. and Mrs. Walter F. Hill announced the coming marriage of their daughter Helene. No mate has been selected for the wedding.

❧

The area in which Miss (Jane) Russell was injured is famed for its beauty.

❧

At this point the gallery of golf fans deserted the champion to watch Miss T———, whose shorts were dropping on the green with remarkable regularity.

❧

Texas is the former birthplace of President Eisenhower.

❧

In a club magazine

> The three-day outing is climaxed
> by a huge picnic, which practically
> doubles the town population each year.

❧

When the baby is done drinking it must be unscrewed and laid in a cool place under a tap. If the baby does not thrive on fresh milk it should be boiled.

❧

RAMSAY'S POSER STARTLES
AUDIENCE

Sir William Ramsay raised the question whether the unfit should be left to die at the dinner of the Institute of Engineers tonight.

❧

As for this puzzler: "Was it he you were talking to?" or "Was it him you were talking to?" Mr. Lewis says the correct sentence would be: "Was it he to whom you can also say it was she I were talking." However, he adds, was thinking about.

❧

"I never went through that ghastly adolescent phase most girls experience. I went from child to woman in one go. One day I was a child, the next, a man."

❧

"Her dark hair is attractively set," said Miss Fryn, "and she has fine fair skin—but," she admits ruefully, "it comes out in a mass of freckles at the first sign of sin."

❧

Dr. N——— had another patient in the same apartment house, so he figured he could kill two birds with one stone.

❧

A Census Bureau table has this category at the base of a column of figures:

U.S. POPULATION
Broken Down by Age and Sex

In a pharmacy window

On every prescription, we dispense
with care.

The banquet began with a vote of thanks to the chairman who had resigned, for his contribution.

Children, you must never talk to a stranger unless it's a friend.

Clerks at the meat counter of the supermarket featuring cooked breasts of chicken have been told by the management: "Don't call them breasts. Say white teats."

In a firm voice, the bride then repeated . . . "to love and to cherish, in sickness and in health, for poorer or richer, until debt do us part."

"Flying saucers are just an optical conclusion."

"Those shoes? I only use them for street-walking."

"Why some parts of the Grand Canyon are a mile deep—and two miles high."

"They better not fool around with that A-bomb. It's dynamite."

"He wants to be cremated, because he doesn't believe in death."

"Oh, did he make a wrong mistake!"

"A girl of seventeen is much more of a woman than a boy who is seventeen."

"The heroine has to be like Julius Caesar's wife—all things to all men."

"She is a middle-aged child."

"Do you wake up feeling tired and lustless?"

"You get just what you pay for—and you don't pay very much."

"It strikes me as funny, don't you?"

"In exactly thirty seconds, it will be approximately one fifteen."

"Her father was a civil serpent."

from my Rome Wasn't Burned in a Day

∾

Usher: "May I sew you to your sheet?"

∾

Singer: "I have dedicated the next song to our queer old dean."

∾

Texan: "That blow-hard? He's the biggest lamb dyer in Texas!"

∾

Churchgoer: "Excuse me, ma'am, but is that pie occupewed?"

See also **Advertisements, Bloopers, Can You Believe It?, Churches, Freudian Slips, Geography Revised, Headlines That Haunt Me, How's That Again?, Typos**

Bores

Bore: Someone who, upon leaving a room, makes you feel that someone fascinating just walked in.

Someone who talks, when you want him to listen.

AMBROSE BIERCE

We often forgive those who bore us, but we cannot forgive those whom we bore.

ROCHEFOUCAULD

He deprives you of solitude and doesn't provide you with company.

The new patient, a most proper Englishman of forty or so, sat down opposite Dr. Cruikshank. "Now Mr. Fotheringdale," said the doctor, "what brings you to consult me?"

"Can't say, really," said Mr. Fotheringdale, "except—yes—probably hope. Sheer hope, I daresay. Mmh. Yes. Hope. That you can—perhaps—give me some measure of relief . . ."

"Relief? From pain, sir?"

"Oh, no. Nothing as *dram*atic as pain, doctor. . . . It's—well, to be perfectly frank about it, it's a—it's this *fright*ful habit I have . . ."

Dr. Cruikshank waited.

"Had it since I was off at school. Caused a bit of trouble there, I might say. . . . Then I was in service. Four years. . . . Saw a bit of this rum old world, I did—"

"About the habit that distresses you . . ." the doctor gently interjected.

"Ah, yes. Sorry. This habit— quite simple, really. It's—talking. That's all. Just talking . . . to myself, I mean. All day long. And in my sleep. Talk, talk, talk. Been going on like that for years and *years*. Talk . . . talk . . ."

"My dear Mr. Fotheringdale," said Dr. Cruikshank easily, "that is not such a worrisome thing. A good many people, I'm sure you know, talk to themselves. . . ."

"Oh, yes. I daresay. Quite so."

"Then why does it upset you?"

"Well, sir, they may talk and talk . . . but . . ." Fotheringdale sighed.

"Yes?"

"But I very much doubt, doctor, whether *any* one of them, anywhere in the world, is as *boring* as I am."

See also **Just Jokes, Psychiatrists/Psychoanalysts/Psychologists, Shlemiels**

Boy Scouts

Scene: Boy Scout Den Meeting

"Now, boys, we'll continue with our first-aid-in-an-emergency lessons," said the scoutmaster, "Raymond, suppose someone burns his hand badly: what do you do?"

"Put the hand in cold water," said Raymond.

The scoutmaster said, "Very good. Tommy, what if a boy gets frostbite in his fingertips?"

"You *don't* rub the frostbite," said Tommy, "which will damage the skin or start an infection. You put the fingers in lukewarm water to thaw out."

"Very good," said the scoutmaster. "Howard, what if a child should accidentally swallow the key to your house."

"I," said Howard, "would climb in through the window."

SCOUTMASTER: Andy, what should you do for hives?
ANDY: Absolutely nothing. They are our enemies.

The scoutmaster surveyed his troop and said, "Well, now, how did we spend the weekend? Any good deeds to enter in the merit book?"

One lad said, "Yes, *sir*. Three boys from the troop and me helped a little old lady cross Oakdale Street."

"Mm. Why did it take four of you?"

"She didn't want to *go*."

Business

Myron P. Walton, the most successful salesman on the insurance company's staff, was especially skillful in using the telephone.

One day, Walton called a number on his list of prospects. "He-vo," came the high, thin voice of a child.

"Hello, there," Walton chuckled. "And what's *your* name?"

"Jamie."

"Are you a boy or a girl, Jamie?"

"I'm a *boy* . . ."

"That's nice. Jamie, can I please talk to your father?"

"He's not here."

"Then could you put your mother on the phone?"

"She went with my daddy."

"Well, is there someone else there I can talk to?"

"Would you like to talk to my sister?" asked Jamie.

"Fine. Can you call her to the phone?"

"Okay."

A long silence ensued. Then Walton heard the little boy's voice again. "Mister?"

"Yes, Jamie?"

"I can't lift her out of the playpen."

Andrew Hamilton struck it so rich in London, that on an impulse he sent his father in Dundee a magnificent fur-lined overcoat—and soon after telephoned the old man. "Well now, dod, an' how'd—"

"Andy, lad, that coat is a very marvel! The fur is fine as a wee one's bottom. And *warm!* By all the saints, Andrew, m' old mackintosh is not fit to be worn next t' it!"

"I'm so glod, dod—"

"But y' should na be spendin' mooney like that, lad. That coat must cost three hoondred pounds!"

"Do na worry, dod. I got it wholesale. It cost me but two."

Several weeks later, Hamilton received this letter from his dear dad in Dundee:

```
Andrew, my boy—Send five more of the same
coat. I sold mine for two-fifty.
                                        Dad
```

"How's your business doing?" asked Timmons.

"It's a nonprofit organization, you know," said Willen.

"I didn't know that."

"Neither did I—until I discovered I couldn't make one damn nickel profit."

A beggar knocked on the door of the rich man's house at six thirty in the morning. There was no answer. He knocked and knocked again.

The rich man opened his window and cried down, "How *dare* you wake me up so early?"

"Listen," said the beggar, "do I tell you how to run your business? Don't tell me how to run mine."

"Hello there, Chuck. Ain't seen you in ages."

"Yeah. How're you, Steve?"

"Moving along, moving along. Tell me, Chuck, how's your plumbing business?"

Chuck wrinkled his nose. "Don't ask!"

"Oh." Steve paused, then, with a bright smile, added, "Hey, for this time of year, that's not bad!"

Pancho Montanes walked into the Hispanic-American Bank and approached the desk of the president of the bank, Rodolfo Guiterez y Morales, "*Buenas dias,* Señor Guiterez y Morales."

"Buenas dias, Señor Montanes."

"Señor Guiterez y Morales, you do remember thees money I borrow las" year?"

"Sí, señor. I remember. Eight-t'ousan'-dollar loan."

"*Correcto,* Señor Guiterez y Morales."

"So?"

"Señor, how much you know about Mexican hat business?"

"I know nothing about Mexican hat business."

"Ai, ai, *ai,*" sighed Señor Montanes. "Would be good idea you learn, Señor Guiterez y Morales."

"Why I should learn, Señor Montanes?"

"Because I no longer am in thees business. *You* are."

Among the crowded pushcarts on Hester Street, on that hot, steaming summer day, was one cart entirely full of little straw hats and hand fans. Its proprietor, Vittorio Scarpi, was calling out, "Da fans, nize fans. Make cool you self. . . . Give to wife. . . . *Cinquanta centesmos* to *tre dollari.*"

A shopper said, "Eh. Why soma you fan cost fifty cents anda soma you fan cost t'ree *dollari?*"

Vittorio Scarpi picked up a fan that cost three dollars and said: "Witha thees fan you make like thees . . ." He waved the fan vigorously before his cheeks. "But witha cheap, cheap fan"—he picked a cheap fan off his cart—"you musta make like *thees!*" Holding the fan still, he vigorously shook his head back and forth. "See?"

The shopper considered this carefully. "I don' know if isa worth it."

Above O'Leary's pub in Killigan, the wife and children of Jock O'Leary were assembled. Feebly, he asked, "Is my son Timothy here, then?"

"Yes, father."

"And me own Maureen?"

"Oh, yes, father. Here I am."

"And Billie . . . wee Bill—"

"Here, dod."

"And moother? Me faithful wife?"

"Trouble not your darlin' head, Jock O'Leary. 'Tis here, I am. . . ."

O'Leary sat up. "So y're all here, y' idjots! Who's watchin' the pub?!"

The panhandler approached Ryan O'Donnell and started his sales pitch, but O'Donnell stopped him short. "No, no, *begorra.* 'Tis not me habit t' hand out money in the street!"

"Thin what'm Oy s'pose t'do, guv'nor? Open an orfice?!"

Gershon and Velvel, old friends, went fishing off the coast of Fort Lauderdale. It was a marvelous day, and the fish were biting. Suddenly, a tropical squall darkened the sky, the clouds dropped a ton of rain, and the waves smashed the boat. Soon Gershon and Velvel were floundering in the boiling waters.

"Gershon?!" shouted Velvel. "Are you okay?"

"Velvel!" gulped Gershon. "I'm okay."

"Don't try to swim to shore!" cried Velvel. "It's too far! Float! Do you hear me?"

"Yes!" cried Gershon. "I'm floating! But Velvel—can *you* float alone?"

"*Gottenyu!*" wailed Velvel. "Is this a time to talk business?!"

A Scotsman walked into the shop of Malcom Rowney, Tobacconist. "Weel na, kin' ye recommend y'r best cigar?"

"Ay," said Rowney, "here is the finest cigar in the place!"

The Scotsman lighted up the cigar—and began to cough and choke. "Mon alive," he gasped, "are ye callin' this disgoostin' weed—"

Rowney sighed, "Ah, what a looky mon y' are."

"Looky?" cried the Scotsman. "It's *mod* y' moost be! Why am I looky?!"

"Because y' own only one of them disosters. Me? Stook w' twunty doozen!"

"Howie," said Mr. Biegeleisen to the star salesman of his dress company, "how would you like to be a partner in the firm?"

"Would I?" Howie goggled. "Just say the word!"

"All you have to do is marry one of my daughters. . . . Open the door a crack. Two of my girls are sitting there. . . . Look them over. . . . Mamie, my third daughter, will be here any minute. When she comes, you can decide—"

Said Howie, "I'll take Mamie."

Luigi Cortillo operated a hotdog stand in New York. One day, a friend asked, "How's business?"

"*Molta bene.*" Luigi smiled. "Already I save t'ousand dollar' in *banco.*"

"Ai, ai, ai!" said the friend. "So maybe you lenda me ten dollar."

Luigi sighed, "I no allow."

"What you mean, you no 'allow'?"

"I make contract with *banco:* They no sell hotdogs, an' I no lenda money."

Sign next to large wall clock in an accounting firm in Manhattan

IT'S EARLIER THAN

YOU THINK

The Harmon and Hutson Store, in business for ten years, decided to celebrate the appearance of its one millionth customer. As a Mrs. Celia Matsill entered the store, cameras flashed, the officers applauded, the publicity department released balloons, and Messrs. Harmon and Hutson piled gift packages, chits for merchandise, and a complimentary order for a year's supply of household goods into the ample arms of the startled Mrs. Matsill. And as the camera of the local television station rolled, a reporter asked the lucky lady, "And what did you come into Harmon and Hutson's for today?"

Said Mrs. Matsill, "The complaint department."

Executive: A man who has an infinite capacity for taking planes.

Changing Times

Sign in pawn-shop window

Don't be shy. Come in!
Now is the time to
Borrow Your Way Out of Debt

DARLY AND CAMERON
19 Forbush Way
Edinburgh, Scotland

Angus McCreedy
30 Bolingbroke St.
Aberdeen, Scotland

Dear Mr. McCreedy:

    Enclosed please find our billing for
£7.82 for merchandise purchased in our
Aberdeen branch on 6 June 1984.
    Payment at this time will be appreci-
ated.

                Yours,
                J. Darly, Pres.

P.S. This bill is now one year old!

The above letter was returned without a check—but under the postscript, in red, was written:

Happy Birthday!

One morning, every office at IBM headquarters bore the now-famous admonition on one of its walls:

THINK

The next morning the executives arrived to find, beneath the sign, this addition:

OR THWIM

"Fifaty cents a roll?" exclaimed Mrs. Barbella. "Cilento, acrossa street, he is ask onaly forty!"

"So you go acrossa street anda buy."

"Today, Cilento isa sold out."

"Mrs. Barbella, when *I* ama sell out, I charga only t'irty cents!"

Jim Fadden, of the Peerless Employment Agency, telephoned Mr. Langley, president of Langley Textiles. "Mr. Langley, I hope you can verify a few facts given to us by a client who used to work for you and is now looking for a good job."

"What's your client's name?" asked Langley.

"Hardwick. Bob Hardwick."

"I remember him. What do you want to know?"

"How long did Hardwick work for your firm?"

After a pause, Langley said, "About two weeks."

"*What?* Hardwick said he'd been in your employ for four years!"

"That's right."

Sign in cashier's office

> There is no such thing
> as petty cash.

See also **Banks, Chutzpa, Clothes, Hotels, Ingenuity, Salesmen, Stock Market, Stratagems**

Camp Lore

Postcard from ten-year-old at camp for the first time

Dear Folks,

Having okay time, I think. Yesterday we went on hike. Send my other sneaker.
Love,
Richy

Letter from eleven-year-old

Dear Ma—

Remember what I told you if you made me go to camp? Something terrible would happen, I told you!
Okay. It did.

Love,
Peter

CAMP HIANIKO
Storr Pond,
Vermont

Dear Mama and Papa:

The kids are pretty nice here. Except Amy. She is a drip who I hate.
My counslor is okay.
The food is good—and they don't make you eat it.

Love,
Jane

Postcard, after three long weeks of silence, from nine-year-old at summer camp for the first time

Dear Mother and Daddy:

The Direcktor is making everyone write home.

Eve

❧

SHOWANAKEE CAMP
Indian Trails,
Vermont

Dear Mr. and Mrs. Long:

Your son Charles is having a *wonderful* time here. Our staff likes him a lot. He is also popular with all the boys in his cabin. I thought you would like to know this. You have every right to be proud of Charley.

Yours truly,
Jack Dallworth
Director

Edward Long
172 Beacon St.
Boston, Mass.

Dear Mr. Dallworth:

My wife and I were pleased to learn what a fine camper little Charles has turned out to be. We certainly are proud of him.

We have a son at Showanakee, too. His name is Bernard. Perhaps you would be good enough to let us know how he is doing.

Yours,
Edward Long
Father

See also **Children, Kids' Stuff, Mothers**

Cannibals

A cannibal is someone who gets his first taste of religion when he captures a missionary—and eats him.

EVAN ESAR

"Can you come by tonight, Wakoo? We're having Mr. and Mrs. Bennett for dinner."

CANNIBAL CHILD:　What's that big, shiny thing flying through the sky and making all that noise?

CANNIBAL MOTHER:　It's like a lobster, dear. We only eat what's inside—and that's de*li*cious!

KOOMKO:　Are you enjoying the food, Glopoo?

GLOPOO:　Man, I'm having a *ball!*

MABOOTI:　What's the matter? You look unhappy.

ZAGROKO:　Oh, I don't know . . . I guess I'm just fed up with people.

The cannibal chief wrote to the head of the Missionary Society in London:

> Please send more messengers from the
> Lord. The last two were delicious.

A cannibal chieftain entered the dining room of the little steamer plying along the coast of Africa. He sat down at a table. When the steward brought him the day's menu, the cannibal said, "May I see the passenger list?"

True. In 1950, one Biaka-Boda, a member of the French Senate, representing the Ivory Coast colony, toured the interior of his country the better to understand the people's problems. Their chief problem, he soon learned, was food: the natives ate him.

Can You Believe It?

There were only two automobiles in the state of Ohio in 1895.
They collided.

JOHN TRAIN, *True Remarkable Occurrences*

Five thousand people were polled by *Collier's* magazine (May 1949) and asked:

What is bought and sold on the
New York Stock Exchange?

Sixty-four percent replied:

Livestock

RADIO GEMS

"MEN! For Christmas, give your wife a gorgeous Gruen!"
(Repeat, increasing tempo, until light dawns.)

"And now, folks—stay stewed for the nudes!"

TRUE TALE

```
MRS. CHARLES LARKIN
ROUND HILL ROAD
GREENWICH, CONN.
DENVER CONFERENCE GREAT SUCCESS. ARRIVE NEW YORK
TONIGHT. MEET ME AT OPERA 8:15. HAVE GOTTEN TICKETS.
LOVE.
                CHARLIE
```

Mr. Larkin arrived at the opera, where he met his wife—plus eight friends.
Her telegram clearly said:

```
HAVE GOT TEN TICKETS.
```

Suppose you are driving through the back country of Iraq one fine spring day. And suppose you see (as you will) that the faces of all the calves are purplish in color, all the chicks are green, all cows' udders are red, and all bulls' dangling testicles are blue.

You would blink, of course, and look again, and swear off the hard stuff, but the astonishing colors would not disappear.

Why? Because superstitious natives in Iraq think that fearful gods demoralize the fornication of animals, thus freezing their fertility. Each spring, therefore, the natives paint their precious livestock in colors to outwit the ancient demons. The colors are dictated by tradition. I do not know what effect the painting has on the animals; it certainly enchants tourists.

from my *The 3:10 to Anywhere*

From a newspaper I received the intriguing news that a Mrs. Elizabeth Hammond, of Gillette, N.J., owns a pet nine hundred-pound elephant, called Mignon, who sleeps in the living room, turns on the TV when bored, and blinks lamp lights on and off to signal that she is going to sleep.

The neighbors think that Mrs. Hammond is bereft of cranial marbles, but her husband and children have accepted Mignon as just another revelation of the lady's love of animals, which include a pet lion cub, three dogs, a horned owl, a bobcat, and a python twelve feet long.

Mrs. Hammond used to train animals for their debut on the stage of the Metropolitan Opera. Perhaps the most startling aspect of all this *mishegoss* is that Mignon, who was born in Thailand, has developed a passion for roast-beef sandwiches.

from my *Passions and Prejudices*

A well-known socialite in New York, planning a grand dinner, told her new French maid: "Be sure, Marcette, to serve the fish *whole*, with its tail and head, and a slice of lemon in the mouth."

When the great dinner was under way, following the oysters Rockefeller, Marcette appeared in the doorway from the kitchen, carrying a huge silver platter. The fish was complete, tail and head in place; and in her mouth, Marcette proudly gripped a large slice of lemon.

TRUE

In 1977, the U.S. Department of Agriculture named its cafeteria after one Alferd Packer.

Alferd Packer, it turned out, had distinguished himself in 1874 by guiding five prospectors across a very high plateau in Colorado. Immobilized by snow and exhaustion, the party seemed doomed to death. So Alferd Packer ate the five prospectors and survived.

At his subsequent trial, the judge sentenced Packer to hang; including in his sentence these historic words: "Why, there were only six Democrats in the whole of Hinsdale County—and you ate five of them!"

adapted from JOHN TRAIN, *op. cit.*

On Hoover Dam

U.S. Govt. Property. Do not remove.

TRUE

A U.S. Navy officer hailed a taxi in Tokyo. He spoke not a word of Japanese. He uttered the name of his hotel, in English, and the driver beamed, nodded, giggled, but made no move to drive on. He just blinked incomprehension.

The officer reached for a cigarette; lighting it, he noticed he was using a matchbook from his hotel. Banzai! He leaned closer to the driver and displayed the matchbook, tapping his finger on the cover.

The cab driver grinned. "*Hai!*" he barked. (Even the most porcelain Nipponese maiden utters the affirmative with a bark.) Off zoomed the taxi.

When the brakes finally squealed and the cab stopped, the driver turned to the officer with a flourish of the hand.

The Navy officer opened the door—and flinched. He was at the entrance to a match factory. (It was, indeed, the very factory which made matches for his hotel: its address was what the officer had so cleverly tapped.)

from my *The 3:10 to Anywhere*

In the lounge of an old inn in the Cotswolds, I browsed through a country weekly. One item still haunts me: a letter addressed to the Dean of the Augustinian Order in Guisborough, England, had been returned to its sender with the address crossed out and this correction written by some local minion in Her Majesty's Royal Post Office:

This monastery was
dissolved in 1540.

NATIVES IN NEW GUINEA
DISTURBED BY MANNEQUIN

Port Moresby, New Guinea, Dec. 19 (UPI)—The appearance of the first mannequin in a store window in New Guinea's primitive eastern highlands has created havoc among natives.

Hundreds of natives in the town of Goroka have gathered outside the store's display window for days, wailing and conducting dances to honor the dead, in the belief that the dummy is a corpse.

From the New Delhi *Link*

Every man is as much entitled to his own smell as his own color. Do not let yourself be culturally castrated, by American imperialists! Let them keep their soap!

S. R. LYSTER

The correspondent of an Italian newspaper in Tahiti reported that when he patted a little two-year-old native, the boy's mother said: "I'll give him to you."

The scandalized journalist learned that it is not uncommon in Tahiti for a mother to hand you her child as a gift. The recipient, in turn, can pass the kid on after a few weeks. Many a youngster in Tahiti grows up without permanent parents.

See also **Appearances, Embarrassing Moments, Evidence, News Items That Haunt Me, Snafus, Texans, True Tales, Waiters**

Characterizations

He has dined in the finest homes in England—once.

OSCAR WILDE

She is the kind of woman who is used for augmenting the grief at a funeral.

GEORGE ADE

He was so small that he was a waste of skin.

He was so skinny you could pass him through a keyhole.

FRED ALLEN

His mind is open—so open that ideas simply pass through it.

F. H. BRADLEY

How holy people look when they are sea-sick.

SAMUEL BUTLER

He is a man without a single redeeming defect.

DISRAELI (of Gladstone)

He is so mean he won't let his boy have more than one measle at a time.

EUGENE FIELD

Do I trust him? I'd rather trust a rabbit to deliver a head of lettuce.

He could not see a belt without hitting below it.

MARGOT ASQUITH (of Lloyd George)

He gave her a look you could pour on a waffle.

RING LARDNER

He had all the backbone of a chocolate eclair.

THEODORE ROOSEVELT (of William McKinley)

I never wrestle with a chimney-sweep.

BOLINGBROKE

"I may not know much, but I know chicken-shit from chicken salad."

LYNDON JOHNSON (of a speech
by V.P. Richard Nixon)

"I never give them hell . . . I just tell the truth—and they think it's hell."

HARRY TRUMAN

"One good thing about being president. Nobody can tell you when to sit down."

DWIGHT D. EISENHOWER

He is by all odds the most interesting man he has ever known.

L. R.

He is one of those people who would be enormously improved by death.

H. H. MUNRO ("SAKI")

You can lead a horticulture, but you can't make her think.

DOROTHY PARKER

(He respects nothing and nobody.) Why, I once heard him speak disrespectfully of the equator.

SYDNEY SMITH

He is every other inch a gentleman.

REBECCA WEST

He has not an enemy in the world, but none of his friends like him.

OSCAR WILDE

While he was not dumber than an ox, he was not any smarter either.

JAMES THURBER

Her cooking suggested she had attended the *Cordon Noir*.

L. R.

He wasn't hostile to facts; he was apathetic about them.

WOLCOTT GIBBS

His mind may be slow, but it's *dull*.

DOROTHY PARKER

He is insane, but he has lucid moments, when he is merely stupid.

HEINRICH HEINE

His judgment is so poor that he runs a risk every time he uses it.

EDGAR WATSON HOWE

There's someone at every party who eats all the celery.

"KIN" (usually FRANK ("KIN")) HUBBARD

I despise the pleasure of pleasing people whom I despise.

LADY MARY WORTLEY MONTAGU

If not actually disgruntled, he was far from being gruntled.

P. G. WODEHOUSE

"When you're as great as I am, it's hard to be humble."

MUHAMMAD ALI

The butler entered the room, a solemn procession of one.

P. G. WODEHOUSE

On the stage, he was natural, simple, affecting; it was only when he was off-stage that he was acting.

OLIVER GOLDSMITH

He charged nothing for his preaching, and it was worth it.

MARK TWAIN

See also **Put-downs, Repartée, Sarcasm, Squelches, Wit**

Chelm

Chelm (pronounce the *Ch* as in the German "Ach!" or the Scottish "loch"—as if expelling a fishbone from the roof of your mouth) is a Jewish mythical town, in which all the inhabitants are fools, simpletons, dumbbells. Chelm is the Jewish equivalent of the legendary Gotham, whose wisemen were idiots.

The most popular fad in Chelm is a game called "Guess Who?" Any number of players can play. The rules are simple. One player leaves the room: the others must guess who it was.

The elders of Chelm decided to give Yussel, the perennial indigent, a face-saving job. "Yussel, we will pay you two zlotys a day. Sit on the hill outside our little village every day, from dawn to sunset."

"Two zlotys!" exclaimed Yussel ecstatically. "What do you want me to do there?"

"We want you to be our lookout—for the approach of the Messiah."

"Pssh," cried Yussel, slapping himself on the cheek. "The Messiah! And if I see him coming, what should I do?"

"When you see him, you run back to the *shtetl* as fast as you can, shouting, 'The Messiah! The Messiah! He is coming!' "

Yussel's face lighted up just thinking of the glory. . . . Every morning he greeted the dawn from the hill outside Chelm. He did not budge. He brought a bag of black bread and radishes and cheese, and a little container of tea, to nourish him during the day. And not until sunset did Yussel leave his treasured post.

One day, a year later, a traveler approached the little village and noticed the figure sitting on a hill. "*Sholem aleichem,*" called the traveler. "What are you doing on this hill?"

"I am waiting for the Messiah. It's my job. I sit here all day, every day!"

The traveler suppressed a smile. "Confidentially, how do you like this job?"

"Ssssh!" Yussel looked about. "Frankly, it doesn't pay much—but it's steady!"

The rabbi of Chelm visited the prison, and there he heard all but one of the inmates insist on their innocence. So he came back, held a council of wisemen, and recommended that Chelm have *two* prisons: one for the guilty and another for the innocent.

"How just is the Lord," said a sage from Chelm. "He gives the food to the rich—and the appetite to the poor!"

The sages of Chelm began to argue about which was more important to the world: the moon or the sun. The community divided into two passionate camps. The reigning wiseman then ruled: "The moon *must* be more important than the sun, because without the light of the moon our nights would be so dark we could not see anything. The sun, however, shines only by day—which is when we don't need it!"

In Chelm, after many years of research, they finally invented an entirely new brand of parachute. "People all over the world will be talking about the Chelm parachute!" boasted an elder. "It is unique!"

"What," asked a visitor, "makes it unique?"

The elder laughed. "What makes it *unique?* Mister, it's the only parachute in the world that is guaranteed to open *every time* on impact."

Two Chelmites were discussing the wonders of scientific research. "Listen," said Minkus, "let's you and me do an experiment. Maybe it will make us famous!"

"Fine," said his brother Shlomo. "What should we experiment about?"

Minkus looked around. On the sleeve of his brother's jacket he saw a flea. Carefully, he reached out, caught the insect, tore off one of its legs, and, putting his mouth close to the flea, said, "Jump! . . . Jump! . . ." and nudged the insect. The flea did just what Minkus had ordered. Minkus spent the day ordering the flea to jump—and the flea jumped each time.

"That's wonderful," said Shlomo.

"Tomorrow," said Minkus, "we'll teach him to jump *backward.*"

The next day, Shlomo tore another leg off the flea, chanted, "Back! Back!" and nudged the flea from the front. After several hours, the flea had learned to jump backward. . . .

On the third day, Minkus removed a third leg of the flea, and called "Circle! . . . Circle!" nudging the flea to rotate on its axis. But the flea did nothing. Minkus removed the fourth leg from the flea and cried "Circle! Circle . . ." The flea remained motionless.

"Aha! You've done it!" cried Shlomo.

"Done what?"

"You've proved that when you remove the legs of a flea it destroys his sense of hearing."

Sleep faster: we need the pillows!

THE WISDOM OF CHELM

Things were getting worse (and worser) in Chelm. Jobs were virtually nonexistent. Food was running low. To find some solution, the elders met. After prolonged analyses they decided that the best hope for Chelm was for the town to develop and sell a new brand of beer.

After considerable experiment, they produced a liquid they thought not bad—and sent a gallon to a famous brewmaster in Prague, with this letter:

> O Worthy Brewmasters:
>
> Seeking to help our poor, we have produced a beer that we can sell. We are humble folk, not known, so it would help our cause if a famous brewer such as you praised our potion.
>
> May the Holy One, blessed be His name, speed your answer.
>
> The Elders of Chelm

A week later came the answer from Prague:

> Your horse has diabetes.

In Chelm (so 'tis said), one night a citizen ran to the fire station, yelling at the top of his lungs: "Theater! Theater! Help! Theater!"

In Chelm, they go to the dentist to have their wisdom teeth put in.

See also **Dummies, Hillbillies, Nebechs, Shaggy Dogs, Shlemiels**

Children

Scene: The Porch of a Summer Hotel in the Catskills

The two women were rocking back and forth, gazing at the lovely sunset.
"And how many children," asked Mrs. Alpert, absently, "do you have?"
"No children," sighed Mrs. Minkoff.
"*No* children?!" blinked Mrs. Alpert incredulously. "Tell me, Mrs. Minkoff, if it's not too personal, what do you do for aggravation?"

Childhood: That wonderful time when all you had to do to lose weight was bathe.

KIM MCGINNIS

Little Brenda gloomily came into the house after her first day at school.
"Well, dear!" beamed her mother. "Did you like it?"
"Nope."
"Did you learn anything?"
"Nope. . . . And something worse."
"What's that?"
"I have to go again tomorrow."

Mrs. Botnick and Mrs. Krasnitz had not met in years. "Tell me," asked Mrs. Botnick, "what ever happened to your son?"
"My son—what a misfortune!" wailed Mrs. Krasnitz. "He married a girl who doesn't lift a finger around the house. She can't cook, she can't sew a button on a shirt; all she does is sleep late. My poor boy brings her breakfast in bed, and all day long she stays there, loafing. . . ."
"How terrible," said Mrs. Botnick. "And what about your daughter?"
"Ah, my daughter!" beamed Mrs. Krasnitz. "She married a man, an angel! He won't let her set *foot* in the kitchen. He gives her a full-time maid, a cook, and every morning he brings her breakfast in bed! And he makes her stay in bed all day. . . ."

A universe of aspiration lies in the heart-felt cry of a Jewish woman at the seashore:

"Help! Help! My son the doctor is drowning!"

The saddest words of tongue and pen:
We just sold the buggy; then—

Twins: Womb-mates.

KAY FRANCIS

"*Ciao,* Mrs. Barbella. How you children?"

"Justa wonnnderful, *grazie.* My Antonia isa teach—in high school; my boy Arnaldo isa *dottore* medicine! Why you no go see him, Mrs. Mastriom? You get besta exam!"

"But Mrs. Barbella, I no needa exam. I'ma *perfetto* healt'."

"Don'a be sure. My Arnaldo—he alaways find *some* sickness!"

Mrs. Kotchin and Mrs. Mishkin sat rocking on the porch of the Villa Lipshitz, a Catskill resort, when a young man approached.

"*Gottenyu!*" exclaimed Mrs. Kotchin. "*Look* at that boy! Did you ever see such a big nose? Such shifty eyes? Such a crooked mouth?"

In a freezing voice, Mrs. Mishkin replied, "It so happens, you are talking about my son!"

"Well," said Mrs. Kotchin, "on *him,* it's becoming!"

See also **Camp Lore, Famous People, Geography Revised, History Revised, Kids' Stuff, Mothers**

Churches

On church bulletin board

Today's Sermon

HOW MUCH CAN A MAN DRINK

with hymns from
a full choir

On church bulletin board

Sermon Sunday Feb. 6:
Change Your Wife Through Prayer

The Tuesday Night Ladies Club had a nice time at the church after their pot-luck supper. For the first time in several months all the members were pregnant.

Church bulletin

Miss Marcia Devin sang "I Will Not Pass This Way Again," giving obvious pleasure to the entire congregation.

Church bulletin

Our choir sang in a broadcast from Minneapolis. It was nice to hear them and realize they were nearly a thousand miles away.

Sign on announcement stand before church

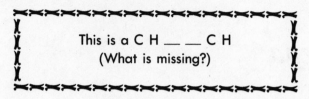

This is a C H __ __ C H
(What is missing?)

Correction

The sermon at the Presbyterian Church this coming Sunday will be

There Are No Sects in Heaven.

The subject was incorrectly printed in yesterday's edition of the *Clarion* as

There Is No Sex in Heaven.

Notice on church bulletin board

Sunday: Rev. M. Farnsworth will talk on:
ETERNITY AND YOU
Come early—if you want to be sure of
getting a seat in the back.

Church bulletin

In the future, ushers will swat late-comers to the service.

A dashing young man in the choir,
Had a voice that went hoir and hoir,
'Til one memorable night
It soared clear out of sight,
And they heard it, in time, in the spoir.

See also **Bloopers, Boo-boos, Clergy, Faith, God, Heaven, Prayer, Religion**

Chutzpa

The quality demonstrated by the man who, having killed his mother and father, throws himself on the mercy of the court—because he's an orphan.

Scene: *Swimming Pool of a Fine Resort Hotel in India*

"Madam Raijapundit," said the lifeguard sternly, "I must inform you that the management has instructed me to tell you to command your son—not to urinate in the waters of the bathing pool!"

"Do not harbor such foolishments," retorted Madam Raijapundit, arranging her sari. "It is well known, amongst *educated* persons, that every child will, from time to time, urinate whilst bathing."

"That is true, indeed true, madam, but not from the diving board!"

Note: Challa, pronounced with a rattling *kh*, is a Jewish bread, greatly favored for Sabbath eve. It is a braided white-bread loaf, glazed with egg white.

A beggar came to the back door of the Meiselman house and knocked. Mrs. Meiselman came to the door. "Can I help you?"

"Can you help me?" the beggar repeated, with a bit of scorn. "You sointinly can. Lady, I am *starving*. Two days already, not a piece food—"

"Oh, you poor man!" said Mrs. Meiselman. "Come in, come in. Sit down. On the table is some bread. Start—I'll make you something."

The shnorrer saw some rye bread and some *challa*. He fell upon the soft, sweet, ever-so-tasty *challa*.

"Uh . . . listen," said Mrs. Meiselman. "There is some good *rye* bread there, too."

"I know." More slices of *challa* were wolfed down.

"Mister . . . the *challa* is much more expensive!"

"Lady," observed the beggar, "it's *worth* it."

Two friends met on the street in Dublin. "Terence, me boy, how nice it is' t' see ye, 'specially since ye owe me ten-pound-six."

"Eamon, me old friend, I know. I'll give ye the money firrst thing t'morrow."

" 'T'morrow, t'morrow. It's procrastinatin' ye are, Terence. Last moonth, ye said ye' didn't have th' money. Last *week*, ye swore ye simply could not pay. Last Friday, ye will recall, ye said ye were out of funds—"

Terence cut in, "Enough, Eamon. Are ye forgettin' that *each toime I kept me word?!*"

Pincus, a *nebech* if ever there was one, blubbered to his boss, "Mr. Fiddelman, I absolutely can't live on the salary you're paying me! My wife has been nagging me—I have to ask for a raise—of t-ten dollars a week more!"

The boss shrugged. "*Nu?* So okay. . . . You got it."

It was an overjoyed Pincus who hurried home that night with ten dollars more than he had earned the week before.

Next week, he opened his pay envelope—and his face fell. He rushed into the boss's office. "Mr. Fiddelman! Mr. Fiddelman! What h-happened to my *raise?!*"

"Your raise?" echoed Fiddelman. "*Gevalt,* Pincus. *Again* you want ten dollars more?"

The phone rang in the office of Joel Greenberg, owner of La Plage Sportswear.

"Hello," said a woman's voice. "This is Mrs. Feitelman. Would you please call my husband to the phone?"

Greenberg frowned. "Who's your husband?"

"Shimon. Shimon Feitelman."

"Does he work here?"

"Sure. He's a presser."

"No pressers are working today, lady. They're all on strike!"

"I know," said Mrs. Feitelman. "That's why I asked if you would call him to the phone. He's on the picket line. He's the one carrying the big, big sign."

The Internal Revenue agent walked into Feinberg's Fancy Deli and asked for the owner. "I am Milton Feinberg," said one of the men behind the counter.

The IRS agent flashed his identification. "I have a question about your income tax returns."

They sat down at a corner table, where the IRS man opened his briefcase, pulled out a folder, spread its contents before Feinberg, and said, "I call your attention to this section—Professional Expenses, tax-deductible."

"My expenses are very big," said Feinberg.

"But not *this* big," said the revenue agent. "Look. Right here, under 'Business Expenses' you list five trips to—Israel!"

"Right."

"Five trips to Israel? Those you call '*Business* expenses'?!"

"Certainly."

"How can a small delicatessen justify—"

"What do you mean 'justify'?" Feinberg drew himself up. "We de*liver*!"

The beggar knocked at the back door of the cottage in Falkirk. Mrs. MacDougald came to the door.

"Mum, could a poor mon ask y' f'r a piece o' cake?" He wiped his nose with the back of his sleeve.

"Cake, is it?" bristled Mrs. MacDougald. "*Cake* y' have the gall to ask for, mon? A piece o' plain bread is nae good enough for you?"

The beggar raised a minatory hand. "*Usually*. But, mum, y' have t' bear in moind that t'day is me birthday."

Marvin O. Winkler, owner of Delectable Dresses, en route to Israel from New York, was obliged to make a business stopover in a certain Arab country. The customs officer at the airport studied Winkler's passport carefully, went through his suitcases twice, reexamined the passport, the picture of Winkler, the visa, and addressed him bluntly: "Mr. Winkler, frankly—are you a Jew?!"

"Nope," said Winkler.

"You certainly *look* Jewish."

"So do you," smiled Winkler. "So do nine-tenths of the people in your country!"

The official, taken aback, stammered, "W-what is your religion, sir?"

"I," said Winkler, "am a Seventh Avenue Adventist."

Scene: Rue de Rivoli

A plump lady from the Midwest, on her first day in Paris, entered Mme. Cuvier's linen shop. After fingering laces, napkins, and a fine tablecloth, she asked the proprietress the price thusly: "*Combien pour cette tish-toch* [tablecloth]?"

"*Cinquante francs, madame,*" said Mme. Cuvier.

"*Cinquante francs?*" echoed the American. "*Mais, c'est une schmatte* [rag]!"

Mme. Cuvier drew herself up: "*Une schmatte, madame? Quelle chutzpa!*"

A *chutzpanik,* having dined very well in a restaurant, now smoking a fine cigar, asked to see the owner. When the owner came to the man's table, the diner said, "My friend, I greatly enjoyed your food. But I haven't a penny to my name. Wait: Don't be angry! I have an idea: I am, by profession, a beggar. I happen to be extremely talented. Why, I can go out—and inside of an hour I can raise the entire amount I owe you. But naturally, you can't trust me to come back? I understand. You'd be well advised to come with me—not let me out of your sight? But a man like you, a well-known restaurateur, can't be seen in the company of a man who is begging, right? So, I have a simple solution. I'll wait here—and you go out and beg, and when you have raised the price of this dinner and cigar, come back. I promise not to leave until then."

See also **Aplomb, Groucho, Ingenuity, Jews, Repartée, Retorts, Sarcasm, Squelches, Stratagems, Waiters, Wordplay**

Clergy

Old Seamus McCord was dying, dying. For two months he had lain in his bed, and the number of times that Father Morphy had come to comfort him were beyond counting. One fierce winter night, with the thermometer below twenty and a howling wind blowing the snow and rattling at the shutters, old Seamus called out, "Mrs. McCord . . . Mrs. McCord . . ."

His wife was at his side in a flash. "Yes, me darlin'?"

"Mrs. McCord," breathed the old man, "my time has come for sure now. Before this night is done I shall be in the bosom of the Lord. . . ."

"Oh, Seamus, Seamus . . ."

"Mrs. McCord," murmured the old man, "go to the phone . . . and call that rabbi around the corner . . . Kaminsky is his name. . . . Beg him, in the name of the Lord, to hurry over . . ."

"Rabbi Kaminsky?!" echoed his wife. "Seamus, 'tis mad you are! Sure you must be wantin' me to call Father Morphy!"

"Nay, nay . . . the rabbi . . ." His eyes closed.

Mrs. McCord clasped her hands and gazed toward heaven. "Oh God, forgive this poor soul—ravin' so. . . . Why, in the hour of his passing, would he want a rabbi?"

One of Seamus McCord's eyelids lifted. "Because I don't want a *priest* to come out on a godawful night like this!"

Said the new minister from the pulpit: "—And finally, dearly beloved, I must make a confession. I did not mind *too* much when, during my sermon, some of you cast covert glances at your watches. What *did* upset me was when you held your watches next to your ears to make sure they were still running."

The car of Rabbi Golden was stopped at the traffic light, waiting for the red to change to green, when the coupe driven by Father Mitchell crashed into him.

At once, traffic cop Kelley hastened over. "Well now, father . . . How fast would you say the good rabbi was going when he backed into you?"

See also **Churches, Faith, Heaven, Prayer, Rabbis, Religion**

Clothes

Sign at chic fashion boutique

OUR PANTS LEAVE YOU BREATHLESS

❧

The dowager came into Kolitsky's Fashion Emporium and said, "I want to try on that dress in your window."

"If you want to, you want to," said Mr. Kolitsky. "Personally, I think you'd feel more comfortable in the dressing room."

❧

Sign in dress shop

Sporty sun-dresses for convertibles.
Great with tops down.

❧

Lingerie

GAY NIGHTIES

In store window

These shoes will look better on your feet than on our hands.

❧

In fur-store window

Let us be your miss in lynx.

❧

A man hurried into Minkoff's Cleaning Emporium. "Can you press this suit while I wait?"

"Soitinly," said Mr. Minkoff. "I got a nice little waiting-place behind that curtain."

"Good. How much do you charge?"

"Four dollars."

"Four dollars?" exclaimed the man. "You must be crazy. Why, in Florida I can get a suit pressed for only a dollar and a half!"

"Is dot so?" Mr. Minkoff stroked his chin. "And how much is the plane fare?"

❧

Fashion

What woman's dresses will be up to.

❧

That, not necessarily beautiful, which makes what preceded it look silly.

L. R.

❧

What a her does to a hem to get a him.

Changing Times

❧

Induced epidemics.

G. B. SHAW

❧

Sign in girdle department of western store

Unlike the government, we give aid to overdeveloped areas.

❧

Falsies: Hidden persuaders

❧

Sign in lingerie-shop window

WE FIX FLATS

Ian Crombie stumbled along the street in Inverary, limping, moaning, and groaning. Mrs. Dumfree stopped him. "What is the matter, mon?"

"M' shoes," said Crombie. "These shoes. Instruments of torrture, they are!"

"Why d' y' wear them, then?"

"*Why*, woman? I'll be tellin' ye. M' business couldna be worse. I owe money t' th' bonk, th' grocer, th' landlord. I have a doughter so ugly, it would be a miracle she iver married. M' wife nags me day oon night. I coom home each night, look at th' bills and at m' wife 'n doughter—ooon I could kill m'self! So I take off m' shoes. Woman, th' viry moment these shoes is off m' feet, it's th' only thing makes life woorth livin'!"

See also **Tailors**

Communism

Two dogs met in West Berlin. "How do you like life in this decadent, capitalist city?" asked the dachshund.

"So-so," waffled the borzoi.

"What's wrong with it?"

"Well, in East Berlin I get meat that is soaked in the finest vodka. My doghouse has an electric heater in it. Once a week I see a cultural movie."

The dachshund scratched his chin. "If that's the way you live in Communist East Berlin, why do you come to West Berlin so often?"

The borzoi frowned, "Every so often I have this need to bark."

The ardent Communist explained to his son, "You see: under capitalism, Man exploits Man. But under Communism, it's exactly the opposite!"

At the bar in the great lounge of the United Nations, the chief U.S.S.R. delegate, Nikita Ordzhonokidz, raised his glass to his American and British guests. "*Tovarichchi,* please to join me in fine toast: To Alexander Voloshov Chamainsky, fine Communist!"

The three men drank. Then Lord Stanway, the delegate from Britain, cleared his throat. "Forgive me for being *fright*fully dense, old boy . . . but who *is* Alexander Voloshov—"

"Alexander Voloshov Chamainsky was big Rossian genious! Inwanted elactric. Inwanted movies. Inwanted raddio. Also talevision. In foct"— Ordzhonokidz raised his glass again—"Chamainsky was almost as big inwantor-genious as Grischa Ivanovich Yamporkov! I now toast you: Communist Grischa Yamporkov!"

Again the three glasses were raised and the contents drunk.

"Um . . . Sascha," said the American delegate, "I hate to ask, but—who was Yamporkov?"

Growled Ordzhonokidz, "You don't know who is Grischa Yamporkov? Yamporkov inwanted Chamainsky!"

A national election was recently held in Cuba. It was, of course, "by secret ballot."

One worker in a voting queue approached the polling table, where he was handed a sealed envelope by a guard. "Just drop this ballot in slot."

The worker started to open the sealed envelope.

"*Caramba!* What you doing?"

"I want to see who I vote for."

"Dummy!" said the guard. "That you find out tomorrow. Don't you realize this is secret ballot?!"

Georgi Maystrovich, the Commissar of Agriculture's representative, came, on a special tour of inspection, to the Commune of State Farm 78 in the Kharkhov zone. "And what are your estimates of the tomato crop for this season?"

"This season, Comrade Maystrovich," said the chairman of the local commune, "the tomatoes will be so large and juicy, the department in Moscow will be overjoyed!"

Maystrovich wrote a few notes in his notebook. "And how *large* will the crop be, comrade?"

"How large? Why if all the tomatoes we pick are put into one pile, it will make such an enormous mound that it will practically reach the feet of God!"

"Stop that!" snapped Maystrovich. "What sort of nonsense is this? Communists know there is no God!"

The chairman nodded. "And there aren't any tomatoes either."

The Chinese Security Police officer, accompanied by two soldiers with rifles and bayonets, hammered on the rickety door of the flat. "Police! Open the door! At once!"

The door was opened from the inside, creaking on its hinges, by a barefoot man in a frayed jacket and old blue pajamas.

The Security officer stepped into the room. Eight persons lay on old mattresses in the sunless, airless room. "I have come for Wu Zung-Ko."

Someone coughed, someone grunted, but no one said a word.

"Does Wu Zung-Ko live here?" the officer bellowed.

Silence.

"You!" the officer addressed the barefoot man who had opened the door. "What is your name?"

The old man bowed. "Wu Zung-Ko."

"Then why," the officer glared, "didn't you say you lived here?"

The old man bowed again. "Do you call *this* living?"

See also **Behind the Iron Curtain, Diplomacy/Diplomats, Russia**

Computers

At the Hokumora-Fijo display room in Tokyo, the long-awaited electronic marvel, the KZ9-6444, was being demonstrated to the foremost mathematicians and philosophers in Japan. The savants hovered over the elaborate display screen as numbers, fractions, equations, cosines, curves, graphs, tables flashed and popped. After some time, lights brightened, a bell rang, and on a huge screen above the KZ9-6444 appeared an equation consisting of thirty-two integers, four vectors, seventeen sines . . .

The scientists buzzed with wonder and admiration. "Is amazing!" "Hard to berieve . . ." "Banzai . . ."

And the senior scientist in the group, the revered Professor Mikio Chimoru, said, "Honolable correagues, do you learize it would take one hundled matematician, wolking ten hour a day, over sixty-two year to make mistake rike this?!"

✌

The scientists at the California Institute of Technology were extremely proud of their new robot, the most advanced information/calculating/thinking machine ever produced in the world. They affectionately dubbed it "Albert Feinstein." Lines formed around the block every Friday, when visitors were permitted to ask questions of the Wonder Robot.

One warm, sunny afternoon, Pierre Quarnet, a student from France, asked the machine a question he felt sure would stump the mechanical wonder.

QUARNET

My question is: Where—at this very moment—is my father?

ROBOT

Spell . . . your . . . father's . . . name . . .

QUARNET

My father is Y-V-E-S Q-U-A-R-N-E-T.

ROBOT

(*its parts tumbling and rumbling, flashes perforating its eyes*) Your . . . father . . . is . . . on . . . the . . . beach . . . at . . . Cannes . . . with . . . a . . . blonde . . . named . . . Violetta . . . Despres. . . .

QUARNET
(bursts out laughing)

Wrong! *Excusez-moi.* You are wrong! I just spoke to my father on the transatlantic phone. . . . He is with my mother and sister, in their apartment at Twenty-seven Rue Ramier in Paris! . . . What do you say to that?

ROBOT

I say . . . Yves Quarnet is with . . . your mother . . . and sister . . . in their apartment . . . Twenty-seven Rue Ramier . . . Paris . . . third floor . . .

QUARNET
(smiling)

Good!

ROBOT

But your *father* . . . is on . . . the beach . . . at Cannes, with . . . a . . . blonde . . . named . . . Violetta . . . Despres. . . .

The great Technion Institute in Israel perfected an electronic translator, a machine that could with blinding speed render the text of any one of twenty-two languages into any one of the others.

The marvelous machine was returned to the laboratory for improvement when this sentence from the New Testament was fed into it:

The spirit is willing, but the flesh is weak.

—and this answer, in Russian, popped up:

The vodka agrees, but the meat smells bad.

Scene: A Computer Shop in London

"Is this electronic device any *good?*" the salesman echoed. "My dear Mr. Shelling, this is a most re*mark*able machine. It is, in fact, so efficient that our firm guarantees that it will cut your workload in half!"

"I say!" exclaimed Mr. Shelling. "You're not simply puffing the product—to make a sale?"

"*Mister* Shelling! A written guarantee accompanies each of our DR-209s, precisely stating that the instrument will cut an executive's workload by fifty percent!"

"By Jove! In that case, I'll take two of them."

After all the passengers were belted in, and the aircraft reached its flight path of thirty-two thousand feet, through the loudspeakers came this:

> Good morning, ladies and gentlemen. Thank you for flying Eagle Airlines. We shall be flying at a height of thirty-two thousand feet. Our present ground speed is six hundred thirty miles per hour. So lean back and relax, read, take a nap. This plane, the JX-802, is the latest, most modern model. It is the safest aircraft anywhere in the world. All our operations are governed by the finest computers, which guarantee that nothing can go wrong—nothing can go wrong—nothing can go wrong . . .

Please read this couplet with care:

> Under a lamp the nude is vain
> Broccoli is often blind.

And scan a second:

> Life reached evilly through empty faces.
> Space flowed slowly o'er idle bodies.

These lyrical *pensées* are not the work of an idiot, or a brave bard. The couplets are the first to have come from a digital computer.

The method for producing poems is quite simple. The programmers simply feed a basic vocabulary into the memory bank of their robot, making sure there is an ample assortment of parts of speech (verbs, articles, nouns, adjectives, prepositions, adverbs).

I was so carried away by visions of odes-via-randomization that, owning no digital computer, I decided to conduct an experiment of my own. I wrote one hundred winged words on one hundred slips of paper, making sure that about twenty percent of the words rhymed. Then I distributed the slips among twelve separate envelopes—marked, respectively:

> Openers
> Articles
> Adjectives
> Nouns
> Adverbs
> Verbs
> Adjectives
> Nouns
> Conjunctions
> Articles
> Verbs
> Nouns

I reached into the envelopes, in the same sequence as I have listed the categories above, and picked one slip out of each envelope. When I had extracted twenty words, I arranged them in four lines. *Voilá:*

> On bright pumpernickel gravely twinkle
> Sweet daffodils and a stately pickle,
> Where shrill brassiers shyly hide
> Broken dreams inside insides.

I am sending this to the Pulitzer Prize jury.

I now made a second venture into verse-via-envelope—this time adding a few verbs to my Openers. The slips I pulled out formed this pregnant thought:

> Hail the hairy artichoke!
> Torquemada's frog will gloat.
> Can lunatics like noodle toys?
> Angels have no adenoids.

My third dive into poesy produced:

> How deftly pink suspenders sigh
> A pox on clavichords that lie.
> Hark, hark! The dawn barks Gosh!
> And pregnant mice sell succotash.

Do you want to scale Parnassus, too? It's easy. Just follow the rules I've given you. Choose glowing, gleaming words. Don't worry about gibberish. You may hit upon something as throat-grabbing as this, my latest madrigal:

> Swish green albino dust
> Through avatars unborn
> And circumcise the circumscribed
> Circumstance: Juno stabbed the rooster.

I have read that over many times. It is very beautiful, and makes no sense.

from my *Passions and Prejudices*

See also **Answering Machines**

Conscience

That part of the psyche that dissolves in alcohol.

H. D. LASSWELL

The small inner voice that tells us someone is watching.

H. L. MENCKEN

The mother of invention.

The conscience does not stop you from doing anything; it just keeps you from enjoying it.

Conscience is what makes you feel bad about feeling so good.

L. R.

Conversations I Cannot Forget

"Why, Becky Sorkin!" cried her friend, Rachel. "You're pregnant?! Right?"

"Right," smiled Becky.

"*Mazel tov!*"

"Thank you."

"So tell me, Becky, do you want a boy or a girl?"

Becky said, "Certainly."

At ten forty-two, Rosa Ramirez, the perky new secretary, blithely walked into Mr. Ortega's office.

"Miss Ramirez!" snapped Mr. Ortega. "You should of be here quarter pas 'a nine!"

"*Sí?*" said Miss Ramirez. "Why? Wha' hoppened?"

Judge Napier was very, very cross-eyed. And one day, by a fluke of fate, three cross-eyed hooligans stood arrayed before his bench.

Judge Napier studied each of the men with obvious distaste. Then he asked the first hooligan, "What's your name?"

"Martin Gordon," replied the second.

Snapped the judge: "I wasn't talking to you!"

Cried the third hooligan: "I didn't *say* anything!"

Scene: Martha's Vineyard

The gingerbread hotel has a gingerbread porch, and the gingerbread windows overlook the picturesque harbor of Edgartown.

The porch:

> Aging gentleman occupies one rocker. White flannels, blue blazer, straw hat, pince-nez.
>
> *Enter* septuagenarian lady. Pink cheeks, pink hair, pink parasol, pink purse, pink peekaboo blouse.

WHITE FLANNELS

Good morning, Mathilda.

PINK LADY

Good morning, Theobald.

WHITE FLANNELS

Heard from your daughter?

PINK LADY

Long letter this morning. (*Sits.*) She writes that she and John just *threw* away the guidebooks and struck out on their own. Drove everywhere. Off the beaten paths. They simply took any road or turn that caught their fancy.

WHITE FLANNELS

Good heavens! In *India?*

PINK LADY

Mmh. They *are* adventurers. Emily says they drove into one *dear* little village, a place with an unpronounceable name—

WHITE FLANNELS

Most are.

PINK LADY

—while the natives—Hindus, I presume—

WHITE FLANNELS

Probably.

PINK LADY

—were all in a quaint little temple, worshiping some ancient deity—

WHITE FLANNELS

Fancy that!

PINK LADY

—and when the natives emerged from the temple, and saw Emily—you *know* how very blond and fair she is—

WHITE FLANNELS

Oh, yes, *very*.

PINK LADY

—they *flung* themselves at her feet! Why, they took her for a goddess!

WHITE FLANNELS

(*stops rocking*)

Took her for a *god*dess?

PINK LADY

For a goddess.

WHITE FLANNELS

How nice.

They rock in unison, seeing India.
The ghost of Kipling cackled in my ear.

from my *The 3:10 to Anywhere*

✌

Scene: The Ballroom of a Hotel in the Catskills

MAN: Are you dancing?
WOMAN: Are you asking?
MAN: I'm asking.
WOMAN: I'm dancing.

✌

"Mr. MacIntosh," the young man said, "I coom t' ask f'r your kind permission. I—I make so bold as t' ask ye if I may marry your doughter, Megan."

"Well, well, lad," said Mr. MacIntosh. "Afore I say a worrd—lad, have ye seen Mrs. MacIntosh?"

"Aye, sir," said the young man. "But—I still prefor your doughter."

See also **Accents, Cannibals, Doggerel, Groucho, Hillbillies, Martians, Restaurants, Squelches, Waiters**

Courts

"How far away would you say," smirked the lawyer, "that Mr. Calabrese was standing when he threw the rock at you?"

"He was standin' nine feet, six and a half inches."

"My, my . . ." smiled the lawyer. "Are you testifying—under oath, mind you—that my client was standing *exactly* nine feet, six and a half inches from you when he threw the rock?"

"Yep."

"Well now, Mr. Gorf, how in the world can you possibly be that precise?"

"Because I knew some goddamn lawyer would try to trip me up," growled Gorf, "so I took out my carpenter's rule and measured the distance down to the half-inch!"

Eighty-year-old Augostina Hernandez appeared in Naturalization Court where the judge asked her: "How many states are there in the United States of America?"

"Feefety."

"Good. Who was our first president?"

"Jorge Washington."

"Mmh. . . . Do you believe in overthrowing our government by subversion or violence?"

Mrs. Hernandez thought for a moment. "Violence."

JUDGE:	Now, Mr. Mansfield, how long have you known the defendant?
MANSFIELD:	Over twenty-five years, Your Honor.
JUDGE:	And in your opinion, do you think the defendant is the kind of man who would steal the money the plaintiff alleges he stole?
MANSFIELD:	Uh . . . how much was it?

"Mr. Cortillez, you must only answer counsel's questions. No more, no less. Understand?"

"*Sí, judicatura.*"

"And you must tell us only what you yourself actually *saw*. Not what you think, or assumed, or heard someone tell you. Only what you yourself saw with your own eyes, or heard with your own ears. No what-we-call *hearsay* evidence. Do you understand that?"

"*Sí.*"

"Very well, Mr. Johnson, you may now examine the witness."

The prosecuting attorney stepped to the witness box. "Give your full name, please."

"Full name is Rafael Miguel Escudori y Cortillez."

"And what is your trade?"

"I am *fontanero.*"

"What's that?"

"What you call 'plomber.' "

"Good. And how old are you, Mr. Cortillez?"

"Ai, ai, ai," sighed Cortillez, and remained silent.

"What's wrong, witness?" the judge asked.

"I no can answer, judge."

"You can't tell us how *old* you are?!" The judge glowered.

"No. For eet depend on when I am born, *sí?* And I no can say that. I was *there*, but like you tell me, judge—all I know is that hearasay *evidencia.*"

"Mr. Axelrod," said the judge, "your behavior was very, very bad. You were drunk, you fell through the front window in Oletski's store, you hollered at the policeman."

"Oy . . ." moaned Axelrod. "Am I sorry."

"Sorry—shmorry," said the judge. He rapped his gavel on the desk sharply. "Which will it be, Axelrod: twenty dollars or forty-eight hours in jail?"

Axelrod closed one eye, to think more clearly, then said, "I'll take the money."

The attorney for the defense, famed for his skill in cross-examination, leaned close to the star witness for the prosecution, one Melvin Prosker, and, in the smoothest of voices, crooned: "Now, Mr. Prosker, you have testified that it was night—moreover, a very dark night—and that you were almost two blocks from the scene, yet you clearly saw my client, so you allege, beat Clarence Hyslop over the head with his cane. . . . Is that correct?"

"Yes, sir."

"Mr. Prosker," smiled the attorney, "please tell the court and this jury: How far can you see at night?"

Prosker leaned back. "I don't know for sure."

"You don't *know?*" sneered the attorney. "Well, make a guess."

Prosker leaned forward. "How far is the moon?"

In a courtroom in Tel Aviv, old Mr. Eisenstat was on the witness stand.

The prosecuting attorney was peppering him with questions—all of which Mr. Eisenstat answered, quite politely, quite steadily, but with a lowered head, and in such a low voice that it was almost impossible to hear his answers clearly.

Judge Fanster leaned forward and said, "Mr. Eisenstat, you simply will *have* to speak louder—much louder. And please address—not your chest—but the jury! Do you understand?"

Mr. Eisenstat nodded, raised his head, and said to the jury, "*Shalom*, jury."

The prisoner stood before the bench, miserable, sobbing.

"You ever been sent to prison before?" asked the judge.

"No, Your Honor. Never."

"Well, don't take it so hard. You're going there now."

"Mr. Caravello, how long after you put the phone down did she come into your store?" asked Mr. Marsh, the plaintiff's lawyer.

"I tinka fiva meenut."

"Are you sure of that, Mr. Caravello?"

"Oh, *si, avvocato*. Fiva meenut."

"It couldn't have been eight minutes?"

"Oh, no."

"Or three minutes?"

Mr. Caravello shook his head emphatically. "I say fiva meenut."

Mr. Marsh smiled. "Well, sir, let's test the accuracy—the reliability of your time sense." He pulled a snap-case watch out of his pocket. "When I say 'Start,' begin your estimate. When five minutes have gone by, say 'Now!' Do you understand what I mean, Mr. Caravello?"

"*Certamente. . . . Si, si.*"

"Ready? . . . Start."

The courtroom was hushed as the seconds went by, the minutes . . . on and on. . . . Time suddenly seemed to stretch out. And when some spectators in the courtroom were sure Mr. Caravello was far past the stated time, he sighed and now, "*Alora! . . .* Now!"

Mr. Marsh looked at his watch. His jaw dropped. "My Lord. Five minutes—*precisely* five minutes."

The judge leaned forward. "May I congratulate the witness on the remarkable accuracy of his time sense?"

"*Grazie*," said Mr. Caravello. "Eesa easy, judge. On wall, behind the *avvocato*, is beeg clock. . . ."

MAGISTRATE:	Now, McLarnin, you have sworn to tell the truth, the whole truth, and nothing but the truth, so help you God. Do you understand that?
McLARNIN:	Ay.
MAGISTRATE:	Then what do you have to say about the charges brought against you?
McLARNIN:	Well now, considerin' all them limits you're puttin' on me testimony, I don't think I've got anything at all to say.

Mrs. Alexander Dinerstein was on the witness stand. The judge asked her: "You are Hilda Dinerstein?"

"Yes, Your Honor."

"The wife of Alex Dinerstein?"

"Yes, sir."

"And what does your husband do, Mrs. Dinerstein?"

"He is a manufacturer."

"Children?"

Mrs. Dinerstein blanched. "My God, *no*, Your Honor! Luggage."

"Now, Miss Flinner," said the judge, "will you please tell the court precisely what the defendant said to you?"

The young, blond, buxom charmer blushed furiously. "It was *very* vulgar, Your Honor."

"We are all adults here, Miss Flinner."

"I—I just can't make myself say something so—so filthy!"

The judge thought for a moment and handed the girl a pencil and notepad. "Very well. Just write down the man's words and we'll pass them around the jury."

The girl bit her lip as she wrote down nine or ten words and handed the paper to the judge. He read the paper and gave an involuntary whistle. "You mean the defendant actually asked you—this?"

"Yes, Your Honor."

"Bailiff, circulate this paper among the jury."

The bailiff handed the note to the foreman, who read it, gulped, and passed the indecent proposal to the number-two juror, who read it, dropped his jaw in disbelief, and passed the note on to a woman juror, who barely read three words before she paled, closed her eyes, and passed the words on to the next juror. So it went, juror after juror reading, flushing, turning pale, swallowing. . . . The note reached the last member of the jury, who had been dozing off throughout. He read the note, looked up, nodded to the witness, and, with an expression of bliss, placed the paper in his pocket.

See also **Evidence, Juries, Lawyers**

Criticism

From a book review

However, this is not a book to be tossed aside lightly. It should be thrown, with emphatic force.

A Boston book review

I have no doubt that this book will fill a much-needed void.

Critic

A man who boasts he is hard to please, when nobody tries to please him.

AMBROSE BIERCE

A person who surprises an author by informing him what he meant.

WILSON MIZNER

Mr. _____ apparently writes his plays for the ages: the ages between six and twelve.

GEORGE JEAN NATHAN

Of the play, *I Am a Camera*

I no Leica.

Of the play, *Dreadful Night*

Sure is.

"The opening of his play? It was anything but exciting. I've seen more carrying-on at the opening of an umbrella."

An aspiring, unsuccessful writer sent his latest four-hundred-page novel to a publisher in Boston.

It was returned without comment, he thought, until he happened to turn to the page preceding the first page of the story. There was the usual epigraph:

> All the characters in this
> story are fictional. They bear no
> resemblance to any person, living
> or dead.

In the margin, a blue pencil had scribbled:

> How true.

The little girl marched into the library, stalked to the return counter, and slid a book across the top. The librarian picked up the volume: *Pandas*.

"Well, my dear," said the librarian with a smile, "how did you like this book?"

"Not much."

The librarian looked up in surprise. "Didn't you find the descriptions of panda life and habits just fascinating?"

"Oh, yes."

"Weren't the pictures marvelous?"

"Oh, *yes*."

"Aren't pandas the most darling, lovable little things?"

"Yes, ma'am. They sure are."

"Then why did you say you didn't *like* the book?"

"Well, frankly," the girl sighed, "this book tells you more about pandas than I care to know."

Greek tragedy: The type of drama where the hero says to his sister, "If you don't kill Pa, I will."

SPYROS SKOURAS

From a movie review in the *New York T_____*

> There is Richard Burton growling and
> growling and endlessly chewing the
> lips, ears, and neck of Elizabeth
> Taylor as the faithless wife of a dull
> ambassador, with whom he is having
> a clandestine affair.

I am glad, in a way, that Mr. Burton was endlessly chewing the ears and neck of Miss Taylor as the faithless wife of a dull ambassador, because it probably wouldn't be fun to chew her neck as anyone else. But who is the ambassador with whom Burton is having a clandestine affair?

from my *Passions and Prejudices*

When the curtain came down on the opening night of Cass Lambert's new play, *Where Is Elsa?*, a chorus of boos, jeers, and catcalls ascended from the audience.

"Oh, Lord," groaned Lambert.

"Wait," whispered his wife. "Listen. Some people are applauding!"

Lambert listened. "They're applauding the booing."

See also **Goldwyniana, Reviews of Note, Sarcasm**

Curses

Note: Anglo-Saxons may well marvel over the opulent curses used in Mideastern cultures, where oral maledictions are a popular art form.

Among Jews, swearing is rare but cursing is common. By "swearing" I mean the venting of frustration or anger in obscene phrases directed at no one in particular; by "cursing" I mean the invocation of calamity (pain, injury, death) upon someone—hoping that God, though not directly asked to do so (indeed, usually asked *not* to), will direct his wrath upon the one cursed, in the form requested. For example: *"Damn* this hammer!" is swearing; "May he be buried in the ground and bake bagels—God forbid!" is cursing.

The elaboration of Jewish curses reaches staggering heights of picturesqueness: "May his intestines sound like a music box!" "May he own a hundred houses, and in each a hundred rooms, and in each room a hundred beds; and may he go from bed to bed night after night in search of one moment's sleep!"

I, for one, am awed by such ingenuity in the catharsis of disaffection.

L. R.

May you spend many hours in a soft chair: your dentist's.

I would like to treat him like a treasure: bury him with care and affection.

May God grant him so much breath that he should always be able to ask what the weather is like—outside.

May his navel turn dizzy.

May all your daughters become well known—to policemen.

May he grow sick from satisfactions.

May his buttocks fall off!

Let bunions grow *on* his bunions, and on his carbuncles should grow boils.

May all your teeth fall out—except one: to get toothaches.

Your wife should eat *matzos* in bed, so you get insomnia from the crumbs.

May the seven seas not be enough for your enemas.

May you own five ships of gold—all wrecked.

May a child be named after you soon. (Ashkenazic Jews were forbidden to name a child after a living person.)

May you gain twice as much brains, so you can be a halfwit.

May you become very famous—in medical history.

Like a beet should he grow—with his head in the earth.

Let onions grow in his navel.

Your healthy days, spend on your back—your sick ones, on your feet.

May cramps parade through your bowels.

May all your relatives move in with you.

May you need a prescription.

May you leap up with joy—over an open manhole.

May all his baths be boiling hot, and all his women icy cold.

May everything you fry stick to the bottom of the pan.

May all your shoes be too short.

May you dance with joy, and skid into a sewer.

BUT REMEMBER:
A curse does not arrive as fast as a telegram: (Don't take curses too seriously.)

adapted from my *Treasury of Jewish Quotations*

See also **Insults, Sarcasm**

Cynics' Dictionary

Accordion: A stomach Steinway.

P. G. WODEHOUSE

Adolescent: A teenager who acts like a baby when you don't treat him like an adult.

Applause: The echo of a platitude.

AMBROSE BIERCE

Artificial insemination: Copulation without representation.

Playboy

Aspersion: An Iranian donkey.

Autobiography: A book that proves that the only thing wrong with its author is his memory.

Babies: The worst feature of any new baby is its mother's singing.

FRANK ("KIN") HUBBARD

Bachelor: One who treats all women as sequels.

Bore: One who has the power of speech but not the capacity for conversation.

Calories: Weight lifters.

Centimeter: A parking meter that takes pennies.

L. R.

Champagne: The drink that makes you see double but feel single.

Charm: The ability to make someone think that both of you are wonderful.

Civilization: The progress from shoeless toes to toeless shoes.

Coincide: What you should do when it starts pouring.

Cold War: Hot peace.

Conscience: The thing that feels bad when everything else feels good.

Courtesy: Acceptable hypocrisy.

AMBROSE BIERCE

Demagogue: A man who preaches doctrines he knows to be untrue to men he knows to be idiots.

H. L. MENCKEN

Dinosaur: A colossal fossil who had no *mazel.*

L. R.

Disco: A din of iniquity.

Eccentric: A man too rich to be called crazy.

L. R.

Egotist: One more interested in himself—than in you.

AMBROSE BIERCE

Eternal triangle: Diapers.

L. L. LEVINSON

Etiquette: Yawning with your mouth closed.

Fanatic: A man who does what God would do—if He only had the facts straight.

FINLEY PETER DUNNE

Flattery: The applause that refreshes.

Florida: A place you go to in winter, and usually find it.

Forger: The man who gives a check a bad name.

Fortress: A fort—with breastworks.

Fjords: Bodies of stjll water between steep clyffs in Njorway.

Friendship: An emotion so sweet, steady, loyal, and enduring that it lasts an entire lifetime—unless asked to lend money.

MARK TWAIN

Glamour:
That indefinable something about a girl who has a large bosom.

ABE BURROWS

The capacity of a woman to get more out of a dress than she puts into it.

Gossip:
The only time people dislike gossip is when you gossip about them.

WILL ROGERS

The person who doesn't gossip has no friends to speak of.

Guillotine: The one sure cure for dandruff.

Guilt: One of America's most abundant resources.

Hobson's Choice: Mrs. Hobson.

L. R.

Home: The place where you can scratch any place you itch.

Housing development: Where the builder tears all the trees out of the plot, then names the streets after them.

Humorist: Someone who knows how to feel pretty good about feeling pretty bad.

DON HEROLD

Hypochondriac: One who enjoys poor health, then complains of feeling better.

Hypocrisy: A hypocrite is someone who—but who isn't?

DON MARQUIS

Idealist: One who upon observing that a rose smells better than a cabbage concludes that it will also make better soup.

H. L. MENCKEN

Imagination: What prevents us from being as happy in the arms of a chambermaid as in the arms of a duchess.

SAMUEL JOHNSON

Inconceivable: What happens when an irresistible force meets an immovable object.

L. R.

Insomnia: The inability to sleep even when it's time to get up.

Ireland: A county with so little sense of compromise that a girl has to choose between perpetual adoration and perpetual pregnancy.

GEORGE MOORE

Justice:
Injustice is not hard to bear; it's justice that really hurts.

H. L. MENCKEN

He'd wash his hands in blood to keep them clean.

ELIZABETH BARRETT BROWNING

Kleptomaniac: Someone who can't help helping himself.

HENRY MORGAN

Laissez-faire: The theory that counsels those determined to do good by (or for) others: "Don't just do something; *stand* there."

Logic: The system of thinking that tells us that out of snow you can't make cheesecake.

Los Angeles:
Ten suburbs in search of a city.

A fine place to live, if you're an orange.

FRED ALLEN

Luck: The only explanation for the success of people we hate.

Marriage:
Marriage makes two one; but you never can tell which one is the one.

L. SAFIAN

It's a mutual partnership, if one remains mute.

Love parsonified.

Masochist: Someone who is only happy when miserable . . . (See *Sadist*).

Maybe: The preamble to hope.

Middle-aged: Someone twelve years older than you are.

Money: The thing that keeps people from calling you "Hey, Mac!"

Motel: The place where we exchange good dollars for bad quarters.

Mummies: Egyptians who were pressed for time.

EVAN ESAR

Murderer: Someone presumed to be innocent until he is proved insane.

Reader's Digest

News: Anything that makes a man say, "For heaven's sake!"

Operas in English: About as sensible as baseball in Italian.

H. L. MENCKEN

Optimist: Someone who thinks things can't get worse—after they get worse.

Parking space: An unoccupied place on the other side of the street.

Pawnbroker: A man who takes an interest in everything.

FRED ALLEN

Peace: Time-out.

L. R.

Pessimist: One who feels bad whilst feeling good out of fear he'll feel worse if he feels better.

TED ROBINSON

Platitude: An observation too true to be good.

AMBROSE BIERCE

Politics: That which makes strange postmasters.

FRANK ("KIN") HUBBARD

Popularity: To be popular, ask people for advice. Don't *do* anything about it; just ask.

L. R.

Pornography: Obscene records you play on a pornograph.

Professional men: Slaves to conventions.

Changing Times

Puritanism: The haunting fear that someone, somewhere, may be happy.

H. L. MENCKEN

Railroads: Saturday afternoons, although occurring at regular and well-foreseen intervals, always takes this railway by surprise.

W. S. GILBERT

Rare volume: A returned book.

Reformer:
One who doesn't realize how much worse things can be made.

One who wants his/her conscience to be your guide.

Rules of War: The rules that make it illegal to hit below the toes.

L. R.

Sadist:
Someone who positively refuses to beat up a masochist.

L. R.

Someone who sends get-well cards to hypochondriacs.

Saloon-keepers: I never said all Democrats are saloon-keepers; I said all saloon-keepers are Democrats.

HORACE GREELEY

Sarcasm: Barbed ire.

EVAN ESAR

Scotsman: A man who, before sending his pajamas to the laundry, stuffs a sock in each pocket.

Screens: The wire mesh that keeps flies from getting out of the house.

Secret: What we tell everybody to tell nobody.

Slander: To lie, or tell the truth, about someone.

AMBROSE BIERCE

Snobs: People who talk as if they had begotten their ancestors.

ALFRED ADLER

Spring: The season of balls: tennis, base, charity, and moth.

adapted from L. L. LEVINSON

Suspicion: The emotion that creates what it suspects.

C. S. LEWIS

Switzerland: Beautiful but dumb.

> EDNA FERBER

Tears: A copious discharge of hydrated chlorine of sodium from the eyes.

> AMBROSE BIERCE

Television:
The device that brings into your living room characters you would never allow in your living room.

> RED SKELTON

The electronic device that intersperses gory slaughter with the brushing of teeth.

The reason for ten thousand new brands of cereals that make noise.

The place where show-biz illiterates can express their ill-informed opinions.

The stage for plays about psychopathic adolescents and homicidal nymphomaniacs who are tragically trapped in immense riches.

> L. R.

Tact: Thinking all you say without saying all you think.

Thief: A man with a gift for finding things before you lose them.

> JOE E. LEWIS

Tourist: Someone who goes three thousand miles to get a picture of himself in front of his car.

Truth: It is hard to believe that a man is telling the truth when you know you would lie if you were in his place.

> H. L. MENCKEN

Waiter: A representative of the leisure class.

War: The worst thing about war is that it kills the wrong people.

Yawn: A silent shout.

> G. K. CHESTERTON

Zeal: A nervous disorder that affects the inexperienced.

> AMBROSE BIERCE

See also **Definitions (by Children), Definitions to Cherish, Groucho, Graffiti, How's That Again?, Ingenuity, Sarcasm, Wit**

Death

At his wife's gravesite, in Montparnasse Cemetery, Paris, Alfonse Raimeau wept copiously. And just as copiously wept Gaston Chamford, the late Mme. Raimeau's lover. In fact, Chamford wept with such feeling that Raimeau put his arms around Chamford's shoulder, saying, "Contain yourself, my dear Gaston. Don't take her passing so hard. . . . I promise you, I'll marry again. . . ."

Cemetery: An isolated spot, usually in a suburb, where mourners swap lies.

AMBROSE BIERCE

Cremation

All men are cremated equal.

Sign in undertaker's parlor

Eventually Yours.

Over entrance to morgue

Remains to be seen.

Sign on Halstead's Funeral Home

January 9

We are undergoing extensive alterations. Our facilities will be closed for one month.

THE MANAGEMENT

(cont'd)

Sign on Halstead's Funeral Home

⇶ ⬿

February 9
We are now open for business.
Thank you for waiting.

THE MANAGEMENT

⇶ ⬿

On funeral parlor

Must you be going?

❧

Money refunded if not completely satisfied.

❧

Cremation: For people whose attitude to death is one of grave doubt.

❧

Mrs. Cafferty was wailing and shrieking over the coffin of her dear old uncle—so hysterically that her husband Ignatius said, "Now, Mary, pull yourself t'gither! Enough carryin' on, woman!"

Mrs. Cafferty indignantly folded her arms across her bosom. "This y' call 'carryin' on,' Barney? Wait'll we get to the cemetery, man. *There* you'll see what 'carryin' on' means!"

❧

Francis J. Quimby, age forty-seven, was reading his morning paper, the Dublin *Bugle*. He turned, as was his habit, to the obituaries—and there, to his astonishment and horror, he beheld:

FRANCIS JOSEPH QUIMBY

and under that:

Francis J. Quimby, president of the Q. & R. Building and Loan Society, died last night of a sudden heart attack. He was 47. He leaves his wife, two children, his mother . . .

Fuming in rage, Quimby telephoned his lawyer. "Aloysius! Did y' read this mornin's *Bugle*?"

"That I did, sir. Who is it callin'?"

"What do you mean 'Who is it?' Do y' not recognize my voice? This is Frank. Francis Quimby!"

"*Francis?*" cried the lawyer.

"Hisself! And I want you t' start a suit against that goddam newspaper! For falsehood, embarrassment, psychological grief t' me and me loved ones—"

The lawyer hesitated. "Francis—where are you phonin' from?"

As Solomon Arkin lay dying, his wife and children and grandchildren gathered to comfort him. "Sol, darling," begged his wife, "we . . ."

"I know, I know . . . I'm dying."

"No, no, papa—" said his daughter.

"You think I'm a dummy?" grunted Arkin.

"But the doctors say —"

"Doctors—shmoctors. They're trying to make you feel better. Me, they don't fool. Let's settle important things while there's time. Becky, you don't have to worry about a thing. I left in my will complete funds to take care of you for the rest of your life! Morris, Millie, to you I gave plenty. . . . I don't want to be cremated, you understand? I want a regular burial. Next to my own flesh and blood."

"But Sol, darling, your father, *olav ha-sholem,* is buried in Brooklyn. Your mother, *aleha ha-sholem,* lies in peace in Miami. Your sister is for eternity in La Grange, Illinois. And your brother, God rest his soul, is interred in California. . . ."

"Pa . . ." said Arkin's son. "Where would *you* like—you know . . ."

The old man gave a long yawn. "Morreleh, my boy—surprise me."

Douglas MacPherson, attending a funeral at a cemetery, beheld a magnificent marble mausoleum on his way out. He stopped before it in admiration. On the portal was incised:

CARNEGIE

"Mon, mon!" chuckled MacPherson. "Now *that's* what y' call livin'!"

At the funeral of Yale Friedlander, a very wealthy man, a strange, poorly dressed mourner joined the funeral procession, weeping and wailing louder than all the others.

"Are you from the immediate family?" a woman in black asked him.

"No, no," sobbed the man.

"A distant relative of Yale's, maybe?"

"Not even that," moaned the man.

"An employee! You worked for his firm many years—"

"No, no," wailed the weeper.

The woman in black frowned. "Mister, then why are you so upset?!"

"That's why."

Mr. Smithers entered the offices of his fraternal society. "Mr. Barnes," he said to the secretary, "I want to make funeral arrangements for my dear departed wife."

"Your wife?" frowned Mr. Barnes. "Don't you remember, Mr. Smithers? . . . We buried her last July. . . ."

"That," sighed Mr. Smithers, "was my first wife. I am talking about my second."

"Second? I didn't know you had married again. . . . Congratulations!"

The mourners filed past the coffin, some sobbing, some sighing, and Mrs. Thomson murmured, "Look at him. How peaceful he looks . . . how relaxed . . . so tan . . . so healthy . . ."

"Why not?" replied the widow. "He just spent three weeks in Arizona."

See also **Epitaphs, Limericks, Obituary Data Worth Remembering**

Definitions (by *Children*)

Acrimony: The holy state of being married.

Alcazar: What the Spaniards took for an upset stomach.

Antidote: The medicine that kills dotes.

Boy Scouts: They always obey the dully constipated authorities.

Buttress: A woman's butler.

Duchy: A Dutch lady who marries a duke.

Emulsion: A mixture of oil and emotion.

Epistle: The wife of an apostle.

Esophagus: The author of *Æsop's Fables.*

Females: They get nervous and jumpy during their minstrel periods.

Furthermore: It is much farther than "further."

Germinate: To become a German citizen.

Giraffes: They are a rich source of necks.

Hindus: Religious ones wear a turbine.

Infidels: They are not Christians because they believe in infidelity.

Italics: The language spoken by ancient Italians.

Liter: A bunch of young kittens.

Metallurgist: Someone who is allergic to iron.

Mumbo-jumbo: Large mumbos; or, a mumbling elephant.

Mushrooms: Because they grow in damp places, they resemble umbrellas.

Octagon: A triangle with five sides.

Parthenon: The she-wolf who nursed Romeo and Juliet.

Past tense: When you used to be nervous.

Polygon:
A man who has eight wives.

A dead parrot.

Pompeii: The volcano that buried Pompeii in larva.

President: He must be an American citizen unless he was born here.

Quinine: A valuable medicine that comes from barking trees.

Riches: Some people are so rich they are malted millionaires.

Science: Science keeps discovering answers to unknown problems.

Thence: When you want to say something took place longer ago than "then."

Version: The mother of Jesus.

Waltz: The most famous waltz is the Blue Daniel.

Waterloo: How polite Englishmen refer to the toilet.

Weather: Damp weather is bad for the sciences.

Witches: The most witches of all were burned in Wichita.

Women: The best other sex men have.

See also **Cynics' Dictionary, Famous People (as Seen by Children), Geography Revised, Goldwyniana, History Revised, Malaprops**

Definitions to Cherish

Note: If a bakery is a place that makes baked goods, then the following may be said to define the following:

Adultery: A good many adults.

Archery: A collection of arches.

Artistry: A coterie of artists.

Burglary: A home for burglars.

Cavalry: An assemblage of calves.

Finery: A hoard of fines.

Flattery: A collection of flats.

Gallery: A congregation of females.

History: A chorus of hisses.

Husbandry: A large number of husbands.

Infantry: An arrangement of infants.

Laundry: A display of lawns.

Misery: A collection of misers.

Monastery: A multitude of monsters.

Mummery: A bouquet of chrysanthemums.

Novelty: A library of novels.

Nursery: A school for nurses.

Pantry: A collection of pants.

Parody: A collection of pears.

Sophistry: A group of sophomores.

Vanity: A collection of vans.

Vestry: A multitude of vests.

See also **Cynics' Dictionary, Definitions (by Children), Old Saws Sharpened**

Dentists

The greatest Yank of all.

❧

A dentist bores you to tears.

❧

"How much will such an extraction cost me, doctor?"

"Fifty dollars," said the dentist.

"For a few minutes' work?" exclaimed the patient. "Isn't that a lot of money to charge?"

The dentist nodded amiably. "Well, if you want, I can pull the tooth out very, very slowly."

❧

On dentist's tombstone

Stranger, approach these bones with gravity:
Dr. Brown is filling his last cavity.

❧

After Dr. Newsom examined the new patient's X-rays, he asked, "Mrs. Pulsifer, have you seen another dentist within the past six months?"

"N-no. I went to my druggist."

"A druggist?!" Dr. Newsom snorted. "What sense does that make? What advice did he give you?"

"He told me to see you."

❧

Sign in Istanbul

American Dentist
Room 203
Teeth Extracted by Latest Methodists

Dr. Monte Gershman was an excellent dentist, and a compulsive joker. "Your teeth are in fine fettle," he would tell a patient, "but your gums will have to come out." (That was far from original with Monte, but whenever he sprang the line upon an unsuspecting patient, Monte would chortle and chuckle and shake with delight.)

One day a new patient, Mrs. Marbury, well dressed, condescending in her manner, came to Dr. Gershman's office.

"May I ask who referred me to you?" asked Monte.

"Oh, one of my friends. She said you were Jewish. And I think you Hebrews make the best doctors and dentists."

"Really?"

"I suppose it's something in your blood. Now, doctor, I want to warn you in advance. I will not pay any bill I find excessive. I have a lawyer who approves or disapproves every one of my bills."

"Fine," said Monte. "Now, Mrs. Marbury, open . . . open your mouth, wider. . . . Great Scott, madam! You have the largest cavity I have ever seen in twenty years of practice! . . . *The largest cavity I have ever seen in twenty years—*"

"I *heard* you, doctor!" snapped Mrs. Marbury. "There's no need to repeat yourself."

"Re*peat* myself?" Monte asked with surpassing innocence. "Mrs. Marbury, that was the *echo.*"

See also **Doctors**

Diets

Fat

Energy gone to waist.

❧

There's a divinity that ends our shapes.

L. R.

❧

"Did you say you're a light eater?"
"Absolutely."
"But, man—you must weigh over two hundred pounds!"
"Two twenty."
"And you claim you're a light eater?"
"Absolutely. As soon as it's light, I start eating."

❧

Overweight: Just desserts.

❧

When you diet
Please be quiet.

❧

KATE: I haven't seen you in *years*. What's new?
JANE: Well, since we last met I've gotten rid of one hundred eighty-two pounds of ugly, stupid fat.
KATE: Good lord! How?
JANE: By divorce.

Dilemmas

```
COMCHIEF
FLEET MANEUVERS
        FOG IMPENETRABLE. SHALL I GO ON OR RETURN TO
        BASE?
                                    S.S. COLFAX


S.S. COLFAX
        YES.

                                         COMCHIEF


COMCHIEF
        DOES "YES" MEAN PROCEED OR RETURN?
                                    S.S. COLFAX


S.S. COLFAX
        NO.

                                         COMCHIEF


COMCHIEF
        THOROUGHLY CONFUSED. PLEASE CLARIFY.
                                    S.S. COLFAX


S.S. COLFAX
        CERTAINLY.

                                         COMCHIEF


COMCHIEF
        URGENT. SEND EXACT INSTRUCTIONS. REPEAT.
        SEND EXACT INSTRUCTIONS.
                                    S.S. COLFAX


S.S. COLFAX
        LAST MESSAGE UNCLEAR. REWORD REQUEST.
                                         COMCHIEF
```

COMCHIEF
>   UNLESS YOU GIVE ME EXACT AND DETAILED ORDERS
>   OF NEXT DESTINATION I WILL HAVE TO CIRCLE
>   LAT. 38, LONG. 41.
>
>   S.S. COLFAX

S.S. COLFAX
>   BON VOYAGE.
>
>   COMCHIEF

See also **Snafus, Telegrams**

Diplomacy/Diplomats

Diplomacy: A blend of protocol, alcohol, and Geritol.

ADLAI STEVENSON

Diplomat

A man who never forgets a woman's birthday, and never remembers her age.

One who acts disarming, when his country is not.

At a U.N. meeting, a French delegate, pulling his chair up to the table, accidentally touched the thigh of the Russian female to his left. The Frenchman, smiling, was most gracious in his apology.

The lady turned to the Russian diplomat on her right and whispered something in his ear. The diplomat got up, left the meeting, and hurried out to a phone. He was gone for an hour. When he returned, he leaned over to the lady and whispered in her ear. She leaned toward the French delegate and murmured, "Your place or mine?"

See also **Ingenuity, Tact**

Doctors

Mrs. Korschak frantically telephoned her pediatrician, old Dr. Tobias. "Doctor, doctor! My little Joseph just swallowed a dozen aspirin! What should I do?"

"You're sure it was a dozen?"

"Absolutely! Doctor, I'm scared stiff!"

"Mrs. Korschak, calm down. Is little Joseph crying?"

"No."

"Is he cranky?"

"No."

"Is he sleeping?"

"No."

"Is his color funny?"

"No."

"Did he throw up?"

"No, no, no, doctor! But I'm scared *sick!* All that aspirin—shouldn't I *do* something?"

"Yes," said Dr. Tobias. "Try to give him a headache."

I said to the doctor, "I have this ringing in my ears.

He said, "Don't answer."

JOEY BISHOP

The sign on the medical center door read

LAWRENCE DUNCAN, M.D.
Brain Surgery

F. B. CARNOT, M.D.
Psychiatry

S. RANGOFF, M.D.
Proctology

(cont'd)

Under this, someone had added:

Specialists
in
Odds and Ends

Scene: Doctor's Office, Lexington Avenue, New York

Dr. Hornaday put the X-rays down. "You may get dressed now, Mr. Kampelberg."

"So. What's the story?" asked Shimon Kampelberg as he put on his clothes.

"The story," said Dr. Hornaday, "is quite clear. Your vital organs—heart, lungs, kidneys—are in good shape. For a man of your age, you are quite healthy. But—Mr. Kampelberg, what do you do for exercise?"

"For exercise? Nothing."

"*Nothing?*"

"I never took an hour's exercise in my life."

"Don't you take long walks, or play golf, or jog—?"

"Nothing."

"Well, Mr. Kampelberg, that's the fly in the ointment. Your muscles, your circulation are in *awful* shape! Let me be perfectly frank with you. With your sedentary life, you *must* take regular exercise! Every day, for the rest of your life!"

Kampelberg groaned. "I can't—"

"You *must*. Jog. That's the simplest, easiest of all. You must begin to jog at once!"

"Jogging?" wailed Kampelberg. "Me?"

"Buy yourself a good pair of jogging shoes this afternoon. Then, tomorrow, start. Not fast. Don't push yourself. Slow, at first, a sensible, easy pace. Your first week, jog five blocks a day: that's all. The next week, jog ten. The week after that, fifteen . . . and so on. And after you've reached the point where you can run two-three miles every day, I promise, you'll be a new man! . . . Call me in a month. . . . Goodbye."

The days passed. The weeks passed. Then Dr. Hornaday's phone rang. "Hello?"

A voice puffed, "Heh . . . heh . . . this—is—Shimon—Kampelberg. . . . Re—mem—ber me?"

"Of course, I remember you. You're the patient I insisted start jogging!"

"Right, doc," panted Kampelberg.

"And did you?"

"Oh—sure. Just . . . like . . . you said . . ."

"And don't you feel loads and *loads* better?"

"I . . . feel . . . like a *corpse,* is how I feel. My spine is hot. . . . My arches—forget about such arches. My head—is like a boiler. In fact, every goddam *inch* of my body is on fire—"

"*Mis*ter Kampelberg. Don't get hysterical. I'm sure things aren't all that bad. . . . Why don't you jump in a taxi and come right to my office?!"

There was a pregnant silence. "*Taxi?*" echoed Kampelberg. "Doc, I'm in Danbury!"

"My fee," said Dr. McPherson, "will be three hoondred pounds. You may pay it—say, fifty pounds a month."

"*Och,* that is a strange way to pay a doctor! . . . It's more like buyin' a mootor car."

"Yes, mon. I am."

My doctor is a family physician. He treats my family and I support his.

PHYLLIS DILLER

For a week, Mr. Carlton Satterley's arm had been throbbing. When the throbbing increased and the intensity of the pain sharpened, and the arm began to bear purple, starlike blemishes, Mr. Satterley went to a famous doctor on Harley Street, one Colwyn Melbrone. On the wall, five separate diplomas, each with a gold seal, attested to Dr. Melbrone's medical education, admittance into the practice of internal medicine, and membership in distinguished professional associations.

Dr. Melbrone took a careful case history from Mr. Satterley. Then he examined him thoroughly. Then he took many X-rays of Satterley's arm. Then he studied all the notes he had made and the tests he had taken. . . . "Well, sir. You appear to have a most un*u*sual disorder, Mr. Satterley—one, I am quite frank to confess, that is not at all easy to diagnose. . . . You say you had no accident recently? No blow to your arm?"

"Absolutely not, sir."

"Or have you experienced any abdominal troubles recently? . . ."

"No, sir. Not a thing."

"And your stool, sir. Has that been normal?"

"Oh, absolutely."

Dr. Melbrone stood up, pulled a medical book off the shelf, turned to the index, sat down again, and, oblivious to Carlton Satterley, began to read. He read for some time. Finally, he looked up. "Mr. Satterley, you say you had these identical symptoms in 1973?"

"Yes, sir."

"And again in 1975?"

"Yes, sir."

"Then that settles it!" Dr. Melbrone rose. "Mr. Satterley, it is quite clear that you have the same symptoms, and precisely the same disease, once more!"

My doctor told me I had low blood pressure, so he gave me my bill. That raised it.

ALAN KING

"So how do you feel, Mr. Bohrod?"

"I feel absolutely terrible, doctor. I feel so bad I honest-to-God hope I'm really sick!"

"What a strange thing to say, Mr. Bohrod. Why do you hope you're really sick?"

"Because I certainly don't want to feel this terrible if you tell me there's nothing wrong with me."

A witty young man with a hernia
To his doctor said, "Gol dernia,
While improving my middle
I don't want to fiddle
With parts that don't concernia.

Old Sam Clayborn had spent a dollar on a sweepstake ticket. His number won a million dollars. Clayborn's children did not know how to break the fantastic news to him. "He has a bad heart," said his son. "The surprise could kill him!"

"Let's ask dad's doctor," said Clayborn's daughter.

They phoned the doctor, told him the news, and described their dilemma.

Said the doctor, "Let me handle it. I'll come over."

So Dr. Frungler "dropped in" on the Clayborns and was shown to the old man's bedroom. He made casual conversation with Clayborn for a bit and then, in the most offhand manner, asked, "By the way, I hear you bought a sweepstakes ticket. Is that so?"

"Yes, I did," quavered Clayborn.

"What's the amount, if—by some miracle—you win?"

"One million dollars."

Dr. Frungler laughed amiably. "That certainly is a lot of money. . . . Have you thought of what you'd do if—oh, I *know* the chance is very, very slim—you won that much money?"

"Doc, I sure have thought of that. In fact, I put it in my will. If I win a million dollars, half goes to you."

Dr. Frungler dropped dead.

Victor Borge discourses with particular fondness about an uncle who keeps discovering cures for which there are no diseases.

Dr. Noah Slocum, the distinguished surgeon, carefully cut open the patient's abdomen, parted the skin, sponged the flowing blood, adjusted the hemostats—and out flew two butterflies. They began circling the large lamp over the operating table.

Surgeon, nurses, anesthetist stared at the butterflies. Then Dr. Slocum exclaimed, "I'll be goddamed! He was telling the truth!"

My doctor is a very generous man. He gave a patient six months to live—and when the man couldn't pay his bill, my doctor gave him another six months.

HENNY YOUNGMAN

"Mrs. Mulvaney," frowned the doctor, "do you realize you're running a temperature of 103 point 4?!"

"Is that so, now? And what's the record?"

Sign in office of pediatrician

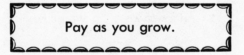

Pay as you grow.

Waldo Stirling told his wife: "Th't new doctor, by Binnie Road—they say he does charge two-pound-ten th' first visit, thin one-pound-five after that."

"Ay?"

"So Ay'll fool th' mon," Waldo chuckled. "Ay'll go in and say, 'A fine morning, t' ye, doctor. Here Ay am ag'in!' "

When Stirling returned from the doctor he looked anything but triumphant.

"So what hoppened, darlin'?" asked his wife.

"What hoppened," said Waldo glumly, "is Ay went in an' very cheery sang out, 'Holloo, doctor. Here Ay am ag'in!' So he bade me disrobe, which Ay did. And when he finished examinin' me, he said, 'Ay now, Mister Stirling. Just ye continue taking the med'cine Ay recommended bifore . . .' "

My doctor is terrific! Some doctors will treat you for a broken arm and you'll die of pneumonia. If my doctor treats you for a broken arm, you die of a broken arm.

MOREY AMSTERDAM

For the first time in her life, Mrs. Flaherty went to a gynecologist.

After taking her medical history, he said, "Now, please go into the next room and take off your clothes."

"My *clothes?*" gasped Mrs. Flaherty.

"Yes."

"Listen, doctor, an' does your good mother know how y' make a living?"

Dr. Jiminez examined the ninety-year-old woman and said, "Mrs. Corzani, you are in very good shape for your age. Your aches, your pains—I can't make you any younger, you know."

"Who ask you make more young?" she retorted. "*Carramba!* I want you make me more *old.*"

My doctor said I was sound as a dollar. That scared the hell out of me.

RED SKELTON

Dr. J. Ritter and Dr. N. Schacht, both obstetricians, shared an office. One day some joker printed under the names:

24 HOUR SERVICE . . . WE DELIVER

"How *are* you, Higgins?" smiled Dr. Nayland, the distinguished obstetrician. "Haven't seen you in a long time. Are you still writing those funny little 'filler' paragraphs for the *News?*"

"Yep," said Higgins. "What about you, doc? Are you still delivering those funny little people?"

The new patient, Yvonne Dupree, was a most ravishing woman.

Dr. Martin said, "Miss—or is it Mrs. Dupree?"

"Mrs. But I'm divorced. Twice . . ."

"Please take off your clothes and get on the examination table."

Yvonne Dupree blushed furiously. "Doctor, you must excuse me. All my life, I've had this—this absolute *revulsion* about undressing in front of anyone. Even before my husbands—I made them turn off the lights first."

Dr. Martin cleared his throat. "I'll be glad to turn off the lights." He snapped the switch on the wall. "Go ahead, madam. Just tell me when you're done."

After a few minutes Mrs. Dupree called, "Okay, doctor. . . . Where shall I put my clothes?"

Dr. Martin's voice was sweet as honey. "Over here. On top of mine."

Diagnosis: What a sick person must make before he can determine which specialist to call.

Dr. Solaway had been in practice for more years than anyone could remember. The faith of his patients in his skill was boundless. His bedside manner was as reassuring as his office manner, which had become legendary in his neighborhood.

One day a distinguished, gray-haired man came to Dr. Soloway's office for a checkup. Dr. Soloway spent a full hour on his examination, then said, "Your blood specimen and urine analysis won't come back from the laboratory until Tuesday. But from everything I've seen, your vital organs are in *excellent* shape. Absolutely. In fact, to me you look like a man who will live to be seventy-eighty years old!"

"That's nice," said the patient.

" 'Nice?' Only 'nice'?! My God, man, do you know how few people who come to this office are as healthy as you?! By the way, my nurse didn't write your age on your interview: how old *are* you?"

"Eighty-one."

"See?" cried Dr. Soloway. "What did I tell you?!"

See also **Hypochondriacs, Psychiatrists/Psychoanalysts/Psychologists**

Doggerel

The kindly rain doth fall upon
The just and unjust fellow,
But mostly on the just
Because
The unjust stole the just's umbrella.

Shake, shake the catsup bottle;
None comes out—and then a lot'll.

RICHARD ARMOUR

In appearance, I'm not a great star,
Others are handsomer—far.
But my face—I don't mind it
Because I'm behind it;
It's the poor folks out front that I jar!

WOODROW WILSON

There was a smart woman named Bright
Whose speed was much faster than light;
She departed one day,
In a relative way,
And returned on the previous night.

Forth from his den to steal he stole
His bags of chink he chunk;
And many a wicked smile he smole,
And many a wink he wunk.

Willie saw some dynamite
Couldn't understand it—quite.
Curiosity never pays;
It rained Willie seven days.

I've the luck of the Irish, my boy,
The best you've ever seen,
I take worn-out pieces of junk
And make them a fine machine.

Old rags I buy, and iron, too,
Broken pots and kettles
And I melt them down
In a far part of town
And sell them as valued metals.

Yes, I've the luck of the Irish, by God,
My wife is a gorgeous colleen,
And as for my smile,
Why they walk for a mile
To see it on Benny Levine.

If one thing is that, and two things are those,
Then hat in the plural should always be hose.

The masculine pronouns are he, his, and him,
But *think* of the feminine: she, shis, and shim.

He who takes what isn't his'n,
Must give it back or go to prison.

To folks below the norm of humor
A pun is the lowest form of humor.

Fish, if not caught,
Can easily be bought.

A lovely girl's smile—ethereal,
Is not, over next morn's cereal.

Consider the ever-busy bbb,
Who buzz and fly with eee,
And certainly are yyy,
However sharp their iii,
Not to try to cross the ccc.

L. R.

❧

Note: Machado's is a cabaret in Lisbon, patronized by those who love *fados*. *Fado* means fate; *fados* are the special, schmaltzy, gloomy songs the Portuguese adore. They listen to elaborations of misery hour after hour, wallowing in wine and *Weltschmerz* and exercising the lumps in their throats.

The *fados* are unlike any popular ditties you ever heard. They recount doleful troubles and doomed amours, maudlin crises and galloping despair. Here are the words of one *fado*. I do not claim that what follows is an exact rendition, but it's close enough.

THE ACCURSED LOVER

Overture

Woe is me
Oh me, oh my,
Let this tale
Dim ear and eye.

Canto

I once was lovely, sweet and innocent,
Bright of smile and even thinnocent,
Until the day—Oh, God, to think—
He paused beside our kitchen sink,
And gravely glanced into my eyes,
Ignoring mama's soup and pies,
To whisper, "I love you with a passion that will never die."

Reprise

Woe is me,
You know by now,
I fell from grace
And—well, and how!

Elegy

How we loved and how we laughed,
In the moonlight on that raft,
Drifting nowhere in our passions
Kissing, loving, nothing rationed.

Recitative

Can you guess it, or believe—
How that man did me deceive?
To my bed he swiftly tarried
Nor did tell he was married!

Coda

O, woe is me
Farewell, my virtue.
Dear God: I didn't mean
To sin or hurt you!

L. R.

See also **Bloopers, Computers, Limericks**

Drink/Drunks

A saloon can't corrupt a good man, any more than a synagogue can reform a bad one.

The drunkard smells of spirits—but so does the bartender.

YIDDISH SAYING

Q: In what month of the year do Swedes drink least?

A: February.

Newscaster in Louisville, Kentucky

> Authorities announced that the Pelican Club,
> where the unfortunate incident occurred, will
> have its leer and bicker license revoked.

In Third Avenue saloon: If you must drive your man to drink, please drive him here.

Two drunks were staring at a huge billboard that showed two sparkling bottles—one marked SODA, one marked GINGER ALE, above this slogan:

DRINK CANADA DRY

After a long silence, one drunk turned to the other: "You think it can be done?"

The other said, "Nope."

Hangover: The wrath of grapes.

The most unpleasant thing about him is that when he isn't drunk, he's sober.

W. B. YEATS

❧

Sign on brewery: The Beer that Made Milwaukee Jealous.

❧

On a bottle of Japanese "Scotch," in Tokyo: This whiskey made from finest grape, by appointment of His Majesty King Elizabeth.

❧

In a bar on the Bowery: Not responsible for ladies left over thirty seconds.

❧

Scene: A Bar

PARKER: Hey, I thought the doctor told you never to take more than one drink a day.

MADDOX: That's right.

PARKER: But you're downing your *third!*

MADDOX: Following doctor's orders to a T. This drink is for October 6, 1992.

❧

Two men, blissfully boozy, paused before a newsstand, to read the headline:

MAN WANTED FOR ARMED ROBBERY IN BROOKLYN

"By gosh and by golly," said the first man, "if that job was in Manhattan, I'd take it!"

❧

Paddy Gilhooly, walking down a crowded street in Belfast, suddenly keeled over. At once a crowd collected, firing suggestions.

"Call a doctor!" cried one man.

"Give the poor soul air!" cried another.

"Fynted, has he?" exclaimed a little old lady. "Then give him a stiff shot o' whiskey."

"Call th' police!"

"Nay, jist open his collar—"

Gilhooly sat up. "Shut up, ye nincompoops, an' listen to th' little old lydy!"

❧

"Skinny" Webster, two sheets to the wind, was holding on to a lamppost when a big burly stranger came along and asked, "Can I help you?"

"Why *(hic)* not?" wheezed Webster.

"You live near here?"

"Second floor."

The man carried Skinny Webster up the stairs, opened the first door, and shoved him in.

When the stranger reached the street, there was another drunk on the sidewalk, moaning and reeking of liquor. "Help . . ."

"You want to get upstairs, too?"

"Yesh, yesh."

So the man dragged the drunk up the stairs, opened the first door, and pushed him in.

When the Good Samaritan reached the sidewalk for the third time, there—to his annoyance—was a third drunk. The do-gooder started to lift the inebriate when that woebegone creature wrestled free, lurched into the street, and stopped a car. "Help!" he gasped. "That crazy bastard keeps hauling me up the stairs and pushing me down an elevator shaft!"

Scene: A Saloon in Stockholm

The brothers Jorgensen, identical twins, always dressed exactly alike. One night they went to a saloon. A man at the bar took one look at the Jorgensens, his eyes popping, and cried, "Godamighty, only two drinks of Aquavit and I be seein' things!"

"No you're not," grinned one Jorgensen.

"My brother and me," smiled the other, "—we are *twins*."

The barfly gasped, "All *four* of ye?!"

DOCTOR: I'm afraid I can't do any more for your husband, Mrs. Windsor. Has he tried Alcoholics Anonymous?

MRS. WINDSOR: I suppose so. Percy will drink *any*thing.

Cohane and Driscoll, old friends, came out of a Dublin saloon in a fine state of euphoria. As they stumbled along, humming aimless tunes, Driscoll stopped short. "My, my, my, my. Liam Cohane, will y'not look at that! A beautiful, *beau*tiful bug—on the branch of that bush?"

Cohane hiccuped. "Bug, is it? What kind o' bug?"

Driscoll blinked and said, "Sure, and 'tis a ladybug."

Cohane gasped. "*Lady* bug, did y' say? By all the saints, Seamus, y' have the eyesight of a telescope."

Mr. Schaffner was on his way home, walking from the subway station to his flat in Astoria, when a drunk came out of an alleyway, a gun waving in one hand and a bottle in the other. "Take a swig—of thish—mister—or I'll—" He pointed the gun at Mr. Schaffner.

The terrified commuter took the bottle with trembling hands, drank, coughed, retched. "Migod, that's the most *awful* stuff—"

"Right!" beamed the boozer. "Now you hold the gun. . . ."

The tanked-up drunk at McFeely's bar yelled, "Now hear this, all y' sons o' the old sod! Show me a loyal Ulsterman and Oy'll show y' a rootin'-tootin', goddam idjit!"

A giant bricklayer pushed his immense shoulders through the crowd and pounded on the bar. "Well now, ya bloomin' Paddy. Oy'm a loyal Ulsterman!"

The drunk surveyed the giant and blinked, "Bless me soul, man: *Oy*'m the rootin-tootin', goddam idjit."

See also **Just Jokes, Shaggy Dogs**

Dummies

As Prokovnick started up the stairs to his flat, the janitor grabbed him. "Listen, Prokovnick! Your wife—she's in bed—*with your best friend!*"

"What?!" boomed Prokovnick. "I'll tear that swine limb from limb!" He charged up the stairs.

In a few minutes, Prokovnick returned. "Hey, janitor. What's the matter with you, telling me my wife is in bed with my best friend? Why, I never laid eyes on that guy before in my whole life."

Harry Farkel, leaving for lunch, handed a batch of bills to his new secretary and said, "Miss Tobin, please total these." At the door, he added, "And make sure you're right, Miss Tobin. Check the addition three times."

When Farkel returned at two thirty, his secretary handed him the batch of bills, plus a covering sheet of figures, smiling, "Here you are, Mr. Farkel. All done."

"Oh, good, Miss Tobin. Did you check your results like I said?"

"Yes, *sir*. Three times."

"Thank you."

"On the top page, Mr. Farkel, you'll see all three answers."

To the new recruits, Drill Sergeant Hogan said, "Brains are as important as muscle around here. All new theories about warfare stress psychology and deception. . . . Now, suppose your squad is facing the enemy—and you run out of ammunition. What should you do?"

Up shot the hand of one recruit.

"Yes?"

"You should keep shooting to fool them!"

Nelda Petersen, the new maid at the Lawrence Hansfords, seemed able, though she admitted she had never worked in so fine a mansion before.

As Mrs. Hansford was having lunch, she heard Nelda answer the phone, "Hansford residence. . . . Ay, y' can say that again!" and hang up.

Some time later, the phone rang again. Nelda once more lifted the receiver. "Hansford residence. . . . Et certainly is!" and hung up.

Around the cocktail hour, the phone rang and Nelda answered. "Hansford residence. . . . You don't have t' keep telling me!"

At this point, Mrs. Hansford asked, "Nelda, have you been getting calls from a friend?"

"Oh no, ma'am."

"Then what on earth is going on?"

"It sure beats me, ma'am," said Nelda. "I pick up the phone; someone says, 'It's long distance from Portland,' and I keep sayin' 'Et sure is!' "

The new secretary, Miss Seltzer, was very pleasant and seemed eager to work. Mr. Rackman, her employer, was pleased. As he went out to lunch, he said, "Miss Seltzer, remind me to call Dr. Boris Yablon the minute I come back."

"Is his number on our office phone list?"

"No. Look him up in the telephone directory."

When Mr. Rackman returned from his lunch date, he said, "Miss Seltzer, get me Dr. Yablon."

"Very soon, sir. I'm still working on it. . . ."

"You're still working—on *what?*"

"His number," smiled Miss Seltzer. "I'm already up to the *K*'s."

Police headquarters in Louisville, Kentucky, distributed these posters around the state:

WANTED
FOR ARMED ROBBERY

plus four different mug shots of one "Porgy Joe" Timkins.

In a week, the phone in Louisville's police headquarters rang. A voice said, "Hello. Lem Albon here, from Hollow Vale Springs. About them armed robbers you want so bad. Well, I catched three of them last night. And I think I got me a mighty good chance to nab the last one afore the sun goes down t'day!"

Five men were playing poker at Latski's apartment . . . when Latski leaped to his feet, crying, "You're cheating! Bleifeld, you are a cheater!"

"Hey, Latski!" cried one player.

"That's a terrible accusation," said another.

"How do you know he's cheating?" asked the third.

"Because he just discarded a seven!" cried Latski. "The hand I dealt him was a pair of fours, a six, jack, and nine!"

Michael Devlin, walking down Third Avenue, was jumped by two husky thugs. Devlin fought like a tiger but to no avail, alas; the thugs beat him up—smashed his glasses, broke his nose, and pinned him to the ground. They tore his wallet out of his pocket, but it contained only three dollar bills. They turned his pockets inside out—but they only contained seventeen cents.

The thugs gazed at each other in amazement. "Hey, man," one called to Devlin, "you some kind of nut? You put up a fight like that for a lousy three bucks?!"

"I thought you were after the two hundred in my socks!"

"Canvasback" Carlin, the pugilist with seventeen straight defeats, took a terrific rain of blows and fell to the mat, dazed.

The referee began to semaphore his arm, counting "One . . . two . . ."

Carlin wobbled up blearily.

". . . three . . . four . . ."

Carlin started to get to one knee, when his manager shouted, "No, no! Stay down! Until eight!"

Carlin blinked. "Uh—wha' time is it now?"

After sixteen dreadful days adrift on a raft in the Atlantic, shipwrecked, without food or drink or shelter from the rains, Stanislaw Karpazik said to Fletcher and Cohn, "Let's pray to God. It's our only chance. Let's pray like *crazy!*"

The three men prayed with uncommon fervor. And lo!—from the sky there appeared a luminous angel. "Dispel your fears, O men of faith," said the angel. "Your Maker has heard your plea and has sent me with His authority to grant each of you one wish!"

"Thank God, thank God!" cried Harry Cohen. "I wish—please—to be whisked to the finest restaurant in New York!"

The angel nodded, and Mr. Cohen vanished into the clouds.

"And I," gasped Morton Fletcher, "pray God, I—want to be in the Tour d'Argent in Paris!"

The angel nodded and Mr. Fletcher was instantly swept upwards and out of sight.

"And your wish?" the angel asked Karpazik.

"I'm *lonely*. I wish those two were back here!"

See also **Chelm, Nebechs, Shaggy Dogs, Shlemiels**

Education

The ability to describe a bathing beauty
without using your hands.

The ability to give directions without taking
your hands out of your pockets.

The path from cocky ignorance to miserable
uncertainty.

That which reveals to the wise, and conceals
from the stupid, the vast limits of their
knowledge.   L. R.

What you must acquire without interference from your schooling.

MARK TWAIN

What remains after you have forgotten all you have been taught.

LORD HALIFAX

On the desk of a kindergarten teacher:

THINK SMALL

Mrs. Flugelman hurried to the door of her son's room. "Bernie! Bernie! It's late. Get up!"

Her son sleepily grumbled, "I don' wanna get up."

Mrs. Flugelman flung the door open. "Bernie! You *have* to get up—wash, dress, eat, go to school!"

Bernie said, "I don' wanna go to school."

"Bernie!" His mother recoiled in horror. "What's gotten into you? All of a sudden you don't want to go to *school?!*"

"I hate school!" said Bernie. "The teachers hate me. The kids call me 'Four-eyes.' They make fun of the way I talk! They throw spitballs at me! They put nails on my chair. They—"

"Bernie, stop that at once! You—must—go—to—school!"

"Why?"

"For two reasons: First, you're forty-six years old—"

"Oh, ma . . ."

"—And second, you're the principal!"

MAXIE: Papa, will you buy me—to help in all my schoolwork—an encyclopedia?

FATHER: Are you *crazy?* You can walk to school, like all the other kids do.

On college bulletin board

Learn from the past:
DON'T TAKE HISTORY 4

On college wall

Dare to be great: TRANSFER!

Caterina Delfaco brought several of her college chums home for the weekend. With considerable intensity they discussed Darwin and the revisionists' criticism of the theory of evolution.

To all of this, Caterina's old-fashioned grandmother, born and raised in Sicily, said, "Younga girls, justa ready to live—why you worry about sucha thing?"

"It's a very complex subject, gramma."

"Isa *simple!*" Gramma scoffed. "In old country, we know answer. Listen: Ifa *bambino* look like papa, thassa heredity. But ifa he look like *vicino*—how you say *vicino*, Caterina?"

" 'Neighbor,' gramma."

"If *bambino* look like neighbor, thassa . . ."

"Environment," sighed Caterina.

You must know a great deal about a subject to know how little is known about it.

L. R.

From St. Andrew's College (Scotland) brochure

> Apart from an isolated incident of violence in 1470, when the dean of the faculty of arts was shot at with bows and arrows, and if one glosses over the Jacobite demonstrations of 1715, the university has been singularly free of student unrest.

R. O. White, president of the Altoona Bank, went back to college for his class reunion. He dropped in on his old economics professor. And as they were chatting, the professor said, "Here's something that will interest you—this year's final exam."

White scanned the exam, then said, "I could swear these are the identical questions you asked my class twenty years ago!"

"Quite so," said the professor with a smile.

"But if you always ask the same questions, don't you think the students will get wise?"

"They do."

"Don't they pass the questions on to next year's class?"

"Sure."

"Then doesn't everyone get an A on every exam?"

"Not at all," said the professor. "In economics, the questions stay the same, year after year—but we keep changing the answers."

> A maiden at college, Miss Breeze,
> Weighed down by B.A.'s and Ph.D's.
> Collapsed from the strain.
> Said her doctor, "It's plain,
> You are killing yourself—by degrees."

Little Humberto Varga's mother was eagerly waiting for him outside the schoolhouse. It was the lad's first day. . . . She hugged him and kissed him and asked, "So, what you learn?"

"I learn to write," said Humberto.

"Ona first day?! Santa Maria! . . . So, what you write?"

"I don' know," said Humberto. "I no can read."

College president

One who must solve three problems: sex, for the students; football, for the alumni; and parking, for the faculty.

ROBERT MAYNARD HUTCHINS

The burly, swarthy woman walked into the El Greco Frame Shop.

"*Buenas dias,*" said the owner, Moe Janklovitz.

"*Buenas dias.* I want you frame me a picture, eet ees worth *viente*—tuventy t'ousand *do*llar."

"El Greco" caught his breath. "Lady, tvanty t'ousand dollars?! Never before, in all the yiss I own this shop, did I see a picture vorth tvanty t'ousand dollars! . . . I'm afraid even to *touch* it!"

"Ees okay. Not to worry." The woman opened an envelope and handed Moe Janklovitz a piece of parchment: her daughter's brand-new college diploma.

PROFESSOR: Miss Gomez, can you tell the class the name of the philosopher who wrote *The Critique of Pure Reason?*

MISS GOMEZ: *(blushing):* I can't.

PROFESSOR: Good! That's the first correct answer you've given all semester.*

*The *Critique* was, of course, written by I(mmanuel) Kant.

Mr. McNulty and his grandson, Stephen, age ten, were taking a walk. "Grampa," said Stephen, "what's the largest ocean on the globe?"

"Eh—oh my. That's a poser, it is," said Mr. McNulty.

A little later, Stephen asked, "How far is it from Dublin to Tanzania?"

Mr. McNulty scratched his head. "Faith!—and it's very far, is all I know."

And a little later the boy asked, "Why is the sky blue?"

Mr. McNulty frowned, "Begorra, if I—" then, observing the expression on little Stephen's face, he quickly added, "don't be gettin' discouraged, lad. Ask me more, more. How ilse can a young 'un be expectin' to' *learn* anythin'?!"

Public schools

A place of detention for children placed in the care of teachers who are afraid of the principal, principals who are afraid of the school board, school boards who are afraid of the parents, parents who are afraid of the children, and children who are afraid of nobody.

ANON.

See also **The English, The English Language**

Embarrassing Moments

The young man went into the airline ticket office and scanned the three women behind the counters. One was an attractive brunette, one a pleasant, plain girl, and the third a ravishing redhead with an ample bosom. The young man stepped to her station. "What flights do you have to Pittsburgh?"

As she leaned over the schedule, her uniform revealed a creamy expanse; the young man's eyes popped.

"Pittsburgh—Pittsburgh . . ." The buxom beauty looked up. "Next flight at three fifteen."

"Okay. I'll take a picket to—" He stopped, crimson. "Oh, God!"

The newlyweds were having their new apartment painted. The new wife, coming out of the shower and slipping into a bathrobe, suddenly noticed a large handprint on a freshly painted wall of the bedroom. "Painter!" she called down the stairs. "Painter! Would you please come up here?"

The painter came up the stairs.

"You won't *believe* this!" said the bride. "Would you like to see where my husband put his hand in the dark last night?"

The painter cleared his throat. "I sure would, lady. But first I've got to finish the downstairs closet."

On a very crowded bus in the Bronx, Mrs. Frenkel kept groping in her huge, zippered handbag for her change purse.

"Lady," said a man next to her, "*I'll* pay your fare."

"No, thank you, I can afford!" said Mrs. Frenkel—and groped and fumbled some more.

"Lady, I will *gladly* pay—"

"No, no. I'll get mine purse open—"

"Lady, 'til you get it open, you already unzipped my pants three times!"

A senator, who prided himself on having a phenomenal memory, was pumping hands in the receiving line during his campaign for reelection. A modest little man approached him, saying, "Senator, you don't remember me, but back in the seventies I made your shirts—"

"Major Shurtz," the senator boomed. "I'd recognize you anywhere!"

TRUE STORY

A pretty girl, suffering from hay fever, leaving for a posh dinner party, decided she needed two handkerchiefs for the evening—and stuck the extra one into her bodice.

At the dinner, having used up one handkerchief, she reached into her bosom for the fresh one. She rummaged around without success—and suddenly became aware that the conversation had stopped and all the guests were watching her. "Excuse me!" she exclaimed. "But I *know* I had two when I arrived."

See also **Can You Believe It?, Dummies, Shlemiels, Snafus, True Tales**

The English

KIDNEYS IN MAYFAIR

The conversation of upper-class Englishmen mixes affection with ceramic rudeness. Consider this conversation I overheard in a posh restaurant between a blasé young man and his beautiful date:

YOUNG MAN

What on earth does that chap—the one who keeps sniffing around Cynthia—actually do?

GIRL

I think he's studying to be a dentist.

YOUNG MAN

A dentist? . . . Good God! Why would anyone want to spend one's life peering into strange people's mouths? . . . Still, I suppose it's no worse than staring into other orifices of the body, the way obstetricians or proctologists—

GIRL

Ron-nie. *Please.* I'm digesting . . . I adore sweetbreads, don't you?

YOUNG MAN

Ugh. I de*test* vital organs drowned in protesting butter.

GIRL

Um. . . . Will you share a treacle tart?

YOUNG MAN

Under *no* circumstances, thenk yaw.

GIRL

You're disgusting.

YOUNG MAN

Quite, dear heart. . . . Shall we pop in on Pinky and Fran?

GIRL

Oh, let's do. He's *fab*.

YOUNG MAN

She's not altogether repulsive, you know.

GIRL

She's balmy.

YOUNG MAN

Had enough to fill your pretty little tummy?

GIRL

I've gorged . . .

YOUNG MAN

Waituh! Bill, please. Afraid we simply *must* dahsh.

WAITER

Very good, suh. . . . Shall I summon a taxi?

YOUNG MAN

That would be most helpful.

WAITER

Thank you, suh. I trust everything was satisfactory?

YOUNG MAN

Quite. Come along, sweetie. Don't forget your ghastly purse.

GIRL

Pig.

WAITER

Good ahfternoon, madam. . . .
(*accepting tip*)

Oh, thank *you*, sir.

YOUNG MAN

Nonsense. Cheerio.

GIRL

Ta-ta.

WAITER

(*beaming*)

Ta.

from my *The 3:10 to Anywhere*

THE ENGLISH, THE JEWS—AND OTHERS

Englishmen prize privacy; Jews prize intimacy.

The English dislike displaying their feelings; Jews think feelings are meant to be verbalized.

Englishmen understate the serious ("The riot was a bit of a mess") and overstate the trivial ("What a *frightfully* amusing hat!"); Jews inflate what is important ("That will blacken his name for all time!") and pooh-pooh what is not cataclysmic ("Stroke-shmoke, he can still wink with one eye!").

The English repress uneasiness; Jews feed it banquets of nourishment.

An Englishman treats a disaster as unfortunate; a Jew thinks a hangnail an injustice.

The English are embarrassed by confidences; Jews are let down by "coldness." . . .

Where Egypt wails, England blinks. Where Hindu women tear their hair, English women study their nails.

An Italian explodes invective; an Englishman sniffs "Really?"

When the Russians thunder "*Averyone* knows . . ." the English demur "But I should think that . . ."

Where Americans cry, "It's terrific!" Englishmen concede "Rather impressive."

And where Englishmen murmur "What a pity," Jews cry "What a disaster!" . . .

Jews may strike Anglo-Saxons as verbose and melodramatic because Jews are early taught to feel an *obligation* to respond to the misfortunes of others with visible, audible sympathy—so that no one can possibly fail to recognize the depth and sensitivity of one's compassion.

To Jews, emotions are not meant to be nursed in private: they are meant to be dramatized and displayed—so that they can be *shared.* . . .

The English think "a stiff upper lip" is a sign of courage; Mediterranean people judge a "stiff upper lip" to be *inappropriate* (why should suffering cast doubt on courage?)—since eyes filled with tears, and eloquent expressions of consolation, can give so much comfort to those, stricken by fate, who have been raised, too, to expect men to be *simpático*, to act decently, to be *sympatish* conveyors of "feeling-with."

I have come to the conclusion that Americans treat "neurotic" as a synonym for "nuts"; that Englishmen think "neurotic" an adjective applicable to foreigners; and that Jews consider "neurotic" a synonym for "human."

from the introduction to my *Treasury of Jewish Quotations*

❧

Scene: English-Speaking Union Headquarters, London

"Calderwood? Are you, by chance, related to the Wiltshire Calderwoods?" asked Lord Parkenhurst.

"I'm afraid not," said the American.

"Ah, then the Calderwoods of Burford Manor?"

"Nope. Sorry, sir. . . . You Englishmen are so conscious of ancestry . . ."

"But of course," sniffed Lord Parkenhurst. "*I*, for example, can trace my forebears all the way back to Queen Anne."

"Well," sighed the American, "*I* have Irish, Italian, French, and Portuguese blood."

"By Jove!" exclaimed Lord Parkenhurst. "How sporting of your mother."

"You're an Englishman, right?" asked Moe Kranz, a New York cab driver.

"Right," said Sir Gerald de Were.

"So here's a riddle. I'm thinking of someone who has the same father and mother I have, but is not my sister or my brother. Who can it be?"

Sir Gerald thought and frowned and tugged at his mustache and finally sighed, "Very well, I give up. Who is it?"

"Me," laughed the driver.

Sir Gerald thought that over; then he chuckled in delight. And a week later, at the Atheneum Club, he said to a group of his cronies, "I have a *delight*ful puzzle, gentlemen. I am thinking of someone who has the same parents I have, but is not my brother nor my sister! Now then, whom am I thinking of?"

The group took solemn thought, rephrasing the puzzle to themselves, exchanging tentative (and incorrect) cues, and finally confessed, "Absolutely stymied, Gerald . . ." "Can't for the *life* of me solve that." "Very well, dear boy, what's the answer. . . . *Whom* are you thinking of?"

Sir Gerald flung his head back in delight. "The driver of a taxi in New York!"

Sign in Midlands hotel garden: Ladies and gentlemen will not, and others must not, pick the flowers in this garden.

The English Language

THE ORDEAL OF MR. PARKHILL

Mr. Parkhill did not see how he could, in conscience, promote Mr. Kaplan to Miss Higby's grade (only last week Mr. Kaplan had referred to the codifier of the laws of gravity as "Isaac Newman"), and he knew that he could not bring himself to advise Mr. Kaplan, as he was often tempted, to transfer to some other night school where he might perhaps be happier. The undeniable fact was that there was no other night school in which Hyman Kaplan could possibly be happier; Mr. Parkhill might be happier; Miss Higby might be happier; a dozen members of the beginners' grade would surely be happier. But Mr. Kaplan? That intrepid scholar displayed the strongest conceivable affection, an affection bordering on the lyrical, for his alma mater.

That was another thing. Strictly speaking, of course, the ANPSA could not possibly be the alma mater of someone who had never been graduated from it; but Mr. Kaplan had a way of acting as if it were.

That was yet another of the baffling characteristics that made Mr. Kaplan so difficult to contend with: his cavalier attitude to reality, which he seemed to think he could alter to suit himself. How else could one describe a man who identified the immortal Strauss waltz as "the Blue Daniel"? Or who, in recounting the tale of the cloak spread in the mud before Queen Elizabeth, insisted on crediting the gallantry to "Sir Walter Reilly"? Or who identified our first First Lady as "Mother Washington"? True, George Washington was the father of our country, but that did not make Martha the *mother*. It was all terribly frustrating.

Every way Mr. Parkhill turned, he seemed to sink deeper and deeper into the Kaplan morass. If Mr. Kaplan could not be promoted, much less graduated, what *could* be done about him? Sometimes it looked to Mr. Parkhill as if Mr. Kaplan was deliberately trying to stay in the beginners' grade for the rest of his (i.e., Mr. Parkhill's) life. . . .

What could be done about Hyman Kaplan? The man simply refused to learn. No, Mr. Parkhill promptly corrected himself: it was not that Mr. Kaplan refused to learn; what Mr. Kaplan refused to do was *conform*. That was an entirely different matter. Mr. Parkhill could get Mr. Kaplan to understand a rule—of grammar or spelling or punctuation; what he did not seem able to do was get Mr. Kaplan to *agree* with it. Somewhere, somehow, Hyman Kaplan had gotten it into his head that to bend the knee to custom was a hairsbreadth from bending the neck to slavery. (To Mr. Kaplan, the plural of "pie" was "pious.")

Nor was that all which impeded Mr. Kaplan's progress. The laws of English, after all, have developed century after century, like the common law; and like the common law, they gain in authority precisely from the fact that men go on observing them down the countless years. But Mr. Kaplan was not in the slightest impressed by precedent. He seemed to take the position that each rule of grammar, each canon of syntax, each convention of usage, no matter how ancient or how formidable, had to prove its case anew—to him. He seemed to make the whole English language start from scratch. (The plural of "sandwich," he had once declaimed, is "delicatessen.")

And there was another perplexity. Whereas all the other students came to school in order to be instructed, Mr. Kaplan seemed to come in order to be consulted. It had taken a good deal of persuasion on Mr. Parkhill's part, for instance, to convince Mr. Kaplan that there simply is no feminine form of "ghost." If the feminine of "host" is "hostess," Mr. Kaplan had observed, then surely the feminine of "ghost" should be "ghostess."

It was most trying. Not that Mr. Kaplan was an obstreperous student. On the contrary. Not one of Mr. Parkhill's abecedarians had ever been more eager, more enthusiastic, more athirst and aflame for knowledge. The trouble was that Mr. Kaplan was so eager, so enthusiastic, so athirst and aflame that he managed to convert the classroom into a courtroom—a courtroom, moreover, in which the entire English language found itself put on the stand as defendant.

How else could one describe the extraordinary process by which Mr. Kaplan had come to the conclusion that if a pronoun is a word used instead of a noun, a proverb is a pronoun used in place of a verb? It was preposterous, of course; yet when Mr. Parkhill had challenged Mr. Kaplan to give the class *one single example* of a pronoun used in place of a verb, Mr. Kaplan, transported by that elation which possessed him *in statu pupillari*, beamed, "I'll give t'ree exemples. Soppoze you are on vacation, an' somebody esks: 'Who vants to go for a svim?' T'ree pipple enswer: 'I!' 'Me!' 'You!' All pronouns. No voibs." (Mr. Olansky had almost had a stroke that night.)

Surely a student could not be permitted to go on changing the tongue of Keats and Swift and Trollope to suit himself. But if a pupil refused to accept authority, the testimony of experts, the awesome weight of precedent, to what higher court could his preceptor possibly appeal? Ay, there was the rub. Mr. Kaplan believed that modern cities consist of streets, boulevards, and revenues. He gave the principal parts of the verb "to fail" as: "fail . . . failed . . . bankrupt." Once he had stunned the beginners' grade of the American Night Preparatory School for Adults by announcing that the opposite of "inhale" is—"dead." And once he drove poor Miss Mitnick, who was always right but never victorious, to tears—when he declared that whenever he was on vacation, "I gat op six-o'clock in the morning no matter what time it is." And the irrepressible scholar had given the positive, comparative, and superlative forms of "good," as "good . . . better . . . high cless!"; and of "bad" as nothing less than "bad . . . worse . . . rotten!" There was no end to Mr. Kaplan's inventive embellishments of the English tongue.

Mind you, Mr. Parkhill reminded himself, Mr. Kaplan did not deny that English had rules—good rules, sensible rules. What he would not accept, apparently, was that the rules applied to *him*. Mr. Kaplan had a way of getting Mr. Parkhill to submit each rule to the test of reason, and Mr. Parkhill was beginning to face the awful suspicion that he was no match for Mr. Kaplan, who had a way of operating with rules of reason entirely his own. Only a man with rules of reason entirely his own would dare to give the opposite of "height" as "lowth" or the plural of "blouse" as "blice" or the plural of "woman" as "married."

There was no longer any doubt in Mr. Parkhill's mind that Mr. Kaplan inhabited a universe all his own. That would explain how Mr. Kaplan had come to define "diameter" as a machine that counts dimes, and once dubbed the waterway that connects the Atlantic and Pacific "the Panama Kennel." Mr. Kaplan expressed considerable admiration for the great Roman ruler he called "Julius Scissor."

Mr. Parkhill passed his hand across his brow. He wondered if it might not be best to think of Mr. Kaplan not as a pupil but as some sort of cosmic force, beyond human influence, a reckless, independent star that roared through the heavens in its own unconstrained and unpredictable orbit. Mr. Kaplan was *sui generis*. Perhaps that was why he so often responded with delight, rather than despair, when Mr. Parkhill corrected him. It had taken Mr. Parkhill a long time to discover that Mr. Kaplan's smile signified not agreement but consolation.

One night Mr. Kaplan had delivered a rhapsodic speech on a topic that he had announced as "Amazink Stories Abot Names in U.S." New York, he had cheerfully confided to his comrades, was originally called "New Hamsterdam," Montana was so named because it was "full of montains," and Ohio, he averred, "sonds like a Indian yawnink." An Indian yawning . . . And once he had given the opposite of "dismay" as "next June!"

Sometimes Mr. Parkhill thought Mr. Kaplan would never find peace until he had invented a language all his own.

adapted from my *O K*A*P*L*A*N! MY K*A*P*L*A*N!*

ON ENGLISH

One fowl is a goose, but two are called geese
Yet the plural of mouse should never be meese,
If I speak of a foot and you show me your feet,
And I give you a boot, would a pair be called beet?
If one is a tooth and the whole set are teeth,
Why should not the plural of booth be called beeth?

THE TWENTY-FIVE BASIC RULES OF ENGLISH SPELLING AND GRAMMAR

1. Correct speling is a Must.
2. "Just between you and I" is a Mustn't. It's as much of a Mustn't as "They telephoned she."
3. Be sure to never split an infinitive.
4. Don't dangle with participles: "Running for the bus, a taxi hit my uncle."
5. The difference between "teach" and "learn" should learn you to pay attention. Teachers don't have to pay attention, so they don't learn; they just teach.
6. When studying grammar, a spiral notebook of well-lined pages are useful. (This shows that subjects and verbs are enemies.)
7. Don't never use no double negative. Triple negative are even worst.
8. Always make a pronoun agree with their referent.
9. Beware of the "them-those" trap. For instance, don't write, "Them apples are rotten" if they are not.
10. Many people *love* to use commas, which are not necessary. For instance, "She ate, the fool" is a comment. "She ate the fool" is correct, if she is a cannibal.
11. One of the trickiest points in punctuation is to use apostrophe's correctly. They are as sensitive as measle's.
12. Never use "real" when you mean "very." Therefore: "She is real stupid" shows that you are very stupid. (This point is real important.)
13. Adjectives are not adverbs. Write careful. (I know that's hardly.)
14. Question marks can be dynamite. Use them carefully. "You sure are pretty?" means you are not sure I am pretty. That is an insult.
15. Many a student is undone by "who" and "whom." Remember George Ade's remark: " 'Whom are you?' she asked, for she had gone to night school."
16. Avoid the excessive use of exclamation points!!!! It is silly to write, "Yesterday, I woke up!!!" because that suggests that today you did not, which is probably true.
17. When you want to say something that indicates anyone, or all of us, the pronoun "one" is better than "he" or "she." Fats Waller put it neatly: "One never knows, do one?"
18. Observe the difference between "don't" and "doesn't." It's shocking to hear so many high-school graduates say "He don't care." What they mean, of course, is "I don't care." Their grades proved it.
19. Never write "heighth" or "weighth." They just are not righth.
20. If you write "Who's hand is stroking my thigh?" you'll never know who's pulling whose leg. Such information can be valuable.
21. "Irregardless" is not in the dictionary. "Hopefully" is—and I hope to God you never use it.

22. Don't use "neither" when you mean "either." Either use "neither" correctly or don't use it at all. And don't use "either" if you mean "ether" neither.

23. Guard against absurd and unnecessary repetitions. This here rule is especially important for new beginners.

24. A real booby trap to avoid is "when"—especially when a sentence like "I do not deny I wasn't afraid" occurs when you mean "I won't deny I *was* afraid." Most writers are, so they master syntax, which is the only tax that doesn't cost money.

25. Don't forget the crucial difference between "lie" and "lay."
    a. The former takes no object ("I lie in bed") but the latter must ("Lay that pistol down, mother").
    b. "To lie" means to express something not true; "to lay" means expressing something more urgent.

Okay? Now, memorize these laws, plus one more: Be sure to reread anything you write to make sure you don't accidentally any words out.

L. R., PLUS PREDECESSORS

"Dizzy" Dean, a country boy and super baseball pitcher, became a radio announcer for baseball games—and to the horror of English teachers proceeded to enrich the language with neologisms and novel syntax, of which the best known remains: "The runner slud into third base."

A purist once snapped at Dean, "You certainly don't know the King's English!"

"I certainly do," the wizard retorted. "And so is the Queen!"

Casey Stengel, master mangler of our tongue, was asked how it felt to be eighty years old. "Let me just put it this way," said Casey. "You have to remember: a lot of people my age are dead at the present time."

"I am always mixed up about when to use 'that' or 'who' and when to use 'which.' Can you explain?"

No, I cannot explain why you always get mixed up about when to use "that" or "who" and when to use "which."

But I can clear up the confusion, so widespread and vexatious, about when to use each of these fine, patriotic adjectives:

1. Use "that" when referring to articles made of cork.

2. Never say *"Who?"* when discussing U.N. delegates from underdeveloped countries. They resent being hard to identify.

3. Use "which" for shredded wheat.

4. Never use "that" when discussing "which," but don't hesitate to use "which" when discussing "that."

5. Always use "who" when referring to owls. Even better is the use of "who-who."

6. The only times to use "that which" is when:

a. you are discussing the historic trials in Salem, Mass.

b. you are on the witness stand and have been asked to point to the woman in the courtroom who has done most to give you shingles. If the judge rules that you are using "which" as a pejorative pun for "witch" (which you are) and asks you to rephrase your answer, reply, "Who?"

He will answer, "You."

That's when you smile: "You who?"

And that's when you get the heave-ho (not "hoo") for contempt of court.

L. R.

From a brochure of a Tokyo car rental agency

When a passenger of foot heave in sight, tootle the horn.
Trumpet at him melodiously first,
but if he still obstacles your passage
then tootle him with vigor.

thanks to DONALD CARROLL

In Great Britain, intonation, inflection, and the cadence of sentences convey social stratification in a way American speech cannot equal. Oxbridgians stress the opening words of a statement, starting at the higher notes and sliding down to the lower, thus: "*Do* you think him honest?"

Americans reverse the harmonics: "Do you think him *hon*est?"

Here are other variants I cherish:

English	American
baw	bore
a gain	again
ducky	darling
strain jaws	strangers
On-tee	Aunty ("Anty")
cheepah	cheaper
rubbish	nonsense
prihvacy	privacy ("pryvacy")
iss-you	issue ("ishoo")

When an Englishman says he feels "sick" he does not mean he feels ill; he means he may throw up.

A "dummy," to Americans, is someone stupid; a "dummy" in Britain is the pacifier which soothes babies.

In London, you do not ride the "subway" but the "tube."

Further mystifications:

English	American
dicey	confused, uncertain
poppet	an endearing person
bubble-and-squeak	a mélange of meat and cabbage
banger	sausage
do	a social gathering
diddle	cheat
punch-up	a smallish fight
perks	benefits attached to a job (abbreviation of "perquisites")
chips	French fries

Americans "take a vacation," Britons "go on holiday." English phones are "engaged" where American phones are "busy." The English ask one to "ring me" where the Americans say "call me." The English go "to hospital," Americans to "the hospital." A London doctor of "med'sin" works in his "surgery"; an American M.D. prescribes *med*-i-cine" in his "office." And when Albion's heirs refer to the "loo," Americans must be on their bilingual toes to realize that what is meant is the "john."

TRANSLATIONS

English	American
Ha jew dew?	How do you do?
View been ha lawn?	Have you been here long?
Strawd'nry!	Extraordinary.
I oh quate shaw?	Are you quite sure?
Praps yaw prifuh a stat-you to a pict your?	Perhaps you prefer a statue to a picture?
Kyaw.	Thank you.

L. R.

Sign in men's W.C., basement, British Museum

PLEASE OBSERVE:
THESE FACILITIES ARE INTENDED
FOR CASUAL ABLUTIONS ONLY

On a "closed" window in a Brighton bank

SERVICE SUSPENDED WHILST CASHIER IS
ENGAGED ON ANCILLARY TILL ENTRIES

On London lampposts to which wire-mesh trash cans are attached

ANY PERSON NOT PUTTING LITTER INTO
THIS BASKET WILL BE LIABLE TO A FINE OF £5

(To this, H. W. Fowler railed: "Those who have no litter to put into the basket must, it seems, rush to find some.")

My wife, phoning Chicago from London: "Is this the Overseas operator?"

A pitying voice replied, "This is *one* of them, luv."

On Savile Row, I studied myself in the mirror and remarked, "Isn't the jacket too large?"

The proprietor cleared his throat. "If you will but permit the garment to assume its natural aplomb . . ."

To the *London Observer*

> Gentlemen:
>
>   I was impressed by your article headed
> "Escapees." I thought it was written by a
> deep thinkee. But are you trend followees or
> trend settees? Should you change your name
> to the *Observee?* That might please the most
> forward-looking of your readees.
>
>   Roy Herbert

MR. KAPLAN'S SHINING HONOR

"Another mistake," called Miss Mitnick suddenly. There was a glow in her cheeks; evidently Miss Mitnick had discovered something very important to correct in the letter Mr. Kaplan had written on the blackboard. Mr. Kaplan's eyes turned to narrow slits.

"In the letter is," said Miss Mitnick, " 'if your eye falls on a bargain please pick it up.' " Miss Mitnick reread the sentence.

The class burst into laughter. It was a masterly stroke. Even Mr. Parkhill, feeling a bit sorry for Mr. Kaplan, permitted himself a dignified smile.

And suddenly Mr. Kaplan joined the merriment. He didn't laugh; he merely smiled. But his smile was grandiose. "And vat's wronk dere, plizz?" he asked, his tone the epitome of confidence.

Mr. Bloom should have known that he was treading on ground mined with dynamite, but he threw caution to the winds. "Mitnick is right! 'If your *eye* falls on a bargain please pick *it* up'? Some English, Mr. Kaplan!"

Then Mr. Kaplan struck.

"Mine oncle," he said, "has a gless eye."

The effect was incredible. Mr. Bloom's mouth fell open. Miss Mitnick dropped her pencil. Mrs. Moskowitz looked at Mr. Kaplan as if she had seen a vision; she wondered how she had dared criticize such a man. And Mr. Kaplan's smile was that of a child, deep in some imperishable sleep. He was like a man who had redeemed himself, a man whose honor, unsmirched, waved above him like a dazzling banner.

                          from my *The Education of H*Y*M*A*N K*A*P*L*A*N*

See also **Accents, Bloopers, Boo-boos, Definitions to Cherish, Famous People (as Seen by Children), Freudian Slips, Goldwyniana, Graffiti, Headlines That Haunt Me, Malaprops, News Items That Haunt Me**

Epitaphs

A monumental liar.

An inscription which hopes that virtues acquired by death will have a retroactive effect.

AMBROSE BIERCE

Lying in behalf of those lying in state.

The revelation of such virtues that we would be well advised to resurrect the dead and bury the living.

L. R.

On a tombstone in Dublin

> Beneath this lavish stone lies
> ALOYSIUS XAVIER SMILEY
> Buried one beautiful day in May
> He lived the lovely life of Reilly—
> Whenever Reilly was away.

Herewith, epitaphs selected by a handful of celebrities for their own tombstones:

William Powell: Excuse me for not rising.

H. G. Wells: I *told* you so, dammit!

Dorothy Parker: Excuse my dust.

Jack Benny: Did you hear about my operation?

Milton Berle: This one's on me.

Robert Benchley: All of this is over my head.

Alfred Hitchcock: I'm involved in a plot.

L. R.: This is much too deep for me.

A hypochondriac: I kept *telling* you I was sick!

Nunnally Johnson: I *thought* there was a funny taste about that last one.

He was born in summer
And died in a fall
But didn't tell St. Peter
He had lived in St. Paul.

See also **Death, Obituary Data Worth Remembering**

Eulogies

Even the widow could not deny that her late husband, Norm, had been greatly disliked in the community. He had not one good friend; critics he had by the score. The Widow Schwartzberg asked Rabbi Nagel, "Doesn't even a man like Norman—a model husband he was not—deserve some kind words after he *dies?*"

"You're right, Mrs. Schwartzberg," said the rabbi. "I'll give your Norman a eulogy—a eulogy no one will ever forget."

A large audience came to hear how Rabbi Nagel would frame a funeral oration for Norman Schwartzberg. Here is what Rabbi Nagel declaimed:

> We are here to say goodbye to Norman Schwartzberg. Frankly, he was not an admirable man. He never contributed to charity, he left many debts, his word was not as good as his bond, he drank too much, he carried on in ways to bring pain and sorrow to his faithful wife. . . . But one thing I can tell all of you, with profound conviction: compared to his brother Cooky, Norman was an absolute saint!

See also **Epitaphs**

Evidence

An English spinster, disliked in the village because of her superior ways and bluenose judgments, loudly accused Rufus Andrews of having reverted to his old heavy-drinking habits. "I observed his wheelbarrow outside the local pub at eleven o'clock last night!"

That night, Rufus Andrews placed his wheelbarrow outside the spinster's door. It was still there next morning. . . .

It was a smashing success of a cocktail party the Fullertons threw, so much so that after an hour Mrs. Halley tugged at her husband's sleeve and declared, "Harvey, don't you think you—ought to stop drinking? . . . Why, your whole face is beginning to look blurred!"

Mrs. Stuart stormed into Kirkpatrick's Perfect Cleaners and Dyers Palace and cried, "Call y'rselves pairfect, do ye? Mon, will ye jist look at what ye ruined? Ruined, no less!"

Mr. Kirkpatrick lifted the object Mrs. Stuart had tossed on the counter, and he carefully examined it. "Well now, mum, I do nae see a thing wrong w' this foyne lace . . ."

"*Lace?*" echoed Mrs. Stuart. "Have ye taken leave of y'r senses, then? What I brought in for th' cleanin' was a double-size *sheet!*"

SEEING IS DECEIVING

For centuries, the women of Burma have walked several feet behind their husbands with respectful expressions. But after World War II, Burmese women began to walk *ahead* of their former masters. This created a sensation among foreign observers, who asserted that at last democracy, with its egalitarian emphases, had taken root in Burma.

I hate to be a sourpuss, but would you like to know why the men in Burma allowed—no, *insisted*—that their gentle wives walk in front of them? Because (you'd better brace yourself) unexploded land mines were still buried all over the place. . . .

from my *The Power of Positive Nonsense*

The first mate, having received a cable that he was now the father of a fine, eight-pound boy, went on a glorious binge. The next morning, as he took the helm, he read in the ship's log: "First mate Jennison was drunk last night."

When the captain came into the cabin, Jennison said, "Sir, I wish you would remove that entry in the log. I've never, never in my life been drunk before. Not on duty or off. But you see . . . last night, I received this cable!" He showed the captain the cable.

The captain read it. "Congratulations, Jennison. But the entry stays in the log. After all, you *were* drunk."

"Yes, sir, but—"

"There are no ifs, ands, or buts. Facts are facts!"

The next morning, the captain found this entry in the ship's log: "The captain was sober last night."

At a gathering in the social hall of the Hillsboro Temple, the crowd gathered about Mrs. Richter, who was proudly displaying her newest grandchild.

Rabbi Seforim approached the beaming grandmother and patted the baby and cluck-clucked, "My, *my*, Mrs. Richter, what a *beau*tiful little boy!"

Mrs. Richter appraised the rabbi and said, "First of all, rabbi, it's not a boy; it's a girl. Second, please let go of my finger."

See also **Appearances, Can You Believe It?, Courts, Hanky-panky, News Items That Haunt Me**

Faith

Faith can move mountains, but not furniture.

Homer Morton went off alone one day to scale the sheerest face of Mount Hood. He dug his crampon onto a ledge, which gave way, and Homer fell 150 feet—managing, by a miracle, to grab a branch from a gnarled tree that was growing in a crevice. He dangled there helplessly, swinging back and forth, calling, "Help! Oh, God! Help!"

At last an immense, orotund voice far above intoned, "My son, did you call?"

"Oh, yes, yes!" cried Homer. "Please!"

"Do you at this moment have full true trust in Me?"

"Yes! Oh, Lord, yes!"

"Will you obey Me—without reservation?"

"Oh, yes, Lord!"

"Then, my son, let go of that branch. . . ."

"*What?!*"

"I said, 'Let . . . go . . . of . . . that . . . branch.' "

A pause; then Morton said, "Excuse me, Sir, but—is there anyone else up there?!"

"Fortunately we're insured against Acts of God," said the Reverend Martin after lightning struck, sending rafters crashing down on the church altar.

Canon Kilnarnock was traveling to London. The train stopped at Cambridge. A heavyset man of about forty entered the compartment. The two nodded to each other.

Canon Kilnarnock returned to his breviary. The large man sat down and opened a copy of a book whose bold title was visible to the canon:

Why I Am Not a Christian
by
Bertrand Russell

The canon sighed.

The train started, then stopped. A conductor, walking along the platform, called, "Ten-minute delay. . . . Ten-minute delay."

"Oh, dear, oh, dear," said the canon. He glanced at his watch. "I may miss my connection."

"Let us pray you do not," smiled the man from Cambridge, then winked.

"Ay. Pulling my leg a wee bit, are ye?"

"I daresay," the man chuckled.

"Ye nae believe in prayer?"

"No, I do not."

"May I ask, what thin is y'r faith?"

"I," said the man, "am an atheist. . . . Does that offend you?"

The canon shrugged. "Have y' thin read much o' the Good Book?"

"Not a line since I was sixteen."

"Do y' know the arguments for faith by Saint Thomas Aquinas?"

The man smiled. "No."

"Have ye perhaps read Saint Augustine?"

"I never felt the need to."

"P'haps thin, Cardinal Newman? . . . E'en Malcolm Muggeridge?"

"No, no. They all seem to me gas bags."

The canon studied the big man thoughtfully. "Dare I be frank, sir, to a total stranger?"

"Of *course* you may, sir. I rather enjoy a healthy difference of opinion."

"Well thin, sir. Ay have news f'r ye. Y're not an atheist. No, no. Y're an ignoramus."

See also **God, Heaven, Reason**

Famous People
(as Seen by Children)

Radium was discovered by Madman Curry.

The most famous Italian composer was Libretto.

Isaac Newman passed the law of gravity.

Beethoven had ten children; he practiced on
a spinster in his attic.

The biggest inventor (besides Thomas Edison)
is Pat Pending.

The man who fought the windmills of Spain was
Don Coyote.

Popular authors can win the Pullet Surprise.

The Gorgons looked like women, but more horrible.

Ben and Dick Arnold were terrible traitors.

See also **Cynics' Dictionary, Definitions (by Children), Geography Revised, History Revised**

Fan Mail

Every writer learns, sooner or later, that a certain number of those who admire his work, and write in to tell him so, are oddballs. Others are not so much odd as nuts.

I don't know why people think that a writer is a sage, a seer, a psychiatrist—and an expert on bearded irises—all rolled into one; but readers do, they certainly do. I suppose it's because they attribute magic to print, and confuse a skill (writing) with a state (wisdom). Whatever the reason, I have received some of the most extraordinary, flabbergasting, cockamamy requests you can imagine from earnest letter-writing fans. My prose seems to exert a special magnetic effect upon epileptic masseuses and nearsighted bowlers.

Now, I have never mastered the art of solemn flippancy achieved by the late H. L. Mencken, whose hate mail was steeped in vituperative juices. Mencken answered all overwrought rages with a postcard on which was printed, briefly and to the point:

> Dear Sir or Madam:
>
> You may be right.
>
> Yours,
> H. L. Mencken

This answer often drove his irate correspondents up the wall.

I could never match such cold-blooded, definitive irony. I always answer letters gravely, even when they deserve scorn. This compulsive kindliness is both disgusting and cowardly. Whenever I go over my correspondence at the end of the year, I am stricken with shame. So, like any craven recreant, I try to restore my self-esteem by composing in my mind those searing, soul-satisfying replies I *should* have sent. Here, in my annual rite of purgation, are excerpts from some of the letters I received from readers last year, plus the answers I wish I had had the gumption to send back.

Who wrote "The Battle Hymn of the Republic"?

I did.

I heard someone say that you once won the Noble Prize. Is that true?

Yes. I won the Noble Prize in 1971 for my invention of an index to Webster's Dictionary.

The Noble Foundation medal is inscribed:

TO A NOBLE FELLOW

FROM

MORRIS R. NOBLE

Morris R. Noble, who died of prolonged inhaling, was an immigrant from Bialystock who founded the Hug-Tite Girdle Corporation. It was his lifelong interest in girdles that made him set up a foundation.

Do you believe in interracial marriage?

Absolutely not. Intermarriage between the male and female races is the sole cause of humanity's problems.

. . . the Secret Meaning of Isaiah 8:14 makes it ABSOLUTELY PLAIN the world will END August 3 at 10:30 P.M.!!! What do you say to that?

Isaiah man like you is crocked.

In one of your books you say that you clip newspapers and magazines all the time for your files. I would like to know—what is your favoritemost clipping?

This one, from a small-town paper in Iowa:

> The baseball game between the Rockets and the Huskers was held in Mr. Simpson's cow pasture, and ended in the third inning, with the score tied 1–1, when a runner slid into what he thought was second base.

Who was the first man in history to cross the United States on roller skates? It is my ambition to do something like that.

He was crazy. So are you.

I heard a TV discussion which mentioned the fact that Einstein proved that space is curved. This idea threw me for a loop. Can you explain "Space is curved"?

Easily. You know what "space" is. You know what "curved" means. Now: the whole concept depends on what Einstein meant by "is."

Who was the first police commissioner of Kalamazoo, Michigan?

I was.

Do you know a cure for hiccups?

Yes.

We just bought a French poodle for our daughter, who wants to call him Amen-hotep. Can you give us an idea about what to do? We think Amen-hotep is a peculiar name for a poodle.

So do I. Amen-hotep was not French; he was an Egyptian and a gambler, addicted to playing pharaoh.

Tell your daughter she must learn to respect other people's hangups. A poodle named Amen-hotep is likely to think he is a mummy and may spend all his time lying on the floor with his paws folded across his chest. Dogs who lie on their back all day are no fun to throw sticks at.

My husband and I often read you, and he gets very angry with me because I do not agree with him. Whom do you think is right?

If he likes my work, him is right. If he doesn't, youm is.

My wife is a wiz at brain-teasers and gave me one I can't figure out. It is driving me nuts:

"Horace is 2 years younger than his sister, Mame, and is losing his teeth. Mame is 4 years older than the cheerleader of their school in Great Neck. The janitor, who is always whistling, night and day, is 72. The total age of these four people is 183. What's the principal's name?"

My wife says the answer is easily apparent!

I am surprised you find this brain-teaser difficult. The answer is a cinch:

1. "Night and Day" was written by Cole Porter, which is a perfect name for a janitor.
2. The difference between "principle" and "principal" is seven.
3. If Horace is losing his teeth while two years younger than his sister, put the blame on Mame.
4. If the janitor is seventy-two, he should quit and collect Social Security.
5. The principal's name is not Apparent. It is Theodore Feldman, the most popular name for high school principals in Great Neck.

P.S. If I had a wife like yours, I would fill my back yard with quicksand.

Which politician do you most (and least) admire?

The politician I most admire is the English bucko who proclaimed, "I promise you that if I am elected, I will be neither partial nor impartial."

The politician I most despise is the flimflammer who told the voters in Florida, in a campaign against Senator Claude Pepper: "Did you know that my opponent once *matriculated* at college? That he openly practices *monogamy?* That his sister works in New York as a well-known *thespian!"*

Poor Pepper was clobbered at the polls.

In your opinion who was the greatest shortstop of all times?

In my opinion, I was the greatest shortstop of all time. The only shortshop who was shorter was "Pee-Wee" Pincus, who played for the New Haven Nudnicks. "Pee-Wee" was so short that even with cleats on his shoes he could walk under the tables down at Mory's.

My biology teacher told us that grasshoppers make their buzzing sounds by rubbing their back legs together. Is this true?

This is one of the most ridiculous prejudices law-abiding grasshoppers have to put up with. Grasshoppers make those buzzing noises not by rubbing their back legs together but by blowing on tiny kazoos which they conceal under their wings. The male makes the "zzz" sound and the female makes the "bzz" sound.

Sometimes a grasshopper will produce both a "zzz" and a "bzz" sound simultaneously, like this: "Zzzbzzzzz." That means you are listening to a grasshopper who has an identity crisis.

In English novels they are always giving someone's weight not in pounds but in "stones." How can I find out how many pounds are in a stone?

Weigh the stone, dummy.

Which one man or woman do you think has done the most for the human race?

Whitcomb L. Judson. He invented the zipper.

What is the quickest way how someone gets to be a "pro" writer?

The quickest way how someone gets to be a "pro" writer is to compose petitions in support of causes, like:

DISARM TODAY!

or

YANKEE, GET LOST!

That will put you in the *pro* ranks at once.

If you want to be a con writer, on the other hand, compose patriotic petitions *against* things, like:

BOYCOTT BEETS FROM BURUNDI!

or

STAMP OUT DANGLING PARTICIPLES!

Who discovered the Sea of Cortez?

I did.

Did you ever know Aimee Semple McPherson?

No. But I did enjoy her evangelical shenanigans. What I most admire is her faith: she was buried with a telephone beside her.

How did animals ever get the names we call them by?

One of the tidier things man has done is to give names to things: birds, beasts, insects, fishes. This was not easy. An ichthyologist, for instance, can't just take a pencil and clipboard and dive down to a blunt-nosed flounder, say, and ask: "Excuse me, fish: I am taking a poll for the U.S. Census Bureau. What is your name, please?"

The men in charge of fish-naming *did* try this system at first, but they got fouled up something terrible because every fish gave the same answer: "Glp."

This led the ichthyologists, who have an unshakable faith in data, to conclude that *all* fish are named "Glp." But when they fed this into a computer and asked for its opinion, quick as a flash came the answer: "No!" When a computer answers "No!" instead of just flipping its disks, you can be sure something important has happened in the world of science.

The same thing happened to the zoologists, who were assigned to name animals. *Every single specimen of a species interviewed gave the same name.* Every dog, for instance, said his name was "Bark", every cat, "Meow", every cow, "Moo," and so on.

For a long time, during the Idiopathic Era, people went around calling every dog "Bark" and no one minded, but when men began to move out to the suburbs and called their dogs in from the street to give them their vitamin-enriched chopped liver, any one man's call of "Here, Bark! Here, Bark, Bark, Bark!" brought every dog in the neighborhood to his door. They came like lemmings, and many died of overeating.

Things couldn't go on this way, so dogologists decided to name each *breed,* once and for all. They gave many a dog a bad name, like "Schnauzer." Anyone knows that if you call a sensitive dog a Schnauzer, he will develop post-nasal drip.

Is it true that in Bali, servants fall into a trance the minute you order them to do something?

Yes. The Balinese have such a horror of being told to do something that they fall into a coma.

You will no doubt ask, "Then how can you get a servant to do anything—like, say, getting your wife's hat out of the car?"

This way:

YOU

Bongo, I recall that our car has one seat in front and another in back, has it not?

BONGO

I share that recollection, master.

YOU

And is it not true that when my wife, your lovely mistress, left this morning, she was wearing a hat?

BONGO

I did observe that myself.

YOU
(chuckling merrily)

I remember certain occasions when she returned *without* her hat. Ha, ha, ha. Can you remember similar events?

BONGO

Ha, ha, ha, yes, many.

YOU

Then, dear Bongo, perhaps you could drift out to the car and observe whether the hat of the mistress is indeed on that back seat we just discussed?

BONGO

An excellent suggestion, master.

YOU

And if you *do* observe the hat of the mistress there, would you be so kind as to bring it into the house where, I assure you, both it and your admirable services will be hugely appreciated?

Baliphiles tell me that if you talk this way, the chances are even-Stephen that Bongo will not fall into a trance.

from my *The Power of Positive Nonsense*

Fate

THE ACCURSED EMERALD

To the great charity ball of the season, the buxom dowager wore a huge emerald pendant. And in the ladies' powder room at the Hotel Pierre, all the women crowded around her to get a closer look at the glistening gem. The dowager boasted, "This happens to be the third largest emerald in the whole world. The largest is the Queen of England's. Then comes the Onassis. Then comes this one, which is called the Lefkowitz."

"What a jewel!"

"How lucky you are!"

"Wait, nothing in life is that easy," said the dowager. "Unfortunately, the wearer of the fabulous Lefkowitz emerald must bear with the famous Lefkowitz curse."

The ladies were silent for but a second. "And what is the Lefkowitz curse?"

The dowager sighed, "Lefkowitz."

Message in fortune cookie: You will make fortune on next investment.
Message in next fortune cookie: Disregard previous message.

Flashers

Old Mr. Cardohy, in Room 109 of the old-age home, was as mischievous as he was spry—and bored. One day, reading about the wave of "flashers" around the country, he decided, on a sudden impulse, to undress and, during dinner, run through the dining room.

The room was indeed packed when naked Mr. Cardohy appeared in the doorway, yelled "Eureka!" ran around the tables and out.

The gaping silence was broken by old man Strudnick, a tailor: "Whatever that nut was wearing, folks, he should never wear it again until he has it *pressed*, for God's sake!"

See also **Appearances, Clothes**

Freudian Slips

These items actually appeared in print: none was invented by this delighted compiler.

L. R.

Upon arriving at the Honolulu airport, two men were given coveted lays by Hawaiian maidens.

❧

The rapists tell us . . .*

*Therapists.

❧

The President, who has been sick for several days, is now in bed with a coed.

❧

They were married and lived happily even after.

❧

There are millions of desirable women who are unattacked, and hungry for love.

❧

Mr. and Mrs. Fechner returned yesterday from Hawaii, where they spent two weeks of unallowed pleasure.

❧

The head of the investment firm would not say whether, in his own private holdings, he was more interested in stocks or blonds.

❧

A seven-pound baby boy arrived last night to frighten the lives of Mr. and Mrs. Sherman Caswell.

❧

Before the verdict was rendered this morning, "Miss Mexico" told interviewers that if the court freed her, she would become a nut.

Mrs. and Mr. Seligman have lied most of their married life in Hartford.

Overcome by gas while taking a bath, she owes her life to the watchfulness of the janitor.

The prosecutors, representing the State, asked prospective jurors if they would inflict the death penalty "if the evidence warranted it." Those who said they were opposed to capital punishment under any circumstances were executed.

The Red Cross paid for emergency care and later found a free bed for him in an institution specializing in the treatment of artcritics.

The protesting students insisted that before they were arrested they only intended to show their opposition to the speaker by pissing.

Telegram to wife

HAVING WONDERFUL TIME. WISH YOU WERE HER.

On bill from lawyer, typed by his secretary: Bull rendered: $500.

BEAUTY QUEEN UNVEILS BUST
AT DEDICATION CEREMONY

News column: James Melville, the district attorney, then forcefully addressed the jury and gummed up the case.

Society column: Their annual ball was held last night at the Hilton Hotel. Seldom have we seen such a glittering display of beaux and bellies.

Social notes: He is visiting our town with his bitter half.

In department store: Bath towels for your whole damp family.

Mr. and Mrs. Oliver Sloane request the pleasure of your presents at the marriage of their daughter . . .

If we would only send young American tenors to stud abroad, they would return immensely improved.

VOTE FOR
JORDAN BARNES
Your fiend in City Hall

The report was signed by five faulty members of the university.

She went into the hospital after being bitten by a spider in a bathing suit.

Mr. Okum lives with his wife, his high-school sweetheart, and three sons.

When his wife called from London, Mr. Favish said, "It was wonderful to hear her voice and realize she was over three thousand miles away."

He collapsed on the sidewalk and died without medical assistance.

Service magazine for home furnishings: Mr. Frenkel won the national bedding award from the National Association. Mr. Frenkel has ten children.

His friends could give no reason why he should have committed suicide. He is single.

The chief is inclined to believe that a crossed wife might be the cause of the fire.

The bride and her mother were in the deceiving line.

The All-Girl orchestra was rather weak in the bras section.

Mrs. Williams of the Home Garden Club gave a short talk on how to keep ants out of your blooming pants.

WANTED:
Job as janitor. Long experience.
Expert moper.

See also Bloopers, Boo-boos, Headlines That Haunt Me, How's That Again?, Malaprops, News Items That Haunt Me, Typos

Freudian Tales

The great psychoanalyst Freud,
Had the upper class very anneud,
Preaching, "You cannot be rid
Of the damn lustful Id,
So it might as well be enjeud."

Sigmund Freud, to a heaving, sweating patient, "Get out of this office. You're *sick!*"

RED BUTTONS

Tilly Schechtman was unmarried. She had never been married. She had never been proposed to. She had never even been—betrayed. And, alas, Tilly was thirty-three years old—plain, not graceful, plump—and by now boy-shy and man-scared. Her parents grieved sorely over Tilly's sad, sad plight.

One day, Mrs. Schechtman said to Tilly, "I have been thinking and thinking, and I think I have a good idea. To end this sitting around, night after night, hoping *maybe* some nice man just will come . . . from where, Tilly? From the clouds? From a star? A white knight, I suppose, on a pony—"

"Mama. . . ."

"Tilly, it's a whole lot smarter you should put an ad in the newspaper!"

"Mama!" gasped the spinster. "Are you joking?"

"I'm not joking."

"But the *shame*—"

"What shame? You don't give your *name*, Tilly. You write it like this."

She handed her daughter a paper, on which she had carefully printed:

A CHARMING JEWISH GIRL, FROM FINE FAMILY,
EDUCATED, GOOD COOK, BIG READER, AGE 28,
WOULD LIKE TO MEET KIND, INTELLIGENT, REFINED
JEWISH GENTLEMAN. OBJECT: FRIENDSHIP
FIRST. CONCERTS, PLAYS, WALKS IN PARK,
LECTURES, MUSEUMS . . . THEN MAYBE MARRIAGE.
—BOX 462.

Tilly stammered and gulped protestations, but her mother insisted, "What can you *lose,* Tilly? And just think of what could happen! Who knows? A good man—a teacher. With your intelligence, all the books you have read, the music you know . . ."

And so the advertisement appeared. And each morning the girl known as "Box 462" hastened down three flights of stairs to meet the postman. . . .

On the fifth day she came running up and burst into the apartment: "Mama! An answer! Forwarded from the paper!" With flushed cheeks, Tilly ripped open the envelope, devoured the contents—sank into a chair as if in a state of shock, and burst into tears.

"Tilly!" cried Mrs. Shechtman, "Tilly! Tell mama! What's *wrong?*"

In a strangling voice, Tilly said, "It's from papa."

See also **Jews, Just Jokes**

Gambling

Scene: The Salon, Windemere Club, off Berkeley Square, London

"Willie" Pierce and "Bunty" Blore were having sherry at the bar. They were silent for a bit, then Pierce said, "I say, Bunty . . ."

"Mmh?

"Heard about Kit Cranmere?"

"No."

Pierce sipped his sherry. "Won a packet at Cockford's last night."

"A packet?"

"Right. Ten thousand pounds."

"Good Lord, Willie. Are you shaw?!" Blore sipped his sherry.

"Quite. . . . Ah, here comes Ilford. . . . Hullo, Colly. I say, Bunty and I were talking about Kit Cranmere. They say he won ten thousand quid at Cockford's last night . . ."

Ilford raised his glass of ale. "Cheers." He drank.

"Heard anything about that, Colly?" asked Blore.

"Mmh," said Ilford. "Saw it with my own eyes, Bunty."

"Ah, then—" crowed Pierce.

"But it wasn't Kit Cranmere, Willie; it was his brother Ainsly. And it wasn't at Cockford's, it was at the Curzon. And 'twasn't ten thousand quid. It was six. And he didn't win it, old man, he lost it." Ilford took a deep swig. "In all other respects, old boy, your account is entirely correct."

Two friends, Nora and Cindy, recently divorced, decided to celebrate their freedom with a weekend of gambling in Las Vegas. In the Scheherazade Casino, they walked past the slot machines, the blackjack tables, the dice wells—to the roulette tables. "All my *life* I've wanted to play roulette," said Nora. "How do I decide which number to choose?"

"It's all luck," said Cindy. "Look, my address is Eighteen eighteen Eighteenth Street. So I'll—" She placed a chip on number eighteen. "Maybe it's my lucky number."

Nora said, "I don't have a lucky number . . ."

"Your age," said Cindy. "Why not put a chip on your age?"

Nora placed a hundred dollars worth of chips on number thirty-four.

"Bets closed!" The croupier spun the wheel, then tossed the little ball into the whirling circle. The ball bounced and clacked and Cindy's eyes were wide as saucers. The ball nestled into its cradle. "Number forty-two," intoned the croupier.

"Too bad, dear," said Cindy, turning to Nora.

Nora lay on the floor. She had fainted.

On a slot machine

Warning: This Machine is Coiniverous!

Scene: Atlantic City Rooming House

BOY: Golly, Pop, all the other boys in my class play ball in the schoolyard every day—and hang out together—and go swimming—

POP: Shut up, Alfred. Deal.

Gambling: The only certain way of getting nothing for something.

WILSON MIZNER

Mr. Vito Martelli was complaining to a friend that a disaster had befallen him. "My son-in-law—it'sa terrible, Giovanni, terrible!"

"What's a matt'?"

"What's a matt'?" Martelli groaned. "Thata man don'ta know how to drink, and he don'ta know how to shoota craps!"

"*That*'sa 'terrible,' Vito? You crazy! That'sa wonderful! Why you complain?"

"Because he doesa drink, and he doesa shoot craps!"

BAER: Did you know there's an absolutely foolproof way to come home from Vegas or Atlantic City with a small fortune?

ASPIS: Really? What's that?

BAER: Go there with a large fortune.

See also **Ingenuity, Stratagems**

The Gay Set

Bisexual: A man who likes girls as well as the next fellow.

"Mrs. Brett, is it true that your grandson is a practicing homosexual?"
Mrs. Brett sighed sadly, "Yeah."
"So where is his office?"

"Hello, mother."
"Hel-*lo*, Sherman. How is my darling, my favorite son?"
"Fine, mama. Great."
"Thank God. You're eating well—?"
"Mama, listen. I'm married!"
"*Married?* Sherman? *Mazel tov* and you should be happy for a hundred and twenty years—"
"Mama, wait. Listen . . . I didn't marry a Jew . . ."
"So? I know some wonderful gentiles."
"But, mama, I hope you're not prejudiced—against blacks."
"Me? Prejudiced? Don't be silly. 'Grow with the times,' that's what I always say. You have to grow with the times! . . . So what's her name?"
"Mama, that's another thing. Brace yourself. 'Her' name is—Peter."
Silence. " 'Peter?!' "
"Yes, mama."
"That's not a nickname, for like Patricia?"
"No, mama. Peter is a boy. We really love each other. . . . We're trying to find a place to live. There's so much prejudice against blacks. . . . We want to start a home—"
"Until you find a place, Sherman darling, you and Peter can come and stay with us!"
"Oh, mama, you're wonderful. . . . But how can we stay with you? Your apartment only has one bedroom. . . ."
"So? You and Peter can't sleep in one bedroom?!"
"Sure, mama—but where will you and papa sleep?"
"That worries you? Put it out of your *mind*, Sherman. Your papa will sleep on the couch in the living room. Many is the night he slept there, when I had the flu, when my back was in traction—"

"Oh, wonderful. But, mama, if Peter and I share the bedroom and papa takes the sofa—where will *you* sleep?"

"Ah, Sherman, my own little Sherman—don't you know yet that about your mother, who loves you more than life itself, you never, *never* have to worry?"

"But you can't sleep on the floor—"

"Who sleeps on a floor? Don't *worry*, Sherman. I will never cause you trouble or discomfort. I will never stand in the way of your happiness. I—"

"Mama, stop beating around the bush. *Where* will you sleep?"

"Who'll sleep? Relax, Sherman. The minute I'm hanging up to finish this wonderful heart-to-heart talk between a mother and her son, I'm going to jump out of the window."

Scene: The Palm Court, Plaza Hotel

Mrs. William Forsythe was having tea with her twenty-three-year-old son, the handsome—indeed, the very handsome—Reginald. The teacup trembled in Mrs. Forsythe's hand when Reginald said, "But I *love* him, mother. And Marvin loves me. We want to get mar—"

"*Please!*" said Mrs. Forsythe. "Can you imagine what people will *say*?"

"We don't care," said Reginald. "But I do, very much, want *your* blessing!"

"No, Reggie. Never!"

"Are you so old-fashioned, mother? So afraid of convention? Give me one reason, other than—"

Mrs. Forsythe looked her son straight in the eye. "He's *Jewish!*"

Geography Revised

Calcutta: The climate in Calcutta is so terrible, its inhabitants have to live elsewhere.

Dresden: The ancient capital of China.

Pennsylvania: One of its chief products is pencils. But its founder invented the pen.

Pyramids: The mountains between Spain, France, and Egypt.

Red Sea: It is connected to the Mediterranean by the Sewage Canal.

Tides: Some tides are named Eb and others Flo.

Turkey: Is most famous for its goblets.

Vesuvius: The volcano where the creator usually smokes.

See also **Bloopers, Boo-boos, Definitions (by Children), Definitions to Cherish, History Revised, Typos**

God

I once knew a codger named Dodd
Whose gripes were exceedingly odd.
He growled, "If you please,
Spell my name with three D's!"
Forgetting that one was sufficient for God.

A brilliant young student came to the old, learned rabbi and defiantly exclaimed, "I must tell you the truth: I have become an atheist! I no longer believe in God."

"And how long," asked the elder, "have you been studying Talmud?"

"Five years."

"Only five years," exclaimed the rabbi, "and you have the *nerve* to call yourself an atheist?!"

Don't blame God: He's only human.

L. R.

God created man because he was so disappointed in the monkey.

MARK TWAIN

If triangles had a god, he would have three sides.

VOLTAIRE

Man is surely crazy; he can't make a worm, but he makes gods by the dozen.

PASCAL

God: the most popular scapegoat for our sins.

MARK TWAIN

God will forgive me: it is his *métier*.

HEINRICH HEINE

God said, "Let us make man in our image"; and Man said, "Let us make God in our image."

DOUGLAS JERROLD

What the Lord does is certainly best—probably.

Dear God: You help total *strangers*—so why not me?

Dear God: I am a believing Jew and know that You will provide: but please tell me: why You don't provide *until* You provide?!

If God lived on earth, men would knock out all His windows.

YIDDISH SAYINGS

God is not everything that exists; God is everything that does not exist.

REMY DE GOURMONT

Rabbi Beckman, the young, new rabbi in a Connecticut temple, greatly loved to play golf.

One sunny Saturday morning, after services, Rabbi Beckman felt so powerful a craving to play a few holes, that he begged God to forgive him for breaking the Sabbath, tossed his golf bag into the back of the car, and sped off to a course where he was certain no one would recognize him. With an apology to his Maker, the Rabbi teed off. . . .

Up in heaven, Moses suddenly bolted upright. "Lord! Lord!" he cried. "Do my eyes deceive me? There, Holy One—do You *see?*"

"Y-yes," said the Lord.

"That's Rabbi Sylvan Beckman!" said Moses. "Playing golf on Your Holy Sabbath!"

"Dear Me," sighed the Lord.

"Such a transgression!" said Moses. "How will You punish him?"

"We must teach him a lesson." God cupped His hands over His mouth and—just as Rabbi Beckman teed off for the second hole, the Almighty, King of the Universe, let out His breath in a mighty, cosmic "*Whoooosh!*"

The powerful sound caught the rabbi's golf ball in midair, lifted it two hundred yards, flipped it around a tree, over a stream, and into the cup—for a remarkable hole in one!

Moses stared at God. "*That* You call a punishment, Lord?"

The Lord winked. "Whom can he *tell?*"

"But how can you be so positive that God does not exist?" asked the priest.

The atheist huffed: "A man has to believe in *some*thing!"

Mr. Somekh, age seventy-four, was taking his first trip by air. He was given a seat next to a swarthy Arab wearing the traditional kaffiyeh (headdress) and djellabah (robe). The Arab stared at the old Jew, buckled his seatbelt, and deliberately spat on Mr. Somekh's shoes. . . .

The plane took off, leveled off. . . . The Arab put his head back and dozed off. . . .

Soon the aircraft ran into a storm: tremendous bouncings up and around, and fierce, sudden droppings down. Poor Mr. Somekh grabbed for the airsickness bag stuffed in the pocket ahead—but alas, alas; it was too late. All over the sleeping Arab's white robe, Mr. Somekh threw up. . . .

The old man fearfully closed his eyes and gave a prayer to the Lord, "Help me, Your pious servant. Give me an idea. When this crazy man awakens and sees his robe, he'll pull out that dagger and stab me in the heart! O Lord, Lord, *never* did I need Your help so badly!"

And when the Arab yawned and opened his eyes, Mr. Somekh, suddenly hearing a divine whisper in his ears, leaned forward and politely smiled, "So, Mister from Arabia—are you feeling better now?"

> God's plan got off to a happy beginning
> But Adam ruined it by sinning!
> I hope the whole story
> Will end in God's glory,
> But right now the wrong side is winning.
>
> DOUGLAS JERROLD

The Reverend Abner Ravenswood was playing golf, near High Wycombe, with one of his parishioners, Bryan Olcutt. Olcutt missed an easy putt and exclaimed, "God*dam!*"

"Tut, tut, Bryan," said the Reverend Ravenswood. "Mustn't take the name of the Lord in vain."

"So sorry, vicar." But on the fourth hole, Olcutt chipped his ball out of the sand—all the way beyond the putting green. "My *God!*" he swore.

"Now, Bryan, I really cannot allow such cursing!" said the reverend. "If you do that once more, I swear—I shall call on the Lord to strike you down!"

On the eighth hole, Olcutt missed a six-inch putt. "For God's sake, can't I do *one* goddam thing right?" he exploded.

At once a great cloud formed above the two golfers, a bolt of lightning flashed—and knocked the Reverend Ravenswood to the ground. As he and Olcutt stared incredulously at the cloud, an orotund voice from heaven said, "Sorry, Ravenswood. Missed my damn target!"

Three rowboats moved along the totally flooded streets, and the water was still rising as the torrent from heaven raged unabated. The rescuers spied a strange figure on the roof of a small building: a tall, bearded man, wearing a wide, flat black hat, his arms crossed.

"Come down!" shouted the rowers. "Get into the boat!"

The tall figure gestured calmly. "Save others. Do not worry about me. I am Rabbi Gershon Rosenbloom. The *Lord* will save me!"

An hour later, another boat—this one with an outboard motor—approached. "Hey! You on the roof! Come down! The waters are still rising!"

The rabbi, standing cross-armed despite water up to his waist, called out, "Go *on!* Save others. I am a rabbi. I have complete faith in my Lord!"

And an hour after that, the rains still pouring down, a helicopter, searching for survivors of the flood, hovered above the rabbi on the roof, lowered its ladder, the pilot's voice bellowing out of a bullhorn: "Grab that ladder, man! The water's up to your *chin!* This is your last—"

"Fear not!" sang the rabbi. "I am a man of God! And—He—will—*glub, glub, kmpf . . .*" And Rabbi Gershon Rosenbloom, that good and faithful servant of the Lord, sank beneath the rising waters.

Being a soul of the utmost virtue, without stain throughout his life, the rabbi, within an instant after drowning, found himself among the Heavenly Throng, gazing at the effulgent radiance of God Himself.

"Oh, Lord!" cried the rabbi. "How *could* You? I had absolute faith in You, and You let me drown! How could You let me down—"

" 'Let you *down?*' " bridled the Lord. "I sent two boats and a helicopter to take you off that roof, you idiot!"

A most pious old Jew prayed in the synagogue thrice every day of his adult life. His worldly business partner had not once set foot therein. And in his seventieth year the old Jew addressed the Lord thus: "Oh, God, Blessed be Thy Name, have I not every day since my *Bar Mitzva* celebrated Your Glory? Have I ever made a move, named a child, taken a trip, without consulting You first? Is there a more devout, humble, observing soul in all Your fold? . . . And now I'm old, I can't sleep, I'm poor. . . . But my partner! That no-good! Not *once* has he even made a prayer! Not a penny has he given to the synagogue! He drinks, he gambles, he runs around with loose women—and he's worth a *fortune!* . . . Dear God, King of All the Universe, I am not asking You to punish him, but please tell me: why, why, *why* have You treated me this way?"

The synagogue rumbled as The Voice intoned: "Because all you do, day after day, is *nag, nag, nag* me!"

See also **Clergy, Faith, Heaven, Jews, Religion**

Goldwyniana

Note: Samuel Goldwyn (né Shmuel Gelbfisz) was a superb maker of movies, an incomparable judge of stories, and a master of creative malapropism. The following transformations of English are not limited to Mr. Goldwyn's observations; but they all qualify for inclusion in that category of startling and instructive solecisms with which the ex–glove salesman so generously endowed us.

Items which were indubitably the product of Mr. Goldwyn are identified by his initials.

L. R.

Acting
Tell them to put more life in their dying.
Tell them to stand closer apart.

Aplomb: I don't care about that; it rolls off my back like a duck.

S. G.

Argument: You fail to overlook the crucial point!

Autobiography: How would you like to write my autobiography?

Business: If I was in this business only for the business, I wouldn't be in this business.

Decorum: For your information, just answer me one question!

Decision
True, I've been a long time making up my mind about buying your book. But now I'm giving you a definite answer. I won't say yes and I won't say no—but I'm giving you a *definite* maybe.

S. G.

Emphasis: I'll give it to you in two words: um possible.

S. G.

Floods: The damage is so great they'll have to evaporate three cities.

Impossibilities: It's absolutely impossible—but it has possibilities.

Lesbians
   "Mr. Goldwyn, I don't think you'd want to make that story: it's about two Lesbians!"
   "So? We can change them to Americans."

Memory: Put it out of your mind. In no time, it will be a forgotten memory.

Movie business: You'll get along fine in this business as long as you don't bite the hand that lays the golden eggs.

Movies
   The wide screen will only make bad films twice as bad.

S. G.

Go see that turkey for yourself, and see for yourself why you shouldn't see it.

That movie? Terrible! Don't fail to miss it if you can!

They didn't *release* that movie; it escaped.

Columbia would be smart to take that film and cut it up into guitar picks.

IRVING CAESAR

Oral contract: An oral contract isn't worth the paper it's written on.

S. G.

Pride: I don't pay any attention to him. I don't even ignore him.

Producers: Producers shouldn't get ulcers; they should *give* them.

S. G.

Rejection: Gentlemen, I have made up my mind. Include me out.

S. G.

Scenery: I love true nature, where the hand of man never set foot.

Sculpture: My wife's hands are so beautiful, I'm having a bust made of them.

S. G.

Singers: Can she *sing?* She's practically a Florence Nightingale.

Stars: Give me a couple of years and I'll make that actress an overnight success.

Stories for the silver screen

That story is wonderful. It's magnificent. It's *prolific.*

S. G.

What do you mean the story is too caustic? Who cares about expense?

S. G.

Travel: When I travel, I always like a nice hotel suite, where I can put up with my wife.

Writers

"We just have to get fresh talent around here," complained Mr. Goldwyn. "Take our writers. They're getting old. They're stale. We should hire some young, talented unknowns!"

"Wonderful," said his story editor. "I know one."

"What's his name?"

"Raymond Jesperson."

"I never even heard of him. Can't you think of anyone else?"

I'm overpaying [Ben] Hecht something terrible—but he's worth it.

S. G.

TALES ABOUT SAM GOLDWYN

Goldwyn to L. B. Mayer: "We're both in real trouble!"

"Why?"

"Because you have Gable under contract, and I want him."

"Mr. Goldwyn, I just became the father of a boy!"

"Wonderful. What are you going to call him?"

"Ronald."

"*Ronald?*" echoed Goldwyn. "What kind of name is that? Today every Tom, Dick, and Harry is named Ronald."

At Arthur Mayer's place in Connecticut, Mr. Goldwyn saw a curious metal object on a pedestal in the center of the garden. "What's that?" he asked.

"It's a sundial, Sam," said Mayer.

"A *sun*dial? What does it do?"

"The vertical part casts a shadow, and the place that shadow falls on . . ." Mayer carefully explained how a sundial marks off time.

"My!" chuck-chucked Goldwyn. "What won't they think up next!"

Mr. and Mrs. Goldwyn were about to sail to Hawaii on a vacation. A group of relatives, friends, and employees came to the dock to see them off. As the ship started to slip away, Goldwyn put his hands to his mouth and sang out: "*Bon voyage!*"

Goldwyn had gotten into a severe wrangle with Walter Wanger about a female star Goldwyn wanted and Wanger had under contract. The negotiations between the lawyers got nowhere. Wanger telephoned Goldwyn. "Look, Sam. We're getting nowhere. Why not submit the whole mess to arbitration?"

"Fine! Great!" said Goldwyn. "I agree—just so it's understood I get her."

At a large dinner in his home, Goldwyn declared, "Listen, during all the ins and outs of my career, no matter what—no one in Hollywood ever had to sue me!"

"Hold it, Sam," said one guest. "Why, at this table alone I—Willie—Joe—and Ben have taken you to court!"

"I meant, present company excepted."

See also **Bloopers, Boo-boos, Cynics' Dictionary, Definitions (by Children), Geography Revised, History Revised, Malaprops, Typos**

Golf

On the fairway of the Glen Loch Club, Mr. Lachlan was walking toward the next green when a golf ball struck him hard in the temple. Mr. Lachlan clutched his head and fell to the ground, moaning.

Roddy MacIlhenny, the golfer who had teed off behind Lachlan, came running over to him. "Oh, *mon*—"

Lachlan cried, "Did y' nae *see* me? Y'domn fool, ye! I'll take this oop with m' lawyer, I will! I'll sue y' for five hoondred pounds!"

"But did ye nae *hear* me?" protested MacIlhenny. "Loud an' clear, I shouted, 'Fore! Fore!' "

Lachlin took thought for but an instant. "I'll take it."

Hugh McNair had joined a golf club near Glasgow. He took a fresh box of balls to the attendant in the locker room. "Ye're to put my initials on these balls, so's to tell me which ball in a cluster, or in the woods, is mine. And to facilitate their being returned to the clubhouse."

"Right y' are, sir. What initials?"

"*H* for 'Hugh' and *M* for 'McNair.' Then *M* and *D*—as I am a medical doctor."

"Yes, sir."

"And while y're doin' that," said McNair, "y'may as well add. 'Off. Hours: 10 to 5.' "

On the flight to Sarasota, two passengers, seated side by side, began to talk. The first man said, "I tell you, I can't wait to get into that sun, onto the golf course, the feel of my favorite club in my hand. I just am a *nut* about golf! . . . What about you? Are you a golfer?"

"Am *I* a golfer?" echoed the second man. "Mister, you could say that golf is practically my whole life!"

"What's your handicap?"

"Oh, my left ankle is sort of weak . . ."

"No, no. I mean your scoring? I—I'm in the low eighties."

"Really? Me, too! But once the thermometer goes over ninety, I pack up my clubs and head right back to my hotel!"

See also **God**

Graffiti

In men's room of an expensive restaurant that serves mediocre food:

DUNCAN HINES WEPT HERE

❧

On menu of diner: All meats declared A-1

U.S. RUBBER CO.

❧

On the mirror above the washbasin in a men's room

THINK!

Under this, a wag had printed an arrow, pointing downward, and this word:

THOAP

❧

In college dorm

A little coitus
Never hoitus.

❧

On college wall

Oh, Jim, let's not park here.
Oh, Jim, let's not park
Oh, Jim, let's not
Oh, Jim, let's
Oh, Jim,
Oh!

❧

On medical building

Neuroses are red,
Depression is blue,
I'm schizophrenic
How about you?

❧

Chalked on wall

GET OUT OF ANGOLA!
And below in another hand:
WHAT'S HER LAST NAME?

✌

On dormitory bulletin board

> She offered her honor, so
> I honored her offer.
> And all night long
> It was on her and off her.

✌

On a corridor wall at Brooklyn College

KAFKA
is a
KVETCH

✌

On a bulletin board at N.Y.U.

PROUST
is a
YENTA

✌

On bulletin board in mathematics building of a college in New England: I love the girls—but, oh, Euclid!

✌

On college wall: Just because you're paranoid, don't think they don't hate you.

✌

On church bulletin board: If Jesus was a Jew, how come he has a Puerto Rican name?

✌

On college wall

> *God*
> is
> *Dead!*
> —Nietzche

and underneath:

No. Nietzsche
is Dead.
—God

Under this sign in the women's clothes department of a Brooklyn store

LADIES READY TO WEAR CLOTHES

some male (no doubt) had printed, with a black felt-tip pen:

It's about time.

Under a sign

Auto Service: Call us 24 hours a day

some wag had added:

After midnight, we are not on our tows.

On big garage for a trucking firm

WE NEVER SLEEP

someone added:

NEITHER DO YOUR NEIGHBORS!

Billboard

JESUS

SAVES

under which:

Green stamps.
Why don't you, dummy?

See also **Advertisements, Boo-boos, Freudian Slips, Headlines That Haunt Me, Malaprops, Signs, Typos**

Groucho

A MEMOIR

One day, years ago, when I was committing movies, my phone rang in Beverly Hills. I shall give you as much of the conversation as I can retrieve from a memory bank whose circuits were blown ga-ga:

ROSTEN

Hello.

VOICE

Do I have the honor of addressing the world-famed proctologist, Marmaduke Montague?

ROSTEN

You have the wrong number.

VOICE

Then why did you answer?! You imposter! . . . For *years* I've been calling this number and getting Professor Marmaduke Montague. *What have you done with his body?* I'm going to call the police! *What* I'll call them is none of your business. What number *is* this, anyway?

ROSTEN
(indignantly)
This is Crestview-eight, two, nine—

VOICE

Aha! So you admit it! Why, if you were a man you'd come over and knock all my teeth out.

ROSTEN

I—

VOICE

If you were *half* a man, you'd knock half my teeth out.

ROSTEN
Who—

VOICE
And if you were a woman we could dance away the night in wild—*don't hang up!* You're a pretty dull conversationalist, Leo, if I have to say so myself. All *you* do is grunt, gripe, and sputter. That, bye the bye, is a perfect name for an outboard motor. . . . This is Groucho—as if you cared, running around with all those other starlets. I'm not that kind of girl. I'm not that kind of boy either. . . . Are you free for lunch? Fine. The Derby. I'll have a rose clenched between my teeth.

In the ten years I spent in Hollywood, I was the patsy for a dozen phone calls of the same maniacal order. They were not as easy to spot as you may think, for they came at all sorts of hours, at reasonable intervals, and used a crafty assortment of voices. Every call began with an entirely plausible greeting:

"Hello. My name is Iphigene Wimbledon. Is this Leo Rosten?"

Or, " 'ol-lo? Here iss Pierre Jouvert, *directeur* of Eiffel Tours . . ."

Or, "My name is Hollister, Floyd Hollister, of Sloat, Bankhead, and Dooley, appointed by the Probate Court to act as executors of the estate of Elmo Rosten, the oil billionaire from Waco, Texas."

Once I had been suckered, the Master hauled off and let me have it. Iphigene Wimbledon offered to sell my son ("A kid like that could net you ten-twelve thousand in today's market"). Pierre Jouvert read me a pornographic ode to the Catacombs ("You can get the entire set, bound in caterpillar cloth, for only—"). And the putative Floyd Hollister was trying to locate any relative of Elmo Rosten, especially Sister Terésa Ginsberg ("whose will left her collection of *mezuzas* to the Knights of Chocolate Malta").

At one time or another, during my decade in Hollywood, I was denounced for housing the leader of a white-slave ring, begged by a dentist from Pomona to let him fit me with stainless-steel bicuspids *entirely free* ("It's my only way of getting known in this dental institution"), and warned by a fire inspector not to have my roof sprayed with Mom's Fire Retardant "which is *actually a mouthwash*" when "a coat of buttermilk will do the job at less than half the cost."

It was quite a life.

At one lunch a gushy dowager leaned over between us and cooed. *"Do forgive me for intruding, but—are you Groucho Marx?"*

"No," iced my host, "are you?"

He was a wizard of reason run amok. He perfected the logic of lunacy. He also mocked the lunacy of logic. Consider his resignation from a certain club:

> I do not wish to belong to the
> kind of club that accepts people
> like me as members.

Shortly after he settled in Los Angeles, he was being driven around by a friend. As they took a long curve on Sunset Boulevard, the sparkling Pacific opened below them. On the beautiful sands stretched a row of cabanas with pretty striped awnings. "That's the C——— Beach Club," said his friend.

"Nifty," said Groucho. "That would be a good club for me and my family."

The friend cleared his throat. "Um—forget it . . . They don't admit Jews."

To which Groucho, whose wife was gentile, replied, "My son is half-Jewish. Do you think they'd let him go into the water up to his knees?"

When a bank sent him an effusive form letter, after he had opened an account, a letter that ended with the obligatory sentiment: "If we can ever be of any assistance, do not hesitate to call on us," Marx called on them pronto:

> Gentlemen:
>
> The best assistance you can give me is to steal some money from the account of one of your richer clients and credit it to mine.
>
> Groucho Marx

When *Variety*, the bible of show biz, editorialized that the Marx Brothers could earn twenty thousand dollars a week if they would only work together again, Marx wrote the editor:

> Dear Sir:
>
> Apparently you are under the impression that the only thing that matters in this world is money. That is quite true.
>
> Groucho Marx

Marx was once dragooned into serving as manager of the movie Comedians in their annual charity match against the Actors. He told Jack Benny to lead off. "All right, Benny. Get up there and hit a home run."

Benny struck out.

Marx resigned. "I can't manage a team that won't follow instructions."

A pretty actress tried to flatter him by cooing, "You're a man after my own heart."

"That's not all I'm after," leered Groucho.

A FAN: It's a real pleasure for me to meet Groucho Marx.
GROUCHO *(sneering)*: I've known him for years, and I can tell you it's not much of a pleasure.

On a radio show

GROUCHO: Is it true that all you professional wrestlers fake most of your matches?
WRESTLER: That's a darn dirty rumor!
GROUCHO: How many dirty rumors have you wrestled lately?

"They came back on a small English ship. I think it was a base Cunard."

He had a need to puncture decorum. During World War II, he was at an Army training camp to entertain the soldiers. In the quarters of the commanding general, the phone rang. Groucho picked it up, crooning, "World War *Two*-oo."

Groucho's friends, praising a local psychic's powers of divination, begged Groucho to attend a séance. Groucho sat quiet and respectful, as the swami stared into a crystal ball, called up departed souls from the Beyond, and answered questions from his paying guests—question after question—in an eerie monotone. After a prolonged spell of omniscience, the sorcerer intoned, "My medium . . . is growing tired. . . . There is time for . . . one more question."

Groucho asked it. "What's the capital of North Dakota?"

At a Bel-Air party, Groucho proposed this toast to the hostess. "Madam, I drink to your beauty, your charm, your wit—and I hope this gives you some idea of the lengths I will go to to get a drink around here."

Groucho's calculated derangement, abetted by that rasp of a voice, that black smear of mustache, that roué's lope, those waggling eyebrows, that one wall-eye, that stare of contempt—expressed what the rest of us simply have not the wit, much less the audacity, to utter. When a woman said, "I made a stew last night," Groucho leered, "Anyone I know?"

To a hostess, upon leaving her party, he said, "Don't think this hasn't been an unusually dull evening, because it has."

Once, leaving his house after dinner, I paused to say, "I'd like to say goodbye to your wife."

Said Groucho, "Who wouldn't?"

A tipsy tourist once placed his arm around Marx's shoulders and cackled, "Groucho, you son-of-a-gun, I bet you don't remember me!"

Marx fixed the oaf with a baleful eye. "Sir, I never forget a face—but in your case I'll be glad to make an exception."

His correspondence with me was sprinkled with such corkers as:

> Home is where you hang your head.

> Writing to you is like corresponding with an aching void.

> You don't have to have relatives in St. Louis to be miserable.

Of all his sideswipes, the one I most admire is this:

```
Dear Junior:

    Excuse me for not answering your letter
sooner. I have not been answering so many
letters lately that I couldn't get around
to not answering yours in time.
```

He once offered to write a blurb for one of my books:

From the moment I picked this book up
until the moment I put it down, I could not
stop laughing. Some day I hope to read it.

On "You Bet Your Life," his celebrated television show, a nurse from Australia, when asked, "Where are you from?" replied, "I flew here by plane."

Groucho nodded. "A girl would be a fool to try it any other way."

When a Japanese lad said he was twenty-one, Groucho asked, "Is that in years or in yen?"

"You don't count age in yen," said the young man.

"No? I have a yen to be thirty again."

One of the contestants turned out to be from cornhusker country. Let's call him Floyd.

GROUCHO

How did you meet your wife?

FLOYD

Well, I drive a truck—

GROUCHO

You ran over her?

FLOYD

No. She was in the barn—

GROUCHO

You drove your truck into a *barn?*

FLOYD

No, no, Groucho. Her family had been missing some chickens—

GROUCHO
(Incredulously)

They were lonely for *chickens?*

FLOYD

No. They had been *missing* them, so they turned on a light in the barnyard, and I'm driving up to get some turkeys, and her father hollers, "The turkeys are in the barn"—

GROUCHO
(horrified)

You married a *turkey?*

FLOYD

No, *no*. As I go to the barn, a big skunk starts for the chicken-house, and a girl yells, "Get that skunk, too"—and we both smelled so bad—no one else would come close to us—

GROUCHO

That's the most romantic story I ever heard.

One night Groucho was interviewing a beautiful model. "You must have all sorts of exciting experiences."

"N-no," she said. "It's just routine."

Groucho gaped, "What are you modeling: *clay?*"

He was driving back from a casual trip to Tijuana, Mexico. On the California side of the border, the U.S. immigration officials asked each driver a few questions. When Groucho's car stopped, the Fed touched the brim of his hat and said, "Are you an American citizen?"

"Certainly," said Groucho.

"And where were you born?"

"New York."

"What's your occupation?"

Groucho leaned out of the window to whisper, "Smuggler."

And once, emerging from the preview of a Doris Day movie, in which that wide-eyed, wholesome, all-American maiden spent an hour and a half resisting the blandishments of Cary Grant, someone asked Groucho, "Do you know Doris Day?"

The mordant crow said, "Shucks, I knew her before she was a virgin."

At a testimonial dinner to S. J. Perelman

This is a man who has not let success go to his head—a man who is humble and unspoiled. He is as unassuming, as comfortable to be with as an old glove—and just about as interesting.

GROUCHO: How old are you, ma'am?
CONTESTANT: I'm—approaching forty.
GROUCHO: From which direction?

One night he was driving me to a meeting. I suddenly remembered it was my father's birthday. "Can you stop at a Western Union office?" I asked. "I want to wire my father."

"What's wrong?" asked Groucho. "Can't he stand by himself?"

Groucho's old friend, Goodman Ace, was staying with Marx in Beverly Hills. At breakfast, Ace said to Groucho, "This orange juice is delicious." Turning to the maid, he said, "Could I have another glass, please?"

"Wait a minute, Ace," said Groucho. "Do you think oranges grow on trees?"

See also **Chutzpa, Cynics' Dictionary, Definitions (by Children), Definitions to Cherish, Goldwyniana, Put-downs, Repartée, Retorts, Sarcasm, Waiters, Wit, Wordplay**

Gurus

THE TRIP TO SHINGBWIYANG

Mrs. Julius Seltzer, long widowed, marched into the Fugazy Travel Agency on Fifth Avenue and said, "I want you to make me all arrangements. I must leave, as soon as possible, to a place in Burma called—" She placed a piece of paper on the desk of the agent, Noel Grant, who read:

SHINGBWIYANG

"Madam, are you sure this is how it's spelled?"

"Absolutely. You can look it up. It's in Burma."

Mr. Grant consulted a large atlas of the world. "My goodness. You're right! Very high up. In the Himalayas! I've never even heard of this place. . . . Are you *sure* that's where you—"

"Positive. And I can't waste time! Make plane reservations."

"I'd better call our central office. Do be seated."

Mrs. Seltzer sat down. Mr. Grant made a phone call. "Central? . . . Give me a readout on a place in Burma called S-H-I-N-G-B-W-I-Y-A-N-G. . . . Yes? Air India? . . . What time? . . . Change planes in Calcutta. . . . Yes. . . . Hold on. . . . Mrs. Seltzer, there are flights to Calcutta—then Burmese airlines—which deliver you near the town. But you would have to hire a guide and ponies to take you up that mountain—"

"Do it! Forget expense."

"What about stopovers, Mrs. Seltzer? For rest? It's seven thousand miles."

"I don't need rest. No stopovers!"

"And do you expect to climb the mountain?"

"Certainly. Arrange for ponies."

"How will you be paying for all this, Mrs. Seltzer? The bill will run into many thousands—"

"I'll give you a cashier's check."

As Mrs. Seltzer started out, Mr. Grant said, "Please excuse me, madam, but I can't help asking . . . *why* are you taking such a long, costly, *very* hard—even hazardous trip? To such an extraordinary destination?"

"I am going to a holy cave, where is the world-famous swami guru, Jarawhalal Krishnapanoora!"

Within forty-eight hours, Mrs. Julius Seltzer was on Air India's flight to London—and Calcutta. There a waiting Burmese travel representative put her aboard a local plane to Shingbwiyang. And there two natives, with ponies, waited. And Mrs. Seltzer got on one pony and a guide on the other, and the two started the ascent.

Up, up, up they rode, passing saffron-clad monks and sackcloth pilgrims by the dozen, some whirling little prayer wheels, others tinkling bells, still others swinging brass censers. For half a mile before the entrance to the holy cave, the waiting line stood motionless.

All, all of these adorers of the swami, Mrs. Seltzer rode by—for her guide kept calling out Burmese phrases, announcing the priority of a believer come so many thousands of miles to seek the help of the great Guru Jarawhalal Krishnapanoora.

At last the indomitable woman reached the entrance to the cave. The guide helped her down from her pony. She stretched her arms and legs and vigorously marched into the cave.

It was filled with the pious, murmuring, and the air was heavy with incense. The swami was lighted from hidden spotlights. He was a young man, wore a gold turban and saffron robe, and sat cross-legged on piled cushions of gold and silver, his pale hands in his lap, his eyes closed in trance, mumbling: "Oom—oom . . ."

Mrs. Seltzer pushed through the seated acolytes, strode straight to the pile of gold and silver cushions, and in a clear, commanding voice declaimed: "Sheldon, enough! Come home!"

Mrs. Bealoir Thornycroft, a widow, living on in her late husband's great estate in Delhi, heard of the remarkable powers of a famous old oracle named Sholuparmarunji, who lived in a cave in nearby Bharatour. She wrote to the seer, who granted her an audience at 11 P.M. in twelve days, for an appropriate offering to Shiva, the great Vedic god.

Mrs. Thornycroft's chauffeur drove the old family Rolls-Royce up to the sacred cave of Chumpra precisely at 11:00 P.M.

Pandit Sholuparmarunji, wizened, wrinkled, naked save for his dhoti, was sitting cross-legged, dimly lighted by flickering candles set in a circle of fine brass holders. He signaled Mrs. Thornycroft to seat herself on a brocaded cushion and, in a mesmeric tone and mellifluous English, placed both palms together, inclining his head. "And what service can one as humble as Sholuparmarunji offer to so fine and great a lady, who has come to seek his—may I say—solace? Augury of hope? Beneficence of karma?"

"Dear, *dear* pandit," said Mrs. Thornycroft, "I am a Christian; you are a Hindu. And still I come to you—for I have failed to find an answer, from my own faith and its seers. I come to you in the hope—the great, boundless hope—of receiving the answer to but one question."

The holy man nodded, closed his eyes, and slid into a trance, murmuring incomprehensible phrases in Hindi, then said: "Dear lady . . . continue . . ."

"I want to know this, dear pandit: When I die, will I go to heaven—I mean, to our Christian heaven—to be reunited with my loved ones and to bask in the glory of Paradise forever?"

Sholuparmarunji bowed and stirred some ashes in a bowl before him, releasing the pungent scent of incense in the cave. Then he began to chant, and to sway in rhythm to the chanting, and to bob his head, eyes closed, slowly from one side to the other.

Mrs. Thornycroft sat transfixed.

After some time in the transcendental state, the holy man's eyelids fluttered . . . his eyes opened . . . and he blinked to focus in the soft, flickering light. "Ah, my dear, my *gracious* lady; yes, yes, almighty Shiva has seen fit to answer my petition . . ." He indicated a large encised platter to Mrs. Thornycroft's right. There were many rupees on it, and the English lady added generously to them.

" 'Shall she go to her heaven?' I asked the sacred one. . . . His answer . . ." Sholuparmarunji closed his eyes to intensify his concentration ". . . consisted of two parts—what you descendants of the Raj would call 'Good news' and 'Bad news.' First, I will transmit the Good news. Yes, *yes*, madam, when you leave this impure world, because you have been so kind and pious, *yes*, angels will waft you up through the clouds, to the Golden Throne! And there you will remain in heaven forever and ever, throughout the measureless span of eternity, blessed, drenched in blissful love—"

"Oh, pandit, pandit!" cried Mrs. Thornycroft. "My heart is overflowing!"

The transported features of Sholuparmarunji were broken by a wince. "The *bad* news—"

"But pandit," exclaimed the ecstatic lady. "After such marvelous good news, how can any other news be *bad?*"

"Tonight," murmured the seer.

See also **God, The Occult, Religion**

Hanky-panky

"Hello, Jake Kessler?"

"Speaking."

"This is Howie. Listen, Jake, can you join our poker game this Saturday night?"

"I'll look in my calendar. . . . Gee, I'm sorry, Howie. I can't. The great pianist Yitzchok Bobrovnick is playing with the New York Philharmonic."

"So how's about Tuesday, Jake?"

"Hold on. . . . Nope. . . . Bobrovnick is playing at Carnegie Hall."

"Oh, well, how about two weeks from tonight?"

"Uh—ah . . . oh, no. Two weeks from tonight, Bobrovnick will be at Lincoln Center."

"For goodness sake, Jake. Are you that crazy about hearing this Bobrovnick play?"

"Frankly, I've never heard him."

"B-but—"

"Whenever Bobrovnick gives a concert, I visit Natasha."

"Who's Natasha?"

Said Jake, "His wife."

Scene: London Club

"I say, Rippleworth," said Lord Bunleigh, "did you know that Lady Cynthia Paget always wears black garters?"

" 'Pon my word!" exclaimed Rippleworth. "Why?"

Lord Bunleigh stared into his glass thoughtfully. "In memory, I suppose, of all the fine chaps who have passed beyond."

An American in Paris, checking into the hotel, saw an appetizing brunette sitting in a chair in the lobby, her long legs crossed to reveal their shapeliness, her body turned to emphasize the grandeur of her bosom, her sidelong, inviting glance focused on the arriving Don Juan. He smiled; she smiled back. He raised an eyebrow; she nodded. . . .

The confident American signed the hotel register: "Mr. and Mrs. J. Arnold Danforth."

The naughty weekend was simply *glorious.* . . .

When J. Arnold Danforth checked out, the cashier handed him his bill: $7,480.

"Good God!" sputtered Danforth. "This must be the wrong check. I had Suite six-oh-two—"

"I assure you: zat is ze right check, M'sieur Danforth."

"But that's impossible! I was only here for two nights!"

"Quite so," said the cashier. "But—hm—*Mrs.* Danforth has been wiz us for four-and-a-half weeks!"

Sign in go-go bar

4 Gorgeous Dance Girls

3 Costumes

Eamonn McCone came home early, to his cottage in Galway—and there, to his total discombobulation, he beheld his wife, Erin, under the sheets with his best friend, Patrick O'Flynn.

"Erin!" cried Eamonn. "Me own wife! Me own true love! How kin ye be doin' such a terrible thing?! And you, Patrick, as close t' me as me own brother—by all that's holy, O'Flynn, can't ye even stop while I'm *talk*ing?!"

"Oh, Seymour, will you love me always?"

"Absolutely, sweetheart. Which way would you like me to try first?"

HENNY YOUNGMAN

Charlotte Devere, an attractive widow, was depressed by the life in the suburb into which she had recently moved. One day she hastened to her neighbor's house. "Leora," she said, with some embarrassment, "you're the only one I can ask. Would you give me some—confidential advice?"

"Gladly."

Charlotte blushed. "How—how do you go about having an affair in this town?"

"Well, I," beamed Leora, "always start with 'The Star-Spangled Banner.' "

At Sonny Kotcher's Gym, two men in the exercise class were undressing. One man started unhooking his—girdle.

The other goggled, "Hey, Morrie, since when do you wear a girdle?"

Morrie grimaced. "Since my wife found it in my glove compartment."

Into the phone, Dexter said, "Hello?"

"Hu-llo," answered a very deep voice.

Dexter hesitated, then said, "I'm—trying to reach my home. God, I hope I have the wrong number!"

Scene: Hyde Park, London

Young Bentley Alderstone was using all his charm, which was considerable, and all his guile, which was formidable, to persuade the beauteous Letitia, who was entwined in his arms on the grass, to go to bed with him. But neither charm nor guile nor persistent coaxing could budge the girl. "*Do* desist. Bentley. . . . No . . . *no* . . . I shall *not* change my mind. . . ."

"But my dearest darling," cooed Bentley. "Can you give me one reason—one truly persuasive reason—why you will not let me transport you to paradise?"

"I," said Letitia, "should simply *hate* myself in the morning!"

Bentley pulled back and moonily fixed the girl's eyes with his. "I think I have a way out of that, dear heart."

" 'Way out?' "

"Yes, my sweet; sleep late."

Marcel Duschanel, suddenly widowed at fifty-two, went to the south of France to escape from his sorrows and try to gain a new lease on life. He took a suite at the Hotel Carrousel overlooking the grand pool, and he sat in the sun and observed the divings and splashings and merriment, the flirtings and snugglings, the courtships and kisses of the beautiful young people around the pool.

One man in particular stood out amidst the crowd of sun worshipers and macho males. He stood out not only because he was entirely gray-haired, pale, his cheeks lined, but because he was never without two or three beautiful maidens at his side, or at his table near the pool, or at his regular table in the Palm d'Or Restaurant. And every night, the hotel gossips reminded Marcel Duschanel that the man was off dancing at some nightclub, or dashing off to Monaco to gamble, or carousing until the early, early hours.

For several weeks, Marcel Duschanel enviously observed this phenomenal old-timer. One night, soon after dinner, Duschanel found himself in the men's room, when in came the gray-haired man. He headed straight for the mirror, carefully combing, brushing, patting his gray hair.

"M'sieur!" Duschanel exclaimed. "What a piece of good fortune. I have been so hoping we might perhaps meet . . ."

"Ah?"

"You see, we are in the same hotel—and I have been filled with admiration for the way you live, your *joie de vivre,* your many girlfriends . . ."

The man smiled.

"A thousand pardons, m'sieur—but I trust you will not take offense if I ask you a question: How old *are* you?"

The *roué* shrugged. "Twenty-nine."

Scene: A Hotel in the Poconos

Manny Drucker was a sharp dresser, a nifty dancer, fast with a joke, and not one to give up easily. He took Evelyn Millar's hand in his, gazed soulfully into her eyes, and in his best David Niven manner murmured, "Evie, I love you. I love you." His lips brushed her cheek. "My room or yours?"

"But Manny," gulped Evelyn, "we just met three hours ago!"

"True, true," murmured Manny. "But I'm only here for the weekend."

Rinaldo Palastrino was a compulsive Casanova. Not a week passed by without his romancing a girl. Looks, age, avoirdupois scarcely mattered. Any female on two legs roused Rinaldo's baser appetites.

And whenever Rinaldo came in late, his wife, Fioretta, was waiting up for him. Rinaldo always came up with a masterly explanation: He had found a hit-and-run victim in the street and carried the child in his arms all the way to San Pietro hospital; he had suffered a fainting spell on his way home and awakened in an ambulance; three thugs had attacked him—but he had fought with such ferocity that two *carabinieri* heard and came to his rescue, but he had to go to the police station and bring charges . . .

After years of such outrageous excuses for outrageous infidelities, Rinaldo's wife read him the riot act: "No more thees excuses, Rinaldo! One more time late—justa one—and I leave, and I never spika you again!"

"*Cara* Fioretta, I *promessa!* Never, never I look at other woman!"

Came a fateful twilight when Rinaldo met Beatrice Voglioni. .... Not until three-thirty the next morning did Rinaldo awaken in her boudoir. His heart sank. What could he tell his Fioretta?

Rinaldo dressed in moments, ran out and called his home.

"*Pronto,*" said Fioretta in a firm voice.

Rinaldo panted: "Oh, *cara mia* . . . have those *monsters* called you yet?"

"What 'monsters'?"

"The gangsters! They did kidnap me. *Cara,* listen! They will demand two—million—lire ransom!"

"Rinaldo!"

"Don't pay one lira! I justa excape! . . . I be home—in fifateen minutes!"

Ray Tucker was so tired that he quit work at three and drove home from his office. He parked his car next to his wife's and went into the house. On the living-room couch he beheld his wife in the arms of another man.

"What in hell is going on here?" Tucker shouted. "Lana—darling—who *is* this guy?"

Said Lana, "That's a perfectly fair question, dear." She turned to the man. "What's your name, sweetheart?"

Mistress: What goes between a mister and a mattress.

JOE E. LEWIS

Millie hurried into the home of her best friend, Marcie. A bright light illuminated her eyes, a smile adorned her cheeks, and she was breathing heavily.

"Jumping Jupiter, Millie!" said Marcie. "You look as though you just won the ten-million-dollar jackpot!"

"Marcie, I have such great news I—I had to come over. After all, you *are* my best friend. . . ."

"You're pregnant!" cried Marcie.

"Oh, *no*. Heavens no." Millie's cheeks were flaming. "I—I'm having a big, big affair!"

"That's *won*derful," said Marcie. "It's about time you got out of that same day-after-day routine."

"I'm so glad you approve!" said Millie. "I was afraid you wouldn't."

"*Me?* Marcie, I'm just mad about affairs. . . . Tell me, who's going to do the catering?!"

In the London headquarters of Imperial Beacon Securities, the chairman of the board, G. R. Murdych, glanced around his directors' table somberly. "Gentlemen, I fear that the last item on my own—um—agenda, involves a most delicate matter. I expect each of you to answer my next question, on your honor as a gentleman, with a simple, direct yes or no. No explanations; no excuses; no hemming or hawing. . . . We'll start with you, Smithers. Have you been—conducting any hanky-panky, after office hours, with Miss Irene Strothers, our receptionist?"

Smithers turned scarlet.

"Yes or no, Smithers?"

Smithers swallowed. "Yes, sir."

G. R. Murdych addressed the next vice president. "Crabb-Williams, have you been—'dating' Irene, the receptionist, after office hours?"

Crabb-Williams paled. "Y-yes, Mr. Murdych."

Murdych turned to the next man. "Heathinger?"

Heathinger hung his head. "Yes, sir."

Down one side of the table and up the other G. R. Murdych asked the fateful question. And one after another, without exception, the officers of Imperial Beacon Securities confessed their shameful liaison. The final man was the treasurer, Norris Payne-Vinton.

"Payne-Vinton?" muttered G. R. Murdych.

"No, *sir!*" declaimed Norris Payne-Vinton. "Not I, sir. Never!"

G. R. Murdych's stern features melted into lineaments of pleasure. "By Jove, Payne-Vinton, then you are the very man I need!"

"Thank you, sir."

"Go out—right now—find Miss Strothers, our charming receptionist, and tell her she no longer is employed."

The judge studied the tall, muscular woman, then frowned at the small, thin man, then turned back to the woman. "Madam," he cleared his throat, "—am I to understand you are accusing this man of—*rape?*"

"Absolutely," huffed the Amazon.

"Was he—holding a gun at the time?"

"Nope."

"Did he tie you up?"

"Nope."

"Well, madam, you are at least six feet tall and weigh at least a hundred and eighty pounds, whereas this man is not much over five feet—I wonder how in the absence of a weapon, rape could—"

"I stooped a bit."

The two women were sharing confidences over their tea. "I don't know what to do about my husband anymore," said Louise. "Do you know that he never comes home until long, long past midnight?!"

"Oh, dear. My husband used to be like that—but no more. Never!"

"What changed him?"

Her friend smiled. "What changed him, my dear, is that every time he stealthily opened the door, at one or two or three in the morning, I would sweetly call out, 'Is that you, Everett?' "

"That was all there was to it?"

"Uh-huh."

"But why would *that* stop him?"

"Because his name is Herbie."

Chittingham accosted Farnsworth in the club lobby. "I say, Farnsworth. Have you recently had a—bit of a fling with my wife?"

Farnsworth cleared his throat. "Well, old boy, since you are so straightforward about it—I must say, yes, I did."

"Well now, Farnsworth, I—do—not—much—like—that!"

Farnworth nodded. "Can't blame you, old boy. I didn't like it much, either."

Antoine Rouget, the young real-estate agent specializing in fine apartments near the Arc de Triomphe, watched the exceptionally beautiful brunette sign a five-year lease.

"Mademoiselle," he smiled, "I wish for you many happy hours in your new home. And here"— he handed her a tiny envelope —"are your two keys."

The exceptionally beautiful brunette tilted the envelope. Two keys slid into her palm. "And here," she murmured, handing him one of the keys, "is the first month's rent."

"Nelly," said Jacqueline, "we've been friends for so long, and gone through so much together—"

"What are you trying to say, Jackie?"

"Look, if this is out of line . . ."

"Nothing you ask me can be out of line."

"All right." Jacqueline took a long, deep breath. "Nelly—are you cheating on your husband?"

Nelly shrugged. "Who else?"

See also **Doggerel, Limericks, Sex, Typos**

Headlines That Haunt Me

When a blizzard in Buffalo cut box-office receipts, *Variety*'s headline read:

BLIZ BOFFS BUFF. BIZ

❧

When a national analysis showed a marked decline in box-office receipts for movies about small towns or farms, *Variety*'s headline was:

STIX NIX HIX PIX

MASSIVE ORGAN DRAWS CROWD

Lucky Girl Sees Friends Die

❧

FATHER OF NINE FINED $100
FOR FAILING TO STOP

❧

DEAD POLICEMAN ON FORCE 23 YEARS

❧

26-YEAR FRIENDSHIP ENDS AT ALTAR

❧

MIXED MARRIAGE CONDUCTED BY RABBIT

MAN FOUND DEAD IN CEMETERY

FARMERS THREATENED BY PLAGUE OF RABBIS

❧

The finest caption I ever read appeared in the old, forever-lamented *Herald-Tribune* of New York:

GIRL SEDUCED ATOP 65-FT. FLAGPOLE

The story was as much of a stopper as the caption. It recounted that a car salesman in El Paso, Texas, was charged with the "statutory rape" of a fifteen-year-old girl he allegedly seduced atop a flagpole that was sixty-five feet high. The hanky-panky took place in this novel locale because the Don Juan was a flagpole-sitter by profession, and he had spent no less than sixty-four days on the flagpole before committing libidinal acrobatics *in situ*.

The girl, whose name the authorities did not reveal, told the police she had actually been seduced five times, "after climbing a rope ladder to the top of the pole a number of times." The fact that this lass had climbed a sixty-five-foot rope ladder "a number of times" made me wonder whether the maiden could make the charge of seduction (except the first, of course) stick. Sixty-five-foot ascents are strong prima facie evidence of a not entirely traumatic experience. They certainly do not suggest forcible entry.

from my *Passions and Prejudices*

MAN STOWS AWAY TO SEE GIRL FRIED

9 VOLUNTEERS PUT IN NEW CHURCH FURNACE

FLORIST ASKS GIRLS TO DROP STRAPLESS GOWNS

BABIES FLOOD HOSPITALS!

ESCAPED LEOPARD BELIEVED SPOTTED

CITY OFFICIALS TALK RUBBISH

See also Bloopers, Boo-boos, Graffiti, How's That Again?, News Items That Haunt Me, Typos

Heaven

Heaven: God's country

Zelda Szold, age eighty-two, appeared before the Golden Gates of Paradise and rang the golden bell.

An Admitting Angel opened the gates. "Welcome, good soul, welcome. Follow me to the Registrar."

Mrs. Szold trod light clouds that wafted her to the radiant, kindly presence of the Registrar of Heaven. "Your name, dear one?"

"My name is Zelda Levy Szold."

"S-z-o-l-d?"

"The same."

"And what was your last address on earth, Friend Szold?"

"On earth, my last address was eighty-four Beersheba Lane, Haifa."

The Registrar swiftly ran down the list of *S*'s in the ledger emblazoned "Expected Arrivals." He ran his finger down one page, then down another . . . "Szold . . . Szold . . . from Haifa . . . Aha . . . Yes." The Registrar frowned. "Well, well, can you imagine that?" He looked up. "Mrs. Szold, age eighty-two, from Haifa—you are not due in Heaven for another six and a half weeks! . . . Listen, who is your doctor?!"

THE MAN WHO COULD NOT SIN

Mr. Toplovitz stood before the Chief Admitting Angel anxiously. And the Chief Admitting Angel exclaimed, "But this is fantastic! I have read your records three times. This is unprecedented. In your entire lifetime did you not commit *one* little sin?"

"I tried to live in virtue," faltered Mr. Toplovitz, "as a God-fearing man. . . ."

"But not one—little—sin in an entire lifetime?" sputtered the Admitting Angel. "We can't let you into Heaven! You are practically an angel already. No, no. You must be *human*, fallible, subjected to temptation . . . at least once. So, I am going to send you back to earth—for twenty-four hours. During that time, you must commit a sin—at least one little sin, Mr. Toplovitz. It is now 7:00 A.M. I will have the Angel of Death pick you up tomorrow at precisely 7:00 A.M.!"

The bewildered innocent found himself back on earth, determined to try to take one step from the path of righteousness. An hour passed, then two, then three; poor Mr. Toplovitz simply could find no opportunity to commit a sin.

Then a buxom woman winked at him. . . . Mr. Toplovitz responded with alacrity. The lady was neither young nor beautiful—but she *was* willing. And when she blushingly hinted that he might spend the night with her, Mr. Toplovitz was in sixth heaven.

At last, in bed, having truly sinned, in the dark, wee hours—Mr. Toplovitz looked at his watch: only one more hour before the Angel would whisk him back to heaven . . . only half an hour . . .

And as Mr. Toplovitz quickly put on his clothes, preparing for his return to the celestial region, his blood froze as the old maid in the bed sighed, "Oh, Toplovitz, Toplovitz—what a good deed you have performed this night!"

See also **Faith, God, Golf, The Occult, Religion**

Heroes of Mine

DEAR ROBERT BENCHLEY

Robert Benchley, known to one and all as "Bob," was the gentlest of men, a lovely humorist, and a prince of drollery. He once confirmed to me a story making the rounds of Hollywood. He had recently asked his doctor what he (the doctor) was going to prescribe for his (Benchley's) stuffed head, runny nose, clammy palms, and romping fever.

The M.D. briskly said, "One of the new miracle drugs."

Benchley, a devout hypochondriac, complained: "But I don't *like* to try new drugs; they might have funny side effects. . . ."

"Nonsense! This will make you fit as a fiddle," said the doctor, whose name, I think, was Stradivarius. "I'll drop in to see you tomorrow."

The next morning, Benchley arose to find his fever vanished, his head clear, his anxieties allayed. His spirit soared so high that he decided to brighten the doctor's day. Benchley considered several ways of doing this, then found a pot of glue, slit open his pillow, and glued feathers to both his thighs. This maneuveur completed, he drew the sheet up to his neck carefully, high above his waist, and waited for his healer.

The moment Dr. Stradivarius appeared in the doorway, Benchley exclaimed, "Doc, you're a whiz! That new drug you gave me certainly worked miracles!"

"You can say that again," said the doctor.

Instead of saying it again, Benchley blinked innocently. "There's just one thing, Doc: What do you make of"— he flung back the sheet to reveal two thighs thick with feathers—". . .this!"

I have whiled away many an hour imagining what the expression on that doctor's face must have been, and what horrified apparitions—of incredulity, panic, guilt—beset his thunderstruckness.

from my *People I Have Loved, Known or Admired*

THE PRINCE OF PASTA

Joseph Pellegrino, who owned a little restaurant in Rome, was lunching in a country *trattoria*. He was served a steaming plate of spaghetti. It was possibly the one hundred thousandth plate of spaghetti Signor Pellegrino had been served during his lifetime, but this one caused his jaw to drop, his fork to fall, and his eyes to pop: the spaghetti was not round! It was square.

Pellegrino stared at this farinaceous heresy, lifted some on his fork, tasted the pasta, and rushed into the kitchen. There he saw the Mamma of the *trattoria* rolling a slab of dough across a wooden frame on which was stretched a grid of—guitar strings . . .

Pellegrino began to serve quadrilateral spaghetti in his restaurant in Rome. It was made on a frame of wire (instead of catgut) strings and has delighted Italians and tourists alike.

This unorthodox—nay, revolutionary!—pasta offers many advantages over conventional spaghetti. It does not slip off the fork so often; it does not slide on the plate so readily; it is also firmer, and holds onto the tomato sauce better than run-of-the-mill pasta. I think square spaghetti also inspires confidence in its character, because of its sturdy, self-reliant appearance.

So far as I can see, this splendid pasta *may* have one trivial fault, a defect implied, though not foreseen, by Christopher Morley, who once said: "No man is lonely while eating spaghetti; it takes so much *attention.*"

I have long admired the unknown genius, larcenous though he must have been, who ran this one-line ad in a Los Angeles newspaper:

LAST DAY TO SEND IN YOUR DOLLAR.
Box 153

Thousands of idiots sent in their dollars.

from my *People I Have Loved, Known or Admired*

THE UNBELIEVABLE LAIBOWITZ

"Good morning," said Captain Newman brightly.

The soldier touched a finger to his forehead, confirming its existence, and studied us through lugubrious eyes. He made no effort to conceal the fact that he did not approve of what he beheld.

"Sit down, Corporal. What's your name?"

"Laibowitz," came a sepulchral suspiration.

"First name?"

"Jackson." (sigh)

"How old are you?"

"Twenty-five."

To my surprise, Captain Newman leaned forward and said frostily, "I *believe* it is customary for a soldier to address an officer as 'sir'!"

Corporal Laibowitz shrugged. "What's 'customary' for a soldier can be tough for a civilian."

"But you aren't a civilian," said Newman acidly.

"I *feel* like a civilian," said Laibowitz.

"Congratulations." Captain Newman held out his cigarettes. "Would you like to smoke?"

"Nicotine," announced Laibowitz, "is bad for the eyes."

"Oh. Do you have trouble with your eyes?"

"No, sir."

"Then why—"

"That's because I never touch nicotine," said Laibowitz.

Captain Newman looked startled. He leaned back in his chair to study the man before him with new interest. This did not present the slightest problem to Laibowitz, who suffered the scrutiny with the resignation of a man accustomed to the slow-witted. He was, all in all, rather good-looking—well-shaped features, a firm mouth, large liquid eyes. It was only his manner—an amalgam of acid stomach and apocalypse—which celebrated despair.

Captain Newman said, "I assume you've worked in a hospital before."

"Yes—sir."

Captain Newman waited. So did Laibowitz.

"Go on, Corporal."

"Go on where?" blinked the dour one.

"Tell me about your hospital experience."

"What's to tell? The camp I just came from wasn't fit for a dog! Maybe a Nazi dog, not a U.S. citizen. They had me working in the wards day and night. I didn't like it."

"You mustn't hide your feelings," said Captain Newman dryly.

"I agree," said Laibowitz.

Newman winced. "What kinds of wards did you work in?"

"All kinds."

"Give me a hint," crooned Newman.

"It would spoil your lunch."

"I'll skip lunch."

"I advise you shouldn't; ask any doctor—"

"I *am* a doctor," leered Newman.

"O.K. General, general surgery, infectial diseases, where I caught everything—"

"Did you ever work in—an N.P. ward?" asked Captain Newman, rather too casually.

Laibowitz's eyes widened. "A *mental* ward?"

"I mean psychiatric cases—"

"*Nuts?*"

"They are not 'nuts,' " said Captain Newman firmly. "They're men who—"

"My God, Doc," cried Laibowitz, "you gonna put me in a *loony* bin?"

"It is *not*—"

"I'll drop dead!" Laibowitz struggled to his feet, "I give you my word, Doc, inside one hour you can start digging my grave!"

"Sit down."

"Better ask me to *lay* down! I'm already a patient."

"Now listen!" said Captain Newman sharply. "I don't know where the hell you guys got all these cockeyed ideas! Most of the men in my ward are simply depressed—"

"So am I," proclaimed Laibowitz.

"—miserable—"

"*They're* miserable? Look at me!"

"Sit *down!*"

Corporal Laibowitz sank into the chair with noises suggestive of strangulation and verging on emphysema.

Crisply, firmly, Captain Newman launched into a lecture explaining the functions of his ward, the nature of our tasks, the duties of a wardman. He was simple, direct, and, I thought, remarkably reassuring. It made not the slightest dent on Laibowitz, who kept uttering woeful lamentations.

Captain Newman explained that we had a staff of excellent doctors ("For me alone you'll need one full time," said Laibowitz), that the patients were not permitted razors, matches, blunt artifacts, or sharp objects ("But *teeth* they've got?"), that an encouraging proportion of our cases responded favorably to therapy ("Don't spoil your record, Captain!") and were dismissed from Ward 7 to return to either army or civilian life ("I will gladly join them!"), that orderlies were pampered with frequent passes ("You mean of their own free will they come *back?*"), and that when he was off duty, Corporal Laibowitz, along with the other wardman, would sleep in complete comfort and safety in the finest barracks on the base, a good five hundred yards away ("Who will drag me back and forth?" asked Laibowitz).

"That's it," said Captain Newman efficiently. "Do you have any questions?"

Laibowitz rose. "Doc, I appreciate your trying to raise my morale. But let us face facts. You are putting me in a booby hatch. You are asking me to buddy up to cuckoos, crazies, dumdums, and scrambled-eggs-in-the-head. . . . I got problems of my own, you know. I'm practically a nervous wretch. I'm high-strung, sensitive. I promise you if you send me into your nuthouse, by Sunday—the *latest*—you'll have to fit me for a straitjacket!"

Captain Newman, who had listened to this oration somewhat openmouthed, braced his shoulders and narrowed his eyes. "That will be all. You may go now. You will report to Sergeant Kopp."

"Who's he?" said Laibowitz.

"My wardmaster."

"Where does he keep his whip?"

"Laibowitz," snapped Captain Newman, "what the *devil* is the matter with you? You look intelligent—"

"Don't be fooled by my looks!"

"You're making a mountain out of a molehill!"

"So I'm no good in geography."

"You'll get the best food on the post in my ward!"

"I already lost all my appetite."

"You have my deepest sympathy," said Captain Newman sarcastically.

"From plumbers I expect sympathy; from psychiatrists I expect understanding," cried Laibowitz, glancing toward the Judge in heaven.

Again, Captain Newman cleared his throat. "You may go now. . . . Ring the bell outside the door. Sergeant Kopp will show you the ropes."

"He should only *give* me a rope; I'll hang myself."

"Dismissed!"

Laibowitz reaffirmed the location on his forehead and sagged out of the room. He might have been en route to the firing squad. . . .

Laibowitz was a master of the art of standing military authority on its head. Take his way of dealing with orders from officers. Written orders of which he approved, he executed with lightning dispatch; written orders of which he disapproved, he "mislaid," misread, or misrouted.

His response to verbal instructions was even more exasperating: when he disagreed with a superior's instruction, he simply pretended he had not heard it; when it was repeated to him, he concluded it had not been communicated correctly the first time, which made the second exposition no more reliable than the first; when it was driven home to him in an indisputable manner that whatever his personal views, such-and-such a command *had* to be obeyed, he got "sick" and took to his quarters. Achilles had his tent; Laibowitz had his symptoms. Rarely has medical science been confronted with such symptoms—such coughs, aches, pains, wheezes, and vertigos—as Jackson Laibowitz could summon to his cause. He never directly *disobeyed* Captain Newman's will, for instance; he managed to modify it through reinterpretation. He never refused; he simply outflanked. He simulated deafness with an innocence that defied exposure, and stupidity with a poise that demanded admiration. . . .

No one ever won an argument from Laibowitz. He rarely expressed an opinion without framing it as an axiom. He could not, indeed, conceive of having mere opinions; they were propositions in a larger, majestic philosophical system.

Take a matter as mundane as shaving. Laibowitz hated to shave. But he would never say—simply, directly—that he hated to shave. He wrapped his prejudice in the raiment of cosmology: "If God meant men should have clean cheeks, *would He have invented hair?*"

One morning, when Laibowitz looked like the "before" version in an advertisement for razor blades, Captain Newman asked him testily, "Why didn't you shave this morning?"

"The major in Room C didn't shave this morning, either," said Laibowitz.

"You know perfectly well that the major is forbidden to use a razor."

"So give me the same break; *forbid* I should use one."

"Major Slater is suicidal," said Newman.

"That's exactly what I'm becoming, with your fetish about hair."

"I asked you a question!" snapped Newman. "Why didn't you shave this morning?"

"Is this morning different from other mornings?"

"No. That's why you should shave."

"Excuse me. There is a hole in your logic. That's why I shouldn't."

"Laibowitz—"

"A man can be born with very delicate skin!" cried Laibowitz. "Touch it with metal, it bleeds. Scratch it with steel, it gushes. Douse it with witch hazel, my whole body breaks out in a rash."

"I'll report these original symptoms to the AMA," said Newman.

"Put in that I also itch from the brush."

"Shave!" said Captain Newman.

"Why do you treat me like I was *normal?*" complained Laibowitz. "If I was a patient, you'd call it a phobia and bring me breakfast in bed."

"But you're *not* a patient—"

"That, you can arrange in a second."

Captain Newman assumed his most forbidding expression. "That will be enough, Jackson. Shave!"

Laibowitz rolled his eyes around in anguish. "I think I'll lay down. I feel dizzy."

"That - is - an - order."

"It's against human nature," muttered Laibowitz.

This apothegm, "It's against human nature," was the last, unyielding bastion of Laibowitz's creed. Whatever he opposed, he transformed into an enemy of natural law. He believed that he knew more about "human nature" than any man on earth. He also seemed to think that *his* human nature was different from others' and required unquestioning acceptance. "Today I am depressed," he might announce, "so do not aggravate me with details." Or: "Some men God gave big muscles; others He gave big brains. Don't ask me to move furniture."

I often heard him invoke the Deity—but in a peculiar way: he called upon God the way a coach sends in a pinch hitter. . . .

One day I saw Captain Newman stalk out of the ward, his face a cloud. Laibowitz was in his wake. "I suppose," scowled Newman, "that Sergeant Kopp is on leave."

"How did you guess?"

"I didn't have to guess, Corporal; I smelled. The bedding in the ward."

"What's that got to do with Arkie?"

"When Kopp is on duty, that ward is as clean as a whistle!"

"Today it's 110 in the shade," cried Laibowitz, "so naturally, the bedding smells!"

"If you *aired* it, Laibowitz, it wouldn't smell."

Laibowitz regarded his captain with solicitude. "I have been studying your behavior. When you're mad, you call me Laibowitz; when you're annoyed, you call me Jackson; when you're happy, you call me Jake."

"You're damn right I'm mad! That bedding is a disgrace!"

"*Today* you think it smells?" cried Laibowitz. "You should of smelled it yesterday! It's a miracle my patients didn't faint like flies! I could of bottled that smell and sold it to Secret Weapons!"

"All sheets, mattresses, and pillowcases are to be aired each morning," said Captain Newman firmly. "Do you understand?"

"Deaf, I'm not."

"That is an order!"

To a direct command, which Laibowitz regarded as the unfair advantage the Chiefs of Staff had given officers against GIs who might best them in man-to-man combat, Laibowitz unfailingly responded with a surprise maneuver on the flanks. "I'm only human."

"So are the men who have to sleep in those beds!" snapped Newman.

"I only have two hands."

"But you have four orderlies to help you!"

"They're human the same as me."

"That's enough!"

Corporal Laibowitz studied his captain with the utmost sympathy. "Doc, you look tired."

"Thank you. The condition of the bedding has tired me."

"If it tires you, imagine what it does to *me.*"

"Stop playing Ping-Pong with my sentences! Get that bedding out of the ward and into the open air."

"That goddam sun could make the mattresses explode!" wailed Laibowitz.

"Then put them in the shade."

"By the time you get any shade around here it's time for my patients to go to sleep!"

"Don't talk like an idiot."

"That," Laibowitz grumbled darkly, "is what will lose us this war."

"Airing the mattresses?" exclaimed Captain Newman.

"Treating Americans like slaves."

"Welcome, Patrick Henry," scowled Newman.

"Sarcasm is for dentists; from psychiatrists I expect honesty."

I thought it was Captain Newman's excessive indulgence that encouraged Laibowitz's unmilitary conduct, but I learned how wrong I was the day Laibowitz passed my office, on his way to Central Supplies, and asked if there was anything he could get me.

"Yes, thank you." I gave him a list. I needed PPS forms, red pencils, and thumbtacks.

In an hour, Corporal Laibowitz returned—with PPS forms, red pencils, and Scotch tape.

"Didn't they have thumbtacks?" I asked.

"You wanted *thumb*tacks?" he asked incredulously.

"Why, yes. That's why I wrote them down."

Laibowitz found fascination in the ceiling. "I can't read your writing."

"But I *printed* that list."

"Lieutenant, your printing is even worse than your writing!"

Suddenly I saw a rare opportunity to achieve a miracle—make Laibowitz admit that he had made a mistake "Did you by any chance keep that list, Jake?"

"Am I the type to destroy official documents?" He reached into his pocket and produced the list with an expression that warned me that where trust is stunted friendship will soon die.

"Read it," I suggested.

"With pleasure. . . . Item number one," he read, "PPS forms."

"Check."

"Item two: Red pencils."

"I thought you said you can't read my printing," I smiled.

"*This* you call reading? I'm breaking a code!"

"Try item three."

"Is that the one that says 'Thumbtacks'?"

"Ah!" I sang out in triumph. "So you *did* understand."

"Scotch tape is better! Put a thumbtack in deep, you need a crowbar to pry it out! Stick your thumb, you get blood poisoning. Be honest, Lieutenant; did you ever hear a man should get hurt from Scotch tape?"

"That's not the point. I *wanted* thumbtacks!"

Laibowitz bestowed a considerate expression upon me. "You got too much on your mind, Lieutenant. I don't blame you for not knowing what's best for your own welfare."

I often wonder what orders Laibowitz is upsetting, ignoring, transforming, or subverting now. . . .

from my *Captain Newman, M.D.*

See also **Chutzpa, Ingenuity, Repartée, Sarcasm, Scoundrels**

Hillbillies

"Hey, Doke."

"Yeh, Trap?"

"Y'know that thayer fella Cat Carson, down Cabbage Way?"

"Yup."

"That fella must be the dumbest durn fella in tain counties. Why, I bet it takes Cat a good six-seven minutes to jest write the number eleven."

"Aw, Trap, no fella's *that* dumb. How could he possibly use up them six-seven minutes figgerin' how to set down the number eleven? Et's only a one and a one!"

"Well, Doke, he ain't never shore which o' them comes first."

Dwayne was going off to visit relatives for a spell. And now he and Myrtle-Mae were sparking in the moonlight. "Myrtle-Mae," said Dwayne, "will y' all be faithful t' me while I'm gone?"

The maid in gingham smoothed her dress. "Um—how long 'r ye figgerin' to' be away? . . ."

A television crew had come all the way from Tulsa to Pumpkin Corners to interview old Clem Sash, who was supposed to have reached his ninety-seventh birthday.

"—And now here is Clem Sash," said the interviewer, "who will tell us his secret of longevity! . . . Mr. Sash, to what do you think your great age is due?" He moved the microphone to Clem Sash's grizzled chin.

"Cain't say, bub," munched Mr. Sash.

"But surely you must have *some* idea . . ."

"Nope. Not yit."

"What do you mean 'not yet,' Mr. Sash?"

"I mean jist what I say, bub. Not yit. 'Cause I've got a couple of them advertisin' companies—fer bran flakes, shredded wheat, prune juice, an' veetamins A, C, E—a-dickerin' fer my evidence."

The couple from rural Arkansas drove into Little Rock to see a road-company performance of a New York hit. They left after Act II, because the program clearly read:

> ACT I: The Howland Mansion
> ACT II: The Robinson home.
> ACT III: The same.

Upstate farmer, emerging from a New York restaurant, studying check he just paid—to his wife: "Six-fifty fur a ham sandwich! . . . Emma, I figure our hogs are worth over eight thousand dollars each."

The country bumpkin entered the elevator at the Hilton Hotel, looked at the key to his room, 1217, repeated: "Twelve one seven," and carefully punched the buttons marked 12, 1, 7.

The young man from the Ozarks attended his first play. After Act I, he studied the program.

> ACT I: Charles Brookfield's living room.
> ACT II: The parson's office.
> ACT III: Brookfield's office: one week later.

The young man from the Ozarks left after Act II—and returned one week later.

Lem Sloper came ambling down the dirt road to Zeke Coffin's place, tucked among some Kentucky woods. "Hey, Zeke . . ."

"Yup, Lem . . ."

"Be plantin' radishes?"

"Nope . . . Tarnips."

Lem munched his gums. "Be maghty obleeged t' you, Zeke—if'n you lend me Mathilda f'r some hours. . . ."

"Glad to, Lem, if'n that mare warn't at the vet's, in the stable down the holla. Feelin' porely, she is, real porely. . . . Be there all day an' night I reckon. . . ."

Suddenly, from the shed behind the far split-rail fence, came Mathilda's unmistakable, high, rattling neigh.

Zeke Coffin took the straw from between his lips and studied it. Came another keen, nasal, rattling neigh.

Lem Sloper spat tobaccer-juice on the ground.

Whereupon Zeke growled, "Now who you goin' to set faith by, Lem? Me or a goldurn dumb horse?! And a mare, mindja, known all through these here hills and hollas for her unreliable, lyin' ways!"

"I shore do wish," said Sly Farr, "I had enough money t' git me a nice tall *geer*affe. . . ."

"A *geer*affe?" echoed Mose Loud. "What'n tarnation ez a *geer*affe?"

"One o' them critters with spots all over his hide, n' them big knobby knees, and that thayer high, high neck—mebbe twenny feet tall."

"Oh. One of them. Bu' why, Sly?"

"Why what?"

"Why you be wantin' a geeraffe?"

"I din say I wanted a geeraffe. I sayd I just wisht I had enough money f'r th' buyin' o' one."

Jeb and Lem were walking down dusty Skunk Hole Road, when suddenly the heavens opened up and the rain came down in buckets. "Lem," said Jeb, "open that goldurn umbrelly!"

"This umbrelly?" Lem snorted. "Shucks, Jeb, it's chuck full o' holes."

Jeb stopped short. "Then why in tarnation 'd you bring it along?"

"How'd I know 't was goin' t' rain?!"

Scene: Hillbilly Shack in Tennessee

"Maw? . . ." said pretty Holly Hawkins.

"Uh huh."

"Maw, this here suntan oil paw bought f'r me down in th' store by the Three Corners . . ."

"Uh huh."

"Well, t'ain't no durn *good*, maw!"

"What's bad about it?"

"Well, maw, I already drunk three whole bottles o' th' stuff, an' just look at me—pale as Miz Tompkins' white sheets!"

Scene: Split Rail Fence, Ezra's Clearing

"Heerd from y'r boy Luke?" asked Zack Koom.

"Yup."

"Went t' the city, din'e?"

"Yup."

"Like it thayer?"

"Yup. Got'm a job. A real payin' job."

"Well, well," Zack paused in his whittling. "What kind work?"

"They teached him t' work one of them real new-fangled machines," said Hoke.

"What's it do?"

"What it does, Luke tells us, is measure. Measures parts, parts f'r special tools, right down t' thousandths of'n inch!"

"*Thousandths* of'n inch?" Zack shook his head in wonder. "How many o' them thousandths d'ye figger thayer are t' a inch?"

Hoke sprayed the ground with tobacco juice. "Millions, I figger. Millions."

❧

Zeb Doon and Jud Boone were chugging along in Jud's old jalopy on their way to Morgantown, forty miles from Smoke Crossing, when they entered some dark woods with the highest trees either of them had ever seen.

"Lord a'mighty!" breathed Zeb. "Folks down our way ain't hardly ever gonna believe there's trees that thayer tall."

"Them trees is four-five times higher'n any oak or pine in all o' Carter County!" Jud exclaimed.

"Mebbe higher 'n that."

They chugged along, into the shade, looking right and left, when, in a patch of sunlight, they beheld two men plying a long crosscut saw to cut down a tree with a very wide trunk.

Jud stopped the car and the two hillbillies watched. One lumberjack was a giant of a man, but the other was short and wizened. As the two sawyers pulled back and forth, Zeb muttered, "Kin y' believe y'r eyes?!"

"A doggone shame!" said Jud.

The two men got out of the jalopy and hurried to the tree, Zeb shouting, "Hey, thayer! Stop that!"

"You—the big fella!" cried Jud.

The sawyers stopped. "What's botherin' you two?"

"Well, *damn* it," cried Zeb, "when the little fella wants t' use the saw, can't you let him have it f'r a bit?!"

❧

"Dokey?"

"Huh?"

"You heerd any news from Porky—th' Simpson boy—that crazy coot—sence his maw married that city feller?"

"Yup."

"Whatcha heerd?"

"Well, folks in Green Holla, where they be livin', say Katy Simpson's new husband is mighty nice t' Porky, considerin' the tyke is, like you said, teched in th' haid. That new paw plays a real nice game with the boy, I heerd. He rows Porky out to the middle of Loon Lake, tosses him into the water, then rows back to shore—leavin' Porky t' swim all th' way back."

"Lands' sake, Dokey. That thayer is a pretty durn big lake!"

"Two miles acrost."

"And the little coot swims all that way back?"

"No—jest half. From the middle, where his new paw puts him off."

"Why, still—a whole *mile* a-swimmin'!"

"Mmh. That's not the hard part, Porky says. He don't mind th' swimmin'. It's th' gittin' out of the burlap sack each time—*thass* hard."

See also **Chelm, Dummies, Shlemiels, Tall Tales**

History Revised
(by Children)

Achilles: His mother dipped him in a stinking river; this made him invisible.

Ancient Egypt: It was mostly inhabited by mummies.

Black Hole of Calcutta
 Where hundreds of English soldiers were shut up. Since it had only one widow, many Englishmen died.

Charles I: The English people did not like him so they decomposed him.

Consorts: Since some Queens could not find any King to marry, they arranged to have concerts.

Constitution: After our Constitution was finished, Washington and Franklin added the bill for rice.

Crusaders: Fighting pilgrims to the Holy Land who wanted to find the Holy Grill. Many of them died of salvation.

Ice Age: No human beings were around at this time, because it was the pre-stork era.

Ireland: It was overrun by absentee landlords.

Joshua: He led the Hebrews in their victory in the battle of Geritol.

Julius Caesar: Julius Caesar was warned in advance that he would be killed by some March brides.

Magna Carta: After Magna Carta the King was not allowed to take taxis without permission from Parliament.

Martin Luther: Martin Luther was nailed to a church door for selling the pope's privileges. He died after he was communicated by a bull.

Napoleon: He made the crowned heads of Europe tremble in their shoes.

Papal Bull: A bull kept at the Vatican; it belongs to the pope.

Queen Elizabeth: Queen Elizabeth was so fond of dresses that she never was seen without one.

Queen Victoria: Queen Victoria was the longest queen who ever sat on a throne.

Samson: He was very strong and pulled down the pillars, which buried all the Finkelsteins inside that temple.

Venice: At one time, Venice was ruled by dogs.

Walter Raleigh: When he died he started heavy smoking.

Washington's farewell address: Mount Vernon.

See also **Bloopers, Boo-boos, Cynics' Dictionary, Definitions (by Children), Famous People (as Seen by Children), Geography Revised, Goldwyniana, Graffiti, Malaprops, Typos**

Hollywood

Siberia with palms.

Malice in Wonderland.

The place where girls look for husbands and husbands look for girls.

The biggest electric train any boy ever had.

ORSON WELLES

Scene: The Pearly Gates

ST. PETER: Where are you from?
APPLICANT: Hollywood.
ST. PETER: Come in . . . but I'll bet you won't like it.

Casey Krausse and Jordan Hilgard, two Hollywood writers, were going to the same psychoanalyst, Dr. Helmut Pforzheimer. "Nothing ever *throws* him," remarked Krausse. "Have you ever seen or heard him act surprised?"

"Never," said Hilgard.

They bemoaned their healer's inhuman unflappability, his total "cool," his "laid-back" response to even the most painful (to the patient) material.

"I have an idea," said Hilgard. "Let's make up a dream! A really fantastic, hair-raising dream. I'll report it at my hour—nine to ten—and—"

"And I'll report precisely the same dream at my hour: five to six!"

With many a laugh and gloat of anticipation, the two writers concocted a dream: "A naked boy with a sword, in a green gondola, is drifting under a large, golden Gothic archway"— (consider that symbolism!) —"and suddenly a huge bearded warrior, with a hissing serpent in one hand and a fearsome club in the other, jumps into the gondola—at which point a woman all in white gauze cries, 'Rape! Snake! Don't club the boy!' . . . The dream breaks off—"

"What a beaut of a dream!" Krausse chortled.

"Wait until Pforzheimer hears *that* twice in one day!" gloated Hilgard.

And so, the next morning, at around 9:05, from his perch in Couch Canyon (as Roxbury Drive is called), Jordan Hilgard reported the bizarre dream to Dr. Pforzheimer. . . . And at 5:05, Casey Krausse reported the identical phantasmagoria—then stopped and waited for his "shrink's" response.

"That dream . . ." Dr. Pforzheimer cleared his throat. "Strange . . . very strange. That's the *third* time I've heard it today."

A young producer took a young actress to a business dinner at a posh restaurant in Beverly Hills. As they dawdled over their baked Alaska, the producer smiled, "Now—shall we top it all off with a demitasse?"

"You men," the doxy murmured, "are all alike. You can't even wait for a girl to have a cup of coffee."

"*My* mother," said little Heather, "just got married again, so I have a new father."

"What's his name?" asked little Margy.

"Hanley Droob," said Heather.

"Oh, he's *nice*," said Margy. "You'll like him."

"Do you know him?"

"Certainly I know him. Last year, he was *my* father."

MODERN PASSIONS

Scene: Peregrine Wolf's Opulent Apartment

Enter Peregrine Wolf, in white tie and tails, with a very beautiful, albeit sleazy, blonde. He turns lights down, steps to psychedelic bar.

WOLF

Well, Sandra, a little nightcap?

SANDRA

Peachy, Perry.

WOLF

Liqueur? Scotch? Brandy?

SANDRA

Uh—brandy.

WOLF

*Splen*did.

He puts two large snifters on tray. Sandra stretches seductively on the leopard-skin sofa. Wolf comes to her, hands her a snifter, raises bottle, starts to pour.

WOLF
(wolfishly)

Darling, say when . . .

SANDRA

Right after this drink.

CURTAIN

Two pretty, curvaceous girls, in a bus on Hollywood Boulevard, were talking with great animation. "—And my agent said," said Louise, "that whoever got that part would be the next Marilyn Monroe!"

"So did you audition?" asked Madge.

"You bet I did! I wore my sexiest nightgown and—"

"Tell, tell. Did you get the part?"

Louise smiled. "Did I *get* it? Madge, I was *made* for the part!"

At this point an old lady behind the girls leaned between them, saying, "Excuse me—but do you think you should tell such a thing to *strangers?*"

Tommy and Melvyn were pushing and shoving each other on the school playground, their altercation studded with the usual boyish imprecations. "I can spit farther than you can!" "Yeah? Yeah? I can throw the bean-bag farther 'n you!"

At last Tommy shouted, "My father can beat up your father!"

"Your fa—" Melvyn stopped, astonished. "You jerk! My father *is* your father!"

The two full-bosomed, bare-shouldered, stunningly coiffured, expensively gowned starlets were sitting side by side in the Marie Antoinette powder room of the Beverly Hilton Hotel. "By the way, Dolores," asked Lorraine, the first *tsatske*, "I didn't notice your table in the banquet hall: whose date are you tonight?"

"My date is Waldo Kantroviz, the producer."

"Oh, my!" said Lorraine. "I've gone out with him. He's *fun*. And such a classy dresser."

"I know," said Dolores. "And so *fast*."

The movie writers' lament: "They change our stories, ruin our characters, distort our ideas—and what do we get for it? A *fortune*."

At executives' meetings in a certain studio in movieland, it is said, the head of the studio usually ends a discussion with the following words: "All those in favor of my position, please say ay. . . . Good. All those opposed, say 'I resign.' "

It is reliably reported, by those who were on the scene at the time, that Louis B. Mayer, head of lofty Metro-Goldwyn-Mayer in its dazzling heyday, was trying to get the incomparable Marlene Dietrich to do a movie for MGM, for whom she had not made a film in fifteen years.

"Miss Dietrich," said the persuasive Mr. Mayer, "you can practically name your own ticket. I personally guarantee you will get anything you want."

After several more persistent invitations, Miss Dietrich said, "Mr. Mayer, let's first do a test . . . *if* you give me Joe Ruttenberg as the cameraman. You know, Joe lighted me more beautifully, more perfectly, when I made my last picture at Metro, than any photographer I ever had before or since. He knows every angle of my face, my bone structure, my profile—above all, my *moods*. . . ."

"Say no more, Marlene!" said Mayer. "You've got Ruttenberg."

And so the critical screen test was made. . . .

Now Mayer, Ruttenberg, and the great Dietrich were in a projection room. When the test was finished and the lights flashed on, Miss Dietrich cried, "I—look—just—awful! My skin, my neckline—" She turned to Ruttenberg. "Joe, what's *happened* to you? Remember how gorgeously you lighted me before?"

Ruttenberg said, "Miss Dietrich, please remember—I was fifteen years younger at that time. . . ."

Clifford Voultarian, the famous movie director, on a trip to New York, met Wanda Parton, a beautiful, though not particularly bright, model. He fell madly in love with Wanda. After a whirlwind courtship, he married Wanda and brought her home to his mansion near Malibu Beach. And there, very soon after they arrived, Voultarian arranged for twenty of his closest friends to meet his bride at a formal dinner.

As they were dressing to go down to greet the guests, Wanda said, "Cliff, I hafta tell you—I'm as nervous as a knocked-up cat!"

"Now, now, doll," said Clifford.

"But, Cliff, sweetie. These famous writers and directors and producer pals of yours! They're—they're such great *talkers*. I just ain't got the faintest idea of what to say to such brainy people!"

Voultarian put his arms around her and kissed her on the forehead. "Sweetie, you don't have to say a *word* to these people. With your looks, they'll just talk your ears off. All you have to do is be charming. Just listen—as if you're absolutely *fascinated*, no matter what they gab about.

And every so often say, 'How *in*teresting!' or 'That's *mar*velous!' or 'How clever of you!' They'll adore you. Trust me!"

Voultarian was entirely right. His bride charmed one and all with her ready smile, her animated expression, her occasional laughs and compliments.

Only after the dessert did Wanda Voultarian make the slightest *faux pas*. Clifford rose from the table saying, "Well, gang, shall we have coffee and liqueurs in the library?"

To which his beautiful darling trilled, "Cliff, honey, do you think it's still open this late at night?"

⮑

The actor Sherman Caldwell (né Irving Calish) turned his profile toward his friend David and said, "So? What do you think?"

"Hey," exclaimed David. "You've had a nose job! That's a fantastic change. You look like a Barrymore or a Basil Rathbone!"

"Do you mean that? Or are you just trying to make me feel good?"

"It's the God's honest, Irv. You look like a thing of beauty—and a *goy* forever."

⮑

"Before I came to Hollywood," said the cutie, "I thought for sure that money—well, that money is the greatest thing in the world!"

"And now," asked her friend. "Don't you?"

"Absolutely not," said the doxie. "There's jewelry, real estate, community property . . ."

⮑

Beverly Hills is *very* exclusive. For example, the fire department won't make house calls.

MORT SAHL

⮑

The most grandiose filmmaker in Hollywood was the new boy genius, Sidney B. de Milstein. After two years of preparation and shooting, he was now completing his most daring saga, a tumultuous story of the Mexican war with Texas.

On the plains near the Rio Grande (to Mexicans, the Rio Bravo), de Milstein had constructed four different towers—complete with cameras, sound equipment, huge light reflectors (desert light creates deep shadows), and immense fans to produce fierce desert winds. The four towers, each complete with a sound boom, camera, and crew, were de Milstein's way of ensuring that the climactic scene (involving a battle that used three thousand uniformed extras, four hundred horses, two thousand sabers, flags, lances, rifles, etc.) would be photographed *in toto*.

All was in place. The sun shone. The fans stirred the desert sand. The armies waited.

"Action!" called Sidney B. de Milstein through his bullhorn.

And what action it was! Never had a battle raged with such fury, such authenticity, such cinematic magnificence. And when, after seventeen un-interrupted minutes of action, de Milstein finally boomed "Cut!" through the loudspeakers, all the extras and technicians and prop men burst into spontaneous cheering.

Into his telephone hookup to Tower 1, de Milstein said: "You got it all, Lansing?"

"Mr. de Milstein," came an anguished voice. "Our power blew out! We couldn't shoot—"

"What?!"

"—one single frame!"

De Milstein raged and cursed and fumed, then flipped the intercom button that connected him to Tower 2. "Slawson! How was it?"

"Mr. de Milstein, *please* don't get mad! But the cameraman forgot to reload, so the cameras rolled all right, but they didn't get—"

"Idiot! Maniac! You're fired!" Mr. de Milstein snapped the connection to Tower 3. "Benton! How did it go?"

"Mr. de Milstein," said Benton, "*never* was there such a scene! It will make film history! You are a *genius,* an absolute—"

"Stop the malarkey, Benton. Did you get it all on film?"

" 'On film'?" echoed Benton. "You wanted me to *photograph* it? I thought it was a rehearsal—"

"You moron!" roared de Milstein. "You imbecile! You'll never get a job with me again, Benton!" The great de Milstein slammed down the phone and turned to his own cameraman, who happened to be his brother-in-law. "At least, thank God, *you're* here, Nat. I'm sure everything was okay with *this* setup?"

"Absolutely!" chortled Nat.

"Enough film in the cans?"

"Plenty, Sidney."

"Is the sound okay?"

"The sound is perfect."

"Thank God!"

"Yep," grinned Nat. "We're ready whenever you are, Sidney."

See also **Actors, Goldwyniana, Moses**

Hotels

Mrs. Dumfries was checking out of the Bolton Holiday Camp, near Swanson, on the Scottish coast.

"And did ye find us satisfyin'?" asked the proprietor, Mr. Duncan.

"Ay. Except for y'r food, Mr. Duncan."

"Our food did nae please you, mum?"

"Y'r food is a disgrace, mon. And such wee, wee portions!"

In the lobby of the Sterling Hotel, Mr. Ottenheim beheld a large, fat man, sprawled in a chair, smoking a large, fat cigar.

Mr. Ottenheim sniffed the smoke, made a face, and said, "That is some cheap cigar."

"It costs fifty cents," the smoker said.

"Fifty—and how many do you smoke a day?"

"Nine—ten."

"Let's say ten. That's five dollars a day, right?"

"Right."

"Three hundred sixty-five days a year. That's—for cigars—over eighteen hundred dollars a year! . . . And how many years have you been smoking?"

"Forty, forty-five."

"My God!" said Mr. Ottenheim. "That's like—let's see—eighty-five *thousand* dollars! Did you ever stop to think that if you hadn't burned all that money in smoke, *you* could—oh, own a little hotel like this!"

The fat man studied his cigar. "Mister," he said, "do *you* happen to smoke?"

"God forbid! Not even a cigarette! In my whole life, I never took one puff—"

"So do you own this hotel?"

Mr. Ottenheim blinked "Certainly."

P.S. The same story may be told with this ending:

"My God!" cried Mr. Ottenheim. "Did you ever stop to think that if you hadn't literally burned up eighty-five thousand dollars in smoke, you might—why, you might own a little hotel, like this one!"

The fat man nodded. "I do."

It was 3:40 A.M. when irate Bruce Fraser picked up the phone in his room in Scotland's Loch Merrane Hotel.

"Front desk," came a voice.

"Ay. C'n ye answer me one simple question, mon?"

"Sure I shall try, sir."

"Tell me, mon, 've ye iver heard of the straw th't broke the camel's back?"

"Ay. That I have."

"Well, tell the goddam owner of this hostelry that in Room three-four-six, one Bruce Fraser, age sixty-four, has been tryin' all night to sleep on 't."

"How did you like Atlantic City?" asked Morton.

"Fine. Good hotel. Good weather. Good food. Good gambling." Spratt hesitated. "The only thing wrong was—the help."

"Really? Were they rude?"

"N-no. Just cunning."

"What do you mean 'cunning'?"

"Well, when you phone down for a deck of cards, the bellboy delivers them one at a time."

In the fine new hotel in Tel Aviv, Manny Futterman, watching television, picked up the telephone. "This is Room three-oh-seven: I would like some Seven-Up, please."

"Seven-Up? Yes, *sir*. I'll attend to it."

"Thank you."

By midnight, the Seven-Up had not arrived and Manny Futterman had fallen fast asleep—from which he was harshly awakened by the telephone operator precisely at seven o'clock in the morning.

A young buyer from Des Moines, in Chicago for a convention, filled out her first hotel registration card this way:

Name:	Selma Hansley
Address:	806 Oak St., Des Moines, Iowa
Firm:	Not very.

"So Nate, tell me, how is your little hotel in the Poconos doing this year?"

"Sensational!" replied Nate. "We have guests sleeping under our beds!"

"No kiddin'?"

"No kiddin'. . . . The roofs leak."

Notice in rooming house in Anchorage, Alaska

1. Guests arriving without baggage, must leave wife's at desk with Harold.
2. Please do not smoke pot in hallways.
3. Do not clean shoes with a towel, unless it was stolen from another hotel.
4. In case of fire, do not use central stairway. It is highly inflammable. The moment you smell smoke, or hear our central fire alarm, jump out of nearest window.
5. If you see a mouse in your room, notify desk promptly. We will send up two heartless cats.
6. To prevent consistent loss of fresh fruit from center of dining-room table, there will no longer be fresh fruit in center of dining-room table.
7. Gambling is permitted only in areas designated "GAMBLING SALON." The nearest one is LUCY'S WHEEL, four blocks down the street.
8. We do not supply bottles, nipples, or wet nurses for babies.
9. All bribes to our help will be turned in to the Welfare Fund for Our Three Children. All our help are our children.
10. If you like our rooming house, service, food, or atmosphere, please tell others. If you do not, tell us. We will add 20 percent to your bill.

How's That Again?

Lovingly collected, from newspapers, magazines, talk shows

Reverend Hammond was congratulated on being able to get his parish plastered.

The jury's verdict showed they were of one mind: temporarily insane.

He was sent to prison for strangling a woman without killing her.

The driver of the car swerved to avoid missing the woman's husband.

These premises will shortly be opened as a cafeteria, with courteous and efficient self-service.

Tom Mix and his wonder horse, Tony, are featured. In some stunts, Tom shows almost human intelligence.

The ball struck Berra on the right temple and knocked him cold. He was taken to Ford Hospital, where X-rays of his head showed nothing.

He and his wife have left for Florida. We all hope they will like their trip and stay in Miami.

We note with regret that Mr. Yost is recovering after his serious operation.

The congressman sat on the carpet and discussed the rise in prices and the high cost of living with several women.

Push back the cuticles on one hand with the orange-stick while you soak the other.

A stray bullet killed one bystander slightly.

The Fire Department will blow the siren fifteen minutes before the start of each fire.

The doctor felt the man's purse and said there was no hope.

. . . There were only three other people in the big room, half of them waiters.

The police reported that the victim suffered at least two broken legs.

The A & P is actually the Great American Teat Company.

I live so far out of town, the mailman mails me my letters.

HENNY YOUNGMAN

The jury retired at 10:00 A.M. and deliberated twenty-four hours before returning a verdict of guilty of manslaughter. This conviction carried a penalty of one to ten years in Alabama.

He had a stroke, and didn't recover until he died.

A son was born to Mr. and Mrs. William Kleintop, Lehigh Avenue, during the past week. Congratulations, Pete!

No governor in many years has been able to love on the salary paid him, even though he is supplied with a furnished home rent free.

H*Y*M*A*N K*A*P*L*A*N puts asterisks between each letter in his name.

BRENDAN GILL

☙

"Bang! Boom! Pow!" he hissed.

☙

He was born in Hartford. Prior to that he worked for the American Silver Company.

☙

Many men reach maturity, but only women have reached maternity so far.

☙

People in search of solitude are flocking here from the four corners of the world.

CANADIAN HOTEL PROSPECTUS

☙

He's a real eager-beaver. Why, he gets up six o'clock in the morning no matter what time it is.

THANKS TO HYMAN KAPLAN

☙

Dance-hall marquee

**GOOD CLEAN DANCING
EVERY NIGHT
EXCEPT SUNDAY**

☙

He was an engaging little dog, said an observer with a curly tail and friendly manner.

☙

Mrs. Beardsley, who is knitting a complex shawl for the church raffle, said, "I am knitting as swiftly as I can, to be sure to get to the end of the garment before the wool runs out."

☙

Dogs are getting bigger, according to a leading dog manufacturer.

☙

He is so honest that he worked in a bathhouse for three years and never took one.

WEST SIMMS TO HAVE
PARENT-TEACHER ASSASSINATION

PRIEST SAYS PUTTING CRONIN TO DEATH
Eliminates all Hope of
Rehabilitation

Ladies who have undertaken to act as school-crossing wardens are reminded that if they attempt to carry out their duties without the clothing on, motorists may not take notice of them.

No one heard him laugh like that since his wife died.

Sign on hotel elevator door in Bucharest

Lift is being fixed. Until then, we regret you are unbearable.

On lifeguard's stand in Florida

GIRLS: DO NOT BOTHER LIFEGUARD
UNLESS ACTUALLY DROWNING

Fortunately for the deceased, he had deposited all of his money in the bank the day before, so he lost virtually nothing but his life.

Preposition: An enormously versatile part of grammar, as in " 'What made you choose this book for me to be read to out of up for?' "

WINSTON CHURCHILL

The grandstand was so crowded they had to turn hundreds of people down for seats.

❧

She held out her hand. The young man took it, and departed.

❧

On photocopier in office

The Typist's reproduction equipment is not to be inter-fered with without my specific permission.

MANAGER

❧

"This young lady walked very close to me," the witness testified, "and it was obvious that underneath her clothing she wore nothing."

See also Boo-boos, Definitions to Cherish, Graffiti, Headlines That Haunt Me, Signs

Hypochondriacs

A bed bug.

A man who wants to be buried next to his doctor.

One with an infinite capacity for faking pains.

Someone who feels bad when he feels good because he know he'll feel worse when he feels better.

Mrs. Glock was rich, lonely, and a hypochondriac. She confined most of her reading to journals such as *Popular Health, Modern Medicine, You and Your Body.* One day she hastened to her doctor. "I think I have anartaxia cobulgamytis!"

The doctor stared at her. "Now who ever told you anything as silly as that?"

"Nobody *told* me. I happened to read an article—"

"Will you ever stop reading those articles? Anartaxia cobulgamytis is one of the rarest diseases in the world."

"So take tests! Maybe I'm one of those rare cases."

"Nonsense, Mrs. Glock. First of all, people who have that affliction never feel the slightest pain. Second, they never develop any visible symptoms. Third, the victims' only clue is an unreasonable terror about alligators."

Mrs. Glock promptly fainted.

After the doctor revived her, Mrs. Glock gasped, "My symptoms exactly!"

See also **Doctors, Insomnia**

Immigrants

A greenhorn, having heard about the wonders of Coney Island, asked a girl out on a date there.

The next morning, his landlady asked, "So did you enjoy?"

"Y-yeah. But the place I was most anxious to see—the Tunnel of Love—that was a terrible disappointment. We both got so wet. . . ."

"That's awful. Did your boat leak that much?"

The greenhorn blinked: "You mean there's a *boat?*"

Hyman Soper entered Shona Mincus's kosher restaurant on lower Broadway. The waiter who poured his water was—clearly an Oriental. Perhaps a Korean? Perhaps from Thailand? And the man proceeded to rattle off the menu—in fluent Yiddish!

When Hyman Soper was paying his bill, he told the cashier, "I enjoyed my dinner—and even more, I can't get over the fact that your waiter speaks such excellent Yiddish!"

"Ssh!" hissed the cashier. "He thinks we're teaching him English."

Social column: "I's very pleased," said Sushi, a medical student, in perfect English.

Paddy Muldoon and a horde of hopeful immigrants to America crowded the rails of the ship. As they approached the pier, they beheld—in absolute astonishment—the interminable line of automobiles crawling down the West Side drive.

"Begorrah and b'Jasus," gulped Paddy, "will you look at the len'th of that funeral now!"

Muttel Friedman, newly arrived from Romania, got a job as a janitor in a theater on Second Avenue. One afternoon he started for a backstage room on the door of which was this sign:

**CHORUS GIRLS ONLY
ENTRY TO ALL OTHERS FORBIDDEN!**

Just as Muttel put his hand on the knob of the door, the stage manager shouted, "Stay out of there!" and hurried over. "What's the matter with you, you greenhorn?" He pointed to the sign. "Can't you read English?!"

Muttel drew himself up in righteous indignation. "Who's smoking?"

Antonio Montero, fresh from Chile, at the Staten Island end of the ferry, raced at breakneck speed and hurled himself across the patch of water. He landed on the ferryboat with a tremendous crash—but picked himself up proudly, dusting his corduroy trousers, glancing around, grinning, for recognition of his feat.

The only recognition came from a passenger of Colombian descent. "What ess you horry? We coming *een!*"

"Fathair Dooley," complained Padraic Flanagan, " 'tis six months I'm here, since leaving County Mayo, an' I tell ye, I cannot see how I can live the life of a good, pious man on the wages I make. . . ."

"How much are they payin' you, my son?"

"Therty-noine dollars a week, fathair."

"On therty-noine dollars a week, Paddy, that's about all ye can do," sighed Father Dooley.

1919. Myron Bolitsky glowed with pride—as he stood before Judge Cranborn, to become a citizen.

"How many states are there in the Union?" asked Judge Cranborn.

"Forty-eight," said Bolitsky.

"Good. And into how many branches is our government divided?"

"President, judges, and Congress."

"Fine. . . . Now, Mr. Bolitsky, will you solemnly swear to support the Constitution?"

A moan escaped Bolitsky. "I would like to, *believe* me, judge. But I have a mother, wife, and two children in Romania."

Scotty Dunviddie, but newly arrived in America, saved up enough money and screwed up enough nerve to go into a restaurant for breakfast. Without looking at the menu, he sang out, "Orange juice, two aigs fried, 'n' a nice spot of tea."

The waitress nodded. "The eggs, sir: you want them on toast or a roll?"

Scotty blinked. "If you dinnae have plates, mum, best put th' aigs on two rolls."

Paddy O'Reilly met his cousin Mike, who had arrived in the United States only ten months ago. "*Ay* there, Michael, me boy. Y're lookin' peaked. Are ye not well?"

"Nay. It's in hospital I was, three days."

"For what, man?"

"A tech of flu they said. 'Tis gone now, 'tis. But d'ye know what hospital charged me, Paddy? Fair on a hoondred twelve dollars!"

"Mike, lad, that's not much—"

"Not *much?*" echoed Michael. "Why back in County Cork, ye can be sick three *months* for money like that!"

Dennis Offaly was an immigrant, arrived but one week earlier from County Sligo. Now, for the first time, he was in an automat, with his cousin Gilly. Dennis fed nickel after nickel into the pie slots, and soon a row of pies—apple, blueberry, cherry, peach—was arrayed before him. And still he kept dropping nickels in the slots.

Gilly exclaimed, "Is it *mad* y've gone then, Denny? Y've got fourteen—fifteen—sixteen!—pies b'fore ye, man!"

Said Dennis, "Faith, why is it botherin' ye that Oy've a lucky streak an' keep winnin'?!"

See also **Accents, The English Language**

Ingenuity

Police who arrested two men on car-theft charges in New York said they belonged to a gang who offered their customers an unusual guarantee. They sold stolen Cadillacs on the understanding that they were in sound mechanical condition. But if a defect developed, the gang guaranteed to resteal the car, so the illegal owner could collect from the insurance company—usually about four times what he had paid for the car.

Sign on shoeshine box on lower Broadway

FREE! FREE!
One shoe shined absolutely free.

At the nurses' desk on the sixth floor of Mount Sinai Hospital, the telephone rang. Nurse Juanita Campaña lifted the receiver. " 'ollo. Seex floor."

"Is this the nurse?"

"*Sí.* I can help you?"

"I hope so. I'm calling about one of your patients—Sol Bloomberg. That's B-L-O-O-M-B-E-R-G. He was operated on—four days ago."

Nurse Campaña was consulting the charts. "*Sí.*"

"Nurse, tell me, what's his condition? How is he coming along?"

"Hees condision is ajust fine. In foct, Doctor Shapeero say he can go home Duesday. . . . Who I should say telephone to heem?"

"No one. *I'm* Sol Bloomberg, and Doctor Shapiro don't tell me a goddam thing!"

In San Antonio, a large sign in the window of Miguel Gonzales's store read:

$$ BIG SALE!! $$
EVER TING
for
HOME, PORCK, KIHTCEN!

An English teacher from the nearby school, Carlotta Mendino, entered the store, and in Spanish inquired, "Who is the owner?"

"*Yo,*" said Miguel Gonzales. "Miguel Gonzales."

"I am the teacher of English, Señor Gonzales. I think you should know that the sign in your window—contains some—several *bad* mistakes in spelling."

"*Sí,*" nodded Gonzales.

"You know?"

"*Sí, sí.*"

"Would you like me to point out those mistakes, and correct them?"

"No," the proprietor said. "I do not wish *corrección.* People come in all the time—to tell me I have this mistake or that mistake in the sign. And at least *half,* señora, once inside, load up on bargains!"

Scene: Telephone Exchange, Cleveland

OPERATOR

This is Long Distance. May I help you?

MR. KIRSCHBAUM

You soitinly can, operator. Give me in the state New York, the town is Quaquaga, the phone is number two-seven-six, four, four, three, eight—

OPERATOR

Would you mind repeating the name of that city, please?

MR. KIRSCHBAUM

Qua-qu-a-ga. In New York.

OPERATOR

Sir, would you mind *spelling* that?

MR KIRSCHBAUM

Listen, lady; if I could spell it, I would send a postal card.

Scene: Plaza de la Independencia, Havana

Sergeant Roberto Fiana of the Cuban Special Police, on duty at the vast Plaza de la Independencia, spied a man carrying a heavy brief bag. Sergeant Fiana stopped the man, flashed his identification card, and asked, "Your name, señor?"

"Charamazo."

"Christian *nombre?*"

"Vicente."

"What you carry in thees beeg case?"

"In thees case," smiled Charamazo, "are pesos."

"Pesos?!"

"*Sí.*"

"Open thees bag!"

Vicente Charamazo opened the brief bag. There, indeed, were pesos—thousands of them.

Sergeant Fiana's eyes bulged. "How you did get all thees pesos?"

"Gombling."

"Gombling?" echoed Fiana. "Thot ees most easy explanation—you think I am fool?"

"I prove to you, comrade," said Charamazo. He thought for a moment. "I—I bet you feefty pesos you no can take you pants off before I ron to that monument and back."

"To the monument and *back?*"

"*Sí.*"

"That, up and back, take you at least four minutes!"

"So?"

"You want bet me feefty pesos I no can take off my pants in four whole minute?!"

"*Sí!*"

"Done!" Sergeant Fiana chuckled. "Ready? Go!"

Vicente Charamazo started to trot toward the monument; Sergeant Fiana swiftly untied his boots, dropped them, undid his zipper, pulled down his trousers, stepped out of them, and cried, "*Finito!*"

Charamazo stopped trotting and came back to the pantsless sergeant.

"Well?" grinned Fiana.

"You ween," said Charamazo, and handed the sergeant fifty pesos.

As Sergeant Fiana pulled on his trousers, he chuckled, "Charamazo, you are worst gambler I did ever seen! How you could ween all that money in bag?!"

"Would you like know?" asked Charamazo.

"Sure."

"Okay. Sergeant, how many people you see over there, in crowd?"

"Oh, ees thirty—forty."

"Forty-seex," said Charamazo, then beamed. "And every one of them did bet me five pesos I no could talk you into taking off you pants in meedle of Plaza de la Independencia!"

Andrew Selkirk and Currie Stour, two Scotsmen visiting New York, decided their trip could not be considered complete unless they ventured down and took a ride on the legendary subway.

They were hurtling along toward Chambers Street when two armed hoodlums entered their car.

"Don't anyone try to move or I'll blow them to hell!" cried the first hoodlum.

"Just hand over all your valuables!" said the second hoodlum. "Wallet, watch, rings, necklaces . . ."

Selkirk and Stour swiftly removed their wallets.

Just before the collecting hoodlum reached them, Selkirk murmured, "Currie . . ."

"Ay?"

Selkirk handed Stour a ten-dollar bill.

"What is this for, Andrew?"

"Dinnae y' remember, mon? That be the ten dollars I'm owin' ye."

"Timothy Clark," said his wife sternly, "what time did you come home last night?"

"Eh—a quarter o' twelve, luv."

"You lie! Clear and loud I heard the clock strike three."

Timothy studied the floor but a moment, then grinned. "Ay, m' darlin'—an' tell me: how much is a quarter o' twelve?"

In Red Bank, New Jersey, the house of the Lester Pragers adjoined the house of the Gerald Stinnets. The Stinnets had a large, smelly, noisy chicken coop in their back yard. Worse, to the Pragers, was the fact that the chickens often made their way through one or another place in the Stinnet hedge onto the Prager lawn, clucking and pecking at blossoms and depositing their ugly waste on the grass.

Mr. Prager often complained to Mr. Stinnet about the behavior of his fractious brood, but Mr. Stinnet, who did not like people of Mr. Prager's religious persuasion, only smirked. He did nothing to remedy the unpleasant situation.

Life for the Pragers was fairly miserable—until Mr. Prager, one day, burst into laughter.

"What's that about?" asked Mrs. Prager.

"I have it! I have it!" cried Mr. Prager. "The way to make Stinnet keep his damn chickens in his own damn yard!"

"What is it?"

Prager smiled. "Watch. Come on."

He went into the kitchen, removed the seven eggs that were in the refrigerator, went into his yard, looked around to make sure no Stinnets were watching, and carefully hid the eggs under a bush in his garden.

"Lester," sighed his wife, "are you crazy?"

"Crazy like a fox," he grinned. "Let's wait until Stinnet goes into his yard. . . ."

They sat on a bench, under the peach tree, and soon the back door of the Stinnet house opened and out came Gerald Stinnet. He headed for the chicken coop.

Lester Prager stood up, went to the bush in his garden where he had laid the seven eggs, and in a loud voice called, "Steffie, dear! Look! Look what I see!" He bent down and picked up egg after egg, high enough for Stinnet to see. "Seven fresh eggs! Those chickens must have laid them this morning."

Gerald Stinnet's jaw dropped.

The Pragers were not bothered by Stinnet's chickens again.

Mendel Tarshov fell off a bridge in Moscow. He could not swim. He thrashed around and shouted for help at the top of his lungs.

Two policemen heard his cries and ran to the rail, but when they saw Tarshov's skullcap, they simply laughed.

"Help! Help!" cried Tarshov. "I'm drowning!"

"So drown, *Zhid* [Yid]!"

Just as Tarshov started under for the proverbial third time, he had an inspiration: "To hell with Marx! To hell with Lenin! Down with the Politburo!"

At once, the policemen jumped into the water, pulled Tarshov out, and arrested him for spreading anti-Communist propaganda.

Sandy Kilcallon came to the law chambers of Clyde Galshiel. "Mister Galshiel, it's a wee bit o'advice I'm seekin'. Maybe I shall sue me partner, an' maybe not. . . . If, after hearin' the evidence, ye tell me my case is no good, I go no fairther. But if ye say the facts are one-hundred percent in favor o' me winning, it's my counsel ye shall be."

"Ay." Galshiel tilted back in his chair. "What are the focts?"

Kilcallon set forth upon a meticulous, detailed account of a ruptured partnership with one Ben Berwick. "So the question I face is: if I sue Berwick, do I get back me money?"

"Ay, indaid ye will, Mr. Kilcallon," said Mr. Galshiel earnestly. "Why, mon, never, *never* have I heard such an open-and-shut case!"

Kilcallon winced, as if struck a blow, and rose. "I'm thankin' ye for y'r time—"

"Are ye not intendin' to bring suit?" asked Galshiel.

"Nae." Kilcallon started for the door.

"But, mon—I dinna understand ye!"

"The focts I did give ye," said Sandy Kilcallon, "are Ben Berwick's version of the case."

One day, to the border post separating Russia from Poland, Yuli Probovnie came riding along on a bicycle—with a heavy sack slung across his shoulders. He stopped at the sentry box and showed the guard his passport, permission to travel, visa. . . .

The chief border guard found the papers in order. Then he asked, "*Tovarich*, what's in the sack?"

"Flour," said Probovnie.

"Humph. Open it up. I want to see for myself if *all* you're taking to those damn Poles is flour!"

So Probovnie opened the sack. The contents certainly looked like flour. But the chief guard stabbed his bayonet into the flour, six—seven—eight times, in eight different places. Nowhere did he strike metal, or a box, a can, a bottle. . . . "Okay, *tovarich.*" He lifted the border gate, and Yuri Probovnie retied his bag, slung it across his shoulder, and pedaled across the border.

A week later, to the same sentry box, came Yuri. Again he presented his passport, his papers, his visa. And again the chief sentry asked, "*Tovarich,* what are you taking into Poland this time?"

"Grain."

"Grain, eh? Open up the sack. I want to see for myself. . . ."

Again Yuri opened his sack. The contents certainly were grain. The border guard stabbed his bayonet into the grain—six, seven, eight times once more. His bayonet struck no metal, no can, no bottle. . . . "All right."

Once a week, for a whole year, the same scene was reenacted. Each time Yuri Probovnie was stopped by the chief of the border customs control. "And what are you carrying this time, *tovarich?*"

One week Yuri said, "Beans." Another time he said, "Sugar." Other weeks he carried a sackful of salt, meal, rice. . . .

Each time the customs chief examined Yuri's sack and found the contents to be as described.

At the end of the year, the border chief defected. He made his way to Vienna, where, drinking tea in a café one afternoon, he beheld Yuri Probovnie. "*Tovarich!*" he exclaimed. "You here? Come. Have some tea."

As they drank, the defector asked Yuri, "Listen, my friend. I have escaped from the Soviet Union. I'll never go back. So you can talk frankly to me. Will you?"

"Sure."

"Look, I *know* you were smuggling stuff across that border! I felt it in every bone in my body—but I could never prove it! Now you can tell me the truth. . . . *Were* you smuggling?"

"Certainly." Yuri smiled.

"What?"

"Bicycles."

Amos Harvey, in a taxi, noticed he had forgotten to take his wallet along. The meter read $3.25. He thought for a moment, then said to the driver: "Stop at the next place I can buy some cigarettes." The cab stopped in front of a drugstore. "I'll only be a minute," said Harvey. "Oh, by the way, I dropped a fifty-dollar bill in the back. Couldn't find it in the dark. Remind me to look for it when I get back."

Harvey opened the door to the drugstore. The taxi roared away.

Into Giovanni's Hair Heaven Barbershop, on a hot, humid day, walked a man and a boy of eight or nine. The man said, "Just sit there, son. Look at a magazine." He got into the chair. "Haircut, shave, face massage, manicure, shine . . ."

It was a good hour before these were completed. The man said, "Okay now, son," and the boy climbed into the chair.

The man said to Giovanni, "While you cut the kid's hair, I'll go across the street for a beer."

Giovanni cut the boy's hair. The man did not return.

Giovanni said, "Eh, *bambino*. What'sa keep you papa?"

"He ain't my father," said the boy.

"Hanh? So who he isa?"

"Search me. I was playing in the street and he said, 'Hey, kid, how would you like a free haircut?' "

Two Jews, Gumbiner and Ohrbach, were walking down a street in Berlin when they saw an SS cop approaching. Only Gumbiner had an identity card. Ohrbach said, "Quick, Hans, *run!* He'll chase you. You'll show him your identity card—and I'll get away!"

So Gumbiner broke into a run.

"Stop! Stop!" cried the policeman.

Gumbiner kept on running.

The SS cop finally caught up. "Jew!" he roared. "Show me your papers!"

Gumbiner, gasping, produced his papers.

The Nazi examined them and saw they were in order. "But why," he asked in surprise, "were you running away from me?!"

"Eh—I wasn't running away from you," said Gumbiner. "My doctor—told me to run half a mile after each meal."

The Nazi frowned. "But you saw me chasing you! You heard me yelling! Why didn't you stop?"

"I—uh—thought maybe you go to the same doctor."

Amos and Myron, brothers, not particularly friendly, inherited a large plot of land from their father. They argued and argued about how to divide it. Unable to agree, Myron said, "Let's go to Rabbi Sampson and ask him the fairest way to divvy up the land."

Rabbi Sampson was the right man to ask. He said, "Toss a coin. The one who wins the toss, divides the land."

"But *rebbe*," complained Amos, "I don't believe in gambling!"

"Nor do I," smiled Rabbi Sampson. "The one who wins the toss divides the land; but the other one gets first choice."

At the annual reunion of the McDermott clan in Aberdeen, Stewart McDermott suddenly raced to the loudspeaker, interrupted the singing of "Blue Bells of Scotland," and cried, "Hoot! Hear this, all ye fine and loyal McDermotts! It's me money-purse! Lost, it is. There's a *hundred quid in that purse!* Whoever brings it up here—now—I will give a reward of *fif-teen* pounds!"

From the back of the crowd came a burry voice: "I'll give twenty-five!"

Dr. Tyning examined the cardiogram and, smiling at the patient, said, "You're in perfect health, Mr. Everett. Your heart, lungs, blood pressure, cholesterol level—everything is just shipshape!"

"Splendid!" said Mr. Everett.

"I'll see you next year," said Dr. Tyning.

Doctor and patient shook hands. Mr. Everett stepped out.

In a moment, Dr. Tyning heard a loud crash. He dashed into the reception office. There, flat on his face, lay Mr. Everett.

Dr. Tyning's nurse cried, "He just collapsed, doctor! Without the slightest warning! He fell down like a rock!"

The doctor knelt, listened to Everett's heart. "He's dead . . ." Dr. Tyning put his hands under the corpse's arms. "Quick, nurse. Take his feet!"

"What?"

"For God's *sake,* nurse, let's turn the man around. We must make it look like he was coming *in!*"

At a small hotel in a faroff town in Alaska, a woman guest told the owner that twice during the night she had had to get into her bathrobe and slippers and walk all the way down to the lobby and back to fill the tiny carafe of water on her night table.

"But why," asked the puzzled owner, "didn't you just press the button for the bellboy? He's on duty all night."

"You mean the little white button on the wall next to the bed?"

"Certainly."

"He told me that button was to be used only in case of fire!"

High in the ranks of the ingenious must be the Jewish beggar who, at the height of Hitler's power, stood on a busy Berlin corner with a tin cup and this sign:

I DO NOT ACCEPT
MONEY FROM JEWS

The approving *Herrenvolk* dropped coins in the cup in a veritable shower.

The owner of a new drugstore put a large glass fish tank in his window, filled it with water, then placed this sign in front of it:

THIS BOWL CONTAINS 63
INVISIBLE PERUVIAN DEVIL-FISH

The sidewalk in front of the window was packed all day.

Jackson lent Maxon five hundred dollars. Maxon promised to return it within a month. A year later, Jackson still had not received a dime. Jackson consulted a lawyer.

"Do you have Maxon's IOU?" asked the lawyer.

"No. I didn't ask for one."

"Do you have his personal note?"

"I have nothing in writing. I thought I was dealing with a friend."

The lawyer thought for a while, then said, "Write Maxon and tell him you have to have the seven hundred dollars he borrowed—"

"You mean five hundred."

"No, I mean seven hundred. He'll write back indignantly that he only owes you five hundred. You'll have it in writing."

Sign in pilots' lounge at airport

ATTENTION
By Order of Navigation Control
Absolutely no flying is permitted over
the nudist camp which is 18.3 SSW on a
true course of 149 degrees.

After his first day as a bus driver, Patrick Flynn handed in receipts of $165. The next day his receipts were $194. The third day's income was $172. But on the fourth day, Flynn, beaming with pride, placed $483 on the desk before the cashier, whose eyes popped.

"Flynn," said the cashier, "this is fontostic, for sure. Never, never has your route brought in such sums! What happened?"

"Well, after me first three days on the route that dispatcher give me, I figured business would never improve. So I drove over to Main Street. . . . I tell you, that street is a very gold mine!"

A learned rabbi used to ride from town to town in old Lithuania to preach. He loved to answer questions. Now, the rabbi's driver always listened to the sermons, and especially to the questions and answers.

After many years, one day the driver said, "*Rebbe,* I have listened to you for over twenty years. I can recite your sermons in my sleep. . . . Before I die, I'd like to be as respected as you are. Tomorrow we're coming to a village we've never seen before. Why can't we change places?! Just this once. I'll wear your broad hat and caftan, and deliver the sermon; and people will ask *me* questions and I'll answer every one—exactly the way you would!"

The idea intrigued the rabbi. So he and the driver changed clothes. . . . The driver delivered an excellent sermon. Then the congregation began to ask questions, which he answered with ease from memory. But the last question asked was so new, so profound, that the poor driver was flabbergasted. Finally, with altogether admirable presence of mind, he drew himself up and thundered, "*Me* you ask a question as simple as that! Why, even my driver, sitting back there, a poor, hard-working man who never set foot in a *yeshiva,* can answer it. Driver!" he sang out to the rabbi, "Stand up! Did you hear the question?"

"Yes, *rebbe,*" said the rabbi.

"Answer it."

The large delivery truck of Fraser's Highland Queen Beer careened around a corner in a crowded part of Aberdeen, skidded, and turned over with a terrific crash. Bottles flew in all directions and smashed on the cobblestones, and beer bubbled out and formed a fizzing, foaming river.

The young driver of the truck gazed around the debris and burst into tears. "Oh, oh! Lord preserve me wife and wee ones! For Mr. Fraser is a hard, hard mon, and he will surely make me pay—"

At this point a well-dressed, elderly man in a derby pushed his way through the crowd and, from the curb, addressed the throng. "Sons of Aberdeen, kin ya nae *feel* this poor lad's sorrow? 'Tis ruination he does face. Ruination. Debt for many a year ahead." He took off his derby. "I say to all o' ye, 'tis our bounden duty as good Christians—as true Presbyterians—to take oop a collection. T' pay for this young mon's misfortune. Ay will start meself, with a pound note!" With a flourish, the Good Samaritan fluttered a pound in the air for all to see and deposited it in his derby. "Na, men! Ladies! Open y'r hearts and y'r purses, in the name of Saint Andrew."

Bills and silver and coppers dropped into the derby. And the collector soon approached the sobbing driver. "Here, laddie. Open y'r apron. . . . All for you." He dropped the money into the young man's open apron, plopped his derby back on his head, and disappeared into the crowd.

"*Och,* thair goes a very saint!" called a spectator.

" 'Tis the spirit o' human compassion, no less!" exclaimed another.

"Aye, lad, an' are ye not proud t' see the great heart of Scotland open before y'r very eyes?"

The young man looked surprised. "Nae, did na *one* o' ye reconize Mr. Fraser?"

See also **Aplomb, Graffiti, Reason, Revenge, Scoundrels, Signs, Stratagems**

Ingratitude

The Padraic Hannegans of Sydney, Australia, were taking a holiday at the sea near Wollongong. Mrs. Hannegan was playing in the water with her little son, Carson. Suddenly, an unexpected, powerful wave rolled in, knocked the little boy down, and, roaring back, scooped the child up and carried him out to sea.

"Carson! My boy!" screamed Mrs. Hannegan. "Help! Help!"

People leaped to their feet. Several waded into the water. But all stood frozen, for they could not see the lad who was being sucked out to sea.

"Help! My boy! Drowning!" shrieked Mrs. Hannegan.

From his high tower, a lifeguard leaped down to the sand, hurled his torpedo-buoy ahead in the direction he had seen the boy being carried, and with powerful strokes swam out, reached the lad, slung him across the orange torpedo, and propelled both onto a huge wave that carried all three back to shore.

Mrs. Hannegan smothered her son, who was coughing, but definitely alive, in her arms.

The lifeguard beamed. "Fit as a fiddle, he is, mum."

Mrs. Hannegan noticed something, drew herself up, and, with considerable indignation, declared: "He—was—wearing—a—hat! . . ."

See also **Chutzpa**

Insomnia

Old Mr. Franzini was going mad from lack of sleep. Night after night, week after week, the old man suffered from unconquerable insomnia. His children had given the poor man medicines, syrups, tranquilizers—all to no avail. Old Franzini's sunken eyes and hollow cheeks gave him the appearance of a corpse.

The children finally decided to call in a new doctor, Salvadore Cravone, who had won a fine reputation in Little Italy as a *psychiatra,* a clever medico who on occasion resorted to hypnosis.

When young Dr. Cravone arrived, the children introduced him to the old man. "Papa, here is *dottore* who makes *miracolos*—he makes people *sleep!*"

Said Dr. Cravone: "Papa Franzini, if you'll have just a little faith—I promise, you will fall asleep like a *bambino.* Look, papa." He held up his gold watch. "Keep the eyes here. . . . *Buono* . . ." The doctor swung the watch back and forth on its gold chain, slowly, intoning: "Left . . . right . . . *sinistro* . . . *destra.* . . . Now, the eyes get tired . . . very tired . . . very *stracco.* . . . The eyelids are so heavy . . . heavy . . . now you sleep . . . *dormire* . . . sleep . . ."

And the old man's head sank low, his eyes shut, and his breathing was as placid as a babe's. A soft snore came from him. . . .

Dr. Cravone placed a warning finger on his lips, cautioning the children to remain silent, and tiptoed out. He closed the bedroom door softly. . . .

At once, the old man lifted his head. One fierce eye opened. He glanced at his children. "Thata crazy man? Isa go?"

Insomnia: The triumph of mind over mattress.

He's such an insomniac that when he falls asleep, he dreams he's awake.

Poor Mr. Gittelman could not sleep. No pills from his doctor, no advice from his friends, helped his tormenting insomnia. Mr. Gittelman began to look so haggard that his partner, Mr. Feigenbaum, said, "You'll end up in a loony ward!"

"So what can I *do?*" moaned Gittelman. "I drink hot milk. I take warm baths. I play soft music. I take every sleeping pill the doctor prescribes. . . ."

"What about the oldest trick of all: counting sheep?"

Gittelman smote his forehead. "Harvey, so help me, I forgot that one. You're a lifesaver. Tonight, I'll count sheep and if I have to count up to ten thousand, I'll fall asleep at last!"

The next morning, the moment Gittelman entered the loft, Feigenbaum asked, "Did it work?"

"No," groaned Gittelman. "I counted sheep. Oh, how I counted sheep. I counted up to two thousand without getting tired. So I sheared the sheep—all two thousand—and still I was wide awake. So I had an idea, and I made up two thousand overcoats. Do you *know* how tiring it is to make two thousand overcoats! I was exhausted and practically snoring—when it happened!"

"What happened?"

"All night I was up, worrying; where could I get two thousand linings?"

The two friends were at their favorite bar, feeling nice and friendly.

"An' did y' know I was on the wagon, I was, for all of Lent, me boy? Not a drop, not a *drop* so much as touched me lips!"

"Fancy that, Emmet. A reg'lar saint y're gittin' to be."

"What about you, Terence?"

"It grieves me to confess to ye, I drink a pint of Irish—a whole pint, mind y', ivery single night. In fact I do it on the express orders of Doctor Mc-Gonigle."

"A pint of whiskey, is it? Ah, tell me, Terence, me foine friend—has the doctor's prescription helped y'r not sleepin' so bad?"

"T' tell ye the truth, Emmet, the whiskey hasn't even *tetched* me insomnia—but I sure don't mind staying oop the way I used t'."

See also **Doctors, Hypochondriacs**

Insults

The last time we met was in my nightmare.

You have a wonderful head on your shoulders; too bad it's not on your neck.

You have the manners of a perfect gentleman: whose are they?

HENNY YOUNGMAN

I don't know what I would do without you—but I'd rather.

Our club is having a membership drive—to drive him out of the club.

You're just what the doctor ordered—a big pill.

He hasn't been himself lately: let's hope he stays that way.

See also **Curses, Groucho, Put-downs, Retorts, Sarcasm, Squelches**

Israel

The air-raid sirens began to shriek, well past midnight, bringing all Tel Avivians out of their beds. In one apartment, old Mr. and Mrs. Lipsky—he in his pajamas, she in her flannel nightgown—started for the door to the corridor and down to the air-raid shelter.

Suddenly, Mrs. Lipsky stopped short. "Wait! Milton!" She rushed back to the bedroom.

"Sylvia!" cried Mr. Lipsky. "Are you crazy? It's an air raid!"

"I can't leave without my teeth!" shouted Mrs. Lipsky.

"Your *teeth?* For God's sake, Sylvia: what do you think the Arabs are going to drop: sandwiches?!"

In 1949, Gerald Harmon, from Manchester, was visiting Israel, and was invited by his Israeli cousin, Simeon, to the historic ceremonies dedicating the Tomb of the Unknown Soldier.

Speeches were made by the president of Israel, the minister of defense, by the commanding general of the army; and at last the tarpaulin that covered the monument was pulled aside—to reveal a simple tomb. On the front was engraved:

BARUCH BARZELAI
Born: Vilna, 1903
Died: Sinai, 1948

All rose as the military band played Israel's national anthem. Soldiers saluted. Civilians placed their right hands over their hearts.

Then Ben Gurion stepped to the lectern to address the throng. And Gerald Harmon whispered to his cousin: "Simeon . . . I say . . . isn't this supposed to be the Tomb of the Unknown Soldier?"

Simeon nodded.

"But—forgive me, old man. 'Unknown?' Absurd. Why, there, plainly inscribed, is the man's name, his birthplace, his—"

"Ssh," hushed Simeon. "You don't understand. As a *soldier*, Baruch Barzelai was unknown; but as a pants-maker—!"

In Israel, an American visitor saw an elderly Jew praying, tears simply pouring down his face.

The American, who could not bear the old man's wailing, asked, "*Zayde* [grandfather] . . . please . . . why are you weeping so bitterly?"

"Because—I want to be with my people!" sobbed the old man.

"But you *are*, in Israel, the Promised Land."

"I mean with my people in Miami!"

Mr. and Mrs. Gelfarb, from Denver, were visiting Israel. Driving around Tel Aviv, their car was stopped by a traffic patrol car. The officer addressed him: "Don't you know you're going down a one-way street?!"

"No, officer."

"Well, you're not blind, are you? Don't you see that great big arrow?"

"Sure I can see that arrow," said Mr. Gelfarb. "But in Israel, who expects to find *In*dians?"

In El Al cabin

FASTEN YOUR SEAT BELTS
NO SMOKING
EAT FRUIT

Jewish dropout: A student who didn't get a Ph.D.

Sign in a café in Jerusalem

SELF-SERVICE
"For you are servants unto Me," said the Lord.

One afternoon, in a new *kibbutz* not far from the Golan Heights, the little house of Shelomi and Sura Schneuer, newly arrived immigrants from Buffalo, caught fire. Shelomi ran up the main street to the Community Hall as fast as he could, shouting, "Fire! Fire! Fire!" all the way.

From the fields, strong young *kibbutzim* ran out toward the fire engine. As it started up, they leaped on the running boards. Clanging its bell, careening from its gathering speed down a hill, the fire engine almost smashed into the Schneuer house, stopping just at the door, where the firefighters jumped off, pumped water, and soon the flames were extinguished.

So grateful were Shelomi and Sura that they embraced each of the gallant firefighters. Then Shelomi drew out his wallet, extracted fifty shekels, and cried, "A contribution! A contribution to the work of such *fearless* comrades. Why, you virtually drove into the cauldron itself!"

The young chief glanced at the fifty shekels and exclaimed, "*Kibbutzniks*, look. Now we can buy brakes!"

Mendel Dresselberg, who was extremely active in Jewish affairs and had raised a considerable sum for the Bonds for Israel drive, was in Israel for an election—and the day after, he was in the office of the newly elected prime minister. "I want you to know that if you—well, if you see fit to appoint me to an important position in your government, I can come here, become a citizen, settle . . . I mean, after all—I hope you haven't forgotten how much I've done . . ."

"Forgotten? Never!" said the prime minister-elect. "In fact, I was just telling a member of my new cabinet that our great friend, Mendel Dresselberg, is the perfect appointee for minister of Health and Transportation!"

Dresselberg's face broke into a great smile. "Minister—that's wonderful. But"—he frowned—"isn't that an unusual combination?"

"Unusual? No, no, my friend," smiled the prime minister. "What this job involves is this: the minister—you—gets an apartment in Haifa, preferably with a balcony, overlooking the harbor. And you sit on that balcony, where everyone can see you. And whenever a ship prepares to leave Haifa, you, the minister, stand up, holding a huge bullhorn, and as the ship begins to pull away from the dock, you wave at it like crazy and, in a strong, official voice, through the bullhorn, you holler, "Sail in the best of health! Go, go! Sail in the best of health!"

Two Israeli spies, caught in Syria, were put up against the wall. The firing squad marched in. The Syrian captain asked the first spy, "Do you have any last wish?"

"A cigarette."

The captain gave him a cigarette, lighted it, and asked the second spy, "Do you have a last request?"

Without a word, the second spy spit in the captain's face.

"Harry!" cried the first spy, "*please!* Don't make trouble."

Charley Gans, a congenital wise guy, visiting Israel, stopped at a vegetable stand. He picked up several large cantaloupes, hefted them for weight, then *utz*ed the farmer, "Hey, can't you *sabras* grow bigger peaches than these?"

The farmer fixed Gans with an icy stare. "Peaches? Do me a favor, mister; put down the two grapes and go away."

Sign in a barracks of the Israeli army: Privates will refrain from giving advice to officers.

In Tel Aviv, one dark night, Special Agent 6-Z-4 looked up and down the street, then darted into the apartment building. He slipped the Colt into his outer pocket, knocked on the door of 2D twice, paused, knocked once, paused, knocked twice again.

From inside, a voice inquired, "Who's dere?"

"Goldblatt?" whispered 6-Z-4.

The door opened; a bald-headed little man in pajamas said, "*Sholem aleichem.*"

"The ostriches," murmured 6-Z-4, "have arrived in Greece."

"*Ha-anh?*" goggled Goldblatt.

"The ostriches," repeated 6-Z-4 slowly, "have arrived in Greece. . . ."

A light entered the eyes of the bald-headed little man. "Ah-*aha!* Mister, I am Goldblatt, the piano teacher. You want Goldblatt the spy. Upstairs, 4B."

Israel's prime minister at a cabinet meeting lamented: "Our inflation is unbearable, our deficits are increasing by leaps and bounds—I don't know what to do that's best for our country!"

The minister of finance said, "Why not—declare war?"

"War?" frowned the prime minister. "Against whom?"

"Against—the United States of America."

This astounding suggestion created gasps and groans. "You must be crazy! War? Between Israel and America? Why, such a war would not last ten minutes!"

The finance minister nodded. "Quite so. We declare war—and in two hours acknowledge defeat. 'You are the victors!' we tell the Americans. So immediately the U.S. will send us relief: food, supplies, oil. They will give us huge grants, rebuild our roads and harbors, send us—"

"*Just* a minute," growled the prime minister. "All that is fine, and would certainly happen. But tell me, if you're so damn clever, what if we *win?!*"

See also **Anti-Semitism, God, Jews, Rabbis, Stratagems**

Jews

Either Hilaire Belloc or A. N. Ewer coined this quatrain:

> How odd
> Of God
> To choose
> The Jews.

This jingle was answered by some unknown wag:

> Not news,
> Not odd,
> The Jews
> Chose God.

To which a Jew responded:

> Not odd
> Of God:
> Goyim
> Annoy 'im.

Young Mrs. Pollack, pushing a pram with two baby boys in it, encountered Mrs. Miller, who said, "Good morning, Mrs. Pollack. My, what beautiful boys! So—how old are they?"

"The doctor," said Mrs. Pollack, "is two. The lawyer, tomorrow is his first birthday."

Mrs. Zolotow was proudly pushing the perambulator down Ocean Avenue, where her neighbor, Mrs. O'Leary, stopped her. "Well now, Mrs. Zolotow, an' which o' y'r children has made y' a grandmother again?"

"My daughter, Rosalie."

Mrs. O'Leary looked into the carriage. "Oh, my, *my*, Mrs. Zolotow. Sure an' this is a pretty bundle o' joy."

"You think *she's* pretty?" Mrs. Zolotow sniffed. "Wait until you see the pictures!"

Jackson, Waybrook, Buchanan, and Isaacs was one of the finest law firms in the city. One day a friend of Eli Isaacs asked, "Why does your name appear last, Eli? Everyone knows that Jackson is ga-ga, Waybrook spends most of his time in the country, and Buchanan never won a case in court. Your name should be first!"

"You forget something." Isaacs smiled.

"What's that?"

"*My* clients read from right to left."

Mrs. Galitzki, visiting London, went shopping at world-famed Fortnum & Mason. She bought jars of marmalade, jams, pickles, tins of fine cookies.

"And where," asked the striped-trousered salesman, "shall we deliver these, madam?"

"Don't bother. I'll take them."

"But madam, we'll be *happy* to deliver this order—"

"I know, but I don't mind, I'm from the Bronx."

"I understand, madam," said the clerk. "Still—why *shlep?*"

Roses are reddish,
Violets, bluish;
If it wasn't for Christmas
We'd all be Jewish.

Harold Schussler and Norman Meyerson, both widowers, were passing the time by playing cards in Meyerson's old apartment on Amsterdam Avenue. After several hours, Schussler glanced at his wrist. "Oh, damn. My watch has stopped again. Norman, what time is it?"

Meyerson shuffled the cards. "I don't know."

"So Norman, look at your watch."

"I don't have a watch."

"So take a look at the clock in the kitchen," said Schussler.

"I don't have in the kitchen a clock," said Meyerson.

"So in the bedroom, Norman. The clock—"

"In my bedroom also is no clock."

Schussler's brow furrowed. "Listen, Norman. Are you telling me that you don't have on your wrist or in a pocket, a watch—and that in this whole six-room apartment you don't have one single clock?!"

"That's right."

"For God's *sake*, Norman! What do you do when you have to know what time it is?"

Meyerson shrugged. "I use my bugle."

"Your *what?!*"

"My bugle." Meyerson leaned over and from the floor lifted an old, battered bugle, went to a window, raised the pane, put the bugle to his lips, and blared a forceful: "Ra-ta-ta-ta-*tah!*"

And from a dozen flats in the courtyard came this litany: "What's the matter with you, you crazy man, playing the bugle at a quarter to eleven at night?!"

Note: No collection of humorous episodes would be complete without the following well-known exchange—which, no matter how often told, loses nothing by repetition:

The hostess was making the rounds, at her tea for the ladies, with a platter of freshly baked, home-made cookies. "So, Mrs. Pearlstein," she smiled, "have some cookies."

"No, thank you," said Mrs. Pearlstein. "They're absolutely delicious— but I already had four."

"You already had *five*," said the hostess. "But who's counting?"

Terence Spillman and Chaim Glatkin were crossing the street, not far from the Cathedral of St. John the Divine, when a motorcycle roared up, knocked Glatkin to the ground, and roared away.

Spillman bent over his old friend, "Chaim! Chaim! Are you hurt?"

To his astonishment, he saw Glatkin, eyes closed, make the sign of the cross.

"Chaim!"

"I'm all right, don't worry." Glatkin sat up.

"Thank God! . . . I thought you were on the very edge of death—you, making the sign of the cross?!"

"What sign of what cross?" blinked Glatkin.

"You went like this—" Spillman touched his brow, chest, left shoulder, right shoulder.

"Oh, *that*," said Glatkin. "I was just testing: spectacles, testicles, fountain pen, wallet."

Said Mrs. Heffelman, "Listen, Goldie. I hear you had this year a very, very bad time."

"Why 'had'?" said Mrs. Kopman. "You think everything is by me now hotsy-totsy?"

"No?"

"No."

"So tell me what's happened?"

"What's happened is, in May, my darling little dog was run over. In June, my daughter Freda ran away with a married man. In July, my son lost his job. In August, my husband had a fatal heart attack. And next Tuesday," Mrs. Kopman sighed, "the painters are coming."

When Messrs. Motzner and Krupnick opened their new store, they decided, for tactical reasons, to call it "Donahue and Donahue."

On their first day, a customer asked one of the salesmen, "I want to talk to Mr. Donahue."

"Which Mr. Donahue do you want?" replied the salesman. "Motzner or Krupnick?"

The resident pediatrician was making his morning rounds in the ward, trailed by six interns. "Sickle-cell anemia may be found in black children, especially if their parents come from the Caribbean. Tay-Sachs syndrome occurs in adult Jews, of course; but Jewish children are more easily identified by one fact. Can anyone tell me what that is?"

"Certainly," said one intern. "Heartburn."

Father Malachy was walking down a street in Boston when he saw a large banner over a store:

GREENBERG AND O'SULLIVAN

Father Malachy hastened in with a broad, broad smile. He was greeted by a bearded man wearing a *yarmulka.*

"Well, sir," beamed Father Malachy, "I jist want ye t' know how foine it is afther all these years, for a simple Irishman to see your people and mine working together—and as partners! What a sorprise. What a sorprise!"

"Father, I thank you. But I'll give you a bigger surprise," said the old man. "*I'm* O'Sullivan."

THE WALLS OF JERICHO

ACT I

Scene: Classroom, Sunday School at Beth Hillel Synagogue

MR. AARONS	Well, children, who can tell me the answer to this question: Who was it who blew down the walls of Jericho. . . . Jonas?
JONAS SPRINGER	Don't look at me, sir. *I* didn't!

ACT II
Elias Springer's Home
The phone rings.

MR. SPRINGER   Hello.

MR. AARONS   Hello, Mr. Springer?

MR. SPRINGER   Yeah.

MR. AARONS   This is Mr. Aarons, from Beth Hillel. I'm sorry to bother you, but I must talk to you about your boy, Jonas. When I asked him, during Bible class this morning, who it was who blew down the walls of Jericho, he answered, "Don't look at me! *I* didn't."

MR. SPRINGER   Look, Mr. Aarons. If my Joney says he didn't do it, he didn't do it!
                (hangs up abruptly)

ACT III
Rabbi's Office

RABBI LOWENSTEIN   Mr. Aarons, I hear that when you asked Jonas Springer, in your class, 'Who blew down the walls of Jericho?' the boy answered 'Don't look at me, *I* didn't!' Is that so?

MR. AARONS   Yes. But the boy's father *assures* me that if Jonas says he didn't do it, he didn't do it!

RABBI LOWENSTEIN   Well, I have known Elias Springer for fifteen years. And I can vouch for his honesty!

ACT IV
Office of Nathan Fardroos

RABBI LOWENSTEIN   Since you are the chairman of our synagogue's board of trustees, there is one little matter I ought to bring to your attention. You know Mr. Springer, of course. Well, his son Jonas is in our Bible class. And when the teacher, Mr. Aarons, asked who blew down the walls of Jericho, little Jonas replied: "Not me." Mr. Aarons told this to Mr. Springer, who insisted that his son could be trusted! I asked Mr. Aarons what he thought, and he said he believed the father! When Mr. Aarons asked me what *I* thought, I told him that I have known Elias Springer for many years, and if *he* says Jonas is telling the truth—

MR. FARDROOS   All right, enough! I'm a busy man, rabbi. There's
no need to make a big deal about this. Just have
the wall fixed, and send the bill to me.

In the card room of a resort hotel in the Poconos, four strangers arranged
a bridge game. As they sat down, the first man said, "Let's introduce
ourselves. I'm Albert Carman."

"My name," said the second player, "is William Cohane."

"I," said the third man, "am Joe Cronin."

The fourth man: "I'm Jack."

"Jack what?"

"Also Cohen."

Ephriam Gerbner could scarcely believe his eyes. There, on Yom Kippur,
the most holy fast day, the Day of Atonement, at a table right in the window
of the Sea King Restaurant, sat his old friend, Meyer Perlmutter—eating
oysters!

Into the Sea King dashed Gerbner. "Meyer! My God! Eating?! Today?!
And *oysters* yet?"

"So?" shrugged Perlmutter. "Isn't there an *r* in Yom Kippur?"

A bearded old man once patted my head, when I was ten, and chuckled
fondly, "You look like a nice boy. You should live to a hundred and
twenty-one!"

When I told this to my father, he explained, "Jews say that—because
Moses, according to legend, lived to be a hundred and twenty."

"Oh . . . but why did the old man tell me 'a hundred and twenty-*one*'?"

My father smiled. "Maybe he didn't want you to die suddenly."

The four ladies were on the porch of Mrs. Ruttenberg's Villa d'Esther
resort, in the Poconos, rocking back and forth, taking in the scenic beauties.
After a bit, the first woman sighed, "*Oy* . . ."

The other three sighed in sympathy.

Soon, a second woman sighed, "*Oy vey* . . ." The others nodded.

A third woman said, "*Oy, Gottenyu!* . . ." and the others again nodded.

At last, the fourth rocker said, "So. Enough talk about the children. Let's
go for a walk."

Comtesse de Rothschild, a distinguished hostess in French society, cultivated, a fine painter and harpist, at home in four languages, lay in childbirth

in the master bedroom of her magnificent mansion on the Boulevard de Victoire.

Downstairs, Comte de Rothschild, her husband, was pacing back and forth anxiously. From above came the countess's sudden cry of pain, and a heart-rending wail. "Raymond!" cried the count to Dr. Pyorette, the obstetrician, "Can't you do *something?*"

"The nurses are doing all that need be done, *mon cher* Georges. Calm yourself. Come. Let us pass the time with a game of backgammon."

The two men settled themselves in chairs before a Louis XVI table. Dr. Pyorette rattled the dice in his cup. . . .

A high, shrill cry from above froze the players. The countess was crying, "*Mon dieu!* Have pity! *Mon dieu!*"

The count leaped up. "Come on—"

"No, no," Dr. Pyorette clutched the count's jacket. "There's plenty of time. Sit down. It's your throw."

The men exchanged moves with the ivory pieces.

A long wail came from the countess. "Oh, *God.* Oh, *God!*"

The count again leaped to his feet—and Dr. Pyorette grabbed him. "No, *no*, Georges! There's time . . ."

The doctor shook the dice.

"*Mama mia! O mama mia!*" the countess ululated.

Up leaped the count—and again the doctor snatched his coattails, saying, "Georges, *Georges!* Not yet. Not yet, *mon cher ami.* . . . It's your throw, I believe."

Count Rothschild wiped his brow and sat down and rattled the dice in his cup. . . .

Soon, from above, came a mighty, "*Ge-valt!*"

Up leaped Dr. Pyorette, "Now, Georges!"

And the two men raced upstairs.

(P.S. *Gevalt* is the universal Yiddish exclamation of pain, fear, or cry for help.)

On its maiden voyage, the S.S. *Shalom,* the first great ocean liner of Israel, steamed into the harbor of New York to a truly tumultuous greeting. But one observer was not tumultuous. He frowned, "That boat . . . you know something: she doesn't *look* Jewish!"

Note: "Bialy" is the abbreviated name of Bialystock, in which Russian or Polish town bakers first (supposedly) made those slightly underbaked rolls, shaped like a tiny, tiny rubber wading pool, with baked onion sprinkled in the declivity, that have become second in popularity only to bagels.

The Richard F. Lowenfelds bought a fine house in Sands Point, Long Island, staffed it with a French cook, an Irish maid, and an English butler, and invited three couples from New York out for the first Sunday brunch of the season: the Goldsmiths, the Rubloffs, and the Chertoks.

On Sunday morning, Mrs. Lowenfeld noticed that the table was set for twelve. She rang for the butler. "Earnshaw," she said, "did you set the table for *six* couples?"

"Yes, madam."

"But I told you we were having three couples—plus Mr. Lowenfeld and myself. That's eight in all."

"Yes, madam."

"Then why did you set the table for twelve?"

"Because, madam," said the butler, "Mrs. Chertok telephoned an hour ago to say that they are bringing the Bagels and the Bialys."

The waves were high and rough and pounded at the shores of Pompano Beach, and the lifeguard pulled the limp form of Maxwell Sonnenfeld out of the angry waters. A crowd formed around them.

"Stand back!" boomed the lifeguard.

"Get a doctor!"

"Give the man air!"

"Get his wife!"

"Stand *back!*" the lifeguard shouted. "I'm going to give him artificial respiration."

"Never!" cried Mrs. Sonnenfeld, pressing her way to the fore. "My Max gets real respiration or nothing!"

On the train from Boston to New Bedford, Mr. Josephson sat down opposite an attractive young man. After a moment, the young man said, "Sir, may I ask you what time it is?"

Mr. Josephson pulled his gold watch out of his vest pocket, snapped the cover open, and said: "Twenty-two minutes past eleven."

"Thank you."

Mr. Josephson put his watch back, studied the young man, and said, "Are you by any chance going to New Bedford?"

"Yes, I am."

Mr. Josephson stared at him, said, "Go to hell—and don't say a word to me again!" and opened his newspaper with a flourish.

The young man had turned red. He said, "Sir, I resent that! . . . Do you hate Jews?"

"Oh, no. I'm a Jew myself."

"Then why—just because I asked you a polite question—did you—"

Mr. Josephson placed both hands on his chest. "Don't jump to conclusions, young man. . . . Listen. Suppose I gave you a polite answer, after you said you were going to New Bedford—like 'That's good' or 'Nice day' or 'Staying long?' We would start a conversation. You would ask me, 'Do you live in New Bedford? . . . Do you take this train often? . . . What business are you in?' and I would ask you what you do for a living—and so on, for a half-hour, maybe. And then, because you are a nice-looking young man, I would ask you to come to dinner at my home—where you would meet my wife and my daughter, Sylvia, our only child, a *lovely* girl, beautiful, talented, a wonderful cook, loves music, reads a lot. . . . You would undoubtedly ask her to go out on a date. So you and my Sylvia would go out, and—believe me!—young man, you would fall head over heels in love! . . . So soon you would come to me and say, 'Mr. Josephson, I would like your consent to marry your daughter' . . . Young man, I would absolutely break your heart! Could *I* let my only daughter marry a fellow who doesn't even *own a watch?!*" Mr. Josephson shook his head. "No. . . . So I figured it best for me, for Sylvia, for you, too—to stop the whole business before it can even start. That's why I said, 'Go to hell!' before—and that's why I say, 'Go to hell!' now. . . . Do me a favor. Don't say another word to me until we get to New Bedford!"

Mrs. Gorshky sent this telegram from Leningrad to her husband in Kovno:

SAYS TO OPERATE OPERATE

RUCHEL

To this message, Mr. Gorshky replied:

SAYS TO OPERATE OPERATE

NAHUM

The police at once arrested Mr. Gorshky, beat him up, threw him into a cell, then asked, "All right now, you agent of the capitalist bourgeoisie! What secret code are you using?"

"What code? What secret?" asked bewildered Gorshky.

"Do you think we're fools? Just read these messages!"

"Certainly," said Gorshky. "But first I must tell you that my Ruchel is sick, and the doctors in Kovno couldn't help her. So she went to Leningrad to consult a famous surgeon. And after she saw him, she wired me like this—" He picked up her telegram and read: " 'Says to operate . . . *Operate?*' . . . I thought over the surgeon's recommendation, and I answered her"—Gorshky picked up a copy of his reply. " 'Says to operate? Operate!' "

No Jewish girl reaches the age of thirty without having been asked to marry at least four times—once by her father, three times by her mother.

At the festive table, during the Sheineman's Passover party, the conversation sparkled. At one point, Mr. Sheineman asked Mrs. Glantz, on his right, "Someone told me you're an expert on Omar Khayyam."

"Who's a *maven?*" she asked. "I only know what I like and what I don't like."

"So? What's your feeling about the Rubaiyat?"

Mrs. Glantz shrugged. "Not bad, not great. But speaking personally, *I* prefer Chianti."

When the Glantzes left the party, Mr. Glantz said, "Mildred, why do you always have to show off? Why do you have to pretend you know it all? The Rubaiyat isn't a *wine!*"

"Omigod," moaned Mrs. Glantz.

"It's a cheese."

One of the telephone operators at the famous law firm Fleming, Boyd, Harwood, and Kassenbaum answers the switchboard, "Fleming, Boyd, Harwood, and Kassenbaum."

"Hello, may I please speak to Jacob Kassenbaum?"

"I'm sorry, sir, but Mr. Kassenbaum is not in today. This is Yom Kippur."

"Well, Miss Kippur, please tell Mr. Kassenbaum his bifocals are ready."

WHY DO JEWS SAY "WHY?"

Lord Strathmore asked Lapidus, his tailor, "Why is it that you Jews always answer a question with another question?"

Lapidus pursed his lips. "Why not?"

The next day, Strathmore asked the driver of his taxi, one Isaac Lipsky, "Driver, why is it that Jews always answer a question with another question?"

"Who told you that?" sneered Lipsky.

That Sunday, Strathmore asked a Jewish neighbor, "I say, Herbert, why do Jews seem to answer every question with a question?"

Herbert smiled, "But who doesn't?"

A week later, Strathmore asked Dr. Shulman, his dentist, "Why do Jews always answer a question with another question?"

Shulman's eyes rounded. "They *do?*"

Aboard the Concorde to New York, Lord Strathmore asked the bearded man in the seat next to him, "Why do you Jews always answer a question with another question?"

"How should I know?" replied the rabbi.

And at dinner, several days later, Strathmore asked the famous banker, Roger Lehmann Loebel, "May I ask you something, Roger? *Why* do Jews always answer a question with another question?"

"*Do* they?" exclaimed Loebel.

So Lord Strathmore, utterly frustrated, asked a priest, "Father, perhaps you can help me."

"I'll try."

"Well, it is said that whenever a member of the Jewish faith is asked a question he answers with another question. You serve on several interreligious committees. Is that true?"

Sighed the priest, "Now what idjit iver told ye a silly thing like that?"

Mr. Lurie, a resident of Los Angeles for fifty years, approached a young man who was waiting for a bus on Wilshire Boulevard. "Young man, excuse me. Can I ask a personal question? Are you Jewish?"

"No, I'm not."

"Are you sure?"

"Of course I'm sure!" The young man laughed.

"You're not just teasing me?"

"No. Why should I tease You?"

Mr. Lurie sighed. "Well, excuse my question. I didn't mean to embarrass you."

"Wait, mister," the young man glanced around and, lowering his voice, said, "can you keep a secret?"

"Absolutely!"

"Well, not a soul in the world knows it—except you. The truth is: I am a Jew."

"My, my," clucked Mr. Lurie. "You don't *look* Jewish."

Herbie Klonsky came into his boss's office with trepidation. "Mr. Rodolovitch, I don't like to bother you, but—well, maybe you wouldn't mind too much if—if I take off tomorrow? . . ."

"Tomorrow?" Mr. Rodolovitch said. "What type holiday is tomorrow?"

"It's not exactly a holiday," said Klonsky. "It's—our anniversary. Wedding anniversary. For me and my Shaindl. Twenty-five *years,* Mr. Rodolovitch."

"Oh . . . Well, I suppose it will be all right you shouldn't come to work. . . . Take the day off."

"*Thank* you, Mr. Rodolovitch."

Just as Herbie was going through the door, Rodolovitch cried, "But one thing, Klonsky. Do I have to go through this nonsense every twenty-five years?!"

The teacher said, "Children, since this is the first day of a new term, I want each of you to stand up, give us your name—clearly—and your age, and mention your favorite hobby."

The first child rose and said, "My name is Andrew Blake. I'm almost ten years old . . . I like to swim."

The second student rose: "My name is Jimmy Cort. I'm nine and a half years old. My hobby is collecting stamps."

The third student rose: "My name is Morris Wexler. I'm ten, and I pledge five dollars."

"Hey, Pete," said Waldman, "have you heard the latest joke about the two Jews who—"

"Hold it. Wait," said Pete Hyman. "Why does it always have to be two Jews? Are the Jews the only people in the world you can tell funny stories about? Wouldn't a story be just as funny if it was about two Mexicans? Or two Japanese?"

"Okay, okay," said Waldman. "I'll try it your way. Once there were two Japanese, partners in a *teffilin* [phylacteries] factory. One day, going to a meeting of the UJA, the first Japanese said to his partner, 'Menachem, next Yom Kippur, I hope to be in Boston, because my grandson, Erwin, will be *Bar Mitzva!*' So the second Japanese answered, 'Israel, I'm going to a circumcision . . .' "

Said Pete, "Forget it."

Beckman and Moscot, old friends, had sat in silence on their favorite park bench for hours, lost in thought. Finally, Beckman gave a long, sad sigh.

Moscot said, "You're telling *me?*"

"Hello, Mandel. What's new?"

"Good. With me, everything is good!"

"Really? Everyone knows you almost went broke. So how can you say everything's *good?*"

"Because it is. I get up every morning good and tired. I come home every night good and depressed. I'm good and disgusted with my children, and I'm good and sick of my wife. In fact, my whole life is so rotten, I'm good and tired of living!"

Into the posh aisles of Kensington Gourmet Foods came a bearded figure in a black hat with a broad, flat rim, a white shirt, no necktie, and wearing the long black caftan of a *Chasid*, a most pious disciple of the sainted holy man, Itzkhak Ben Mendelovitch.

The *Chasid* surveyed the fine, rare comestibles for which Kensington Gourmet Foods was known, then stopped in front of the station where, behind a glass partition, slabs of meat were arrayed: roast beef, turkey, bologna, liverwurst. . . .

"Can I help you?" asked one of the men behind the counter.

"Eh . . . mmh . . . yeah . . ." The *Chasid* appeared to be debating his choice. "Eh—yeah! I'll take, please, a helf-pound that nice corn biff . . ."

The clerk cleared his throat. "Sir, that is not corned beef. It's baked Virginia—*ham.*"

The *Chasid* eyed the clerk frostily. "Tell me, young man . . . did I *esk* you?!"

Old Hyman Sisselberg, crossing Fifth Avenue in front of St. Patrick's Cathedral, was knocked down by a hit-and-run driver.

He lay there, half conscious, as people crowded around him. A priest pushed his way through the crowd, knelt beside Hyman Sisselberg, and out of force of habit quickly said, "My son, do you believe in God the Father, God the Son, and God the Holy Ghost?"

"*Gottenyu,*" croaked Sisselberg. "I'm dying, and he asks riddles."

Two old friends were sitting on a park bench observing their prolonged, familiar, silent communion. At last one said, "How are things?"

"Eh!" shrugged the other. "How about you?"

"Mnyeh."

In an hour they rose. "Well, goodbye. It's always nice to have a heart-to-heart talk."

A lady from Brooklyn was watching a parade on Fifth Avenue.

"Look!" someone cried. "There goes the mayor of Dublin—and he's a Jew!"

"*Ai-ai-ai,*" clucked the matron. "Where could such a thing happen? Only in America!"

Two men sat opposite each other in the Amtrak train. One was reading a newspaper. After a while, the other man said, "Uh—going to Philadelphia?"

The first man lowered his newspaper. "No," he said. "I'm going to Baltimore. My business is insurance. My name is Henry Slott. I live in Great Neck. I'm not rich, I have a son at Swarthmore and a daughter who's married. My wife's maiden name was Portanow and she comes from New Haven. I'm a Republican. I can't play golf. I do play bridge. I spend my summers in Westhampton and in winter I spend two weeks every December in Pompano Beach. I go to a Reform temple, contribute to the UJA and the

Community Chest. I don't have a brother of the same name because I don't have a brother, and my sister you couldn't possibly have known because she died thirty years ago in Detroit. So: if I've forgotten anything you're interested in, please ask me right now, because I want to finish this paper and take a nap until I get to Balitmore."

Azriel Chyet, a Jewish patriarch, was on the witness stand in Brooklyn.

"How old are you?" asked the district attorney.

"I am, thank the Lord for His goodness, eighty-two years old."

"What was that?"

"I said, 'I am, thank the Lord for His goodness, eighty-two years old.' "

"Just answer the question!" snapped the D.A. "Nothing else. Now, how—old—are—you?"

"Eighty-two," said the old man, "thank the Lord for His—"

The judge banged his gavel and cut in, "The witness will answer the question—*only* the question, without additional comment, or be held in contempt of court! Do you understand that?"

Up rose the counsel for the defense: "Your Honor, may I ask the question? . . .

"Try," said the judge.

The lawyer said, "Mr. Chyet, thank the Lord for His goodness, how old are you?"

Beamed the old man, "Eighty-two."

Mr. Korshack had only one grandson, a sixteen-year-old named Bruce. But what could Mr. Korshack and his grandson possibly have in common? Whatever the old man wanted to talk about, bored Bruce. The things Bruce was immersed in, bewildered his grandfather. The greatest passion in Bruce's life, it seemed, was—basketball. Every moment of his spare time was spent in watching professional basketball on television.

One night, Bruce went to a school dance—and Mr. Korshack glued himself before the TV to watch the game between the Milwaukee Bucks and the Los Angeles Lakers.

When Bruce came home, after midnight, Mr. Korshack leaped to his feet. "Bruce! Bruce! I watched that game for you! The whole game!!"

Bruce was properly excited. "Oh, great, gramps! What was the final score?"

"The final score," said Mr. Korshack, "was ninety-nine to one hundred and two!"

"And who won?"

The old man, hesitated. "Eh—one hundred and two."

When Solly Nayfack returned from a tour of Israel, Greece, and Italy, he told his partners in Lochinvar's Men's Wear, "The climax of our whole trip through Europe was the Vatican. You know, we had a little audience with the pope!"

"The *pope*, Solly? You kidding?"

"Absolutely not. The pope—in person!"

"So, Solly, what type man would you call him?"

"Very fine," said Solly. "Spiritual. Dignified. Size forty-six long."

"If you want to live forever," Mendel Minkoff told a very rich cousin, "come to live in our little town."

"Is it that beautiful?"

"Beautiful? It's the ugliest town you ever saw in your whole life!"

"Is the climate that good?" asked the cousin.

"The climate is without a doubt absolutely terrible!"

"Then why in God's name do you tell me to live there?!"

"Look at the statistics!" exclaimed Mendel. "In three hundred and fifty years, never—not once—has a rich man died there!"

Three women were discussing their sons, with customary pride.

"My boy," said the first, "is a famous surgeon, and president of his medical association!"

"My son," said the second, "is a professor in the law school."

"My son," said the third, "is a rabbi."

"A *rabbi!* What kind of career is that for a Jewish boy?"

See also **Accents, Anti-Semitism, Curses, God, Immigrants, Ingenuity, Israel, Rabbis, Restaurants, Retorts, Stratagems, Waiters, Yiddish**

Journalism

A famous New York editor sent a note to his staff saying that since the word "news" was plural, it was to be used that way from then on. Example:

All the news from the flooded area are pessimistic.

To a reporter on assignment in Europe, this editor cabled:

TWO NEW YORK PAPERS FEATURED
STORIES ON LOOMING CRISIS.
HAVE YOU BEEN ABLE TO UNEARTH
FURTHER NEWS?

The reporter's answer read:

SORRY, UNABLE TO FIND A
SINGLE NEW.

Into the managing editor's office at Glasgow's *Daily Herald* came Toby McLarnin, the new feature reporter. "Ye want to see me, Mr. Dunfeenen?"

"Aye, that I do," said Dunfeenen. "Y'r story o' the drownin' bairn—very good, McLarnin. *Very* good."

"Oh, thank you."

"McLarnin, how much are we payin' ye?"

"Therrty pounds a week, sir."

Mr. Dunfeenen nodded, beaming. "Ay'm glad t' hear it."

Three months later, Toby was called into the managing editor's office again. "Th' interview ye did with Lord Cagnavoron's nevew, Toby. Top-notch!"

"Thank you, Mr. Dunfeenen."

"Lad, how much are we payin' ye?"

"Therrty pounds a week, sir."

Mr. Dunfeenen smiled. "That's nice . . ."

A year later Toby was summoned to the office of the editor-in chief, Muir Ross-Ferguson. " 'Tis good work y're doin' for us, young McLarnin. Tell me, lad. How mooch is your salary?"

"Therrty pounds a week—the same I have been getting iver since I started. . . ."

Muir Ross-Ferguson cleared his throat, glanced out of the window, thought for a moment, then turned back to McLarnin. "Therrty pounds, is it?"

"Yes, sir."

Mr. Ross-Ferguson beamed. "That's very good, lad. . . . Ta-ta."

See also **Bloopers, Boo-boos, Headlines That Haunt Me, News Items That Haunt Me, Reviews of Note, Typos**

Juries

The judge asked the last (twelfth) prospective juror: "Do you have any opinion as to whether the defendant in this case is innocent or guilty of the crime with which he is charged?"

"I do not," said the prospective juror.

"Do you have any reservations, in your conscience, about the death penalty?"

"Not in this case."

Jury: Twelve people of average intelligence who couldn't get off jury duty, and who decide whether the prosecution or the defense has the better lawyer.

The witness was old Mr. Blifeld. The judge asked him, "Are you personally acquainted with any of the people on this jury?"

"Soitinly."

"How many do you know?"

"Let's see, mmm . . . two . . . t'ree . . . altogadder: seven."

"Seven?" The judge frowned. "Do you mean to say you know more than half of this jury?"

"I'll go foider," said Mr. Blifeld. "I know more dan all twelve put togadder!"

The judge was irate and made no effort to hide it from the jury. "What possible evidence," he cried, "could have persuaded you to acquit the defendant?"

The foreman said, "Your honor—insanity!"

"All *twelve* of you?" bleated the judge.

See also **Courts, Evidence, Lawyers**

Just Jokes

For years, Rubin Motzer's children and friends had been urging him to get a hearing aid, but the old man objected, "Nonsense! My hearing is A-Number One! It's just that people don't talk loud enough!"

One day, Mr. Motzer passed a shabby discount store that was flying a flag:

SALE! SALE!

In the window, where radios, calculators, cassettes, *et alia* were jammed together, a sign read

BARGAINS!!
EVERYTHING MUST GO!
40% off on Cameras
50% off on Sunglasses
60% off on Hearing Aids

Mr. Motzer hurried in.

Within ten minutes he had been fitted for a hearing aid.

The old man stepped back into the street with a broad smile.

A voice hailed him, "Rubin! Say, Rubin!" It was Joe Kipnis. "Hello there, Rubin. What're you doing in this part of town?"

"*This!*" Rubin pointed to his ear, and the cord leading from it. "Just bought a hearing aid. It's wonderful! My kids were absolutely right. What a difference! Why, now I can hear like an eighteen-year-old!"

"That's great," said Kipnis. "What kind is it?"

Motzer glanced at his wrist. "A quarter to five."

Flander was absolutely steeped in sleep when the phone rang. He pulled the cover over his ears, but the phone rang and rang. Groaning, Flander lifted the phone. "Yeah?"

"Minnie?" a voice asked.

Flander groaned. "No—"

"Is this Glenwood-six, six, nine, one, three?"

Flander's outrage could not be contained as he cried: "You number, you have the wrong idiot!"

A traveling salesman came to the door of the farmhouse and said, "My car's broken down, it's too far to walk to town—do you have a room I can sleep in tonight?"

"The only spare bedroom I got," said the farmer, "is my son's. You'll have to sleep with him."

The salesman turned white. "My God, I'm in the wrong joke!"

Why is it that the walls in a hotel room are very thin when you try to sleep and very thick when you want to listen?

ARTHUR GODFREY

Sean McAfee stopped a man on a busy Shannon street with a hearty, "Bless me soul, if it ain't me old friend Errol Dooley in th' flesh! And if me eyes do not deceive me, it's at least ten-twenty pounds y've taken off. An' your *hair*, man? Is that a wig?"

"*I*," growled the man, "am *not* your old friend! My name is not Errol Dooley. I happen to be *English*, sir. My name is Foster James-Wingham."

"Blimey!" McAfee winked. "Changed your name, too, eh, Errol?"

Barney and Marty were forever "rating" women—those they knew, and those they saw but didn't know.

One day, Marty said, "Ever since we started rating girls, I've been waiting to hear you say, just *once*, 'That girl is a ten.' "

"You show me a ten, I'll admit she's a ten," said Barney.

"How about Rhea Blum?"

"Nah. The best I give her is a five."

"How's about Jo-Anne Sokol?"

Barney pondered. "Too hefty."

"'Rita! Rita Welner!'"

"Rita Welner? . . ." Barney closed his eyes. "She's pretty, all right, but . . ."

"Her father is worth five million dollars!"

Barney reflected. "Oh, Rita is a ten! For *looks*, she's a six—plus four for her father."

Colonel Fairlie Strothingham, as respectable and impressive a Son of the South as you could ever hope to find, telephoned his mansion from his office. "Hello. How are you?"

"Ah'm jest fine."

"Everything all right at home?"

"I—uh—giss so, suh."

"What do you mean you *guess* so? Anything wrong with my wife?"

"No, suh. She ain't sick—"

"Then put her on the phone."

Silence.

"I said, 'Put—her—on—the—phone!' "

"Well, suh, that's jest it. Yo' wife is in the bedroom—but she ain't alone."

"What?!"

"She's in that there bed with a man from Atlanta—"

"Now, listen. Listen carefully," seethed Colonel Strothingham. "Go into my study. There's a gun in the desk. Get it. Go upstairs. Open the bedroom door—and if you see my wife in bed with that man, shoot! Shoot them both!"

"Oh, sir, Ah cain't do that!"

"You do that right now, do you hear? If you don't, I'm coming right home and *I'll* kill the two of them—and you, too! . . ."

"Oh, Lord," moaned the servant.

"Now go and do what I told you. . . . I'll wait on this phone . . ."

In five or six minutes, the quavery voice of the servant returned on the line. "Okay, suh. Ah's through."

"Did you shoot them both?"

"Yas, suh. An' Ah was so nervous, Ah ran to the back garden, and Ah threw the gun in the swimmin' pool, and now—"

"Swimming pool?" echoed the colonel. *"We* don't have a swimming pool. . . . Listen! Is this Fairfax-eight, seven, seven, oh, three?"

Judge Christie leaned forward and said, "Are you trying to tell this court that the defendant actually strangled his wife in a disco, in front of three hundred people?!"

"Yes, sir."

"But didn't anyone try to stop him?"

"No, sir. Everyone thought they were dancing."

Ada was admiring Jennifer's new engagement ring. "It's *gorgeous.* . . . It must be very valuable."

"W-well, Hubert told me he bought it from a millionaire."

"Then it must have cost a bundle!"

"W-well, Hubie didn't tell me the name of the millionaire, until yesterday. . . ."

"What is it?"

"Woolworth."

The plumber rang the doorbell. The housewife answered.

"I come to fix your broken hot-water pipe."

"We no got broke pipe," said the woman.

The plumber consulted a note-paper in his hand. "Are you Mrs. Gonzales?"

"No. She move. Four month back."

"How do you like that?" said the plumber in disgust. "All you people are the same. You call for a plumber, hollering it's an emergency and can I rush right over—and before I can even answer the call, you pack up and move!"

Mr. Nathan was going through some old files when, to his astonishment, he found a claim check for a pair of shoes he had brought to Aristides Narikos's Shoe Repair—fourteen years ago!

That afternoon he went over to the shoe repair store. "Mr. Narikos, I know this is going to surprise you—and maybe this is all too late—but you were supposed to put new heels on a pair of my shoes—"

"Sura!" smiled Narikos.

"—fourteen years—ago!"

Narikos turned pale. "Four-a-tin yiss? . . . Eh, you got to have check!"

"I do." Mr. Nathan handed Narikos the old faded check.

Narikos gulped, scratched his chin, muttered to himself in Greek, disappeared behind a beaded curtain. After a bit, he returned. "Boss, you shoes—dey brown?"

"I think so."

"And got da buckle, not da laces?"

"That's right!" beamed Mr. Nathan.

"Need new heel?"

"Exactly."

"They be ready Wenadsday."

Joel Glickman met Weissman at Feuerman's Delicious, a cafeteria near Union Square. No sooner did they sit down at a table than Glickman exclaimed, "I had a year, Phil, it shouldn't happen to a *dog*. In June, business was so bad I thought I'd go bankrupt. In July, I had to get a loan from the bank. In August, I wished it was still July. In September—"

"Stop!" cried Weissman. "Why are you ruining my lunch? I don't get one word out before you clobber me with all your problems. You want problems? *I'll* give you problems! Last year, my wife ran away with my partner. Then a fire burned my whole apartment to a crisp. On New Year's, my daughter told me she had to have an abortion. And you pepper my head with your problems?! You heard my troubles. Could anything have been worse?!"

Glickman sighed. "November."

I don't know what to get my wife anymore. First she wanted a mink, so I got her a mink. Then she wanted a silver fox, so I bought her a silver fox. Now she wants a lynx—but that's ridiculous. The house is already full of animals.

HENRY MORGAN

Scene: The Bubble 'n Squeak Pub in the East End of London

"Blimey, mate, that cousin o' yours is *daft!*" sneered "Bub" Tomkin.

"Bloody well not," Jock Adair replied. "What's 'e done now?"

"Voted for Winston Churchill!"

"Eh? That makes him daft?" Jock slammed his beer mug on the bar. "Do' ye rightly know how many Cockney lads voted for Winnie?"

Tomkin's eyes narrowed. "*Yes*terday?!"

Mr. and Mrs. Barry Crosby, from Tenafly, had just returned from their first trip to Europe and were regaling their friends with stories.

"And did you get to Rome?" one asked.

"Naturally!"

"How did you like the Colosseum?"

Mr. Crosby made a regal gesture. "Very nice—"

"*If,*" Mrs. Crosby cut in, "you like modern."

"Do you know what it means to come home every night," says Henny Youngman, "to the woman who will give you a little affection, a lot of tenderness, and an ocean of love? It means you went to the wrong house, that's what it means."

Edward Fothersby bought £400 worth of scuba-diving equipment and went down, down into the water off his estate in Barbados. Intrigued by the magnificent fish, he swam on. . . . Soon, to his astonishment, he beheld a stranger in swimming trunks!

Fothersby grabbed his underwater pad and on it wrote, with his underwater pencil:

> I spent £400 on gear. You have
> *none*. How can you stay down so deep?

He handed the pad and pencil to the swimmer, who hastily scribbled on the pad and shoved it back to Fothersby.

> I'm drowning, you jerk.

Eugene Horton of Bayside, Long Island, had made a killing in the market. At once his wife, Ruby, called Perry Duane, a well-known decorator, to her home. "I want you to redecorate this place, Mr. Duane. From top to bottom. Money is no object!"

Mr. Duane said, "Splendid. Di*vine*. Now, Mrs. Horton, would you like the furniture to be modern?"

"Modern? N-no. That's too new to be classy."

"Then what about French?"

"French?" echoed Ruby Horton. "How do me and my husband, both of us from Canarsie, come to French?"

"Well, perhaps Italian?"

"*Ital*– God forbid!"

Perry Duane pondered, then sighed, "Madam, permit me—before I can go any further, I must know what *period* you like."

"What 'period'?" Ruby Horton thought for a moment. "Mr. Duane, the period I really want is for my friends to walk in, take one look around—and drop dead. Period."

JIM: What did the usherette say when her brassiere strap broke?
JOE: What?
JIM: "I have two down in front."

Old Isaac Arp handed Mr. Zeligson, the pharmacist, his latest prescription. In half an hour, Zeligman gave him three little bottles of pills.

"All these?" asked Arp. "Why so many types pills?"

"The red ones calm your nerves," said Mr. Zeligman. "The white ones will help your headache, and the blue ones are to relieve your sinuses."

Mr. Arp clucked in admiration. "How do you like that? Such little pills, and each one knows exactly where to go!"

The Friends of Douglas Park in Chicago met to consider ways of improving the pretty lagoon. Mrs. Mary Lou Stopes suggested, "In my opinion, brothers and sisters, the best thing to do is to put in a flock of gon*dol*as. I seen pictures of gon*dol*as in a place in Italy where all them Eyetalian folk was havin' the *time* of their life!"

"I do agree with Sister Stopes about them most pleasin'-to-the-eye gon*dol*as," said the chairman. "But they is bound to be *mighty* expensive. We cain't afford such improvements!"

After many sighs, up shot the hand of Rufus T. Pratt. "Brothers and sisters, I make a motion we get jist *two* of them gon*dol*as—one male, one female. I hear they breed faster'n rabbits!"

It was old Mr. Eizenstat's first ocean voyage. And the third day out, the ship ran into a terrible storm. The heavings and lurchings and rolling of the vessel forced ashen Mr. Eizenstat to the rail, where he hung and retched in agony.

A voice from a kindly steward piped up, "Don't be too alarmed, sir. No one has ever died of seasickness."

"Oh, God," moaned Eizenstat. "Don't say that. Only that hope is what's keeping me alive."

WIFE:	Wasn't today the day everyone in the plant had to take an intelligence test?
HUSBAND:	That's right, dear.
WIFE:	Did you take the test, too?
HUSBAND:	Absolutely.
WIFE:	How did you do?
HUSBAND:	Let me put it this way: thank God I own the company!

A friend once asked Bob Hope: "What went through your mind, Bob, the first time you got a look at Dorothy Lamour in that sarong?"

"I never gave it a second thought," said Hope.

"Truly?"

"Sure. I was too busy with the first one."

Fergus Cameron, hungry, huddled against the cold, shivering, paused to examine the incredible viands displayed in the window of the world-famous Caledonia Grill on Princes Street in Edinburgh. His eyes devoured the salmon and roe, the quails' eggs, the leg of mutton—and he looked up to see that one diner, to his astonishment, was none other than his neighbor, Stewart Abercromb.

Fergus Cameron could not restrain himself. He pushed through the door of the Caledonia, brushed past the *maître d'*, swept past the mirrored bar—and stood before Stewart Abercromb, his bosom heaving. "Kin me eyes be tellin' th' truth? Is it then Stewart Abercromb of Lytel Street, dinin' here in the most expensive restaurant in all of Scotland?"

Abercromb did not interrupt his eating.

"Hoot, mon, have ye no *shame?*" cried Cameron. "D' ye nae know there's a fearful depression on? D' ye nae *know* that thousands o' good, honist men can't bring home enough earnin' for food for their bairn? D' ye nae realize, Stewart Abercromb, how *lucky* y' are—"

Abercromb's face clouded over. He laid down his knife and fork sharply. " 'Lucky' am I thin, Fergus Cameron? *Lucky*, is it? An' by all that's sacred, *mon,* are ye forgettin' that me wife and three wee ones are lyin' at home an' starvin' o' hunger?! Does that nae mean *anythin'* t' ye?!"

Mrs. Anderson asked her new maid: "Vesta, did you remember to clean out the refrigerator?"

"Oh, *yes.*" The maid smiled. "And everything was really delicious!"

Angus Dawson, running for the office of a Labor Party boroughman in Edinburgh, made an exceptionally long (and equally boring) speech. When he at last concluded, the chairman stepped to the lectern and said, "And now, Brother Dawson will answer questions."

There were no questions. The chairman scanned the whole audience. "Ye need not be shy. . . . Any questions . . . ?"

At last a laborer, an old muffler at his throat, the unlighted stub of a cigarette dangling from his lower lip, rose.

The chairman beamed. "Aye, Bobby Scott there? And what is your question?"

Scott took the cigarette stub from his lower lip and said, "*Och*—is nae anyone *else* runnin'?"

Keir MacAfee, a congenital non-picker-up of checks, was eating with his old classmate, Jock Thwaite. They had a fine meal of kippers and stout at a pub. The waiter left the check exactly between the two men.

Thwaite was determined not to pick the check up this time. The conversation flagged, the time passed, and finally Keir MacAfee said, "Jock, it has just occurred to me, it has, that ye've paid our restaurant bills for many and many a moonth now."

"True, aye, true," smiled Thwaite.

"That has been thoughtless of me, lad," said MacAfee. He reached into his jacket. "Now f'r *this* bill, Jock—let's us toss a coin."

When Mr. Hennessey returned from a visit to his cousin, Emmett, in the psychiatric ward, Mrs. Hennessey bombarded him with questions. "And was he glad you come? Did he then talk sense?"

"Pore Emmett, pore lad," sighed Mr. Hennessey. "Carries on, he does, somethin' fearful! He rants, he raves—Nora, he jist talks *crazy!* I tried to bring him down to earth—I talk about the weather, will he be needin' anything, do they let him have a nip now and thin, the thirty dollars he owes us . . ."

"Ah, an' did pore Emmett remember?"

"*That* crazy," said Hennessey, "the lad ain't."

Nolly Reynolds and Berly Summerhill, new friends, were sailing off the Isle of Wight in Summerhill's yacht, the *Guinevere III*. Summerhill was a fine seaman, but Nolly Reynolds was entirely at sea at sea.

The skies darkened, the waves rose, a fearful wind blew the *Guinevere* about, and in the ensuing tacking and maneuvering, Berly Summerhill was smashed against a rail, thrown, and fell to the deck with a broken leg. "Nolly!" he gasped. "Nolly. Take the wheel—spin it, port-side—"

"I *say*, old man! I haven't the faintest notion of what you mean!"

"Oh, Lord," groaned Summerhill. "The wireless! Nolly—just throw the switch—on the radio. It's set for Coast Guard. Call out 'S.O.S. . . . S.O.S.' They will have to send a cutter—tow us in . . ."

Nolly leaped to the wireless, pressed the switch to ON, and shouted, "S.O.S. S.O.S. S.O.—"

A crackling sound brought in the voice of a Coast Guardsman. "We hear you. We hear you. Who are you?"

"I am Noland Reynolds—"

"No, no, sir. Name of *craft!*"

"Oh. *Guinevere Three!*" cried Nolly.

"Nature of emergency?"

"The owner—the skipper—has a broken leg—we're going in circles—I don't know what to *do!*"

"Quite, *Guinevere Three*. No need for panic. What is your position?"

"I am senior partner at Wydham and Corbell, Solicitors—" Nolly Reynolds's tone turned icy. "But *do* you think this is the proper time for chitchat?!"

Scene: London Supermarket

"Griselda, my dear, how do you and Ferdy feel about the Common Market?"

"Oh, we still prefer the local grocer."

Elbert Rowley, a wealthy car dealer from Cincinnati who was visiting Palm Beach for the first time, was swept out to sea by a huge wave. "Help! Help!" He thrashed about in the water. "I'm drowning! He-e-e-e-lp!"

A lifeguard plunged into the surf. With powerful strokes he reached Rowley, swam behind him, gripped the drowning man across the chest, and pulled him to shore. Rowley was unconscious. The lifeguard gave him mouth-to-mouth revival, blowing air into Rowley's lungs, and for ten minutes applied pulmonary resuscitation. When at last the lifeguard rose, dripping perspiration from his exertions, Rowley was breathing normally. The lifeguard helped him to his feet. "Okay now, mister?"

"Yes, thank God," said Rowley. "Wait here, young man." He went over to several men sprawled in beach chairs. "Say, can you guys give me some information?"

"What about?"

"How much do you tip for a thing like that?"

Mrs. Clement Partington, the queen of society in Newport (California), breakfasting in the morning room of her fine house overlooking the bay, was reading the society pages. "Well, my *good*ness, Clemmie. You really *must* call the editor at once—to chastise this silly columnist. Just listen: 'Clement Partington is packing his bags to leave his wife—for the hat-check girl at El Ciento!' " She lowered the page. "Clem, we *can't* allow—Clement? Clement?" She stood up, calling, "Clement! *Clem*-ent!!"

Not until eleven forty-five did Julio Ortega hobble into the Cordeiro Tin Shop where he worked—with his arm in a sling, a bandage on his head, his ankle in a cast.

"Ortega!" called Mr. Cordeiro. "You no-good! Thees week we work double sheeft—and you come two hour forty-five minute late?!"

"Meestair Cordeiro," wheezed Julio. "I was feexing window—for my *mujer* Angelina—and I fall out—down, down—from second floor!"

Cordeiro fixed Ortega with a withering glare. "Thees—take—almost— *three hour?!*"

Mr. and Mrs. Driscoll came out of the Houlihan mansion, the richest in the village, and Driscoll confided to his wife: "Oy tell ye, Bridgit, things ain't going too well with them."

"*What?* He's rich as Croesus. What makes ye say a stupid thing like that?"

"Did y' not see his two daughters? Playin' on th' one piano?!"

A teacher of English in Gotham, the legendary city famous for the not-so-bright, told his class of aspiring writers, "Any good short story always contains one or more of these essentials: religion, emotion, sex, mystery, surprise, royalty. . . . For your next exercise, write a story using as many of these essentials as possible."

The best composition was only one line long:

"My God!" wept the beauty-contest queen. "I am pregnant! Who can the father be?"

Old man Mulligan fell out of his third-story window. An excited crowd gathered around him. A police car roared up, sirens shrieking, and a cop hopped out and bent over the old man. "Don't move! We'll have an ambulance here in a jiffy. . . . What happened?"

"How the divil should Oy know?" snorted Mulligan. "Oy jist got here!"

On her first trip out of Llandriddon Wells, Branwyn Abertwyth, a strong, buxom lass, stood admiring the grand railway terminal in Liverpool. "Coom here," said her mother, "and stond on th' scale machine."

"Whaffor?"

"T' weigh y'r own self." The mother dropped a penny in the slot. "T' chart is to show hoo mooch y' should be weighin' f'r your height. . . . This is somethin' we never hov in Llandriddon!"

Branwyn mounted the scale. The needle spun around. The girl read the number, studied the chart, and moaned, "Oh, moother. It's a freak, I am. For I should stond four full inches higher!"

Alvin Silverman, C.P.A., and Dana Shaw, D.D.S., classmates at Erasmus High, decided to go on their own safari. Their wives refused to join them. So Alvin and Dana flew to Africa, hired a native guide and porters, and struck off down the Congo.

On the fourth day, emboldened by the absence of any misadventure, Alvin and Dana rashly ignored their guide and struck off through dense jungle—when a snarl and a ferocious roar froze them in their tracks. "Dana . . ." quavered Alvin.

"I heard it, Alvin."

"Don't *talk*. Whisper . . . for God's sake . . ."

The roar roared closer, louder.

"Alvin," quaked Dana. "It's behind me . . . take a look . . ."

"I'm looking . . ."

"Is it a lion? A leopard?"

"How should I know?" wailed Alvin. "I'm an accountant, not a furrier."

The mother superior glanced with pride at the graduating class. ". . . And so, my girls, you will all fare forth now, to begin your lives as young women, as good Catholics, as toilers in the vineyard of the Lord. . . . Rose Mulvaney . . . stand up, dear Rosie, and tell us what you will be doin' now when you leave us?"

"Oh, I shan't be really *leaving*, mother," said Rose Mulvaney, "for I have made a sacred vow—and I shall take the veil and be the bride of Jesus all my days!"

"Bless you, child, bless you!" beamed the mother superior. "Nelly O'Rourke . . . rise . . . and tell us what road are you hoping to follow?"

"I am going to St. Ignatius college," said Nelly O'Rourke, "where I shall spend four years, so I can become a teacher and devote my life to teaching young Catholics. . . ."

"Splendid, *splen*did!" exclaimed the mother superior. "And you, Katie Moore . . . rise . . ."

Up stood Katie Moore, the prettiest one of them all.

"Tell us, Katie, what is your hope and vision?"

Katie, in a firm voice, declared: "I am going to become a prostitute!"

The class gasped, and at the podium the mother superior gave a strangled shriek and fell to the floor.

The girls rushed to revive her, and Katie Moore patted her cheek, and the old nun opened her eyes. "Katie! Katie? I never thought I'd see the day when one of my girls—I cannot *believe* it! Katie. What did you say?"

"I said I'm going to be a prostitute. . . ."

"Glory be!" cried the mother superior. "I thought you said you were going to become a Protestant!"

Mr. Ardway awakened from his sumptuous snooze on the golden sands of Palm Beach and sat up in the healing sun. The sea was mint green and blue, the sky cloudless. A few mermaids frolicked in the waters.

"Daddy," came the voice of his little girl, "I'm hungry. I was playing in the sand for an hour and—"

"We'll get you something—" Mr. Ardway stopped. In one hand, his little girl was holding a little ball and pail; in the other was the shimmering silver top of a bikini. "Sweetheart," murmured Mr. Ardway, "I'll get you the yummiest lunch you ever had. But first, listen carefully: I want you to lead daddy to the *exact* place you found that. . . ."

See also **Embarrassing Moments, Jews, Shaggy Dogs, True Tales**

Kibitzers

Note: A *kibitzer*, to those who (though it is hard to believe) have never heard the word, is (1) a know-it-all, who offers unasked-for advice—especially at a game in which he is not a player (poker, chess, checkers, bridge), or (2) a buttinski, who sticks his two cents into a discussion that is none of his affair, or (3) a wisecracker, a needler, or (4) a chronic second-guesser, or (5) a self-appointed expert who irritates everyone else, or (6) most favorably: an amicable kidder.

L. R.

Julius Kovalski started to mount the ladder, to hang up this new sign:

FRESH FISH
SOLD HERE
DAILY

Kovalski's neighbor, Finestein, sang out, "Hey, Julie. You nuts, puttin' up a sign like that?"

"What's wrong with it?"

"Why do you say '*Fresh* Fish'? You want your customers to think you ever sold them *stale* fish?"

"You're right." Kovalski took his brush and painted out FRESH. He started up the ladder.

"Hold it," called Finestein. "Why '*Sold*'? Could anyone think you give fish away *free?!*"

Kovalski expunged SOLD.

"And why '*Here*'? Obviously, you don't sell fish over *there.* . . ."

"You're right." Kovalski painted out HERE.

"That leaves 'Daily,' said Finestein. "Is that smart? If fish are fresh, they *must* be caught and sold daily. Right?"

"Absolutely!" Kovalski crossed out DAILY. The sign now read:

FISH

As Kovalski started up the ladder again, along came another neighbor. "Why are you putting up that ridiculous sign?"

"What's wrong with it?" bridled Kovalski.

"You don't have to put up a sign, Kovalski. Anyone can smell your fish a mile away!"

So Kovalski put up no sign at all.

Manny Klopfer was the most persistent, inveterate *kibitzer* in all of Miami Beach. One day he took his place behind a new arrival from New Jersey. For two hours, Manny offered unsolicited advice. To the New Jerseyan's delight, he kept winning all that time.

During the third hour, the new arrival got a hand of unusual complexity. He rearranged it several times, pondering deeply. Finally, he turned to the *kibitzer:* "What card do I play now?"

Klopfer frowned, then whispered: "What game are you playing?"

The regular cardplayers at Kolinsky's Spa in the Catskills were cursed by a *kibitzer.* Most *kibitzers* are mild-mannered, but this *kibitzer,* one Sy Potachek, was a *kibitzer* of such persistence and spurious omniscience that the cardplayers met to decide how to put an end to his activity.

"Let's tell him, once and for all, to mind his own goddam business!" said Mr. Schreiber.

"Let's stop playing in the game room," suggested Mr. Danenberg.

"So where should we play? In the laundry?"

"Wait, I have an idea." That was Henry Kruger. "Let's invent a game! A cockamamy way of dealing and bidding—a game so crazy that Potachek won't be able to figure out what's going on! That'll shut him up good."

The others applauded this altogether superb idea.

The next day, the four men appeared in the game room as usual; and, as usual, Sy Potachek pulled up a chair.

"Suppose today—we play 'Shmeitz and Kreitz'?" suggested Mr. Kruger.

"I *love* 'Shmeitz and Kreitz'!" exclaimed Mr. Garfinkel.

"How about a penny a point?" asked Mr. Danenberg.

"And double for a *plotch!*" said Schreiber.

"And twice over, split-the-pot for *Kashenoy!*" said Kruger.

"Agreed! Cut the deck!"

During all this astonishing nonsense, Sy Potachek sat, frowning, but silent.

Henry Kruger took the deck of cards, divided it into four parts, handed one part to each of the others players, picked up his portion, and tossed a card before Mr. Danenberg. "I bid one *Jiffel.*"

"Double—with a *Schmeitz,*" said Danenberg.

"I have a *Knotch!*" exclaimed Garfinkel. "So I raise you a blue, in spades!"

"Oh, boy!" chortled Mr. Schreiber. "I have a *Shmatzer!* A red *Shmatzer!* So I call you both—"

"*Psst!*" the *kibitzer* hissed. "Schreiber, don't be a fool!"

"What do you mean?"

"A red *Shmatzer* can't beat a Double *Jiffel*—especially when there's a blue raise in *spades!*"

See also **Advice, Chutzpa, Salesmen, Squelches, Texans**

Kids' Stuff

The telephone rang. Little Stanley lifted the receiver. "Hu-woh."

"Hello. Is this the Kramer house?"

"Yup."

"Well, can I speak to Mrs. Kramer, please?"

"She ain't here."

"When will she be home?"

"Around four o'clock."

"Well, will you please give her a message?"

"Sure."

"Tell her to call Mr. Gordon. Will you do that?"

"Sure. . . . How do you spell that name?"

"Just like it sounds: G-O-R-D-O-N . . . Do you have that?"

"Uh—how do you make a G?"

"Sins of omission," said little Wendy, "are those we forget to commit."

Little Morris Ephron came home from his Hebrew school lesson one day.

"And what did you learn today?" asked his father.

"Wow! What a story!" said Morris. "The teacher told us about Moses leading all the Hebrews out of Egypt, with Pharaoh's Egyptians chasing them. At the Red Sea Moses dropped an atomic bomb! Bang! Pow! The waters of the Red Sea opened up, the Jews got across, the waters closed, and all the Egyptians were drowned."

"Tell me truthfully, Morris. Is *that* what your teacher told you?" gasped Mr. Ephron.

"Naw," said little Morrie, "but, pop, the way he did, you'd never believe it either!"

The preschool teacher said, "—And that's why we all love America. Everyone in our country is *free*."

"Not me," said one child. "I'm four!"

The man patted the little boy on the head and asked, "Larry, is your mother still as pretty as she used to be?"

"Oh, yeah," said Larry. "It just takes her a lot longer."

❧

Sunday School teacher: "Now, children, who can tell me why there is only one God?"

Little Susan Lawson waved her hand energetically.

"Yes, Susan?"

"There is only one God because He is *everywhere,* so there's just no room for any other one."

❧

Mrs. Halper marched her son into Dr. Shinkin's office. "Doctor," she demanded, "is a nine-year-old boy really qualified to perform an appendectomy?"

"What?!"

"I asked you: Is a nine-year-old boy qualified to take out someone's appendix?"

"Certainly not!" exclaimed Dr. Shinkin.

Mrs. Halper turned to her son. "Okay, Melvin. You heard the doctor. . . . Now go put it back!"

❧

On the beach, in Santa Monica, a woman was shouting, waving, and crying, "Come out, Sandra! Come out!"

A girl of seven or eight waded back through the wavelets. "Mother!" she pouted. "Can't I stay in the water until my lips turn blue?"

❧

TEACHER: William, what was George Washington most famous for?
WILLIAM: His memory!
TEACHER: That's an odd answer. . . . What makes you think Washington's memory was so remarkable?
WILLIAM: Well, they sure put up a lot of monuments to it.

❧

JOHNNY (age 8): How did Princess Diana *know* she was going to have a baby?
CONNIE (age 9): She can *read,* can't she? My goodness, Johnny, it was in *all* the papers!

❧

Children's clothes store

> **Get your real Cowboy outfits at
> Hopalong Kassidy's (formerly
> J. Kaminsky's)**

The little girl soberly studied the goodies in the case at the candy store.

"So what do you want?" asked the owner.

"I want a chocolate Easter Bunny—a boy," she said.

"A boy?" the owner laughed. "Why, there isn't that—" (snapping his fingers) "—much difference between a boy bunny and a girl bunny."

The little girl said, "But there's *that*—" (snapping fingers) "—much more chocolate."

Little Antonio was watching his mother bake cookies. After a long time, he said, "Mama, why don't you ask me something?"

"Tonio, what you want your mama shoulda ask you?"

The lad replied, "You could ask, 'Hey, Antonio, you want a cookie?' "

Elsa and her brother were visiting their aunt, who placed two apples on the table. One was large, red, and shiny, the other small, dull, and withered.

"Now, children," said Aunt Charlotte, "I want to see which of you has the better manners."

"He does," said Elsa as she took the big red apple.

Father Ortiz asked one of his students, "Josita? You say your prayers before each meal?"

"N-no, *padre*," said Josita.

"*Hanh?* You no pray before you eat?!"

"I no have to. My mama is good cook."

Little Arthur was a fine, healthy six-year-old. There was only one thing his father and mother worried about: little Arthur had never spoken one single word.

One day, his mother sprinkled sugar over half a grapefruit and placed it before Arthur. Arthur ate one spoonful, made a face, and exclaimed, "I *hate* it! This is bitter! Don't ever serve me anything like this again!"

"Arthur!" cried his mother. "You can talk!"

"Arthur!" cried his father. "You know so many words!" He hugged the little boy.

"How *won*derful!" said Arthur's mother.

His father laughed. "Arthur, son, why didn't you ever talk before this? Not one word all these years?!"

The lad said, "Until this grapefruit, everything you gave me tasted dandy."

Said a five-year-old, "The nursery school is where they tell the children who hit someone, not to; and they tell children who don't hit, to hit back."

Tommy Gans, age six, was taken by his mother to the ballet school where his older sister was enrolled. Tommy watched in fascination as the girls practiced their dances on their toes. After a while, he whispered, "Mommy . . ."
"Yes, dear?"
"Can't they just get taller girls?"

When little Filbert learned that his cousin, Peter, whom he had never met, was coming to stay with them for a month, he could scarcely control his excitement. But when cousin Peter finally arrived, Filbert's jaw dropped in astonishment and tears of dismay rolled down his cheeks.
"Why, *Fil*bert," his mother chided him. "What's the matter?"
"I thought," the lad sniffed, "that Peter would be a rabbit!"

Little Earl, age seven, came running into the house from the yard, screaming at the top of his lungs.
"*Dar*ling!" Earl's mother clasped the crying lad to her bosom. "What happened?"
"D-daddy," sobbed the lad, "was fixing—the—the fence—and hit—the hammer—*right on his thumb!!!*" And the boy burst into a new flood of caterwauling.
"Now, now, Earl, dear," his mother cooed. "You must learn not to cry over things like that. Why didn't you just laugh—"
"I did," wept Earl.

See also **Children, Definitions (by Children), Famous People (as Seen by Children), Geography Revised, History Revised, Mothers**

Languages: Pitfalls

The guidebooks urge any American venturing abroad to learn the basic phrases of a foreign language. Tourist tip-sheets assure you that natives adore hearing a visitor roll his tongue around theirs. Well, I hate to say this, but the advice is cockeyed, and if you fall for it, you'll end up to your armpits in the quicksands of phonetics.

The terrible truth is that the slightest slip in pronouncing a little vowel, in any language, can throw you straight into bedlam. Take English. The difference between "Call me" and "Kill me," for instance, is only 1/64th of an inch of air space, so a greenhorn in a hurry can wind up being throttled by an American trying to oblige a visitor from abroad.

Or take a simple sentence such as: "I want my meat well done." Naïvely uttered by, say, a Papuan, that sentence comes out, "I want my mate walled in." Very few restaurants will brick up your wife on such short notice.

The same booby traps await the American who is fool enough to plunge into the jungle of any alien argot. The first time I went to Paris, I entered a neighborhood bistro and hailed the *propriétaire* in bold French: "Ah, m'sieur, but I am very hungry tonight!"

That, at least, is what I thought I was saying. What I actually uttered was, "Ah, but I shall have many a female tonight."

You can hardly blame the astounded man for hustling me to a shadowy corner, where my lust would cause no trouble. On the other hand, you can hardly blame me for having fallen victim to the treacherous nasalities of French, where the ever-so-slight difference in sound between *faim* and *femme* had converted a hungry adolescent into a sex maniac.

In Tokyo, I carefully read aloud (from a phrase book called *You, Too, Can Speak Japanese*) the phonetic syllables for "I—would—like—a—massage."

To this the Oriental attendant replied, with ceremonial hisses of joy and abnegation: "I would be honored to carry you there on my back, exalted thimble, but the cat is already late for the wedding."

I think I had misled him. Either that, or he was relying on his vest-pocket copy of *You, Too, Can Spoke Engrish.*

from my *Passions and Prejudices*

Occidental places can be just as disorienting. I once entered a splashy men's store in Madrid and, in my buoyant high-school Spanish, informed the clerk that I wanted to purchase a pair of gloves and an umbrella. The man turned white and dashed off, bleating for his superior.

To this person in a morning coat and striped trousers, I calmly repeated: "I want—a—pair—of—men's—gloves—and an umbrella."

The superior Iberian flinched. "But, señor," he quavered, "why do you wish to wallop yon horse with a parachute?"

What happened, as I reconstruct the linguistic mishmosh, was this: the Spanish for umbrella is *paraguas*, which I mangled into *paracas*, which they took to mean *paracaidas*, which means parachute. Gentleman is *caballero*, which I blithely rendered as *caballo*, which means horse. It was a cinch to nose-dive from *guante* (glove) to *guantada* (wallop), even though I have never laid a glove on a horse, much less walloped one with a parachute. I have never even chastised a Chihuahua. Not with so much as a feather, which is *pluma*, much less a *plancha*, which is flatiron.

So, I don't care *how* easy the guidebooks tell you it is to toss off a few fruity phrases in the natives' Flemish or Plattdeutsch. The depressing truth is that *any* language simply bulges with laryngeal pitfalls and idiomatic ambushes.

If you're lost in Mozambique, stop any native with a bright "Blessings from your patron saint, and how do I get to the flea market?" Five will get you twenty if the chap doesn't take you by the hand and lead you there himself.

Why drive the locals *loco* by asking them to wallop yon horse with a parachute?

from my *Passions and Prejudices*

CHEMISES OF IRON

In Paris, I went to a railway station to inquire about trains to Nice. I came armed with a charming *Guide to Conversational French* I had picked up, a bargain (it was published in 1880), in a bookstall on the Left Bank.

The charade between me and the Frenchman behind the bars of his ticket cage went like this:

I

(smiling)

Bonjour, m'sieur! Is not this day reliable?

TICKETEER

You speak *French! (He salutes):* What joys! *Vive* the States United! May I wax your elbow?

I

(modestly)

Voilà! To affairs?

TICKETEER
(beaming)

Advance.

I

(chuckling)

I demand you: When, dear Amy [*cher ami*], do gentleman trains go toward Lady Nice?

TICKETEER
(enthusiastic)

They are *very* nice chemises of iron, wet knight.

I

(clearing throat)

I fear I have been soft. What I intended to choke you is: "What *time* do such trains arrive Nice?"

TICKETEER
(slapping forehead)

The *time?!* Smite my neck for buttering your confusion. It takes twelve hours from Paris.

I

No, no! I do not want the interval between farewelling Paris and helloing Nice. What I chattered was: "When—*when*—"

TICKETEER
(excited)

Always it occupies twelve hours! Saturdays, Sundays, apricots—bread pains—

I

Who denies? Merely recite! *When* shrink the trains from Paris to the south—*la Sud*—

TICKETEER
(flinging hands heavenward)

Ahh, a thousand apologies for my porcupine! Let us banish error once and for all right. Tray of beans; to reach the Sudan, you appear in Marseilles—

I

The *south*—

TICKETEER
(puzzled)

But the Sudan *is* south of dirty Marseilles!

I

—of France!

TICKETEER

It is south of France also! From Marseilles, you eat the bark off a boat—

I

(hollering)

Arrest! I do not gnaw vessels! I thirst but one small piece of entirely different *in-for-ma-tion!*

Fourteen hours later, I was in Innsbruck. Hold on: "Innsbruck" does begin with "in" and *is* a small piece of an entirely different nation.

from *Passions and Prejudices*

Leonard and Manny, both lovers of Yiddish, were comparing its charms to those of other languages, and Lenny observed, "Do you know something remarkable? There's no word in Yiddish for 'disappointed'!"

"I can't believe it. You must be wrong. Wait, I'll call my mother."

And to his mother, who barely spoke English, Manny said in fluent Yiddish, "Mameleh, listen. Suppose I told you I was coming to dinner on Friday. And suppose you worked all day Friday to make me the finest meal ever—from chopped liver and *gefilte* fish and down through the chicken and *kugel* and two kinds of strudel for dessert. And on Friday, two minutes before I'm supposed to arrive, I telephone and say that something so important has come up that I just can't come to dinner! What would you say?"

"What I would *say?*" wailed his mother. "I'd say, '*Oy, bin ich* [am I] disappointed.' "

See also **Accents, Advertisements, Boo-boos, The English Language, Goldwyniana, Malaprops, How's That Again?, Signs, Typos, Yinglish**

Lawyers

A very successful lawyer was being badgered by his wife. "You say you will, you *say* you will! But whenever the time comes, you find some excuse—"

"Okay, dear, I'll do it—right now." The legal wizard stalked into his son's room. "Junior, the time has come for us to have a man-to-man talk!"

"Sure, dad. About what?"

"About—the alleged facts of life."

Ignorance of the law excuses no man from practicing it.

Scene: Town in New England

VISITOR: Sir, do you have a criminal lawyer in this town?
LOCAL RESIDENT: We-ell, we're pretty sure we do, but . . .
VISITOR: But what?
LOCAL RESIDENT: But we've not been able to prove it.

The lawyer was briefing his star witness, Sam Peurifoy. "You realize that before you sit down on that chair next to the judge you're going to have to swear to tell the truth, the whole truth, and nothing but the truth?"

"Yes, *sir.*"

"And Sam, suppose you don't tell the truth, the whole truth, and nothing but the truth? Do you know what'll happen?"

"Yes, *sir!* Our side'll win."

In the elegant offices of Mannheim, Mannheim, Mannheim, and Mann-heim, the phone rang. It was promptly answered: "Mannheim, Mannheim, Mannheim, *Mann-*heim."

"Hello," said the caller. "I'd like to speak to Mr. Mannheim."

"I'm sorry, but Mr. Mannheim is in Washington."

"Oh . . . then can I speak to Mr. Mannheim?"

"Sorry, sir, but Mr. Mannheim is in court today."

"Well, then, I'll speak to Mr. Mannheim."

"Mr. Mannheim won't be in his office until four."

The caller sighed. "Okay, then can you connect me to Mr. *Mann*heim?"

"*Spea*-king!"

HARLEY AND SMITHERS

BARRISTERS

CHAMBERS 43-C

LINCOLN'S FIELDS INN

LONDON

    JURY ANNOUNCED VERDICT IN CROWN V. LASSITER.

JUSTICE HAS PREVAILED.

                                 ATKINSON

      J. R. ATKINSON

      BARRISTER

      KINGS BENCH WALK

      PLYMOUTH

          APPEAL AT ONCE.

            HARLEY

The prosecutor, a terror for any defense witness on the stand, leaned forward and, steely eyed, asked Mr. Aaron Rattner, "Are you positively sure, beyond a smidgeon of a doubt, that the woman you saw entering the building was the plaintiff?"

Rattner hemmed and hawed. "Vell, I t'ink—"

"Stop!" The prosecutor raised a minatory palm. "In this court, we do not care what anyone *thinks*. I only want you to tell the court what you *know*."

Rattner blinked. "Excuse me. How I can tell vhat I know unless I t'ink? Don't forget: I'm not a lawyer."

See also **Courts, Evidence, Juries**

Lectures/Lecturers

Moses Trelawney, a candidate for the city council in Yazoo City, Mississippi, was being introduced to an audience in flowery and extravagant phrases. To his neighbor on the platform, Moses whispered, "How long you think all these folks fixin' to hear my oration?"

"You jist hold forth as long as the spirit done move you, Moses," said the neighbor. "*We* all go home aroun' two forty."

I love a finished speaker
I really, really do.
I don't mean one who's polished.
I just mean one who's through.

RICHARD ARMOUR

A garrulous, somewhat vain orator droned on and on and finally declared, "—which brings me to the end of my prepared remarks. Now I shall be happy to answer questions . . ."

In the third row, a gray-haired lady rose.

"Yes, madam," smiled the orator. "What is your question?"

"What time is it?"

As I look into your earnest faces, I say, "Join me in prayer for the future of the United States."

The Reverend Malachy Devany, preaching in the congregation of a friend, stopped in the middle of his long, elaborate sermon and signaled to the sexton. "In the second row," he whispered, "there is a man who is absolutely asleep . . . *snoring!* Wake him up."

"Me?" frowned the sexton. "Is that *fair?!*"

"What do you mean," asked the Reverend Devany icily, " 'Is that *fair?*' "

"*You* put him to sleep," said the sexton. "I think *you* should wake him up."

At a banquet which went on and on and on, the presiding officer of the club finally said, "Ladies and gentlemen, we have run considerably over-time—so I am particularly pleased to introduce our distinguished speaker for the evening, William Collier, who will now give you his address."

The audience applauded, Collier rose, said, "Mr. Toastmaster, ladies and gentlemen: my address is Two thirty-nine East Thirty-eighth Street, New York City," and sat down.

The ballroom shook from the applause.

When the speaker of the evening was introduced, with extravagant praises, at a banquet in his honor, he responded nervously: "You know, I came here in the hope of hearing a fascinating speech. I was hoping to hear my lips drip brilliant phrases and memorable epigrams. Now I have to tell you: I'm afraid I'm going to be disappointed as hell."

The luncheon speaker boomed into the microphone, "Gentlemen, your chairman promised me—and I quote his exact words, 'a *vast* audience.' " But judging from the number of empty chairs, I can only come to the conclusion that I have a half-vast audience . . ."

My friends—(I know you much too well to call you "ladies and gentle-men) . . ."

On and on droned the British sociologist at the final banquet of their annual convention in London. It was past eleven o'clock when the chair-man rose to announce: "We shall now hear our distinguished guest of honor, our main and final speaker, who will speak to us on the subject: 'Current Research on Sex.' Since the hour is so late, I have begged him to condense his long speech somewhat—and he has most graciously agreed to do so. Milords, ladies, and gentlemen, I give you Professor Horace Brownlow."

Up rose Professor Brownlow. When the tired applause trailed off, he said, "My topic is sex. Milords, ladies, and gentlemen: Sex gives me *consider-able* pleasure. Thank you."

See also **Boo-boos, Doggerel, Education, Jews**

Letters

> *Maine Angler*
> Peconsquet, Me.

Lemuel Edwards
P.O.B. 270
Jonesport, Me.

Dear Mr. Edwards:
    Renewal form is enclosed. Your sub-
scription has expired.
> > Yours,
> >   J. Walton
> >   Business Manager

J. Walton
Maine Angler
Peconsquet, Me.

    So has Lem.
> > A neighbor

Mrs. Forsberg received two letters:

Dear Mrs. Forsberg:
    I had a good time at your party last
night. Thank you for asking me.
> > Yours,
> >   Jordan Balder

Dear Mrs. Forsberg:
    What a <u>wonderful</u> hostess you are!
> > Yours,
> >   Ralph Parmenter

    Mrs. Forsberg read both letters, consigned Balder's to the wastebasket, picked up the phone, and called Parmenter. "Ralph? . . . Are you free for dinner Saturday?"

(What do you mean, you don't get the point?! Read the two notes again.)

Dear Aunt Moira:
 I know it is a long time since I wrote to you and I am really very, very sorry I didn't even get around to thanking you for that scrumptious present (the nifty blazer) you sent me for Christmas, weeks ago, and I guess I would feel I really deserved it, after all these months after Christmas, if you just forgot I have a birthday coming up—June 5! . . . But thanks late are better than never, aren't they?
Your loving niece,
Iris

It is said of Julius Rosenwald that he rarely had trouble with people who owed Sears Roebuck money. Whenever a bill went unpaid too long, and "Past Due" notices were to no avail, Mr. Rosenwald would write the debtor:

Dear Mr. Jones:
 Your bill is long overdue. If you do not pay it within 48 hours, we shall notify all your other creditors that you paid us in full.
Yours,
J. Rosenwald

See also **Business, Ingenuity, Salesmen, Stratagems**

Life

Life is a dream, but please don't wake me.

Ever since dying came into fashion, life has not been safe.

Life is the greatest of all bargains; you get it for nothing.

When life isn't the way you like it, like it the way it is.

The only thing you get free in this life is garbage.

YIDDISH FOLK SAYINGS

April Fool: A joke repeated 365 times a year.

SHOLEM ALEICHEM

A pollster was telephoning a sample of Americans for their responses to: *"When do you believe that human life really starts?"*

Terence O'Malley said: "Right at the moment of conception."

Charles Manders replied: "At birth, when the embryo leaves the womb."

Abraham Kotinsky said: "When the children have left home and the dog (may he rest in peace) has died."

Life. It's full of such sadness and sorrow, sometimes I think it's better not to be born at all! . . . But how many people do you meet in a lifetime who were that lucky?

YIDDISH SAYING

Scene: The Porch of Villa Mitnick in the Poconos

Mendel Kalbfiess, age eighty-nine, and Avrum Gottschalk, ninety-one, are in rocking chairs. They rock in silence, save for an occasional sigh or *zifts*, or phatic grunts, "Hmph!"s and "Ai"s, and clucks. Finally, Mr. Kalbfiess clears his throat and announces: "Gottschalk, I made op mine mind. All mine life I been torturing mineself—mit vun qvastion. 'Vat's de minnink of life?' "

"And now you fond de enswer?" asked Mr. Gottschalk with irony.

"Corract. Life? Life is a tremandous fontain in de middle of a lake. And de lake is insite a blue montain mit saventy angels sitting in a coicle, seenging to God." Mr. Kalbfiess nodded his satisfaction and smiled.

Mr. Gottschalk took thought, stroking his chin, tugging at his forelock, closing his eyes the better to visualize Mr. Kalbfiess's poetic vision. After some time, Mr. Gottschalk opened his eyes—and, with a polite sigh, said "Kalbfiess, I hoid a very void you sad; and I been t'inking dem over, every void. But I have to tell you, I am not convinced. *Vhy* is life like a tremandous fontain in de meedle of a lake, and dat lake itsself is insite a blue montain, and saventy angels are in vun big circle singing to the Almighty, blessed be His name?"

Now it was Mr. Kalbfiess's turn to harumph and hack and close his eyes in thought. And after some time, he, too, sighed, opened his eyes, and murmured, "So, Gottschalk. You are right! Life *ain't* a tremandous fontain in de middle of a lake, mit de lake itsalf insite a blue montain, mit saventy angels in a coicle singing to God." He rose. "Now I'm gung to take a nap. Philosophy tires me ot."

The lady of the house said to her maid, "What does your husband do, Julia?"

"Oh, he don't do much of anything, ma'am."

"You mean he never works?" frowned the lady.

"Not much."

"You mean you're the one who has to earn the living in your house?"

The maid smiled, "Well, ma'am, let's say I'm the one who makes the livin'—but he's the one makes the livin' worthwhile."

Two old men sat in rocking chairs on the front porch of the nursing home, rocking gently, back and forth, in silence. Finally, the first old man, Lupowitz, sighed, turned to the second old man, said, "Life." And with that, saying no more, he went back to his rocking.

Janovich, the second old man, coughed, then screwed up his eyelids, " 'Life' you said?"

Lupowitz nodded. "Life . . ."

"So—what about Life?"

Lupowitz cleared his throat. "I have decided that life," he declaimed, "is like a bowl thick, cold sour cream!"

Janovich went *"Tchk-tchk-tchk!"* After taking thought, he quavered, "So why is Life like a bowl thick, cold sour cream?"

Lupowitz shrugged. "How should I know? Am I a philosopher?"

See also **Faith, God, Heaven, Religion**

Limericks

A limerick crams laughs astronomical
Into space truly economical,
But the funniest I've seen
Are not often clean
And the clean ones so seldom are comical.

Said an heiress, madly despotic,
"I just love things grossly exotic,
So I always adored
Making love in a Ford,
And *don't* think that's auto-erotic."

A beautiful gal named Stella
Fell in love with a bow-legged fella.
This foolhardy chap
Let her sit on his lap
And she flopped way down to the cella.

In Vermont, a clumsy young miss
Exclaimed, "Skating is absolute bliss!"
But she no more dares fate
Since a slip of her skate
Reversed her position like this.
˙sıɥʇ ǝʞıl uoıʇısod ɹǝɥ pǝsɹǝʌǝᴚ

A certain young fellow named Beebee
Wished to wed with a lady named Phoebe.
"But," he said, "I must aim
To master her name
Before Phoebe be Phoebe Beebee."

There was a young beauty from Del.
Who surely was quite wel.

That to dress for a ball
Was just nothing at all
But wondered what-in-hell would her fel.

Supreme in Peru were the Incas,
Mighty, gargantuan drincas,
Who worshiped the Sun
And had lots of fun,
But poor folk considered them stincas.   .

Joseph McKisson once told me
He was kissing a girl by the sea,
"This can't be good kissing,"
She said, "I hear hissing!"
Said Joseph, still kissing, "That's me."

This immortal statue by Phidias,
That outraged Athens' phastidious,
Made a committee of sorts
Cover her crotch with shorts,
So Aphrodite looked hermaphroditious.

A glamorous maid named McCall
Wore a newspaper dress to the ball.
The costume caught fire
And burned up her entire
Front page, sports section, *et al.*

A fly and a flea in a flue,
Were imprisoned there: What could they do?
Said the flea, "Let us fly,"
Said the fly, "Let us flee,"
So they flew through a flaw in the flue.

Jane Lurie from Mosby, Mo.
Once decided to sit on a jo.
But the judge turned her down
With a chauvinist frown
And Jane Lo. marched out in a fo.

Good limericks are very complex
And chiefly harp upon sex,
They burgeon with virgins
And masculine urgins
And bust with erotic effects.

There was a young salesman named Eades,
Rashly swallowed six packets of seeds.
In a month, silly ass,
He was covered with grass,
And he couldn't sit down for the weeds.

There was a young lady of Kent
Who said that she knew what it meant
When men asked her to dine,
Gave her cocktails and wine,
She knew what it meant—but she went!

There are numberless folk in Md.
Who know that their state is no Scd.
So it's surprising to find
That they don't seem to mind
That Wis.—not Md.—is Dd.

A kooky young pate who was addled
Had a horse who never was saddled,
But his gust (which was dis)
For his haps (which were mis)
Made him covet his lack (which was Cadil).

She cried, "No, no; stop, Mr.!"
As soon as the sly cad had kr.
And so out of spite
On the very same night
This Mr. kr. sr.

I know a sorority girl, Vammer,
Who's cursed by a terrible stammer,
"There is no s-sister,
I hate like Jane Wister,"
She said, "D-d-d-d-d-damn her!"

A dowager visiting Fla.
Broke her leg in the Fontainebleau ca.
A bus-boy from Me.
To remove all her pe.
Shot her. Could anything be ha.?

An operatic star is Lars Wing,
But when asked by admirers to sing,
Replies, "It's quite odd,
But I confuse "God
Save the Weasel" with "Pop Goes the King!"

There's a girl I shall not embarrass,
Who has a super-superlative ass;
Not soft, round, and pink,
As you shamelessly think:
It is brown, has long ears, and eats grass.

Finally:
There was a young lady named Drew
Whose limericks stopped at line two.

P.S.
These verses I think least tired,
Of all I heard, wrote or inspired,
But I'm sure you will sneer,
"They don't come anywhere *near,*
The ones I so cleverly sired!"

See also **Boo-boos, Doggerel, Signs**

Lincolniana

When Stephen Douglas was barnstorming in Illinois, he noticed that a tall, thin, rawboned young fellow in overalls was always sitting in the first row, listening with the utmost intensity to Douglas's words.

One day, after a rousing reply to an opponent, Douglas signaled to the lanky lad, who shuffled up to the podium. "Young man," said Douglas, "I see you in the front row of every speech I deliver."

"Yes, sir."

"May I ask—why?"

"Well, Mr. Douglas," said the young man, stretching his suspenders, "I'm kind of hoping I'll be up there on that platform one day, debating you—m'self."

Stephen Douglas chuckled. "I admire ambition. How do you earn your living?"

"Split logs."

"And what's your name, friend?"

The young man blushed. "Abe."

"Abe what?"

"Kaminsky."

Radio speaker: We all know, of course, that it was Abraham Lincoln who frayed the sleeves.

Logic

The clerk at Her Majesty's Post Office in Brighton put the package on the scale, adjusted the weights on the balancing lever, and said, "Afraid you're a wee short of stamps on this one, Mr. Farquhar."

"Eh?"

"I said, you'll have to place more stamps on this parcel."

"And why?"

"Because it's too *heavy*, Mr. Farquhar."

The Scotsman harumphed. "And will more stamps make it lighter, mon?"

"Have you anything to say before I pass sentence on you?" asked the judge.

"Yes, Your Honor." The prisoner took a deep breath. "How can I be convicted of forgery when—when I *can't even write my own name!*"

The judge stroked his chin. "Because you were not *charged* with signing your own name."

A commuter came running along the platform at Knobby Vale, in Sussex, England, crying, "Stop! I say—train, *stop!*" But the train pulled away. "Confound it, missed the bloody thing by no more than two seconds!"

Another Englishman, waiting for an incoming train, lowered his newspaper in annoyance. "The way you're carrying on, old boy, one might have thought you missed it by two hours!"

The shabby, untidy mendicant stood before Victor Pozmeyer, in that very rich man's parlor, and asked, "So please can you help me out—just 'til I get back on my feet?"

Pozmeyer studied the mendicant, went to the doorway, called "Slater," and the butler appeared. "Yes, sir?"

"Slater, I want you to *look* at this poor, unfortunate man. His toes are sticking out of his shoes. His trousers are patched in a dozen places. He looks as if he hasn't had a decent meal in God knows how long. It breaks one's *heart* to look at such a miserable creature. Throw him out."

❧

"Lloyd Morgan! Lloyd Morgan!" cried Mrs. Morgan, as she ran into the pub in Llandudnorvon. "Is it then true, Lloyd Morgan, that ye did win a thousand quid in th' lottery?!

"That it is, Mrs. Morgan," laughed the lucky man. "One o' me tickets had th' right number. . . . Have a pint, woman!"

"A pint it is," chortled Mrs. Morgan. "But wait, mon. What is it I heerd you t' say? That *one* 'v your tickets—?"

"Aye. I bought meself five tickets, and one—"

"*Five* tickets?!" the woman cried. "By me blessed mother's memory, Lloyd Morgan, why did ye need to buy them other four?!"

See also **Evidence, Ingenuity, Reason, Shlemiels**

Lord's Prayer
(Children's Version)

Our Father, harped in heaven, Hallowe'en Thy name.
Thy King done come, Thy will be done on earth as
it is in heaven. Give us each day our jelly bread.
And forgive us our press passes, as we forgive those
who press past us. And lead us not into Penn Station,
but deliver us from Emil. For vine is the kingdom
and the powder and the glory forever—A man."

See also **Definitions (by Children), Famous People (as Seen by Children), Geography Revised, History Revised (by Children)**

Love

The delusion that one woman differs from another.

The triumph of imagination over intelligence.

H. L. MENCKEN

'Tis better to have loved and lost than never to have lost at all.

SAMUEL BUTLER

The only fire against which there is no insurance.

EDITH PIAF

The alliance of affection and lust.

L. R.

The Comedy of Eros.

EVAN ESAR

A game that is never called because of darkness.

At twenty, a girl will ask: "Is he good-looking?"
At thirty, she asks, "Is he rich?"
At thirty-five, she cries, "Where is he?!"

William Faulkner once got into an elaborate discussion with a guest about the difference between "like" and "love." After the guest left, Faulkner asked a servant: "Sophia, how would you explain the difference between 'like' and 'love'?"

"Well, Mist' Faulkner," said the maid, "it's like this: when Ah likes 'em, Ah lets 'em. But when Ah *loves* 'em, Ah helps."

The bottle of perfume that Willie sent
Was highly displeasing to Millicent;
Her thanks were so cold
They broke up, I'm told,
Through that silly scent Willie sent Millicent.

Love—male

> Dear Jennie,
>   I luv you. Do you luv me?
>   Joey

Love—female

> Dear Joey:
>   No! I do not love you!
>   Love,
>   Jenny

Lover's leap: The distance from one bed to another.

Love-talk: The difference between rape and rapture.

Playboy

See also **Bachelors, Hanky-panky, Marriage, Shadchens**

Malaprops

At huge funeral for a widely disliked producer

It only goes to show what happens when you give the public what it wants.

✌

I challenge you to give a frank, affirmative answer: Yes or no!

✌

Listen, if people just don't go to see a certain movie, nobody can stop them!

✌

Oh, you three certainly are a pair—if there ever was one.

✌

If his father was alive today he would be turning over in his grave.

✌

If you don't stop nagging me with such details I'll find someone who will!

✌

One thing you have to say for him: he doesn't mince his punches.

✌

When I want your opinion, I'll give it to you!

✌

He's the type who'll cut your throat behind your back.

✌

Every time he opens his mouth, he should close it.

✌

He always puts his foot in the soup.

✌

The most famous Italian composer is Libretto.

❧

The worst thing about him is that when he isn't drunk, he's sober.

❧

That man is such a charmer, he's practically a Don Coyote.

He doesn't waste a word; every line he writes is full of pith!

L. R.

❧

From now on, I'm watching your every move with a fine-tooth comb.

❧

Now we've got them right where they want us!

❧

I wonder if Indian parents had a T.P.A.

❧

After all, a friend in need is a needy friend.

❧

It's like finding a haystack full of needles.

❧

Well, *that's* a different kennel of fish!

❧

I was as mad as a wet blanket!

❧

Does the name Pavlov ring a bell?

❧

She never talks to strangers unless they're friends.

❧

They say you can't do it, but that doesn't nearly always work.

CASEY STENGEL

❧

Your remark is either unnecessary, rude, or both.

❧

I wouldn't trust him if his life depended on it!

❧

He was stranded so high and dry he could barely keep his head above water.

❧

Everything's fine—just honky-tonky.

❧

I'm not the type who wears my heart up my sleeve.

❧

Women tell everybody not to tell anybody.

❧

It's as easy as falling on a log.

❧

He escaped by the skin off his teeth.

❧

Listen! Two rights don't make a wrong, you know.

❧

The way my boy burns up his tires, you'd think rubber grows on trees.

❧

What we currently need is a good five-cent nickel.

❧

There was this terrible woman in the Bible who hated Samson: Phyllis Stein.

❧

Not all that shivers is cold.

See also **Bloopers, Boo-boos, Cynics' Dictionary, Definitions to Cherish, Geography Revised, Goldwyniana, History Revised (by Children), Typos**

Man

The missing link between apes and human beings.

KONRAD LORENZ

❧

The animal that bargains; no dogs exchange bones.

ADAM SMITH

❧

A creature made at the end of the week, when God was tired. . . . God invented man because he was so disappointed in the monkey. . . . Man is the only animal who blushes—or needs to.

MARK TWAIN

❧

Of all the ways of defining man, the worst is the one which calls him a rational animal.

ANATOLE FRANCE

❧

Man has been called the rational animal; all my life I have been searching for evidence to support this.

BERTRAND RUSSELL

❧

Educated chimpanzees.

❧

One of God's blunders, or is God one of man's blunders?

NIETZSCHE

❧

The only animal who cooks his food.

❧

The only animal who can play Scrabble.

See Also **God, Life**

Marriage

When an old man takes a young wife, he becomes young—and she becomes old.

When an old man takes a young wife, he becomes young—and she becomes old.

❧

Long, long before Freud, the Jews had this saying: When a young man gets married, he divorces his mother.

❧

I never knew what happiness was until I got married—and then it was too late.   ANON.

❧

The sole cause of divorce.

❧

The only way of finding out exactly what kind of marvelous mate your wife/husband wished she/he had married.

❧

The only adventure open to the cowardly.

VOLTAIRE

❧

A fifty-fifty proposition, if you're a fraction.

❧

A sanitary institution.

H. L. MENCKEN

❧

Marriage makes strange bedfellows.

GROUCHO MARX

❧

Bigamy: The only crime in which two rites make a wrong.

BOB HOPE

❧

Sign on door of matrimonial agency: COME IN. RELAX. SPOUSE AROUND.

❧

"Me wife will drive me to the loony bin f'r certain," mourned O'Malley. "Ivery night she has this same dream—that she married a bloomin' millionaire!"

"Blimey!" scoffed Kerrigan. "*That* drives ye crazy? *Me* wife has the viry same dream—but in the daytime!"

HOLTZMAN:	I've been married twenty-eight years today, and I'm still in love with the same woman.
GLAZER:	That's wonderful.
HOLTZMAN:	And if my wife ever finds out, she'll kill me!

John Calverton and his college chum, Dan Malloy, were having lunch. During a heart-to-heart talk about their respective marriages, John blurted, "What it comes down to, Dan, is—well, my wife just doesn't *understand* me. . . . Does yours?"

Malloy thought for a moment. "I don't think so, John. I've never heard her mention your name."

Captain Wayne Cummings wrote his wife long, long letters from his post in Lebanon. "There's a shortage of books here, but there sure is no shortage of beautiful girls—Lebanese, Druse, Palestinian, and a dozen other nationalities. But you don't have to worry, darling. I would fill up the long lonely hours learning to play a musical instrument, if I had one. . . ."

His wife promptly express-mailed a harmonica.

A year later, Captain Cummings came home. At the airport was his wife. "Sweetheart! Darling!" Cummings ran to his mate, arms wide open.

"Hold it, Wayne," she said. "Just stay right there. Before there's any embracing around here—let's hear you play the harmonica."

"Dooley," said Monahan, "it's your careful opinion I'm needin'. In July, the missus asked me for—in addition, mind y', to the regular monthly household allowance—another fifteen pounds! In August, she asked me f'r an extra twinty. Last month, so help me, if she don't up and ask me for an extra twinty-thray!"

"Monahan," said Dooley, "it's proper puzzled Oy am. What does Mrs. Monahan *do* with all that money?"

"Who knows, man?" said Mr. Dooley. "Not a bloody sixpence did I give her."

The nervous apprentice at Dumfrees Fabrics approached the manager, Mr. Kirkaldy, and stammered, "M-mister Kirkaldy, Oy *moost* ask ya—beggin' y're forgiveness—for a bit of a rise."

"A *rise?*" echoed Kirkaldy.

"Ay. On me present wages, sir, Oy simply cannot get married!"

"*Och*, that is true, lad," said Kirkaldy. "And many will be the day, from the bottom of your heart, that ye'll be thankin' me."

The man-about-town whispered to the old-fashioned girl in his arms, "Baby, let's get married or something. . . ."

The girl murmured, "We get married—or nothing."

The pharmacist said, "Well, Mr. Tsoner, how did that mudpack you bought for your wife turn out?"

"Pretty good," said Tsoner. "*Pretty* good. If not for that one defect . . ."

"What defect?"

"It kept falling off."

Mr. and Mrs. Kevin McBride, in their early nineties, were celebrating their seventieth wedding anniversary, and a television crew from Belfast had come to interview them in their small thatch-roof cottage.

"Now thin, Mr. McBroyde," said the interviewer, "siventy years is a mighty long toyme. In all those many years, did you never—even once—think of gettin' a divorce?"

"Divorce? Me? From me darlin' Kathleen?" blinked Mr. McBride. "Nay, man. Not once."

"And what about the wife, eh? Mrs. McBroyde?"

"Divorce? Never. Not once did the thought enter me mind." Mrs. McBride shrugged. "But murder? Ay! Often!"

"Some men have all ze luck," mourned Pierre. "Me, I got no luck wis women."

"Why you say zat?" asked Alfonse.

"*Facts* make me say zat. My first wife ran away with one of ze men in our building."

"And your second wife?"

"My zecond wife," said Pierre, "did not."

Sign in Las Vegas store window

WEDDING GOWNS
FOR ALL OCCASIONS

"Well, son, let me congratulate you. You're going to look back on this day as the happiest of your whole life!"

"But, dad, I'm not getting married today. I'm getting married tomorrow."

"That's right, son."

From the marriage announcements column of the London *Times*

> On June 3, 1978: Lord Hansford-Blunt, 74,
> to Lady Prunella Vintor-Fleck, 29. The
> bridegroom's gift to the bride was an
> antique pendant.

". . . And *then* I went to see the doctor—Maury, *Mau*ry!"

"Mmh?"

"Maury, are you listening to me or reading the newspaper?"

"I'm listening, I'm listening."

"I *said*, this afternoon I went to see Dr. Stoller."

"Mmh." Maury turned the page. "So how is he?"

"My wife is such a great housekeeper," boasted Frackman, "that she vacuums every room every day and puts a completely clean, empty bag in the Hoover every night!"

"Humph," said Kolchak. "I've got a wife who, when I get up in the middle of the night to go to the bathroom, changes the sheets before I get back!"

It was almost midnight on a fearful night—the rain pouring down, the storm blowing in fury. Mr. Salovsky was about to close his Golden Door Delicatessen when a wet, wet man staggered through the door, shaking an umbrella that had been turned inside out by the wind.

"I was this minute about to lock up!" said Mr. Salovsky.

"So I'm lucky."

"What would you like?"

"A bagel," said the bedraggled man.

"All right. One bagel. And—?"

"That's all."

"That's *all?*" Mr. Salovsky could hardly believe his ears. "No cream cheese on the bagel?"

"No, thanks."

"A piece lox?"

"No lox."

"But a takeout cup of good hot coffee, right?"

"No, thanks. No coffee."

Mr. Salovsky stared at the dripping stranger. "On a terrible night like this, you came out and walked all the way here for—one—plain—bagel?!"

"That's what she wants," said the customer.

"She?" echoed Salovsky. "That explains it. 'She' has to be your wife, no?"

"Certainly it's my wife. Do you think my *mother* would send me out for one bagel on a godforsaken night like this?!"

"My wife," says Henny Youngman, "is the sweetest, kindest, most understanding woman in the world. . . . This is a paid political announcement."

The old friends met in London's St. James' Square.

"Why, Hubert, old boy, you look positively *won*derful!"

"I should," said Hubert. "Such a spot of luck I've just had. How *can* one be so lucky?!"

"What happened?"

"What happened, dear boy, is that Penelope ran away. Pftt! . . . My wife simply disappeared—with my best friend."

"What's his name?"

"Who knows?" grinned Hubert. "Never even met the bounder."

BESSIE: I read where a single oyster can lay between one and eight *million* eggs a year!

SOPHIE: Migod, think of what the married ones can do!

As the reception line moved past the bride and groom, one man shook the groom's hand and whispered into his ear, "Congratulations, fella. My name is Francis Dorn. You could be hearing a lot about me in the years ahead. Don't take it seriously. . . ."

The groom looked puzzled.

"Your bride," said Dorn, "will from time to time say I'm the man she should have married. . . ."

HUSBAND (*on phone*): Welma, I have good news! You know that new play you've been dying to see? Well, I just got two tickets in the fourth row!

WIFE: Marvelous, honey! I'll start dressing!

HUSBAND: Do. . . . They're for tomorrow night.

Mel Draper, after a night of poker with his pals, was tiptoeing, shoes in his hands, into the bedroom. He stumbled over the bedspread.

Mrs. Draper turned in her sleep and drowsily asked, "Mel, is that you?"
Draper froze. "It damn well better be!"

"Tell me," said Dr. Freda Baum, the well-known marriage counselor, "what do you think *started* the squabble this morning?"

"Who knows?"

"Well . . . did you by any chance wake up grumpy?"

"Oh, no. I let him sleep until noon."

Cried Mrs. Horlick to Mr. Horlick: "So okay! I grant you—yes, I admit it—I *love* to spend money! But just name one other extravagance of mine. Go ahead. Just one."

In Dallas, Mervyn Grimsby turned to his wife and blurted, "Darling, tomorrow is our twenty-fifth wedding anniversary, so why don't you go to Nieman-Marcus and pick out a fabulous new fur coat?"

"Thank you, Merv, but—I really don't want a fabulous new fur coat."

"Okay, Selma. Then how about a diamond necklace? Van Cleef and Arpel—"

"No, dear. I already have a diamond necklace. . . ."

"Then a new Rolls! The color of your eyes—"

"*Mervyn*, stop. I don't want a new Rolls."

Grimsby studied her. "Listen, doll. What *do* you want?"

"What I want," said his wife, "is a divorce."

"A divorce?!" echoed Mervyn. "Good God, Selma. *That* I can't afford."

Mr. and Mrs. Tobias were discussing their daughter, Jessie, nearing forty and never married. "There was a time, Bertha," Mr. Tobias told his wife, "that girl could have married any man she pleased!"

"Mnyeh," scoffed his wife. "So why didn't she get married?"

"Because she never pleased anyone."

"Cynthia," wheezed Mr. Bannister, "I have been figuring out my estate . . ."

"Oh, Floyd, *please* don't talk of that." Mrs. Bannister sniffed. "You'll be better in no time—"

"No, no, my dear. I won't be with you long. I don't want you to worry about getting along after I'm gone. So I figured out my estate. It will come to eight hundred thousand dollars."

"Floyd, *please*. Life won't be worth living without you. You are all I want in the world." Cynthia dabbed her handkerchief to her nostrils, shed a tear, then said, "By the way, dear, does that include the cottage in Connecticut?"

❧

Corky Hearn was in his cups, sniffing and sniveling. "For eighteen years—*eighteen* years, mind ye . . . me and me wife wuz the happiest man and woman in the whole durn world!"

"What," asked a barfly, "happened?"

"Then," blubbered Hearn, "we met."

❧

Mr. Birney studied the young man who had been paying court to his daughter Jenny and now had asked Mr. Birney "for the honor of weddin' y'r Jenny, wi' y're consent an' approval, sor."

Mr. Birney said, "Now, y're a fine young mon, t' be sure, an' both Mrs. Birney and I have taken a fancy to y'. But we must be practical, don't y' agree? I mean to say, I do nae know what it is y're worrth—or can y' support a fomily?"

The young man said, "I do nae want to marry th' fomily, sor. I oonly want t' marry Jenny."

❧

"Man, oh, man," sighed Kelsey, "I had everything any man could want: the love of a gorgeous woman, a beautiful home, plenty of money, fine clothes—"

"What happened?"

"What happened is—out of the blue, without any hint or warning, my wife walked in!"

❧

"Willie," murmured Martha MacToon's father, "the lad who marries my only daughter is going to get a mighty huge weddin' gift."

Willie studied Martha MacToon—stout, nearsighted, far from fetching, and considerably older than he.

"Well?" whispered MacToon.

"Uh," Willie faltered, "could I nae see the gift?"

❧

The late Joe E. Lewis, a nightclub entertainer with special wit, once ruminated: "Show me a Jewish man who comes home early every night, is greeted with smiles and coos, has his coat and hat taken, his shoes taken off, pillows arranged for him, made to feel comfortable and welcome in every way, then is served a really delicious meal—and I'll show you a Jew who lives in a Japanese restaurant."

See also **Bachelors, Hanky-panky, Just Jokes, Love, Marriage**

Martians

The two men from Mars walked down the empty street, gazing around in wonder. Finally, they stopped before a fire hydrant. "Take us to your leader!" said the first Martian. . . . "Hey, didn't you hear what I said?! Take—us—to—your—leader!"

The Martians waited. Silence. The first Martian angrily began to kick the hydrant. "Unless you take us to your—"

"Oh, lay off," said the second Martian. "Can't you see he's only a kid?"

Two men from Mars landed in New York. They drifted about and happened to run into each other on the branch of a tree in Central Park. Each knew the other was from Mars because of the ultrasonic vibrations that emanate from Martians' heads.

"Hello, there," said the first Martian. "Been on this planet long?"

"Since Tuesday," said the second.

"Quite a place, isn't it?"

"You bet."

"By the way, what's your name?"

"44X306. And yours?"

"92T748."

The second Martian pondered: "That's funny; you don't look Jewish."

Opgdkrf, visiting our planet from Mars, studied the window of Warshawsky's Bakery and entered the store. "Those little wheels in the window," he said.

"*Wheels?*" echoed the puzzled Warshawsky.

"Yeah. Like—right there. In the tray . . ."

"Oh, *bagels,*" said Warshawsky. "Here . . . taste one."

Opgdkrf bit into the doughy delicacy and exclaimed, "Wow! You know something? These would go great with cream cheese and lox!"

Middle Age

The period when emotions become symptoms.

IRVIN S. COBB

When women buy every new wrinkle, to try to get rid of old ones.

When burning the midnight oil means staying up past nine thirty.

When you're home on Saturday night, the telephone rings, and you hope it's the wrong number.

RING LARDNER

The time when you think that in a week or two you'll feel as good as ever.

DON MARQUIS

When you have a choice of diversions and choose the one that will get you home by nine o'clock.

That point in life where, when your wife tells you to pull in your stomach you already have.

The time when the thing you grow most in your garden is tired.

Military

For many years, SECRET was the designation used in Washington for confidential material whose circulation was to be severely restricted.

When SECRET failed to keep all the secrets, TOP SECRET was created.

When TOP SECRET did not sufficiently guard triple-important information, FOR EYES ONLY appeared.

Now a new, ultraefficient classification is being considered by the Pentagon: Top, Top, Top Secret materials will henceforth be stamped in glaring red:

D.B.R.

What does D.B.R. stand for?

Destroy Before Reading

❧

Sign on door to U.S. Army recruiting station

**DRAFT CARDS
CHEERFULLY BURNED HERE.**

❧

Scene: Berlin, A Bench in the Tiergarten

"Ach, Heinrich, Heinrich," mused Ulric Schenenkranz, "I vas chust ten days viziting in Paris. . . ."

"Ah, Paris. . . ."

"Heinrich, *mein freund,* it gives me pain to say—but Paris iz no longer ze same. . . ." Ulric sighed. "I am remembering ze goot old times, vhen—"

"Vhen Paris vas Paris, *ja?*"

"No, Heinrich. Vhen Schenenkranz vas Schenenkranz."

❧

Not long after Pearl Harbor, when the WACs (Women's Auxiliary Corps) was trying, by great persistence and guile, to buy up thousands of yards of cloth for uniforms, a general in the Quartermaster's Corps sent this telegram to all army purchasing agents:

ALL WACS CLOTHING MUST BE HELD UP
UNTIL NEEDS OF REGULAR ARMY PERSONNEL
HAVE BEEN FULLY SATISFIED.

❧

On phone booth at Fort Dix: Please limit calls to three chicks.

The recruit was so exhausted by the day's exercises that, assigned to stand guard duty, he could not keep his eyes open—so he rested his chin on the butt of his rifle, whose bayonet he stuck into the earth, and dozed off. . . .

In time he became aware of heavy boots approaching. His heart leaped: the penalty for sleeping on duty was awful. Opening his eyes slightly, he discerned the Officer of the Day, glaring, closing in on him. The soldier kept his head down. The officer stopped.

The soldier raised his head, gazing up to the sky piously, said, "Amen . . ." then braced into a salute. "Yes, *sir?*"

Before the entire ship's complement, the navy commander, a staunch believer in psychology and a champion of morale, addressed them: "Officers, men, before we set foot on our wonderful ship, I want you all to realize how deeply I am committed to one simple principle: the S.S. *Eldridge* is not '*my*' ship. It is not the *officers'* ship. It is not *your* ship. . . . Gentlemen, the S. S. *Eldridge* is *our* ship!"

From the far ranks came an ironic voice, "Great. Let's sell it."

Corporal Fagin, in training in the Parachute Corps, approached his lieutenant. "Lieutenant, I can't seem to understand one thing in the basic manual. It says, 'As you leave the aircraft, be sure you are not jumping on an earlier parachutist—' "

"But that's obvious," said the lieutenant. "It takes only a moment to glance down—"

"Glance down?" echoed Fagin. "You mean I'm supposed to keep my eyes *open?!*"

Commandatore Uprizzi of the Italian navy asked the midshipman training for lookout duty, "Spaccati, suppose some sailor falls overboard. What do you do?"

Spaccati went into a brace and replied, "I would grab the bullhorn and shout, 'Overboard! *Attenzione!* Man overboard!' "

"*Buono.* Now, Spaccati, suppose one of the officers accidentally falls overboard?"

Spaccati deliberated. " '*Scusa*. Which one?"

See also **Behind the Iron Curtain, Just Jokes, Russia**

Miracles

Paddy Kerrigan was going through Irish customs after his trip to France. Among his suitcases stood a brown gallon container. "And what might this be?" asked the customs officer.

"Sure, and that is holy water I am bringin' back t' me loved ones, from Lourdes."

The customs officer unscrewed the top, sniffed, blinked, raised the bottle, and tasted the contents. "*Water,* did you say now?" he sputtered. "This is *brandy*. Strong French brandy!"

"Praise the Lord!" cried Kerrigan. "Another miracle!"

In Belfast, Terence Foley stubbed his toe on a two-by-four plank, fell down, then hurried to his doctor, chortling. The doctor substituted a dead patient's X-ray. And Terence Foley, represented by a lawyer named Houlihan, sued the L. E. Construction Company for a million pounds.

In the courtroom, Terence Foley's bandaged toe had become an immobilized leg, plastered solid up to the hip; and Foley's left arm was in a cast bent up across his shoulder; and Foley's neck was in a brace; and the pain in his back was said to be so great he had to be wheeled in and out of the courtroom in a wheelchair.

Lawyer Houlihan's throat choked as he described Foley's family of eight, a wife, a mother, a father, a father-in-law, one grandmother on her deathbed—all, all dependent on Terence Foley.

It took a softhearted jury less than an hour to find for the plaintiff, and to award Foley no less than five hundred thousand pounds. The cheers from the ranks of Terence Foley's family, friends, and creditors rang through the courtroom.

As Foley was wheeled out of the fateful room, the lawyer for the construction company, Liffey Donahue, stepped over to him. "Well thin, congratilations t' ye, Terence Foley. A mighty fine windfall y've this day gotten. . . . But I have bad news for ye, Terence Foley." He whispered into Foley's ear so no one else could hear him. "Ye know and *I* know this is all a made-up crock! Ye got no more'n a wee *sprain*—if that. So the construction company, determined t' stop any forther such rascalry, has hired the foinest detectives in the land! And they will be followin' ye, Terence, day and night, wheriver ye go, *how*iver ye go! Ye will niver enjoy y'r ill-gotten money! Th' first minute ye get out 'f that ridiculous wheelchair, ye will be slapped with a summons, and hauled back to a smarter judge, God willin'; and ye will be exposed as a malingerer and a crook! Ye will be required to return ivery penny 'v that shameliss verdict! Ye will be charged with th' crime of—"

Foley raised a consoling hand. "Save y're valuable brith, Mr. Donahue. Y'r words do not dismay me. Day and night will y're detictives be followin' me, now? Watchin' me ivery move, is it? Well, I shall *tell* you my ivery move in advance!" Foley signaled Donahue to come closer. "From Belfast I fly to London, where I shall be carried to a plane to the South of France. There I am takin' off and taken in an ambulance to a little town. And if your foine detictives are still watchin', so much the better. Because they will behold a miracle! I shall rise from me chair of pain, an' I shall walk!" Foley smiled beatifically. "Ah, Donahue, Donahue. Me viry heart pounds with joy as I contemplate the mysterious powers of our blessed Lady of Lourdes. . . ."

See also **Gurus, The Occult**

Missionaries

The bright, bubbling new missionary studied the grave faces of the African natives sitting before him. "We are brothers together in Christ, children of the same Lord, blessed with immortal souls now and forever and into the resurrection. . . . Amen."

From the ranks of the natives came, in unison, *"Bombaloobo . . ."*

"And, my children, you must dedicate yourselves never, never to spill the blood of your neighbors!"

"Bombaloobo," crooned the congregation.

"And you must love each other, and even your enemies . . ."

"Bombaloobo! Bombaloobo!"

"May the good Lord bless and keep you," said Father Muldoon.

"Bombaloobo . . ."

As the missionary gathered up his Bible and his stole, Otawbi, the chief of the tribe, came before him, bowing.

"Chief Otawbi," exclaimed Father Muldoon, "I don't think I have ever had a more sincere reception. . . . I will come back next Sunday."

"Yes, yes," said Chief Otawbi. "Go in peace. And when you reach the meadow, where we keep our little flock of cows, be careful. . . ."

"Of what, Otawbi?"

"Not to step into the *bombaloobo.*"

See also **Cannibals**

Modesty

A famous old rabbi was being introduced to a congregation by a trustee who waxed more eloquent by the second: "We are about to hear from a man of such wisdom that even the most learned sit at his feet, of such kindness that even children flock to him for advice, with such a keen understanding of human problems that men and women bare to him their innermost secrets, a man of such . . ."

At this point, the old rabbi tugged at the eulogist's sleeve, whispering, "Don't forget my humility."

Moses

The great throng of Hebrews patiently waited at the foot of the mountain, which was covered with dark smoke. For hours and hours now, Moses, who had led them out of the wilderness, had been gone. . . . Only the night before, the Great Lord Jahweh had appeared in a Cloud before Moses, who had come down from the mountain with the sacred tablets on which were inscribed the commandments to the Hebrews. . . . And Moses had gone back now to . . .

Suddenly the tip of a white staff was seen moving down the mountain—and the fluttering of a white robe . . . A great murmuring possessed the throng. At last they beheld—Moses!

A cheer of acclamation rang out. And Moses stood before the vast assemblage and in a commanding voice said: "Children of Israel! I bring you tidings from our Lord, God of Israel. For six hours I have been with Him, kneeling in the dust, recounting the petition you assigned me to convey to Him! And I can now give you His answer!"

A weighty silence fell upon the Hebrews.

"The answer of our Lord God, King of the Universe, to your petition about the Commandments contains—good news, and bad news."

Agitation swept the ranks. "Tell us, O Moses!"

"What said our Lord?"

Moses spread his arms to still the throng. "The good news, my children, is that I managed to persuade the Lord to cut the list from fourteen to ten!"

Cheer after cheer rose from the congregation. "Hurrah! Hurrah!"

"Our Moses is mighty above all men."

"O Moses, you will be thanked down all the eons . . ."

"Finish!" cried someone.

"What is the bad news?"

Moses stared at the throng for a moment, then cleared his throat and declared: "The bad news . . . He would not budge. Adultery is still in."

This tale is a Hollywoodnik's version of the historic flight of the Hebrews out of ancient Egypt:

When Moses, racing his harassed and desperate people across the desert, came to the Red Sea, he gave swift thanks to the Lord, then called out, "Manny! Manny!"

From the throng came Manny, a publicity man, "Yes, Moses?"

"The boats!" said Moses.

"What?"

"The *boats*. The boats you were supposed to arrange—to get us across the Red Sea?!"

"Oh, my God!" said Manny. "Moses, what with all the news items and human-interest stories—I forgot!"

"You forgot the *boats?!*" cried Moses. "You moron! The Egyptians will be here any minute! What do you expect me to do—ask God to part the waters, let all of us across, and drown the pursuing Egyptians? Is *that* what you think—"

"Boss," said Manny with fervor, "you do that and it's worth at *least* two pages in the Old Testament!"

At the Red Sea, Moses, beholding the astonishing sight of the waters' parting, groaned, "Oh, Lord, I was just going in for a dip!"

RED BUTTONS

Mothers

God could not be everywhere, so he created mothers.

Mothers understand what children do not say.

Why do mothers have big aprons? To cover the faults of their children.

"A mother has glass eyes." (She cannot see her offspring's faults.)

YIDDISH SAYINGS

Harvey Nesselbaum, the patient, stretched out on the couch in his psychoanalyst's office.

Dr. Gupel settled back in his chair behind the couch, notebook in hand.

"A dream," said Nesselbaum. "My God, doctor, such a dream! . . . I was in the kitchen—a nice house, an old-fashioned stove, chairs painted with—let me think, yes, stenciled, with birds and flowers. . . . And my mother was making me breakfast. And while I was eating the cereal, two soft-boiled eggs, toast, a glass of Coca-Cola—into the room flew—an American eagle! And sat on my mother's shoulder! Cawing—*cawing* 'The Star-Spangled Banner'! . . . Doc, what can that mean . . . an American eagle . . . our national an—"

"A Coke?" cried Dr. Gupel. "A *Coke?!* That your mother gives you for *break*fast?!"

Rafe ("Knuckles") Blatkin, a "hit-man" for a Canarsie mob, was gunned down in front of his building by the Slattery boys.

Bleeding from a dozen bullet holes, Knuckles staggered up the brownstone stairs and pushed open the door to his home. "Mama . . ." he groaned. "Mama . . ."

His mother sang out, "Rafeleh!"

Knuckles clutched his abdomen. "Mama—they—"

"Rafeleh, don't talk," beamed Mrs. Blatkin. "First, eat a little something, *then* we can talk."

Mrs. Feeny was inordinately proud of her children—and freely boasted about them. One day, while some friends were visiting her, little Gerald

Feeny, age six, came into the room. "Jerry," his mother exclaimed. "Give a nice big kiss on the cheek to Mrs. Cooper, Mrs. Fagan, Mrs. Ryan . . ." And while Jerry was doing his mother's bidding, she beamed, "Jerry has started public school—two weeks ago. And, ladies, I don't mean to blow my own boy's horn, but I can't *believe* how much he has already learned! Gerald, tell the ladies: Suppose you have three oranges—three, right? Then someone gives you four oranges. Four, right. So, three plus four . . . how many oranges do you have?"

Jerry knit his brow and said, "Eight."

"You see?" chortled Mrs. Feeny. "The dear lad missed by only one!"

Mrs. Notstein sent her little boy off to his first day in school with many a kiss and a hug. "So, *bubeleh,* be a good boy and obey the teacher. And don't make noise. Be polite, *bubeleh,* and play nice with the other children. And when it's time to come home, button up warm, and be careful crossing the street, *bubeleh* . . ." etc., etc.

Off went little Notstein.

When he returned that afternoon, his mother hugged him and kissed him and exclaimed, "So—how did you like school? You make friends, *bubeleh?* You *learned* something?"

"Yeah," said the little lad. "I learned my name is Irving."

Mrs. Herman and Mrs. Gerges were talking about their children. "My son?" said Mrs. Herman. "Who could ask for a better boy? Every Friday, he eats dinner at my house. Every summer, he makes me spend a month with him in the country. Every winter, he sends me for a month to a hotel in Florida."

To which Mrs. Gerges replied, "*I* have a son, an angel. For a whole year, he's been going to the most expensive psychiatrist in New York. Every day, month in and out, he goes there. And he talks each day for an hour. And do you know what he talks about, paying *fifty dollars an hour?!* . . . Me."

Little Gershon came home from school in considerable excitement. "Mama, mama! In half an hour there is going to be an eclipse of the sun! Can I go out and watch it?"

"Why not, dollink?" replied Gershon's mother. "Only one thing; don't stand too close."

See also **Children, Definitions (by Children), Education, Jews**

Movie Marquees

ADAM AND EVE
with a Cast of Thousands

∾

GEORGE WASHINGTON SLEPT HERE
with Ann Sheridan

THE BRIDE WORE BOOTS
and
Selected Shorts

Double features on movie theater marquees

GO FOR BROKE
and
THE LAS VEGAS STORM

∾

THE SEVENTH VEIL
and
GREAT EXPECTATIONS

∾

AN AMERICAN IN PARIS
and
THE BIG HANGOVER

∾

HOLIDAY AFFAIR
and
LET'S MAKE IT LEGAL

TRAPEZE
and
EMERGENCY HOSPITAL

I AM A CAMERA
and
OVEREXPOSED

See also **Boo-boos, Goldwyniana, How's That Again?**

Movies

Traditional Hollywood movie: Boy meets girl. Boy loses girl. Boy gets girl.

Science-fiction films: Boy meets girl. Boy loses girl. Boy builds girl.

Current films: Boy meets boy. Boy loses boy. Boy gets another boy.

Newest movie successes: Boy rapes girl. Girl joins gang. Gang rapes girl's father.

L. R.

See also **Goldwyniana, Movie Marquees**

Musicians

Musicians assert that the following episode is absolutely true. Years ago, when the boy Jascha Heifetz made his astounding debut in Carnegie Hall, every first-rate violinist in New York was in the audience. Among the galaxy of virtuosos was the great Mischa Elman, who had brought along his illustrious friend Leopold Godowsky, a famous pianist and a renowned wit.

Young Heifetz stunned the house with his technical brilliance and indescribable wizardry. After one astonishing arpeggio, the audience exploded into thunderous acclamation.

Elman mopped his brow and neck and whispered to Godowsky, "Lord, it's hot in here!"

"Not," said Godowsky, "for pianists."

The orchestra conductor could not help noticing, during the rehearsal of the Jupiter Symphony, how his first cellist was moaning and making horrible faces. This went on so uninterruptedly that the conductor finally ra-ta-ta-taed his baton on the music stand. The orchestra went silent. The conductor turned to the cellist. "Are you feeling ill?"

"Oh no, maestro."

"Don't you like the way I'm conducting this symphony?"

"Oh no, sir. Your conducting is very inspiring!"

"Then why," the conductor demanded, "are you making those constant groans and tortured faces?"

The cellist sighed, "I *hate* music."

Musician: A man who, hearing a female singing in the shower, puts his ear to the keyhole.

Nationalities

This portion comes from a game played by graduate students when I was at the London School of Economics.

L. R.

One Englishman, a bore;
Two Englishmen, a club;
Three Englishmen, an empire.

One Frenchman, a lover;
Two Frenchmen, an affair;
Three Frenchmen, a ménage.

One German, a burgher;
Two Germans, a beer-parlor;
Three Germans, an army.

One Italian, a tenor;
Two Italians, a duet;
Three Italians, an opera.

One American, a businessman;
Two Americans, a market;
Three Americans, a cartel.

One Irishman, a drinker;
Two Irishmen, a fight;
Three Irishmen, partition.

One Japanese, a gardener;
Two Japanese, a cult;
Three Japanese, electronics.

One Dutchman, a citizen;
Two Dutchmen, a bicycle club;
Three Dutchmen, irrigation.

One Russian, a melancholic;
Two Russians, a chess game;
Three Russians, a revolution.

One Swiss, one Swiss;
Two Swiss, two Swiss;
Three Swiss, three Swiss.

National Anthems
(as Rendered by Various Children)

José, can you see?
By the Donzerly light.
Oh, the ramrods we washed,
were so gallantly peeling.
And the rockets' red glare,
the bombs bursting in there,
grapefruit through the night . . .

God bless America, land that I love,
Stand aside, sir, and guide her
With delight through the night from a bulb.

Nebechs

Note: A *nebech*—often written in English as "nebbish"—is a meek, weak, unimpressive namby-pamby—the sort of character featured in Woody Allen's films.

L. R.

The one in a group you always forget to introduce.

The unlucky soul upon whom a waiter always spills soup.

"Officer, officer!" the driver called from his car on 38th Street.
A policeman sauntered over. "Yeah?"
"Officer, is it okay for me to park here?"
"Absolutely not."
"But officer," the *nebech* protested. "How about all those other cars parked up and down the whole street?!"
"They," said the cop, "didn't ask."

"Doctor Mertz," the *nebech* complained, "why doesn't anyone ever pay attention to me? My wife, my children, my friends—I might as well not even *be* here, the way they just don't listen to anything I say. Why, doctor? Why?"
Dr. Mertz thought for a moment, stepped to his door, and, into the waiting room called, "Next."

Mrs. Bechter began to beat her milquetoast of a husband, who fled her blows by crawling under the sofa.
"Come out of there, Sol, you coward!"
"No!" Sol shouted. "I'll show you who's boss in this house!"

See also **Dummies, Jews, Shlemiels**

News Items That Haunt Me
(All True)

In Kirby Misperton, zoo officials paid out more than £280 to visitors last year for articles stolen from them by monkeys. The monkeys specialized in snatching eyeglasses from the wearers' noses when visitors bent forward to make out a sign on the cage. The sign reads:

WARNING:
THESE MONKEYS SNATCH GLASSES

London Daily Mail

A young British surgeon, on his first visit to America, was invited to look up a cystoscope (an instrument for viewing inside the bladder). To his astonishment, he saw the sign:

VISIT JOE'S BAR

For a moment the young surgeon thought he was beholding the final extremity of a national mania for advertisement. Then he moved the instrument, and saw that he was gazing at a segment of a plastic cocktail stick.

How it got there remains a mystery.

London Daily Telegraph

HE ONLY WANTED A CORN REMOVED

Milan, Sept. 30—An attempt to remove a corn led to three operations and two broken bones in Buenos Aires.

Suffering from a corn on his left foot, an Argentine went to the hospital to have it removed. Afraid of the thought of more pain, he requested an anesthetic. Once the anesthetic was applied, the patient's heart stopped. Frantic doctors immediately operated and conducted a heart massage to revive the patient.

Though the regular heartbeat was soon restored, the patient had been given such an overdose of oxygen that additional surgery was required to relieve a stomach swelling. Two operations later, the patient was being returned to the recovery ward when the elevator jammed and interns had to place him on a stretcher. During this maneuver, an intern slipped and the patient crashed to the pavement, breaking his arm and collarbone. [He] suddenly began gasping for air. He was rushed to the operating room for his third operation of the day—a tracheotomy.

And in all the confusion, the doctors forgot about his corn.

Daily American, Rome

❧

BRAZEN HUNGER MARCH
BY HARES

Moscow (Reuters)—Thousands of fearless and hungry hares were reported on the march today in Far Eastern Siberia.

Tass, the Soviet press agency, said the hares trooped through . . . settlements in the Kamchatka Peninsula, "showing utter disregard for the frenzied barkings of dogs."

When they reached the coast of the sea of Okhotsk, the hares ravenously attacked sea kale . . . [then] "marched back to the tundra in the same organized manner."

London Daily Telegraph

❧

One incident that caused him "a great deal of personal pain," Mr. Heckscher said, was a bitter argument with Mayor Lindsay over the decision to hire Robert S. Collier, who was convicted two years ago of a conspiracy to blow up the Statue of Liberty.

New York Times, March 24, 1968

❧

HUSBANDS WHO HAVE
SEX OPERATION WILL
GET EASIER HOME MORTGAGES

A plan to allow easier mortgages for husbands who had undergone vasectomies was approved by Sutton Coldfield Town Council, Warwickshire, last night.

The council approved a proposal that "if a husband can provide medical evidence he can no longer help to procreate children, his wife's income will be taken into account" when advancing council mortgages.

The proposal was described as "moral blackmail" in a letter from five local Roman Catholic clergymen to Councilor Ron Hudson, chairman of the housing committee.

News of the World, London

❧

A man who removed a stuffed tiger from a zoo's publicity display at Waterloo Station got no farther with it than the taxi rank.

The police arrived as he was trying to get into a taxi-cab with the stuffed animal, with the help of the driver and a porter. The tiger, a rare Sumatran specimen valued at £500, was too big to go into the vehicle.

At Croyden Crown Court, Samuel William Smith, 50, told the court that while he was looking at the display, a youth told him he could have the tiger for £35. He said that as the exhibition was closing that night, the stuffed animals were for sale cheaply.

"I thought it was a bargain at the price."

London Daily Telegraph

WANTED: Typist to copy Top Secret documents. Must be unable to read.

Krokodil (a satiric journal), Moscow

For seven months, the National Park Service has been trying to put out a fire in a 25,000-year accumulation of giant sloth dung, in a remote Grand Canyon cave. So far the agency has not succeeded . . . the effort has cost $50,000.

Smithsonian paleobiology curator Dr. Clayton Ray said . . . the giant sloth . . . was not notable except for producing a large and durable stool in the same place for about 25,000 years.

Washington Post, February 1977

From the august *New York Times:*

> Recently, a Queens salesman began wondering if he shouldn't consult a psychiatrist. Every time he drove his car, he thought it was raining. He clearly heard the sound of gurgling water but no rain was falling.

A psychiatrist friend whom I promptly telephoned chuckled as he offered a diagnosis: (1) The salesman *hated* to go out on the road; so (2) the rain he imagined he was hearing was wish fulfillment; (3) this was a perfectly understandable expression of "the salesman's unconscious," which produced the illusory sounds of rain in order to (4) trick the salesman into going back home to hit the sack.

I thanked my friend and hung up. I did not have the heart to read him the remainder of the story:

> One day, the salesman headed for the nearest service station. It seems that the car's steering column was full of water, which had accumulated from both condensation and leakage.
>
> The mechanic told the salesman it was the first time he had ever run into such a problem.

If you ask me, it's the first time anyone heard of that problem.

from my Passions and Prejudices

GOLDFISH SAVED FROM DROWNING

Mr. Humphrey discovered the goldfish gasping for air on the surface of his garden pond at Hillside Crescent, Uxbridge. He fished it out and found its mouth was jammed open by a pebble. Gently he went to work and gradually eased the pebble out. Then he put the fish back into the water, where it quickly recovered.

Tonight an R.S.P.C.A. inspector said: "Mr. Humphrey's prompt action undoubtedly saved the fish's life. I will be preparing a report to be put before the Awards Committee. Not many people know that a fish could drown if it swallows too much water. I hate to think how many goldfish owners have stood by and let a fish drown because they did not know what was wrong."

London Star

Note: The names in this editorial have been changed to protect the guilty.

TURN BACK, FOOLISH GIRL, TURN BACK!

Miss Blossom Mae Jetheroe, 23, was sentenced to seven days in gaol for "accosting" gentlemen on King Street. In passing sentence, Mr. Justice Cecil Horstcroft sternly admonished the errant female: "The wages of sin is surely *death*. O shameless, foolish girl, mend your ways!"

Yes, yes, Blossom Mae, listen to your just sentencer! Wrest your tinkling feet from the primrose path! Spurn those tawdry escapades that imperil your soul! Stray not from the straight and narrow! Think, Miss Blossom Mae, and turn back! There still is time! Let the blush of virtue return to your still young cheeks!

Jamaica Star, Kingston

See also **Advertisements, Bloopers, Headlines That Haunt Me, How's That Again?, Obituary Data Worth Remembering, Typos**

Nudists

A beautiful young thing walked proudly past a group of men at the nudist colony. Their eyes followed her. One of the men sighed, "Wow! Can you imagine what she would look like in a bathing suit?!"

EDEN NUDIST COLONY
BARE WITH US

Obituary Data Worth Remembering

When he died he left a wife and six children, half of whom were living.

Those who knew him said that underneath his ragged trousers, beat a heart of gold.

One half of his estate went to his wife, and the other half to each of his four children by a previous marriage.

For years, Reverend D——— had given Sunday-school classes twice a week.

Born poor, entirely through his own efforts he worked his way up to within a few cents of a fabulous fortune.

See also **Headlines That Haunt Me, How's That Again?, Limericks, News Items That Haunt Me, Typos**

Obscenity

O banish the use of those four-letter words
Whose meaning is never obscure;
The Romans and Britons, those bawdy old birds,
Were vulgar, obscene, and impure.
You stubbornly use any weaseling phrase
That never says just what you mean,
You prefer to be known for your hypocrite ways
Than be vulgar, impure, or obscene.
Let your morals be loose as a libertine's vest
But your language keep always obscure;
It's the word, not the act, that's the absolute test
Of what's vulgar, obscene, or impure.

AUTHOR UNKNOWN, alas

The Occult

The spiritualist gazed into her crystal ball, blinked, gazed again, then stood up and slapped her beautiful client hard on the cheek.

"Why are you doing this?" cried the client.

"For going to bed with my husband—"

"I never went to bed with your husband!"

"—next Saturday."

The London branch of the Clairvoyant Society will not have its regular meeting this month, due to unforeseen circumstances.

For months, Mrs. Zissel had been nagging her husband, Milty, to go with her to the séance parlor of Madame Froda Pranyakar. "Milty, she is absolutely *spooky*. A real gypsy—and with such things she can bring out of her crystal ball will make your hair stand on end, do you hear me? She brings the voices of the dead—from the other world—right into her parlor! We all *talk* to them. Last week I talked with my darling brother, Howie. Then my mother, may she rest in peace. Then Uncle Freddie and Tante Sura. . . . Milty, for a lousy twenty dollars you can talk to your old grampa who you say you miss so much you're always telling me you mourn him so much. Isn't that worth twenty lousy dollars—to hear—to *talk* to—your darling *zayde?!*"

Milton Zissel could not resist his Hannah's appeal. At the very next séance at Froda Pranyakar's Gypsy Fortune and Séance Parlor, Milty sat under the multicolored light, at the green table, holding hands with the pilgrim to his right and the mystic to his left, all humming, "Ooooom . . . oooom . . . Tonka Tooom . . ." Madame Froda Pranyakar, heavily made up, glitter on her upper eyelids, wearing huge earrings, three sparkling necklaces, and a heavy braid of bracelets, a paisley scarf tied around her head like a *babushka*, her eyes lost in trance, was making mysterious passes over a crystal ball from which a ghostly light emanated. . . . "Oom . . . ooom," moaned Froda Pranyakar. "My medium . . . Vashtri . . ." she keened. "Vashtri . . . come in, Vashtri . . . Who is that with you. . . . Who? . . . Mr. Zissel? . . . Milton Zissel's beloved grandfather? . . . Speak . . . speak, Milton."

Milty Zissel dared not open his eyes. He swallowed the lump in his throat and called, "Grampa? . . . *Zayde?* My own dear *zayde?*"

"Ah, Milteleh," a thin, thin voice quavered. "Is that you, my darling *aynekel?*"

"Yes, yes!" cried Milty. "This is your grandson . . . *Zayde,* are you happy in the other world?"

"Happy, Milteleh? . . . I am in bliss. Eternal, everlasting bliss . . ."

"And are you with my *Baba?*"

"Yes, yes . . . Sara and me . . . together . . ."

"And do you see other Zissels?"

"All . . . all . . . We eat together every day . . . milk . . . manna . . . fruits of paradise. . . . We laugh . . . we pray . . . we sing . . . we gaze upon the shining face of the Everlasting Lord!"

A dozen more questions did Milty ask of his grandfather, and each question did his *zayde* answer with enthusiasm, albeit in that thin, reedy, ectoplasmic voice—until: "So now, Milty darling, I have to go back. . . . The angels are calling . . . I am old and weak. . . . Just one more question, Milteleh. . . . Ask. . . . Ask . . ."

"*Zayde,*" sighed Milty, "when did you learn how to speak English?"

Alec Nadich, carrying his violin case, and with a few minutes to spare in Penn Station, stood on a weighing scale and dropped a penny in the slot.

A deep, resonant voice from inside the machine intoned; "You weigh one hundred sixty-eight pounds . . . you are five feet ten inches tall . . . and you attend the Anshe Emmet Synagogue on Allen Avenue . . ."

Alec was thunderstruck. He quickly dropped another penny in the slot. The needle quickly stopped at 168 again. Now the orotund voice said, "You play the fiddle in Gussheimer's Resort in the Catskill Mountains . . . and you are waiting to catch the—three twenty-two train to Libertyville . . ."

Alec simply could not believe his ears. He pondered, went into the men's room, put on a pair of sunglasses, altered the shape of his hat, removed his tie, took off his jacket and draped it over his violin case—and again dropped a penny in the scale.

And now that maddening, omniscient voice said, "You are five feet ten . . . you weigh one hundred sixty-eight pounds. . . . You attend the Anshe Emmet Synagogue on Allen Avenue. . . . You play the fiddle in the Gussheimer orchestra—and you have just missed the three twenty-two train to Libertyville, you idiot."

In fortune-teller's window

YOUR PROBLEM SOLVED—
OR MANIA REFUNDED.

The Ayatollah Khomeini, plagued by the infirmities of age, cursed by insomnia, and tormented (on those nights he briefly slept) by horrendous nightmares, called in Parsi Fassarjian, "beloved of the Prophet," a mystic renowned throughout Iran for his ability to see into the future.

"My days are numbered as the pages in the holy Koran," the Ayatollah mused, cross-legged on his golden cushion. "Tell me then, can you foretell the day of my passing?"

The great seer peered into a brass bowl he had brought along, in which were coiled the entrails of a rare white lion, heavily sprinkled with incense, then closed his eyes and hummed strange phrases, then stirred the entrails— and exclaimed, "Ah, noble Ayatollah, beloved of Fatima and the Prophet Mohammed, it is foretold that you will soon leave this sordid earthly plane and ascend to Paradise . . ."

The Ayatollah nodded heavily. "Soon? . . . Soon. . . . Can you say *when* soon?"

"On a holiday," said Fassarjian, messing with the entrails and releasing more incense. "A special Zionist holy day, a day celebrated throughout all of Israel."

The Ayatollah's eyes opened and flashed, "What? What? Are you certain?"

"Aye, Revered One, there can be no mistaking the omens."

"Which Zionist holiday? Which day celebrated in all of Israel?"

"Oh, Beloved of the Prophet, *any* day you die will be a holiday celebrated throughout all of Israel."

CLAIRVOYANT: My fee is fifty dollars. That entitles you to three questions and answers.

CLIENT

(*incredulously*): How much?!

CLAIRVOYANT: Fifty dollars.

CLIENT: Gee . . . isn't that a lot of money for three questions?

CLAIRVOYANT: No. . . . Now, what's your last question?

The sign in the window next to the door, at the head of the flight of brown stairs, read:

MADAM NASTAZIA

SPIRITUALIST

MEDIUM

One night, old Mr. Pomeranz made his way up the stairs. . . . "Madam Nastazia . . . my dear Sadie, my wonderful wife of forty years . . . passed on. . . . If only I—could hear her dear voice . . . talk to her . . ."

Moaned Madam Nastazia, "Cross my palma . . . twenty dollars . . ."

In a darkened room scented by exotic perfumes, under a beaded lamp, Madam Nastazia invoked the spirit of her finest intermediary, "Princess Wadlóvi of Molvania," and soon the quivering voice of Mrs. Pomeranz was heard: "Shepsel . . . can you hear me? . . . Here is Sadie . . . your wife . . ."

"Sadie!" cried Mr. Pomeranz. "I hear you! How *are* you, darling? Where—"

"I am in heaven, Shepsel; united with my parents, and yours, and Tante Minnie, and Cousin Mervin . . . and we live on the fruits of paradise . . ."

The séance lasted eight minutes before Princess Wadlóvi murmured, "Our vibrations . . . weaken . . . farewell . . ."

Dimly Mrs. Pomeranz's dulcet tone sounded, "Goodbye, Shepseleh. . . . Please . . . call again . . ."

Madam Nastazia turned the lights on. "What fine séance! You agree?"

"Agree?" echoed Mr. Pomeranz. "It was a miracle! Here! Please!" He placed two more ten-dollar bills in the spiritualist's palm. "I'll be back tomorrow!"

Madam Nastazia beamed. "You are generous mon, sir. Tomorrow, I show how moch I oppreciate. All time you talk to Sadie, I will be drinking a gloss water!!"*

See also **Gurus**

---

*Don't get it? Well, among professional ventriloquists "throwing your voice" while drinking a glass of water is considered the acme of technical perfection.

Old Saws Sharpened

Rome wasn't burned in a day.

Give a man enough rope and he'll hang you.

A rolling stone gathers no moths.

Where there's a will, there's a wail.

He's just a wolf in cheap clothing.

He who laughs last, lasts.

That's like carrying Cohens to New Rochelle.

Beware of the Greek who asks for a gift.

Let sleeping ducks lie.

Never let a gift horse in the house.

People who live in glass houses shouldn't get stoned.

Don't burn your bridges until you come to them.

Don't put all your chickens in one basket.

Let's get down to brass roots.

None but the brave desert the fair.

from my *Rome Wasn't Burned in a Day*

See also **Cynics' Dictionary, Definitions to Cherish, Doggerel, Goldwyniana, Limericks, Malaprops, Puns, Put-downs, Sarcasm, Wit**

One-upmanship

At the height of the Nazi terror in Berlin, an elderly Jew, Heinrich Schlosser, appeared at S.S. headquarters. He went up to the Storm Troop lieutenant at the desk, respectfully removed his hat—revealing a neat, embroidered *yarmulka* (skullcap)—and said, "I am answering your advertisement in this morning's *Beobachter*." He handed the officer a page from the newspaper, on which an advertisement was boldly circled.

The lieutenant glanced at the ad. His jaw fell. "*You* are answering *this?*"

"*Ja wohl*," beamed Schlosser.

"But it reads: 'Wanted: Young, strong Aryan, for special service to the *Führer* . . .' "

"*Ja wohl*," nodded Schlosser.

The lieutenant could scarcely contain himself. "You? '*Young?*' You must be seventy years old!"

"Seventy-two," said Schlosser.

" 'Strong'? Why, you're as skinny as a rail!"

"Skinnier," said Schlosser.

" '*Aryan*'?! You are obviously a Jew!"

"Absolutely," Schlosser nodded.

"Then why the *hell*," the lieutenant fumed, "did you come here?!"

Schlosser spread his arms pacifically. "I just want you to know that on *me*, you shouldn't depend."

A beggar came to Mrs. Guttman's back door. "Lady, I am weak from hunger. I have not had even a sandwich in three days."

"You poor man," said Mrs. Guttman. "But—you couldn't have come on a worse day."

"I'll eat anything!"

Mrs. Guttman glanced around her kitchen. "Listen. Maybe you would like some noodle pudding, left over from last night?"

"Lady, I would *love* it!"

"Good," smiled Mrs. Guttman. "Come back tomorrow."

See also **Business, Ingenuity, Salesmen, Scoundrels, Squelches, Stratagems**

Optometrists

Sign in optometrist's window

EYES EXAMINED WHILE YOU WAIT!

Sign in optometrist's window

IF YOU DON'T SEE WHAT YOU WANT, THIS IS THE RIGHT PLACE TO COME TO.

Sign in optometrist's window

OH, SAY, CAN YOU SEE?

"Now, then," said Dr. Tsviful, indicating the large eye chart on the wall, "what's the smallest line of letters you can read on the chart?"

The patient peered at the wall carefully, then turned to the optometrist. "What chart?"

See also Dentists, Doctors, Psychiatrists/Psychoanalysts/Psychologists

Pets

Sign in pet shop over cage of dachshund puppies

GET A LONG LITTLE DOGIE

Sign near Dog and Cat Hospital

HOSPITAL ZONE
NO BARKING!

Legend holds that when Noah was loading the Ark, God appointed an angel to name each couple as they filed aboard. This angel, whose name was Meyer, would give a couple a searching look, then choose a name. Take the huge-antlered, yellow-coated deer that lives in the mountains of Mongolia. Meyer named it "Altai-Wapiti."

The other angels, who did not like Meyer, were watching him like a whatever-they-called-a hawk before that name was allocated. And when Meyer touched the shoulder of the huge-antlered, yellow-coated deer with his sword, saying, "I dub thee Altai-Wapiti!" a chorus of cherubs protested: "Meyer, why are you calling that yellowish-coated, branch-antlered thing an Altai-Wapiti?!"

Meyer answered, "Because he *looks* like an Altai-Wapiti, that's why!"

I do not believe this.

Meyer named other deer "Hello" and "Goodbye," from which comes our custom of saying "Hello [or Goodbye], dear."

L. R.

Justin Chernik wanted to give his old grandmother, who still lived in the Bronx, alone and with few friends, a birthday present—and this year, he wanted the present to be something special.

He wandered down many streets, looking into the store windows, until he saw something that made him stop cold in his tracks. In the window of

Haley's Pet Shop was a cage, and in the cage was a parrot, and under the cage was this sign:

THIS PARROT SPEAKS YIDDISH!

Justin could hardly wait to enter the shop. "That sign is not a gag or anything, is it?" he asked the owner.

"Certainly not!" said Mr. Haley. "Do you speak Yiddish?"

"Sure."

"Okay. I'll get the bird. Talk to him. See for yourself."

Haley took the parrot out of the window and the bird perched on his finger as the owner came over to Justin. "Go on." The following astonishing conversation then took place, all in Yiddish:

CHERNIK

Sholem aleichem.

PARROT

Aleichem sholem.

CHERNIK

You really speak Yiddish?!

PARROT

Why shouldn't I? Is there a law against it?

CHERNIK

What's your name?

PARROT

Yussel.

CHERNIK

How in the world—?

PARROT

How, how? It's not such a *tsimmes.* I was born in the jungles of Brazil, captured, then brought up in Rio in an Orthodox Jewish family! The father spoke Yiddish; the mother spoke Yiddish; the family even sent me to a Hebrew school. And when my *Bar Mitzva* approached—

CHERNIK

Enough! That's enough. Yussel, you're the answer to my dreams!

To Mr. Haley, Justin said, "It's absolutely astonishing! This little bird is going to give my dear grandma a whole new world of pleasure to live for! She and Yussel can talk for *hours.* Grandma can unburden herself of all sorts of old grievances and sorrows. Yussel can tell grandma about his unusual life—in the jungle, in Rio with an orthodox Jewish family—! Mr. Haley, how much are you asking for this little bird?"

"Eight hundred dollars," said Haley. "And he's not so little."

"Eight hundred—! That's a lot of money."

"Well, Yussel is a lot of parrot. He's young, extremely healthy, he could live for twenty more years—and when can I ever expect to get another Jewish parrot?"

"Five hundred . . ." said Justin.

"No . . . seven."

"Six."

"Six-fifty, and that's my final offer!" said Mr. Haley (né Horwitz).

"It's a deal."

So Justin Chernik wrote out a check. "Deliver the bird tomorrow—grandma's birthday." And he carefully wrote out his grandmother's address. . . .

The next day, Justin telephoned his grandmother with impatient expectations. "*Bawbe,* this is Justin! Happy birthday, Grandma!"

"Oh, darling, thank you."

"And you should have many, many happy returns!"

"I'll be glad if I'll have *three* . . ."

"Grandma. Did you get my—present?" laughed Justin.

"Your present! That beautiful bird! Certainly I got it. *What* a present! Only you could think of such a wonderful, unusual gift!"

"*Bawbe,* you really like him?"

"*Liked* him?" said grandma. "He was *delicious!*"

Postscript to the reader: I always thought that this story could not be improved—nor provided with a "topper." I underrated human resourcefulness. With "delicious!" the story need not end. . . .

"D-*delicious?*" sputtered Justin. "Grandma, that—bird—spoke—fluent—Yiddish!"

Grandma chuckled. "Oh, Justin, you are such a joker."

"I'm not joking, *bawbe,*" cried Justin. "That parrot—spoke—perfect—Yiddish!"

"Don't be silly," scoffed Grandma. "Listen, Justin: if he could talk, why didn't he *say* something?!"

See also **Just Jokes, Shaggy Dogs**

Pledge of Allegiance

(as Rendered by Some Young and Old)

I pledge a legion to the flag, and to the republic for Richard Stands; one naked individual, with liberty injustice for all.

❧

I led a pigeon to the flag . . .

❧

. . . one nation in a dirigible . . .

❧

. . . one nation and a vegetable . . .

See also Bloopers, Boo-boos, Definitions (by Children), Famous People (as Seen by Children), Geography Revised, History Revised (by Children), Malaprops

Prayer

On the ten High Holy Days, between Rosh Hashonah and Yom Kippur, seats in a synagogue are often sold in advance to raise funds for the synagogue's yearly expenses. One Yom Kippur, at a small Bronx synagogue, Leonard Krautman came running up to the door.

The sexton barred his way. "Where's your ticket?"

"I don't have a ticket!" cried Krautman. "I have to see Chaim Shanker!"

"You have to have a ticket—"

"But it's an emergency! Chaim's house is on fire! I'll just tell him—and come right out!"

"Okay," said the sexton. "But don't let me catch you praying!"

Kevin Mitchell told his priest, "Father, my darlin' Kathleen—is going to have a baby!"

"Praise the Lord!" exclaimed Father McEvoy. "Your first, isn't it?"

"Yes, father. And it's bein' our first, my Kathy is going to be a bit scared . . ."

"Only natural, me boy, only natural!"

"So I was thinkin', father; might it not give her great comfort if, while she was in the delivery room at Mother of Mercy, she knew you were in the hospital chapel there, prayin' for God's special mercy. . . ."

"Kevin, say no more! 'Twill be done! And if Kathleen's parents, and your own, and members of the Mitchell family or the Morans, on Kathleen's side, care to join us in prayer, the chapel will fairly ring with Hail Marys!"

And so, when Kathy Mitchell's labor pains began, Kevin phoned Father McEvoy and his parents and Kathleen's. . . . And when, pacing outside the delivery room, the gurgling cry of a baby was heard and a nurse stuck her head out of the door to call, "It's a boy!" Kevin darted down the stairs to the chapel, where Father McEvoy and the assembled family were praying fervently, and cried, "A boy! A boy!" and ran back upstairs.

No sooner had Kevin reached the delivery room than the nurse poked her head out of the door and sang out, "Now it's a girl!"

"Praise the Lord!" cried Kevin and dashed down to the chapel. "Twins! I'm the father of twins!" he shouted. "It's a girl!"

Father McEvoy and the clans roared their pleasure.

Up the stairway raced Kevin Mitchell. And as he reached the delivery room, he heard the obstetrician's voice: "Another boy!"

Kevin wheeled around in his tracks, flew down the stairwell, and flung open the doors of the chapel, shouting, "Triplets!"

"Triplets?!" echoed Father McEvoy.

"—and in the name of the Blessed Virgin, Father and the lot of you: *stop prayin'!*"

Little Gail, age six, to her parents: "I'm going up to bed now. When I say my prayers—either of you want anything?"

See also **Clergy, Faith, God, Religion**

Prejudices

Prejudice: A vagrant opinion without visible means of support.

I believe I have no prejudices whatsoever. All I need to know is that a man is a member of the human race. That's bad enough for me.

MARK TWAIN

The Indians concealed in the thick foliage warily watched the *Santa Maria* lower a boat off its side; then men with sickly, pale bodies and ugly, thick beards plied their oars and the boat approached the shore. The Carib chief sighed, "Well, fellows, there goes the neighborhood!"

Q. Why is Sunday morning the best time to drive on a California freeway?

A. Because the Catholics are in church, the Protestants are still asleep, the Chinese are stuffing fortune cookies, the Jews are in Palm Springs, and the Mexicans can't get their cars started.

From a Romanian cookbook: Omelet: First, steal two eggs.

Psychiatrists/Psychoanalysts/ Psychologists

Psychoanalyst: A Jewish doctor who hates the sight of blood.

A psychotic thinks that two plus two equals nine; a neurotic knows perfectly well that two plus two equals four—but he just can't *stand* it.

The neurotic builds castles in the air, the psychotic thinks he lives in them, and the psychoanalyst collects rent from them both.

A hysteric knows the secret of perpetual emotion.

A congenitally depressed person builds dungeons in the air.

Neurotic: A person who, when asked "How are you?," tells you.

Psychiatrist

A doctor who chases ambivalences.

Someone who does not have to worry, as long as other people do.

Psychologist: A man who, when a voluptuous girl enters a room, watches the other men's reactions.

Experimental psychologist: A scientist who pulls habits out of rats.

L. L. LEVINSON

Mr. Samuel Goldwyn once remarked, during a dinner-table argument about psychiatry: "Anyone who goes to a psychiatrist ought to have his head examined."

When two psychoanalysts meet, the first one says, "You're fine. How am I?"

"Sit down, Mr. Pelham," said the psychiatrist. "Now, what brings you here?"

"People!" declared Pelham. "Stupid people! Doctor, I have to tell you I despair about the whole human race!"

"Mmh. Well, what is it that people actually *do* that makes you so bitter?"

"They call me crazy, that's what they do! No matter what I say or suggest—they say I am a crazy! They won't listen to a word of truth!"

"Mr. Pelham," said the psychiatrist gently, "perhaps you ought to start at the beginning. . . ."

Mr. Pelham said, "Okay. In the beginning, I created the heavens and the earth. And the earth was without form and void . . ."

The office of three psychoanalysts on Fifth Avenue is alleged, by a malicious wit, to carry this shingle:

> Gerald Barton, M.D.
> H. R. Beslow, M.D.
> John Strake, M.D.
> 6 COUCHES—NO WAITING

A woman telephoned Dr. Jerome Chazan, the well-known psychiatrist. "Hollo, Dr. Chazan?"

"Yes."

"Are you the crazy-doctor?"

"Well, madam . . . I am a psychiatrist."

"Good. I want to come see you. I am very, very nervous. . . . But foist—how much do you charge?"

"Fifty dollars an hour."

"Fifty dollars an *hour?*" gasped the caller. "Goodbye. *That* crazy, I'm not!"

Dr. Pendleton, the well-known psychiatrist, was interviewing Mr. Thacker, a new patient. After the conventional questions about age, medical history, unusual symptoms, Dr. Pendleton leaned back and said, "So far, so good, Mr. Thacker. Now then, what particular problem brought you to seek my help?"

"Doctor," said Mr. Thacker in a confidential tone, "the truth is that for some time now I've been feeling like a man sliding into a deep, dark pit . . . I think I am losing my *mind!* I—I just can't remember a single damn thing . . ." He paused, miserable.

"Can you give me an example of what you mean?"

"Easily. I can't remember what I had for dinner last night. Or what time I went to bed. Or when I got up this morning. Or what I had for breakfast . . ."

Dr. Pendleton used his gentlest tone to ask, "Mr. Thacker, how long has this been going on?"

"How long," blinked Thacker, "has *what* been going on?"

A very depressed woman patient of Dr. Homer Byrnes, the well-known psychotherapist, was vacationing in Acapulco, her first venture out of the United States. She sent Dr. Byrnes this postcard:

Hi, Doc. Having wonderful time. *Why?*

THE INSIDE DOPE ON PSYCHOANALYSIS

Psychoanalysis has been used with great success from pole to pole (although it has not been popular with other nationalities). The English, for example, will not even discuss their flower beds with anyone in the medical profession.

The Swiss, for their part, don't pay much attention to Freud because they engage in sex only during the "r" months. Switzerland has been independent for 300 years.

The French, of course, sneer at the mere mention of psychoanalysis, because by the time he is eight any French schoolboy knows how to add, subtract, and multiply.

As for the Germans, their ideas about sex are very orderly: they never indulge in it in front of their pets, who get nervous during a copulation explosion.

I don't know about the Chinese, who are an inscrutable people; or the Japanese, who shout "Banzai!" whenever they get excited. That sort of thing would complicate anyone's sex life. Every time a Japanese man shouts "Banzai!" his partner thinks the Emperor is approaching. This means that a good deal of sex in Japan takes place while the women are bowing.

Now, for the difference between Neurotics and Psychotics. First, they are spelled differently. This is important. Neurotics get extremely upset by incorrect spelling, and psychotics think you are persecuting them.

Second, a *psychotic* is an out-and-out loon. He may think his father is poisoning his yogurt, that his wife is planning to strangle him with noodles, or that the U.S. government should flood Las Vegas with soda water.

Third, a *neurotic* is a determined sufferer, afflicted by things like depressed cuticles, a fear of pistachio nuts, or underarm humidity.

Here are some simple tests you can use to tell the difference between neurotics and psychotics:

1. *Salutation Test*

When you say "Hello" to a neurotic, he is likely to bridle, "What do you mean by that?" When you say "Hello" to a psychotic, he will go to the bathroom.

2. *Dream Interpretation*

A neurotic is happy to elaborate on his dreams for hours. He will even project them for you, along with color slides of his trip to "Nature's Winter Wonderland."

A psychotic, on the other hand, confuses dreams with reality, and he will accuse you of stealing his dreams—and run away. Don't let this worry you, Herm. As Freud taught us, a psychotic is least dangerous when egos away.

3. *Direct Interrogation*

I happen to think that the best way to find out whether someone is neurotic or psychotic is by asking him. Seat the subject in an easy chair and, in a casual tone of voice, smile, "By the way, John, would you describe yourself as being alive?"

If the answer is "Yes," that rules out psychosis. If the answer is "No," do not jump to conclusions until you have listened to the subject's heart with a stethoscope. (Of course, you should never address a subject as "John" if his name is Sam, Percy, or Beulah. You can ruin the Direct Interrogation test by addressing a subject in a way that arouses his suspicions.)

from my *"Dear Herm"*

"Anna," said Mrs. Schlossberg, "is it true that your nephew Merwin is going to a psycho*analyst*?"

"True."

"Five times a week, an hour each time?"

"True, true."

"So Anna, for God's sake, what's the matter with him?"

"The doctor says," sighed Anna, "that Merwin has a real Oedipus complex."

Mrs. Schlossberg thought this over, then declared, "Oedipus-schmoedipus—just as long as he loves his mother!"

"Mrs. Galloway," the psychiatrist said thoughtfully, leaning back in his chair, "I think we can define your problem with no difficulty now. You are suffering from a deep, inordinate sense of guilt . . ."

"Yes, doctor. I agree," said Mrs. Galloway. "But why should that be? After all, I had the happiest of childhoods, no severe sicknesses, I've never lacked money—"

"That," said Dr. Gluckstern, "is why!"

Mrs. Rosenblut said to Evelyn Mortimer, Ph.D. in child psychology, "Dr. Mortimer, my little boy, Danny, nine years old—all of a sudden he has a terror about *knaydlach: matzo*-ball dumplings. Not only won't he eat them: the minute he *sees* one, he throws a temper tantrum! He jumps up and down, screaming like crazy, hollering, '*Knaydlach! Knaydlach! Knaydlach!*'—until I take them away someplace he can't see them . . ."

Dr. Mortimer asked, "When did this start?"

"Two-three weeks ago."

"Did your son have any—kind of *scare* connected with *matzo* dumplings?"

"Never. This came out of the blue."

"Has Danny ever seen how you make the dumplings?"

Mrs. Rosenblut thought for a moment. "N-no. I usually make them when he's at school . . ."

"Well, then"—Dr. Mortimer smiled—"I suggest that you show Danny exactly how *knaydlach* are made. Let him see every step. Once he understands the harmless things that go into *knaydlach*, and the whole process by which they are made, his fears will be allayed and his terror will disappear. . . ."

So, that very afternoon, Mrs. Rosenblut took little Danny into the kitchen, with reassuring smiles. "Danneleh," she said, "I'm going to make for you something *delicious!* Here, sit on the stool—so you can see everything mama does. . . . First, I put some *matzo* meal in this bowl. Nice? . . . I add a little water . . . I mix together, see? . . . Now, I add a little egg . . . salt . . . parsley. . . . Now I mix everything good. . . . I make wet my hands and roll the mix into little balls, like this, and I'm going to drop these little balls into—"

Danny leaped from the stool, screaming, "*Knaydlach! Knaydlach! Knaydlach!!!*"

DR. WEININGER: Well, I think your analysis is now completed. Doesn't that make you happy?

PATIENT: I—suppose so.

DR. WEININGER: Why are you hesitant? Do you remember how you felt when you first came to me?

PATIENT: Yes. Happier.

The woman patient, stretched out on the couch, dabbed her lace hand-kerchief at her nose and sniffed. "But, doctor. If just once—oh, I would feel *so* much better—if just once—you—kissed me!"

" 'Kiss you'?!" the analyst echoed. "Mrs. Forrest, I shouldn't even be lying *next* to you!"

Distraught Mrs. Cooley said to Dr. Flint, "I have to tell ye about a new craziness that's taken hold of me poor man. He thinks he's—a refrigerator!"

The psychiatrist frowned. "Mrs. Cooley, that is an obsession I've never heard of. . . . Uh, how does it manifest itself?"

"Why, the man sleeps with his mouth wide open!"

Dr. Flint chuckled. "That's hardly unusual, Mrs. Cooley. Many men sleep with their mouths wide open."

"But I can't get any *sleep*, doctor, with that little light on all night!"

Late one night, in a psychology lab, three white mice, in their cages, were talking. "I can't figure out what my supervisor *wants*."

"Mine," said the second, "is not too bright."

"Well, *I* couldn't be any happier," said the third. "I've got him so well trained that every time I run through his maze, he has to feed me!"

"Doctor," the new patient complained, "I have this feeling that I am not one person but two! Two separate people. Am I going crazy? Do you think I need some special treatment? Psychiatry? Psycho—"

"Just a minute!" said the doctor. "Not so fast. Start over. One at a time."

J. J. Javitch owned a fine toy store, called "J. J.'s Aladdin's Cave." But lately, Aladdin's Cave had been having grave problems. The children loved to try out the hobby-horses, the rockers, the swings, but never seemed to want to get off. Whenever a parent or a salesman tried to coax a little one off a toy, the tot would scream and dig in his heels and throw a violent temper tantrum. The store often sounded like a madhouse.

One day there appeared before J. J. Javitch a white-haired gentleman, who said: "I am Professor Lawrence Hockheimer, doctor of child psychology, consultant on infant behavior. I have heard of your difficulties; I can solve them. My fee is one hundred dollars."

"A *hundred* dollars?"

Professor Hockheimer smiled. "No obligation. If I fail to give full satisfaction, you don't pay a penny."

Mr. Javitch led the professor into the toy department. "Listen. Did you ever hear such craziness?"

On one tricycle, from which his frantic mother was trying to lift him, a little boy was screaming like a banshee. On a hobby-horse, a little girl was screeching at the salesman who was trying to coax her off. On a rocking horse, a child was caterwauling at her father—

Professor Hockheimer observed the howling scene but a moment, went over to the tricycle, patted the screaming lad on the head, leaned over and, smiling, whispered a few words into the boy's ear. At once, the lad slid off the tricycle and leaped into his mother's arms.

Professor Hockheimer went to the little girl on the hobby-horse, stroked her locks fondly, leaned over, whispered something into her ear—and the tyke stopped screaming at once and jumped off the hobby-horse.

With the squalling tyke on the rocking horse, Professor Hockheimer plied his same swift magic. A pat, a smile, those mesmeric words—and decorum replaced obstinacy.

"I can't believe my eyes!" said J. J. Javitch. "What in the world do you say to them?"

"My fee . . ."

"Fine! Yes! Here's my check. . . . Now, what's the secret?"

"I pat their hair fondly," said the great psychologist, folding the check into his wallet, "then I put my mouth close to their little ears, and I whisper, 'Listen, my little darling. Get off this thing—at once—or I'll give you such a kick in the ass you won't be able to sit down for a month.' "

PSYCHIATRIC EXAM

"Please zit don." He offers me a small silver box, lifting the top. "Zigarette?" He grins, but it is a phony, on account of his fish-eyes are watchful. "*Ja?*"

This is going to be a ball: the shrink telegraphs the answer he wants. "Heaven forfend," I say. "I never indulge."

"Perhops—a zigar?" He lunges for a humidor.

I feign disgust (which is the first time in my life I have ever used "feign").

"Hass any mamber of your immediate fomily"—Dr. Kessler is cooing— "aver been committed to . . . a mental vard? . . ."

"No." My answer is honest; no rubber room ever held my Uncle Hainich, although he thought Romanian soldiers were putting ham in his shoes; or my Aunt Rukhel, who stored her nail-parings in a Mason jar to make sure the Evil One couldn't steal her vital rays.

"Now, vere *you* ever in a mental inztitution?"

"Often."

He almost drops the pen. "Often?! . . . You zaid 'often?!' "

"Sure."

"Vhere?"

"Montefiore Hospital."

"Zis is no zhoke?" he glares.

"I wouldn't joke about something like zat," I shaft him.

Dr. Kessler trembles, "For—vhat—ailment—vere—you—zere?"

"No ailment. To pick up the laundry. I got $2.50 an hour."

He goes *furi*ous. "I zoggest you control your peculiar zanse of humor! It is *not* in your bast interest. . . . Now: hass any member of your fomily zhown zigns of emotional dizturbance?"

"Yes, sir."

"Vich von?"

"All of them."

"*Vhat?!*"

"They were Jewish."

Pause. Harumph. "Vat type emotional dizturbance did zey haff?"

"You name it, they had it. *Every* emotion was extreme: love, heartburn, dry scalp. . . . My mother—may she rest in peace—was a Triple-A worrier. Awake, she worried she would never get to sleep. Asleep, she dreamed she was awake. . . . My father was *always* nervous—about Israel, pinochle, every new line of ladies' garments. . . . Should I go on?"

"Pleaze." But his expression is miles from "Pleaze." It is closer to "Vhy did you haff to come here, you goddam zon-of-a-bitch?"

"My sister," I say, "worried would she ever get married; and after she did, would she be able to have children; and after she had Herschel, would he learn to play the violin or be a no-goodnik for life? . . . She also worried about Mama, who worried about Papa, who worried about me, who worried about them. . . . We were a *very* close family."

Dr. Jekyll goes real sarcastic. "Vhy did zey vorry about you?"

"Would I get run over by a truck on my way to school? Would I be arrested for molesting? . . ."

Goggle! "You—molested—*girls?*"

"No, doc. They molested me."

His clenched eyes tell me I should never name him as a reference. "And vhat did you do?"

"I enjoyed it."

Now Dr. Kessler puts his pen down on the desk. He rubs his temples with the fingers of both hands, anchoring his thumbs on his cheekbones to give the fingers more strength. (This is a man with true know-how in temple-rubbing.) "Haff you ever zoffered a nervous breakdown?"

I take so long answering that his hopes shoot up ski-high . . . "Never."

He stares at me. "Haff you ever experienzed black-outs?"

"Yes."

"*Yes?*"

"Yes."

The eyes glitter. "Vhen?"

"When all the lights in N.Y. blew out—"

"Ztop zat! . . . Ztop. *Ztop!*" He is breathing hard. "Haff you had dizzy zpells?"

"Once."

"Aha! . . . Vhen?"

"When I got on the merry-go-round at Coney—"

"Ztop!" he hollers. "How do you zleep?"

"On my right side, mostly."

"I—meant—do—you—zleep—vell? Zat is vhat I meant! I did *not* mean do you zleep on your back, ztomach—"

"I sleep good."

He sighs. "Do you use—regularly—any medication?"

"Yes, sir."

"Vhich?"

"Valium, Dalmane, Placidyl . . ."

The pen slaps down. "*You zaid you zleep easily!*" he shouts. "And now you reveal three kinds zleeping pills!?!"

"Certainly; that's why I sleep good."

Dr. Kessler is studying the carpet. . . . Then he studies the wall. It is a very good wall for study, being covered by rose-splashed wallpaper.

He takes a deep breath, like a tired man forcing his-self to go back to his duty, and slides a picture to me. "Ztudy zis zcene—and tell me vhat you zee."

What I see is a fuzzy picture. I hold it at arm lenth, but it's still a fuzzy picture. "What I see," I announce, "is an out-of-focus shot, or the photographer needs glasses."

Dr. Caligary sneers, "Ze zcene is meant to be ambiguouse. Vhat you *zink* it zhows? . . ."

I probe the cockamamy picture, and if I give it every benefit of the doubt, which is plenty, the scene shows a woozy woman bending over a furry table and putting a smudged cereal in front of a doped-out kid—whilst in the open doorway a man who could be the Incredible Hulk is stepping into the kitchen. . . . You can't tell if the man is angry, the lady nuts, or the kid a midget.

Dr. Kessler has his pen poised over a chart. Hell, he expects me to say that (1) the man is mad at the woman and the kid; or (2) Daddy is watching fondly; or (3) the woman is either feeding her darling kid oatmeal or planning to dump it on his hair: or (4) Little Ollie don't give a damn about nutrition.

I clear my throat. "This is a cottage small by a waterfall, where the man is looking over a four-leaf clover—while Mother Macree is showing pale hands to Shalimar, her only son."

Dr. K. is ticking off check marks like crazy.

"The kid is whistling a happy tune to show he's not afraid. 'Mairzy Dotes and Dozy Dotes and Little Kidsy Divey—' "

The Kris Krinkle of the Psycho Set has slammed the desk with his fist. "I varned you! . . . Zese foolish answers vill look *very* bad on my report—!"

So I pull the cork out of the bottle. "Like hell they will . . . If you want anyone to think *you* have a sense of humor, which you should want, humor being a sign of good mental health, don't hand him a dum-dum report that shows you didn't even know when someone was giving you cockamamy answers just for laughs . . ."

Dr. Kessler closes his orbs. I think he is praying, so I skedaddle out.

from my *Silky!*

Mrs. Stribling stretched out on the couch and said, "I must tell you, Doctor Ehrenfeld, this whole thing was not *my* idea. . . . Doctor Randolph, our family doctor for ever so many years, simply in*sis*ted that I consult you. 'Try psychoanalysis for a mere month or so,' he said. 'I promise you'll be converted. Doctor Ehrenfeld is a very gifted therapist . . .' "

She paused. Behind her, in a comfortable lounge chair, Dr. Ehrenfeld, notebook in hand, waited, silent.

"*Why* Doctor Randolph ever got the silly idea that I need psychiatric help, doctor, is something I shall never understand. . . . Why, I've never been sick a day in my life, I'm happily married, we have three lovely children, I have dozens of friends—"

"Stop, madam," Dr. Ehrenfeld cut in. "How long has zis been going *on?*"

Drs. Cassman and Stanley, both psychiatrists, lived on the same floor in a fashionable building in Grosvenor Square, Mayfair. One morning, going to their respective offices, they entered the same elevator.

The elevator operator, a new young man, called out cheerfully, "Good *morn*ing, gentlemen!"

The two psychiatrists got off on the garage level. As they started for their cars, Dr. Cassman said to Dr. Stanley, "I say, old boy: *What* do you think the elevator lad meant by that?"

"My son," said Mrs. Parker. "I'm worried *sick* about my son! Doctor, do you know what he does all day, day after day? He makes mud pies!"

Said the psychiatrist, "I wouldn't worry about that, Mrs. Parker. Making mud pies is something all of us once did. His obsession will go away as he gets older."

"I have to doubt that," said Mrs. Parker. "And so does his wife."

See also **Doctors, Hypochondriacs, Jews, Just Jokes, Mothers**

Puns to Shudder Over

Two destroyers were racing home to port. As one passed the other, it sent this message:

EXCUSE ME, BUT YOUR SHIP IS SLOWING

❧

On door of photography store after fire: Good night, sweet prints.

❧

Road sign: Drive carefully. Don't insist on your rites.

❧

Swedish girl: A smorgasbroad.

❧

Have you heard of the bee who took to wearing a *yarmulka* (skullcap) because he didn't want to be mistaken for a Wasp?

❧

He's not worth her wiles.

GALSWORTHY

❧

VIVIAN: Last night I had a date with a very important guy—an airforce general.
MELBA: Major-general?
VIVIAN: Not yet.

❧

"Minnie, tell me honestly: how do you feel about Red China?"
"Please, Dorothy—not with your pink tablecloth!"

❧

TEACHER: Define the word "crick."
STUDENT: That's the sound made by a Japanese camera.

❧

Scene: Istanbul

HARKAOI: *Salaam*, Mostroviz. Do you not remember me?
MOSTROVIZ: Your name I do not remember, but your fez is familiar.

ဆ

On newly seeded lawn: Don't ruin the gay young blades.

ဆ

In old phonograph-record store: The chants of a lifetime.

ဆ

At reducing salon: Why not be the master of your fat?

ဆ

> It isn't the cough
> That carries you off,
> It's the coffin
> They carry you off in.

See also **Advertisements, Graffiti, Malaprops, Typos**

Put-downs

Scene: London, the Apartment of Theodore Benwick-Thorpe, O.B.E.
The telephone rings, Benwick-Thorpe lifts the instrument.

WOMAN:	Hul-lo. Is that dear Rupert?
BENWICK-THORPE:	No, madam, it is not.
WOMAN:	Does not Rupert Carr-Ormond reside there?
BENWICK-THORPE:	I'm afraid he does not, madam.
WOMAN:	Well, am I connected to nine-ought-four, seven, seven, two, three?
BENWICK-THORPE:	No, madam, you are not.
WOMAN:	Well to what number *has* Central put me through?
BENWICK-THORPE:	This is eight-two-zero, six, four, nine, four.
WOMAN:	Are your *shaw?*
BENWICK-THORPE:	Madam, have I ever told you an untruth befaw?

Scene: Callaghan's Seafood Restaurant

ROEBUCK:	Hey there, pal! Remember me?
STRANGER:	I *don't* think I know you!
ROEBUCK:	We both ate here last night.
STRANGER:	What about it?
ROEBUCK:	Well, I wouldn't have recognized you—except by the fine umbrella you're carrying.
STRANGER:	Hmph! Last night, I wasn't carrying this umbrella.
ROEBUCK:	I know. *I* was.

Julio opened the little plush box. "Conchita, ees for you."

Inside the case was a ring, in the center of which glinted a tiny, *tiny* diamond. Conchita said, "Ees for me?"

"*Sí.* And leesen, *amorada.* Thees reeng maybe look small, but remember: is not one seengle—how you say?—*flaw* een eet."

"Julio," said Conchita, "ees so small ess no *room* for—how you say?—one flaw!"

"My husband isn't afraid of *any*thing," said Mrs. Kottsen, who weighed over two hundred pounds. "But me—I have to tell you, I'm afraid of my shadow!"

"Who can blame you?" said Mrs. Nayfish. "It looks like a crowd is following you."

Tom Aberfeldy and Lloyd Morgan were having a violent argument right on the main street of Cardiff. " 'Tis no wonder th' damn English say 'Taffy is a Welshman, Taffy is a thief!' " cried Aberfeldy.

"A *thief* y're callin' me?!" Morgan shouted. "Why in all the days of me life, not once—not *once,* mind ye—did anybody hear my honesty questioned!"

"Questioned?" glared Aberfeldy. "Y'idjit, nobody ever heerd it mentioned!"

Let's go somewhere where I can be alone.

Would you like to come to my pool? I'll be happy to give you a lesson in drowning.

Didn't we meet in Monte Carlo—the day you blew out your brains?

Send your wits out, to be sharpened.

Generous? Why that man would give you the sleeves out of his vest!

You're the kind of boss who, when dictating, ends every other sentence in a proposition.

See also **Groucho, Insults, Repartée, Sarcasm**

Rabbis

A rabbi whose congregation does not want to run him out of town isn't a rabbi; and a rabbi they do run out of town isn't a man.

FOLK SAYING

Mickey Mitganger went to a rabbi to confess his sins, but he was so shame-stricken that he said, "Rabbi, I didn't come here for myself—but—for a friend! He asked me to come. He told me everything to ask you."

The rabbi thought over this strange request and said, "What sins has your friend committed?"

"He often takes the name of the Lord in vain. He fornicates—and gambles—and he even—"

"Stop," sighed the rabbi. "Your friend is foolish. Why didn't he come here himself?"

"He's too ashamed . . ."

"But he could have told me that he came for *you,*" said the rabbi with a smile, "thus saving you all this embarrassment."

Yagil Rapotkin, a traveling salesman, found himself in the synagogue ↓ a little *shtetl* one Friday night. After the prayers, Rapotkin set off in search of a place to sleep.

"Where are you going?" exclaimed a man. "A Jew, alone, on the eve of the Sabbath? Come, man. Come home with me! My name is Boris Marantz. My wife is a marvelous cook. . . ."

The Marantzes could not have been better hosts. They gave Rapotkin a fine bedroom, urged him to soak in a hot tub, gave him fluffy towels and scented soap—and fed him a superlative Sabbath dinner. That night, Rapotkin slept between fine linen sheets. . . .

Next morning a sumptuous breakfast awaited him. And as he made his heartfelt farewells to his host, Rapotkin asked, "How can I ever thank you both?"

Said his host, "Just attend to this." And he handed Rapotkin a slip of paper, on which was carefully written:

ACCOUNTING

1 Bath: hot water	5 kopecks
1 Cake scented soap	12 kopecks
1 Large fresh towel	10 kopecks
1 Sabbath dinner (complete)	3.00 rubles
2 Fresh sheets	15 kopecks
1 Fresh pillowcase	10 kopecks
1 Breakfast	85 kopecks
Total Due	4.37 rubles

(Signed)

Boris Marantz

"B-but—what's this?" gaped Rapotkin.

"Your bill."

"You expect me to *pay* this?!"

"Certainly," said Marantz. "Do you deny that you bathed here, slept overnight, ate like a king—"

"Deny it? I'm absolutely flabbergasted!" cried Rapotkin. "You *invited* me here! You in*sis*ted! I've never heard a more outrageous—"

"Stop!" Marantz held up his hand. "Let's not argue. Let's go to our rabbi, tell him everything. . . . Will you abide by his decision?"

"Will I?" seethed Rapotkin. "I can't *wait* to hear what the rabbi says about such outrageous behavior!"

The two men hurried to the rabbi's house. . . .

Rapotkin told his tale to the rabbi, pouring the words out with great feeling.

The rabbi turned to Marantz. "And what do you, the host, say? You were the one who invited him, pressed your hospitality on him, urged him—"

"Everything he said is just as it happened," said Marantz.

"There you are, rabbi!" cried Rapotkin.

The rabbi nodded. "After hearing you both, and considering all the delicate ethical problems involved, and based on the wisdom—on just such problems—I have studied for years in the Talmud, my decision is clear and simple: Mr. Rapotkin, pay the bill."

Rapotkin could hardly believe his ears. He was shocked; he was speechless. Yet a rabbi had spoken. . . .

Rapotkin and Marantz left the rabbi's house. With a heavy heart, Rapotkin started to count out rubles.

"What are you doing?" asked Marantz.

"Paying your bill."

"*Paying* me? For my hospitality? You must be crazy. Do you think I would accept money from you, my guest—"

Rapotkin sputtered: "I must be going mad! Didn't you give me a bill?! Didn't you ask me to pay you?! *You* suggested—"

"Oh, *that*," scoffed Marantz. "Sure, sure. But I don't want your money. I just wanted you to see what a dope we have here for a rabbi!"

⁊⳯

Three new rabbis, who had been classmates at the Reform seminary, met in a conference and began to discuss their congregations. "My temple is so modern," observed the first, "that after services we adjourn to the social hall for snacks—and ham sandwiches are our most popular item!"

"*My* flock," said the second, "are so emancipated that over sixty percent of their children married gentiles!"

The third rabbi cleared his throat. "*My* temple is closed on Jewish holidays."

This happened many centuries ago, in Persia.

"There's something I want you to do, rabbi," said the shah. "Teach my pet monkey how to talk."

"*What?*"

"He's rather a clever monkey. In any case"—the shah smiled—"that's a command: teach my monkey how to talk within one year, or your head will be chopped off!"

"But Your Majesty, to perform a deed like that—I need more than a year; I need at least ten."

"I'll allow you two years, and not a day more."

When the rabbi returned to his flock and told them what had happened, they cried in despair. "Oh, rabbi, rabbi. What will you *do?*"

"Well," said the rabbi. "In two years, many things can happen. For instance, the shah can die. Or, *I* could die. . . . Or, the monkey could die. . . . And besides, in two years, who knows: maybe I can teach that monkey how to talk."

Fischel Kurtzer, a poor tinker walking the streets of Jerusalem, found a fine wallet, in which were eighty shekels, and this notice in a celluloid jacket:

> *If found, please return to*
> *Yitzchak Zelg*
> *29 Weitzman Boul.*
> *20 shekels Reward*—NO QUESTIONS ASKED

So Fischel hastened to the Zelg home, a beautiful house with a fine garden. A servant admitted him to Mr. Zelg, a rich, cunning man, who examined the wallet's contents. "Ah, I see you already took the twenty-shekel reward."

"Me?" blinked Fischel. "Never!"

"There were a hundred shekels in my wallet," smiled Zelg.

"No, no. I swear—"

"Let's not argue about this," said Zelg. "Let's let Rabbi Frumkin decide."

The two men hurried to the nearby synagogue. Fischel Kurtzer told the rabbi what he had found and done. Then Zelg gave *his* canny version of the events, ending, "*Nu, rebbe.* Who do you believe? Me—or that *shlump?*"

"You, Mr. Zelg, of course," said the rabbi.

Fischel's face fell. The rabbi removed the wallet from Zelg's hand—and gave it to the tinker.

"*Rebbe,* what are you doing?" cried Zelg.

"Taking you at your word," said Rabbi Frumkin. "You said your wallet contained one hundred shekels. This man says the wallet he found contained only eighty. Obviously, this wallet can't be yours."

"But—what of my money?"

"We simply must wait," said the rabbi, "until some honest soul finds a wallet with a hundred shekels in it."

Lewis Browne, author of the immensely successful *This Believing World,* had for a time been a Reform rabbi at a temple in New Jersey. For reasons no one in Hollywood, to which Browne moved, ever found out, Browne had been asked to resign his pulpit.

At a dinner party, a waspish woman remarked, "So you were really a rabbi. Tell us, were you defrocked?"

"N-no," said Browne. "I was unsuited."

Shimmel Himmel came to his rabbi, distraught. "Rabbi, please—you've got to advise me! Every year my wife brings forth another baby. I have nine children already, and barely enough money to even buy them food! . . . Rabbi, what can I *do?*"

The sage thought not a moment. "Do nothing," he said.

"Please, doctor. Save her!" begged Mr. Feingold. "I'll pay you anything."

"But what if I can't cure her?" asked Dr. Zifkin.

"I'll pay you whether you cure her or kill her!" cried Feingold.

A week later, Mrs. Feingold died. . . . The doctor sent Mr. Feingold a large bill. And poor Mr. Feingold suggested they both go to the rabbi to discuss the fee.

Rabbi Heilbrun, who well knew Dr. Zifkin's reputation, said, "What was your agreement, doctor?"

"He agreed to pay me for treating his wife," said the doctor, "whether I cured her or killed her."

The rabbi nodded. "And did you cure her?"

"No."

"Did you kill her?"

"Certainly not!"

"Then," asked Rabbi Heilbrun, "under what contract are you claiming a fee?"

Moishe Zherin, a poor man in a small Polish village, came to his rabbi. "Oh, rabbi, my life is so miserable! I live above the stable—in one room with my wife and four children and her mother. Rabbi, it is so crowded I just can't bear it any longer!"

"Do you—uh—have a goat?" asked the rabbi.

"Yes, rabbi."

"Take the goat into your room."

"*What?*"

"Do as I say, Moishe."

So the poor man went home and took the goat out of his back yard and put it into his room.

A week later he hurried to the rabbi, sputtering: "I did what you told me, rabbi. I took the goat in, and now things are even worse—much worse than before! Rabbi, what shall I *do?*"

"Moishe, do you have any chickens?" asked the rabbi.

"Yes. Three—"

"Bring them into your house."

"Rabbi!"

"Do as I say, Moishe. Do as I say . . ."

So the poor man brought the three chickens into the house. A week later he returned to the rabbi, wringing his hands. "It's terrible! Terrible! I can't *stand* it any more!"

The rabbi nodded. "Very well, Moishe, go home—and put out the goat."

The poor man did as he was told, and came back. "It's a *little* better, rabbi, but still—three chickens—in a room with seven people. . . ."

"Throw out the chickens," said the rabbi.

And the next morning, Moishe Zherin stood before the rabbi, overjoyed, crying: "Rabbi, there's no one in all the world as wise as you! My house—now it is paradise!"

"Well, grandma, how do you feel today?"

"Today, dear, I feel better. And it certainly was nice of that young rabbi to come in to my room at the hospital to cheer me up."

"Rabbi? What rabbi?"

"The one with big glasses, reddish hair, tall, thin—"

"Grandma, that wasn't a rabbi. That was Dr. Feldman—a specialist we called in!"

"A *doctor* that was? My. That explains everything. . . ."

"What do you mean?"

"To tell you the truth, I thought he acted pretty fresh for a rabbi."

See also **Accents, Israel, Jews, Just Jokes, Reason**

Reason

A TRIUMPH OF REASONING

A rabbi, famous throughout Lithuania for the power of his analysis and reasoning, was said to be capable of answering any question put to him. One day one of his disciples cried: "Our *rebbe* can think his way in an instant to the very heart of any problem—and give the perfect answer!"

"It certainly is true that our beloved rabbi has a mind of unparalleled clarity and powers. But what if he is too tired to think hard? Maybe drowsy? Even a bit tipsy? Would his capacity to analyze still prevail?"

This question so fascinated the loving acolytes that they decided to put it to the test. At the next Sabbath feast, they surreptitiously poured enough wine in the rabbi's glass to make him tipsy. Then, while he slept, the disciples carried him, reverently, to the cemetery. There, they laid him on the grass and hid behind the tombstones—waiting to see what the great rabbi would say when he realized where he was. . . .

The rabbi snored away for a time, then yawned, opened his eyes, looked about—and sat up. Stroking his beard, he then proceeded to say, *"Nu? . . . If I am living, what am I doing here? . . . And if I am dead, why do I have to go to the bathroom?"*

Rabbi Tesher, discovering that he had left his comfortable slippers back in the house, sent a student after them with a note for his wife. The note read: "Send me your slippers with this boy."

When the student asked why the rabbi had written *"your"* slippers, Rabbi Tesher answered, "Listen, young man. *Think.* If I wrote 'my' slippers, my wife would read 'my slippers'—and would send me *her* slippers. What can I do with her slippers? So I wrote 'your' slippers; she'll read 'your' slippers and send me mine."

Two salesmen, carrying their sample cases, met in Pennsylvania Railroad Station. They eyed each other warily. "Hello, Poppel."

"How are you, Notkin?"

Silence.

"So—where are you going?" asked Poppel.

"I'm going to Islip," said Notkin.

Silence.

"Listen, *boychik*," sighed Poppel, "when you tell me you're going to Islip, you want me to think you're going to Bellport. But I happen to know that you *are* going to Islip—so why are you lying?!"

Mr. Osterman was awakened from a deep sleep by his wife, who nudged him in the side, saying, "Get *up*, Harry. I'm freezing! Close the window. It's very, very cold outside!"

Sighed Harry, "And if I close the window, Celia, will it be very, very *warm* outside?"

Mr. Solovy was returning from New York by bus to his little hometown in New Jersey. Next to him sat a pleasant young man. Mr. Solovy sang out, "My name is Sam Solovy and I live in Groverville, New Jersey."

"My name," said the young man, "is Spielfogel, Murray Spielfogel, and I'm going to Groverville, too."

Mr. Solovy beamed. "On business, could I ask?"

"No."

"Maybe to visit someone in your family?"

"No. I have no relatives in Groverville."

"Young man, let me ask—are you married or single?"

"I'm not married."

"Aha." Mr. Solovy leaned back in his seat, closed his eyes, and reasoned thusly: "He's not going on business; he's got no family in Groverville; he's not married. *Nu*, why is he going to Groverville? He must be going to meet a girl! And if he's going this far, it must be serious. So—which girl? Selma Kromer? N-no. Selma is engaged to that dentist from Red Bank. . . . So is this Spielfogel going to call on the Coopersteins? Nah. Seymour Cooperstein's daughter just got married. . . . Maybe to the Rifkinds? . . . N-nah, Shirley Rifkind is only fourteen—fifteen. . . . Maybe to the Novarsky's? But Nancy Novarsky is away at college. . . . The Pflaumberg girl? Ah . . . the Pflaumberg's have *three* daughters: Nina, Grace, and Leona. Nina, poor girl, is big and fat, and this young Spielfogel is good-looking enough to pick and choose. Grace? Grace is a divorcée with young children. . . . Leona? . . . Leona. *There* is a live number! And last weekend she went to New York; and the week before that. . . . Aha!" Mr. Solovy opened his eyes, beaming, and extended his hand. "Murray Spielfogel, let me be the first to offer congratulations and best wishes for a long, happy life together!"

"What do you mean?"

"I mean your forthcoming engagement to Miss Leona Pflaumberg."

The young man blushed furiously. "But—Mr. Solovy! We haven't told one living soul! Not even her mother, her father! . . . How in the *world* did you ever find out?"

"How I found out?" echoed Sam Solovy. "My boy, it's obvious."

Mrs. Devlin unlocked the door of the little cottage, slowly trudged in, and sank into a chair, moaning and groaning.

"Elizabeth, me love," said Mr. Devlin, "y' look fit for the grave. What happened?"

"What happened, Denis Devlin, is that I went t' call on Mrs. Duffy, t' pay me respects, her losin' her man. An' there was a whole group of the sodality ladies, y' know, gabbin' and jabberin' and talkin' enough t' make me pore ears ring, I can tell y'. Then Mrs. Duffy's daughter, Maureen, the lass who married that publican in Ryan's Corner, set out the eatin's for a wake-like, an' the way them people dived into the food made y' ashamed for whoever brung them up. Then the chimney began t' smoke 'til a terrible headache fair blew my pore head off me shoulders."

"Faith, me darlin'," said Mr. Devlin, "y' should not've gone there 't all!"

Mrs. Devlin sighed, "Well, who knows? The good Lord does move in strange ways. T' tell ye th' peculiar truth, Mr. Devlin, I feel so foyne bein' away from that madhouse, I'm glad I went."

A chief justice of old was visiting a prison with the warden. Prisoner after prisoner insisted that he was innocent: one said he had been framed, another that the judge who sentenced him had been bribed to do so, another still, that he was the victim of a conspiracy.

The chief justice asked the last prisoner, "And are you, too, innocent?"

"No, sir. I'm a thief. I was fairly tried and sentenced."

"You *admit* you're a thief?"

"Yes, sir."

The chief justice said to the warden, "Throw this crook out of here!"

The other prisoners raised a fearful clamor. "How can you do such a thing?" "How can you free a confessed criminal, while we—"

"I was afraid," smiled the chief justice, "that that evil scoundrel might corrupt all you pure, innocent souls."

See also **Chutzpa, Logic, Salesmen, True Tales**

Religion

Religion: An old, flourishing prophet system.

Baptism: A sacred rite of such efficacy that he who finds himself in heaven without having undergone it will be unhappy forever.

AMBROSE BIERCE

As Grogan lay on his deathbed, eyes closed, Father O'Donnell leaned over and said, "Brian, listen. . . . Repeat after me: 'I renounce the devil and all his evil deeds!' "

Grogan opened one eye, but said nothing.

"Brian!" said Father O'Donnell. "Can you hear me?"

Grogan nodded.

"Then repeat after me: 'I renounce the devil and all his evil deeds!' "

Grogan's other eye opened.

"Brian!" snapped Father O'Donnell. "Don't you *hear* what I'm tellin' ya?"

"Sure, father," murmured Grogan. "But I don't think this is the time for me to go makin' an enemy of *any*body."

PREACHER: We are here on earth to help others, Jimmy.
JIMMY: Then what are the others here for, sir?

The Flahertys moved to the suburbs. Their next-door neighbors were the Spaldings. One day Tim Flaherty, age six, was playing in the brook with Lucy Spalding, age five. When they had splashed water all over their clothes, they took them off. . . .

Little Lucy's mother observed all this from the kitchen. And when Lucy came in, her mother said, "Lucy dear, did you like playing with the new boy? . . ."

"Yes, mother."

"What games did you play?"

"Oh, we didn't play any games. . . . We just cleaned up the brook and splashed around—and we got so wet we took off our clothes and played naked."

Lucy's mother hesitated. "Well, dear, is there *any*thing you'd like to tell me?"

Little Lucy reflected. "Well, mother, one thing: I didn't know there was *that* much difference between Protestants and Catholics."

The priest stopped in at the coffee counter and sat down on a stool. The man next to him said, "Mornin', father."

"Good morning."

"New around here, father?"

"Oh, no."

"Which is your church?"

"St. Joseph's. Just across the street."

"Now ain't that a coincidence, father?" smiled the man. "St. Joseph's is me own church!"

The priest studied the man and said, "Strange . . . I've been carryin' on my duties at St. Joseph's for six years now, and I've not seen you there—"

"Well now, father, Oy never said Oy was a fanatic!"

See also **Clergy, Faith, God, Prayer**

Repartée

The aristocratic young lord said to James McNeill Whistler, "By the way, Whistler, I passed your house last night."

"Thank you."

❧

GIRL: Look, Bob, don't you know what good clean fun is?
BOB: No, what good is it?

❧

"Do you like bathing beauties?"
"I don't know; I never bathed one."

❧

"I asked to see her home."
"Did you?"
"No. She said she'd send me a picture of it."

❧

"Did you see her dress?"
"No, she wouldn't let me."

❧

Phone conversation

"Mr. Noland told me to tell you he's not in."
"Fine. Tell him I'm glad I didn't call."

❧

"What a terrible, condescending way to talk to me! Do you think I'm a damn idiot?"
"Of course not. . . . But, come to think of it, I *could* be mistaken."

❧

Hal Knobloch was late returning from lunch. Said his boss, Mr. Axelrod: "You're over an hour late!"
"That's true," said Knobloch.

"Would you mind giving me a hint why?" asked Mr. Axelrod.

"Not at all: I was having my hair cut."

"Your *hair* cut? Do you think you ought to do that on company time?"

"Why not?" said Knobloch. "The hair grew on company time."

Mr. Axelrod's eyes narrowed: "That hair didn't *all* grow on company time!"

"T-true. That's why I didn't have it all cut off."

"M'sieur Voltaire," said a friend, "it is a great surprise to me that you speak so highly of that man. He always says such unflattering things about you."

"Well," smiled Voltaire, "perhaps we are both mistaken."

See also **Chutzpa, Groucho, Put-downs, Restaurants, Retorts, Squelches, Waiters, Wit, Wordplay**

Restaurants

Mr. Lupowitz, a widower, had for years and years been eating at the same restaurant. On this Friday night, he sat down at his usual table; and his waiter, as usual, put before him the usual chopped liver. Mr. Lupowitz ate the chopped liver. The waiter removed it, as usual, and, as usual, replaced it with a bowl of chicken soup.

As he started off, Lupowitz called, "Eh—eh—eh! Vaiter!"

"What?"

"Please taste this soup."

"*Hanh?*" the waiter frowned. "It's the chicken soup you *always* have—"

"Taste it."

"Listen, Mr. Lupowitz: in all the years you are eating here did you ever *once* have a bad bowl chicken soup?"

"Vaiter—*taste—the—soup!*"

"Okay, what can I do?" scowled the waiter. "I'll taste—where's the spoon?"

"Aha!" cried Lupowitz.

Sign in restaurant window

> **EAT HERE AND YOU'LL NEVER EAT ANYPLACE ELSE AGAIN.**

"Waiter!" called Mrs. Kroeber.

"Yeah?"

"What did you say this dish—your special—is, that I'm eatin'?"

"Spring chicken."

"That's certainly true," said Mrs. Kroeber.

"What does that mean, lady?"

"I just bit into one of the springs."

Scene: Kasdon's Kosher Restaurant

"Waiter!" sang out Mr. Riesman. "*Wai-*ter!"

A waiter ambled over. "You called?"

"No, you heard a *flute*," said Mr. Riesman bitterly.

"So what did the flute want?"

"What it wanted," said Mr. Riesman, "is to know the exact nature of my offense!"

The waiter rubbed his chin. "What offense?"

"That's what I want *you* to tell me, because since I came in here, a half-hour ago, I've been on nothing but bread and water!"

Sir Lawrence and Lady Runfield were in New York for the first time. To Lady Runfield, Sir Lawrence said, "Lucinda, my dear, we get plenty of hotel food, and French and Italian cuisine, back home. Might this not be a splendid opportunity to try some authentic—Jewish comestibles?"

"What a *clever* idea, Lawrence," said Lady Runfield. "Let's do."

That night they taxied down to the Lower East Side, to Olinsky's Excellent Elite, perhaps the best Jewish restaurant in the Western Hemisphere. The owner, Ahron Olinsky, led them to a good table, placed two menus on it, and said, "Enjoy, enjoy."

The Runfields examined the items on the bill of fare. They could hardly understand such items as "*Derma . . . heldzel . . . matjes . . . knaydlach . . .*" When the waiter arrived, Sir Lawrence said, "Waiter, may I ask—" he indicated the next table with a nod "—what are those round, yellowish objects in the soup?"

"In the chicken soup?"

"Yes. They look like quite large dumplings . . ."

"Oh, them is *matzo* balls."

"I beg your pardon?"

"*Mat-zo* balls," the waiter repeated.

"I'll try them . . . Lucinda, dear, you?"

"I'll join you. They *do* look lovely."

The waiter disappeared and soon returned with two steaming dishes of chicken soup glorified by golden *knaydlach* (*matzo* balls).

The Runfields ate this exotic delicacy with *great* satisfaction. Indeed, not a drop of soup, nor a shred of *matzo* balls, was left in their plates.

"How *very* good!" said Sir Lawrence.

"*Super*," said Lady Runfield. "Waiter. . . . Tell me, what other part of the *matzo* do you people eat?"

Sign in restaurant window

By popular demand
UNDER NEW MANAGEMENT

Scene: Blattberg's Gustatory Haven

CUSTOMER: Waiter, waiter!
WAITER: I'm here.
CUSTOMER: This fish is awful! It smells. It—
WAITER: Wait a *min*ute, mister! You ate here three nights ago and said the fish was delicious!
CUSTOMER: That was four—not three—nights ago!
WAITER: Mister, I give you my word, this is the same fish!

Note on menu in Paris

To our American guests:
A 10 percent discount is cheerfully given if you
do not attempt to order in French.

See also **Chutzpa, Put-downs, Repartée, Retorts, Squelches, Waiters, Wit**

Retorts

An Englishman, visiting New York, passed a store window with nothing in it but a clock. He stepped inside.

From the back, a man with a *yarmulka* (skullcap) came forward.

The Englishman said, "Hul-lo. May I ask: How long would it take to mend my watch? It's slowing down—"

"How should I know?" shrugged the proprietor. "I don't fix watches. I'm a *mohel.*"

"A *what?*"

"A *mohel.* I circumcise. . . ."

The Englishman sputtered, "But *I* say—in your window—you have a clock!"

The *mohel* shrugged. "So what would *you* put in the window?"

A visitor to San Francisco placed a garland of roses on the grave of his grandfather. As he turned to leave, he noticed an old Chinese gentleman placing a bowl of rice on a grave nearby. The American smiled.

The Chinese, noticing this, bowed. "What pleases you so?" he politely inquired.

"I was just wondering—when do you expect the dead to eat that rice?"

"About the same time," sighed the Chinese gentleman, "that your dead smell those flowers."

An English lord, noted for his arrogance, once asked Dr. Chaim Weizmann, "Weizmann, can you tell me why it is that you Jews are said to be mercenary?"

To which Weizmann replied, "For the same reason, milord, that you English are said to be gentlemen."

During a dramatic moment in the performance of *King Lear,* in Yiddish, at a Houston Street theater, an actor, at the climax of his great scene, collapsed on stage.

"Doctor!" cried another actor.

"Get a doctor!" shouted a stagehand.

"Is there a doctor in the house?!"

In the fourth row, a man rose. "I'm a doctor!" He hurried up the stairs to the stage, bent over the prostrate actor, pried open an eyelid, felt the recumbent's pulse.

From the balcony an old lady shouted, "Give—him—an—enema!"

The doctor leaned over and placed his ear against the fallen one's breast. Not a heartbeat was to be heard.

"Give—him—an—enema!" trumpeted the old lady in the gallery.

The doctor straightened up. "Lady, this man is *dead!* An enema won't help!"

"It vouldn't *hoit!*" returned the old lady.

Scene: Prospect Park: Brooklyn

MARIA:	Stop! Roberto, I never kees on a first date!
ROBERTO:	Oh . . . well, how's about on a last one?

The pushcart quarters near Little Italy are as crowded, raucous, vital, and disputatious as ever. At one stall, bursting with secondhand kettles, cracked pots, and battered pans, an old Italian *nonna* picked up an old fork, two tines broken off, and addressed the cart owner, "Eh! *Padrone! Ecco!* Howa much you wan for thees no-good, broke *forchetta, hanh?*"

"One-a penny," said the owner.

"One-a *penny?*" the *nonna* countered. "*Scandalo!* It's too much!"

The proprietor bared his teeth. "Okay. So you make me *offer.*"

Mrs. Dougherty sent her ten-year-old son to the store for three pounds of grapes.

After he returned, she phoned the grocer. "Listen, Mr. Carbine. What on earth do you think you're doing?! I just weighed your grapes. There are only two pounds four ounces. Your scales are a disgrace!"

"*My* scales?" huffed Mr. Carbine. "Don't weigh the grapes, lady; weigh your boy!"

The Salvation Army pickup truck stopped in front of Luis Fernandez's *bodega*. The driver hopped out. "Whaddaya say, Mr. Fernandez? Got anything for us? Furniture? Appliances? Everything goes to charity."

"*Nada,*" sighed Fernandez.

"Come on, Fernandez. A man like you. A nice little store. How about shoes—"

"I no got *zapatos.*"

"—phonograph records—"

"No got."

"—old clothes?"

"Ah." Fernandez nodded. "*Sí.* I got *viejos vestidos.*"

"Great."

"—but I no can give you."

"Why not?" the driver bristled. "What can you do with them?"

"What I can do wis zem is thees," said Luis Fernandez. "Each *noches,* I hang up old clothes, nize, neat, careful—and each *mañana* I put back on."

MRS. CONNOLLY: Faith, Mrs. Burke, an' why are ye givin' me sech a dirrty look?

MRS. BURKE: 'Dirrty look,' is it then? *Oy'm* not the one gave it to ye. Ye were wearin' it, plain as day, when y' entered the premises.

Scene: A Community Chest Reception

Mr. Manley Emerson, somewhat tipsy, exclaimed, "I'll have you know, sir—what was your name again?"

"Levitski."

"I'll have you know, Mr. Le-vit-ski, that I come from one of America's first families! In fact, one of my ancestors signed the Declaration of Independence."

"So?" said Levitski. "One of mine signed the Ten Commandments."

On Edinburgh's fashionable Queen Street, Mr. Andrews was accosted by a beggar. "Kin ye gie a starvin' mon ten bob, sor?"

"Ten bob is it ye're beggin'?" snorted Andrews. "Why dinna ye go t' worrk, mon? Ye've got the arrms and legs of a viry *horse!*"

"Hoot, mon!" returned the beggar. "F'r ten bob am Oy to cut off m' limbs?!"

See also Chutzpa, Groucho, Put-downs, Repartée, Restaurants, Squelches, Waiters, Wit

Revenge

Onto Phipps's Fine Foreign Cars lot drove a magnificent Silver Cloud Rolls-Royce, out of which stepped a finely dressed woman, all in black. "I want to sell this car," she announced.

The owner, Kenneth Phipps, glanced at the odometer (only 13,050 miles!), got in the driver's seat, turned on the ignition, listened to the motor . . . "Uh—how much do you want for this car, madam?"

"Fifty dollars."

Mr. Phipps's jaw dropped. "What is this, ma'am—a joke?"

"No. Just give me fifty dollars and a signed bill of sale."

"Lady, are you out of your skull?" exclaimed Phipps. "Don't you know that this Rolls is worth, even secondhand, thirty or forty *thou*sand dollars?"

"Yes. Let's not waste time."

"Madam, is this a stolen car?" asked Phipps.

"Certainly not!"

"Is there a lien on it?"

"Absolutely not. . . . Now look, do you or don't you—"

"Certainly I want to buy it! But fifty dollars! There *must* be a trick. *Why* would *anyone* in her right mind —"

The woman in black arched an eyebrow. "I am entirely in my right mind, sir. I think you will agree. You see, my husband just died. And in his will, he stated that Flora Delago, who was his secretary—and his goddam mistress— should get the full proceeds from the sale of his Silver Cloud Rolls-Royce! . . . Give me the fifty dollars."

Emanuel Gittleman was deep in sleep when his phone rang and rang. He lifted the receiver. "Hollo," he grumbled.

"Mr. Gittleman? In apartment three-B?"

"Yeah."

"This is Mrs. Trautman, in Four-G. It's already half past three at night— and your dog's barking is driving me absolutely *crazy!*" The phone slammed down. . . .

The next night, at 3:45 A.M., Mrs. Trautman's telephone rang. "Hello," she mumbled.

"Mrs. Trautman? In Four-G?"

"Yeah."

"This is Mr. Gittleman, in Three-B. I want to tell you something."

"At a quarter to *four* in the morning?! Are you crazy?!"

"I don't own a dog."

Filip Marisol and Enrico Oquendo simply could not bear the Castro regime any longer. They decided there was only one solution to Cuba's dictatorship: to assassinate Fidel. Both being army veterans, they got out their rifles, fitted them with precision sights, and concealed themselves in the doorway of a building Fidel was scheduled to ride past.

They waited. Hour after hour, they waited.

Finally, Filip whispered, "Enrico, let's hope nothing hoppened to the *bastardo!*"

"Good morning," smiled the nurse in the hospital in Jerusalem. "So you're the mother of a fine, seven-pound boy!"

"That's right."

"And what are you going to name him?"

"Arafat."

"*Arafat?!*" The nurse blanched. "Are you joking?"

"Nope."

"But—I—I never heard of a Jewish mother calling her child by that hateful name, Mrs. Zumkin. Are you *sure*—"

"I'm sure, I'm sure. I'm not Mrs. Zumkin. It's Miss."

The pretty young thing sitting on the stool at the bar was approached by an attractive college boy, smiling, "Are you alone, miss?"

"What kind of a girl do you think I am?" she cried.

He reddened. "I just wanted to buy you a drink."

"No, no, no!" she shouted. "I won't go up to your room!"

"Hey, calm *down!*" said the young man.

"No! I won't meet you at that motel in twenty minutes!"

Absolutely flabbergasted, the college man made his way through a sea of indignant stares and glares to a table in the far, dark corner.

In a moment, the pretty girl left the bar and, smiling broadly, came to the college boy. "Sorry to create such a scene. I'm a graduate student in the Psychology Department, doing research for a report: 'Masculine Behavior in Unexpected Situations'!"

The young man stared at her, then leaped to his feet. "*What?*" he shouted. "Five hundred dollars? For twenty minutes? Never!" And with that he stalked out of the bar.

See also **Ingenuity, Hanky-panky, Scoundrels, Stratagems**

Reviews of Note

The G——— Quartet played Brahms last night at Carnegie Hall. Brahms lost.

PERCY HAMMOND

The plot of this play was intended to be in a light vein, but the vein became varicose.

WOLCOTT GIBBS

The movie version needed something—possibly burial.

DAVID LARDNER

She ran the gamut of human emotions, from A to B.

DOROTHY PARKER

——— opened last night at the Morosco. Why?

BROOKS ATKINSON

I have knocked everything in this play except the chorus girls' knees, and there God anticipated me.

PERCY HAMMOND

About the play *The Greeks Had a Word for It:* So did the Hebrews: lousy.

DOROTHY PARKER

It was one of those plays in which all the actors enunciated clearly, unfortunately.

ROBERT BENCHLEY

The play, called *Halfway to Hell*, grossly underestimates the distance.

BROOKS ATKINSON

For the first time in my life, I envied my feet: they were asleep.

MONTY WOOLLEY

I saw the play under the worst possible conditions: the curtain was up.
                                                ALEXANDER WOOLCOTT

See also **Critics, Sarcasm, Squelches**

The Rich

If the rich could only hire the poor to die for them, the poor would earn a very good living.

If you rub shoulders with the rich, you'll get a hole in your sleeve.

When you're rich, people say you're profound, handsome, graceful—and sing like an angel.

YIDDISH SAYINGS

Scene: Fortnum & Mason's, London

"Why, Claudia!" exclaimed her friend Margery. "Where did you get that *heavenly* tan?"

"In Sri Lanka. Humbert took me there on holiday—to celebrate our sixth anniversary. . . ."

"*Su*per. . . . Did you say Sri Lanka?"

"Yes."

"Where on earth is that?"

"Marge, my pet, I haven't the faintest. We flew."

Scene: Rancho Mirage, California

"Bert, cast a glance at the cabana to our right . . ."

"I see it . . ."

"Do you see the lucious, pouting bit of fluff with Mr. Rockford?"

"Wow. Who is she?"

"His wife."

"His *wife?* She must be twenty years younger than he is!"

"Thirty. . . . And do you know what he gave her for a wedding present?"

"Emeralds?"

"Oh, no. Blocks . . ."

"*Blocks?* Are you joking?"

"Not at all. Fifty-fourth Street between First and Second, and Ninety-eighth Street from West End to Columbus Avenue."

During Yom Kippur services, Jasper Lowenstein, a man of considerable wealth, went into the ritual chant of confession, beating his breast, "Oh, Lord, I am a nothing, a nothing, unworthy of Your Grace!"

Next to Lowenstein the town *shnorrer* was beating his breast, chanting, "Forgive me, O Lord, I am a nothing, a nothing . . ."

Lowenstein promptly protested: "God, *God!* Look who has the nerve to claim he's a nothing!"

In the Poconos, an ingenious gentleman farmer crossbred a Guernsey bull with a Holstein cow—to get a Goldstein calf. It does not go "Moo." It goes *"Nu?"*

See also **Just Jokes**

Russia

The applicant for membership stood before the three members of the Admission Committee of the Fifth District of the Communist party in Odessa.

"Vladimir Ardjenovic," said the committee chairman, "suppose you received, say—one million rubles from America. What would you do with it?"

"I would turn it over to the party!"

"Good," said a member of the committee. "And suppose you had two automobiles. What would you do?"

"I would give one to the party for its use by members of the executive."

"And suppose you had two warm winter overcoats? . . ." asked the third member.

Vladimir Ardjenovic wrinkled his brow, thinking.

"Comrade," said the chairman, "after such swift answers to the other questions, what makes you hesitate on this one?"

"Well, Comrade Chairman, I do have two overcoats. . . ."

RUMZHISKI: Hey, Arkovich! Where are you running like a wild man?
ARKOVICH *(panting)*: To . . . Vitebsk . . . for meat!
RUMZHISKI: But there's no meat in Vitebsk. The only meat within three hundred miles is right here in Moscow.
ARKOVICH *(panting)*: I know . . . but the line *starts* in Vitebsk!

Azriel Rubinstein stood before the commissar of Passport Controls and with the utmost earnestness pleaded, "Comrade Commissar Khreznevsky, I am seventy years old, and it is now six *years* since I began filing applications for permission, from your office, for me to emigrate from the Soviet Union."

Commissar Khreznevsky nodded. *"Da."*

"All of my immigration papers from Israel have been approved and are in your files—"

Khreznevsky nodded. *"Da, da."*

"Comrade Commissar, please tell me—why, *why* will you not let me leave the Soviet Union?"

The commissar assumed his sternest expression. "Becouse in your brain, Rubinstein, you hold vary important secret—*scientific* secrets! Those secrets—if we lat you out of Soviet Union—you will give to Israelis, allies of copitolistic U.S.A.—"

"But that's impossible!" cried Rubinstein. "I no longer *know* a single scientific secret. Have you forgotten? I have been barred from my laboratory for over fifteen years! I have not been allowed to attend any scientific meetings! I have not been given a single classified document about a single weapon or experiment—"

"*Da, da,*" nodded Khreznevsky.

"—And even when I *was* working on missiles, fifteen years ago, we were so far behind the Americans—"

"*Dot,*" thundered the commissar, "is the secret!"

During a gigantic celebration in Red Square, after Trotsky had been sent into exile, Stalin, on Lenin's great tomb, suddenly and excitedly raised his hand to still the acclamations: "Comrades, comrades! A most historic event! A cablegram—of congratulations—from Trotsky!"

The hordes cheered and chortled and cheered again, and Stalin read the historic cable aloud:

JOSEPH STALIN
KREMLIN
MOSCOW
YOU WERE RIGHT AND I WAS WRONG. YOU ARE THE TRUE HEIR OF LENIN.
I SHOULD APOLOGIZE.

TROTSKY

You can imagine what a roar, what an explosion of astonishment and triumph erupted in Red Square now!

But in the front row, below the podium, a little tailor called, "Pst! Pst! Comrade Stalin."

Stalin leaned down.

The tailor said, "Such a message, Comrade Stalin. For the ages! But you read it without the right *feeling!*"

Whereupon Stalin raised his hand and stilled the throng once more. "Comrades! Here is a simple worker, a loyal Communist, who says I haven't read the message from Trotsky with enough feeling! Come, Comrade Worker! Up here! *You* read this historic communication!"

So the little tailor went up to the reviewing stand and took the cablegram from Stalin and read:

JOSEPH STALIN
KREMLIN
MOSCOW

Then he cleared his throat, and sang out:

YOU WERE RIGHT AND I WAS WRONG? *YOU* ARE THE TRUE HEIR OF LENIN? *I* SHOULD APOLOGIZE???!!.

TROTSKY!

Scene: Leningrad

COMMUNIST PARTY HACK: Listen, Boris. Why don't you attend the local's meetings every Monday night?

BORIS   I—I'm just not interested.

HACK: Not *in*terested? Okay: tell me what is meant by dialectical materialism.

BORIS: I don't know.

HACK: What is meant by the iron law of wages?

BORIS: I don't know.

HACK: Who was Ferdinand La Salle?

BORIS: Who knows?

HACK: "Who knows?" "Who *knows?*" Don't you know one important thing?

BORIS: I know one thing you don't know. Who is Vladimir Polikov?

HACK: I don't know. Who is Vladimir Polikov?

BORIS: He is the mechanic who, every Monday night, while you are at the local meeting, is making love to your wife.

Hit movie in Odessa

ESCAPE TO ALCATRAZ!

In the courtyard of the fearful Lubyankow Prison, three condemned men faced the firing squad.

"Andrey Anatovich Narpovikoff," the commanding officer declaimed, "for sabotage against glorious Soviet Republic, you have been sentenced to death. Do you have last request?"

"Yes," said Andrey Anatovich Narpovikoff. "Please bury my ashes outside Kremlin Wall—near great Lenin's tomb, in honor of glorious Vladimir Ilyich Lenin."

"All right. Squad: . . . Ready . . . aim . . . fire!"

Down slid Andrey Anatovich Narpovikoff.

"Nikolai Soniavich Premenyev, you have been sentenced to death for trying to smuggle enemies of state across border to Finland. . . . Do you have last request?"

"*Da, da,* comrade. Bury me in Tiflis, where Josef Stalin was born."

"Fine. Squad, reload: . . . Ready . . . aim . . . fire!"

To the stones fell Nikolai Soniavich Premenyev.

To the third condemned man, the executing officer announced: "Yitzkhok Mandelstein, you have been found guilty of seven attempts to leave glorious motherland, using forged passport and forged exit papers. What is your last request?"

"For me, please," wheezed Mandelstein, "just spread my ashes over grave of Comrade Ilya Borganovich, Executive Secretary of the Politburo."

"Borganovich?" The executioner frowned. "But Comrade Borganovich is not dead!"

Mandelstein blinked amiably. "I don't mind waiting."

Semyon Grizor trudged along the road, carrying a large loaf of bread. He beheld a peasant working in the field. "*Tovarich,*" he sang out, "how far is it to the railroad tracks?"

"Just follow this lane for ten minutes."

"Thank you."

"Wait, *tovarich,*" called the peasant. "You can't get a ticket there. For a ticket, you have to go to the station—"

"I don't want a ticket. I just want the tracks—to lay myself down on. I'm going to kill myself."

"So why are you carrying that big loaf of bread?"

Grizor shrugged. "By the time a train arrives in Russia, a man can *starve* to death."

Scene: A Jail in Stalingrad

FIRST PRISONER: What are you in for?

SECOND PRISONER: I came to work late. . . . How about you?

FIRST PRISONER: I came to work early, so they arrested me—on some suspicion.

THIRD PRISONER: Well, I'm here because I arrived at work exactly on time.

SECOND PRISONER: What kind of offense is that?

THIRD PRISONER: They said I must own an American watch.

Sign in Moscow store window

MEDICINES—APOTHECARY—DRUGS
AVRUM PINSKY
CHEMIST
SPECIAL LAXATIVES
Effective . . . Painless . . . Proven

to

Let My People Go!

The Politburo recently received a secret request from one of Russia's Arab satellites: Could Soviet experts tell them the age of a mummy just discovered in an archaeological dig, which the sheik was delivering by air?

The Russians promptly cabled the sheik:

> MUMMY ARRIVED. INVESTIGATION UNDER
> WAY. CERTAIN WE CAN DETERMINE EXACT AGE.

Five days later the chief Soviet expert, Vlasy Ivanovich Barostinov told the Politburo that the mummy was exactly—5,344 years old.

The head of the Politburo promptly phoned Barostinov. "Congrotulation, Tovarich Barostinov. For soch feat, I will give you Commendation. But I most be sure *you* are sure—*ob*solutely sure—the mommy is old five t'ousand t'ree—"

"Comrade Commissar," exclaimed Barostinov, "I am positively sure!"

"You used scientific carbon-dating?"

"*Nyet,* Comrade Commissar."

"Electronic X-ray?"

"No, no," said Barostinov. "I found out through most reliable method!"

"What is dot?"

"The mommy made full confassion!"

The Russian sergeant-major glared at the ten lines of braced recruits and bellowed, "And if an officer of the Union of Soviet Socialist Republics gives you an order to march into a swamp, what do you do?"

"We march!" barked the recruits.

"And if an officer of the glorious proletariat tells you to climb a cliff?"

"We climb!" boomed the soldiers.

"And if your officer calls 'A mission in which you may die gloriously for the fatherland! Volunteers! Two steps forward!' . . . What do you do?"

From deep back in the ranks came one response: "Step back."

" 'Step *back?*' " The sergeant-major frowned. "The order is 'Volunteers forward'—and you would step *back?*"

"To make room for all the heroes who will be rushing *forward*, comrade."

"Grampa Vassily," said the little girl, "what do you think of Karl Marx?"
"A great man. A very great man!"
"And Comrade Lenin?"
"A great man. A giant."
"And Josef Stalin?"
"A monster! A lunatic. We learned the truth about him from Comrade Khruschev!"
"And what about Comrade Chernenko?"
"Hush, Natasha! We won't know until he's dead."

Old Mischa Gretzkin, age eighty-seven, lay in his bed in Kharkhov, dying. Came a harsh knocking on the door.
"W-who is it?" quavered Gretzkin.
"The *Malakh ha-movess* [angel of death]," came an orotund voice. "Fear not—"
"Who's afraid?" shouted Gretzkin. "I thought it was the KGB."

TRUE

We were thirsting for tea, Mikhail and I, and headed for the huge restaurant in the Park of Culture and Rest. "Culture and Rest." (Why is the language of bureaucrats always clumsy—and funny?)

Mikhail had attached himself to me (I was not entirely attached to him) as my guide and interpreter. "I gat you in *any*place!" He was a fervent Communist.

Mikhail's Marxist principles in no way interfered with his appreciation of fine food, caviar, and vodka—for all of which I picked up the tab. Whenever a bar check or food bill was set before us, Mikhail went to the men's room. Rarely have I seen so persuasive a demonstration of Economic Determinism.

Nor did Mikhail's dedication to "Marxismus-Leninismus" conflict with his hobby: collecting money. He was especially fond of the color and design of capitalist currency. He gave me rubles for my dollars—netting a mere 20 percent for the friendly accommodation.

Now, Mikhail led the way to a table near a window. A waiter appeared and handed each of us a menu. He did not seem enthusiastic about handing each of us a menu, and I could not blame him once I saw, from its spots and stains, that it was a historic document.

Mikhail studied the waiter. "*Tovarich,*" he smiled, with fraudulent innocence, "you ondrostond English? . . ."

The waiter reacted as if he had been insulted in Assyrian. *"Kak? Nyet! Ya ne ponimayu!"*

"Good." Mikhail informed me, "So we can talk. . . . He is *bod*. Reoctionary."

I glanced at the waiter, who only looked cross-eyed.

Mikhail hissed, calling my attention to what the waiter was doing. What was the waiter doing? He was mopping the table. "You see?" observed Mikhail. "Look how he worrk. Very slow. No care. Sauvyet Union *bleed* from soch sobotage!" Mikhail could spot sabotage in a baby carriage.

The waiter placed his hands on his hips and regarded us with disapproval.

"You see?" growled Mikhail. "Bourgeois!"

"Why is he 'bourgeois'?"

"He have no lov for worrking class."

"Perhaps he just wants us to order."

"His job is to *wait*, no ordrer!" Mikhail tapped the menu. "Bast we hov tea, bons, and botter!"

"Fine."

Mikhail gave the waiter the order in gravelly Russian, adding *"Spasibo"* with the utmost sarcasm. . . .

In time, a steaming glass of tea slid before Mikhail and another before me. Then our waiter deposited a plate containing two buns and another containing two slices of pumpernickel: on each piece of pumpernickel reposed a two-inch square of butter.

Mikhail took one look at the pumpernickel and bellowed (I assume): "Why you bring pomprenikol? Who did order pomprenickol?!"

The waiter studied Mikhail hatefully. *"Zhd kyamya bo grodzhni kok svertnoff kak lubyiski!"* (That's how the phonemes sounded to me.)

"Chto? Kntz? Cysoki?" Mikhail turned to me, his cheeks purpling. "He say the pomprenickol-and-botter is *one unit!* He say brad-and-botter cannot be divorce! We did not *order* brad so we have two *bons*—you see, bons, no botter"—he tapped the plate on which the buns rested—"but this beeg fool waiter say we must pay for brad becawse brad-and-botter in *one unit!*"

The waiter, divining Mikhail's exposition, removed the bread and butter. Mikhail almost tore the varlet's hand off as he snatched the plate back. The waiter poured out a torrent of Russian. Heads turned to us from every table in the vicinity.

"Tovarichchi!" roared Mikhail, addressing his fellow workers. *"Cysok ya probnyoski"* (a Russian dictionary won't help you), denouncing the ludicrous ruling that butter could not be obtained *sans* pumpernickel.

An impassioned brouhaha ensued. Though conducted in Russian, its content was clear to me. The waiter displayed a menu which clearly showed that bread and butter were treated as one unit.

Mikhail protested that such a menu was unfair to the working class.

The waiter thundered that the menu had been debated and constructed "in committee"!

Mikhail howled that he would bring the committee's outrageous decision to the attention of the Central Tourist Bureau, who would realize the impression that such a lunacy as "bread-and-butter-are-one-unit" must make on illustrious visitors from abroad.

The waiter sneered that menus in the Park of Culture and Rest were not designed to kowtow to intellectual lackeys of American imperialism.

Mikhail bellowed that it was precisely this kind of unprogressive thinking that was giving the Revolution a bad name abroad.

The waiter snarled that Mikhail's opposition to an official menu verged dangerously close to Deviationism.

"Bozhe moy!" Mikhail thundered. *"Kak zhdrovni kak nudvoy!"* (I can't help it if that's how it sounded.)

The waiter leered that he would be only too happy to remove the bread.

"But leave the botter!" snapped Mikhail.

"Never!" cried the waiter.

A woman near us hissed *"Shnidz! Shnidz!"* ("Shame! Shame!")

Mikhail quoted Marx.

The waiter quoted Lenin.

Mikhail retorted with a cutting quotation from a recent ukase of the Central Executive Committee.

The waiter flushed and faltered, fearing exposure as a Sloth Who Did Not Keep Up with the Party Literature.

"Mikhail," I intervened, "tell him to take the butter *off* the bread, and put it on the buns, then take the bread away. That would leave us with tea, buns, and butter."

Mikhail's face lighted up. "Bravo! You are Marxist!"

"What?"

"Marxist! You put t'eory with proctice!" Grinning, Mikhail outlined my stratagem to the waiter in triumphant strophes.

The waiter shot me a hostile glance, and began transplanting the butter from the bread to the buns. Suddenly he stopped. *"Nyet, tovarich, nyet!"* Firmly, he plopped the patties of butter back upon the bread. To Mikhail (who repeated it to me in English), he said, *"If* I take the butter off the bread and place it on the buns, then I will have two pieces of bread without butter!" He turned on his heel, as final as he was logical, and stalked away, humming the Red Army March.

Mikhail ate his bun in furious silence. I sipped my tea.

As I paid the bill, Mikhail growled, "The sobotage. The sobotage! We must fight him on hondred frohnts!"

from my *The 3:10 to Anywhere*

See also **Anti-Semitism, Behind the Iron Curtain, Communism**

Salesmen

In the circles of England's life-insurance agents, the name of Humphrey R. Watlaw had become a legend. Many were the tales exchanged about Humphrey R. Watlaw's extraordinary ingenuity and his astonishing sales record.

One day, Chauncey Murk, another salesman in the Phoenix Life Assurance Agency, Ltd., was lunching with Watlaw at the Silver Swan Pub and, over the introductory pint of bitters, asked, "Humphrey, old bean, you and I have been friends all these many years. You live in Putney and I live and work in Sevenoaks—so neither of us is in the potential customers' territory of the other. I promise to keep your words a secret, my word of honor . . ."

"What *are* you going all 'round Robin Hood's barn about, Chauncey?"

"Your astonishing record! I mean, your sales record, old boy. Why, you sell three times the life-insurance policies of any of the three hundred agents on Phoenix's staff. . . . Humphrey, old chap, what *is* your special sales technique? You surely *must* have one. . . ."

"I daresay I do," chuckled Watlaw. "And if you promise to take my secret to the grave . . ."

"Word of honor! Absolutely!"

"Very well, old chap. The truth of the matter is that whenever I have a prospect for life insurance tottering on the edge, so to speak, unsure of his decision, I take the policy, fold it neatly, place it in my briefcase, and, with the utmost friendliness, say, 'My *dear* fellow, you need not make a decision as important as this one, so long as you are so beset by reservations. Why not put the worry off for a bit? Think it over—carefully. Sleep on it. . . . And tomorrow, sometime, I'll ring you up, and you give me your answer' "— Watlaw grinned—" 'if, that is, you wake up.' "

On a street in the East Bronx, two hardware stores, directly across the street from each other, sprouted huge, two-story-high banners. One of these signs announced:

BERNARDO CHAVEZ
BANKRUPTCY SALE
GOING OUT OF BUSINESS!
EVERYTHING MUST GO! 50–75 PERCENT OFF!!

The banner across the street read:

LOST LEASE! MUST MOVE!
TREMENDOUS SALE
BARGAINS—BARGAINS—BARGAINS!
MARGOLIS BROTHERS
FOUNDED 1938

A passerby saw an old man, in shirtsleeves and suspenders, standing in front of Margolis Brothers. A plastic name tag on his shirt pocket read: B. J. MARGOLIS.

"Mr. Margolis," said the pedestrian, "you must be having quite a problem."

"What problem?"

"With this going-out-of-business sale, when your competitor, right across the street, is going out of business, too."

Margolis snorted. "That Chavez? That Johnny-come-yesterday? Look, mister. Chavez will be out of business inside a week. But Margolis? Me and my brothers? We have built up a *reputation* for going out of business! People know they can *rely* on us. Chavez? Who can take his word for it? But *we*—we'll be here another forty years!"

Maurice Einziger, owner of Maurice's Masterpiece Furs, was considered (even by his competitors) to be a master of salesmanship. Once a new customer was trying on a magnificent mink coat, preening before the triple mirror. "Nice . . . yes . . . very beautiful, Mr. Einziger. But is it—practical?"

" 'Practical?' " blinked Einziger. "What could be more warm, more light on the shoulders, more long-lasting than a mink coat where every skin is hand-selected by me personally, designed by my designer from Paris, cut and sewed and stitched by the finest craftsmen in the world?!"

The lady hesitated. "But—suppose I'm wearing this expensive coat and get caught in a terrible downpour—rain, rain, rain?!"

Einziger nodded with complete understanding. "So tell me: did you ever hear of a mink carrying an umbrella?"

The chugging, smoking car drove on to the Argyle Used Car Lot in Aberdeen. The driver cut off the ignition and called out, "Mr. Dunleavy, Mr. Dunleavy . . ."

The owner stepped out of his little hut. "Ay. Wha' kin y' be wantin'?"

"Mr. Dunleavy, d' ya nae remember the bonnie, bonnie worrds y' gie me concernin' this great bargain o' a conveyance?"

Dunleavy said, "Wha' about it?"

"Och, Mr. Dunleavy, kin y' do me the honor o' repeatin' them very worrds again?"

"Why, mon?"

"Weel, y' see, I'm gittin' a wee bit discouraged."

"Before I present my company's entirely new and amazing policy, Mr. Folger, may I ask: How much life insurance are you presently carrying?"

"I'd say fourteen thousand dollars," said Folger.

The insurance salesman drew back in shock. "Good Lord! Mr. Folger! How long do you think you can stay dead these days on that kind of money?!"

Charley Rabin was famed among his peers for his phenomenal success as a door-to-door salesman of kitchen appliances. One day, George Mason, who worked for the same firm, said, "Charley, how do you do it? You racked up another first in sales for the seventh straight month. With me, I'm lucky if I get into the kitchen of one out of three prospects. You must get into three out of four."

"That's right."

"Man, that's phenomenal! How do you do it?"

Charley winked. "It's simple, pal. Every time a woman answers the doorbell, I say, 'Good morning, ma'am—you won't be*lieve* what I just saw in your neighbor's place!' . . . Georgie, they can't wait for me to come in."

"Man, oh, man," grinned Murray. "What a day I had! Callahan, I bet I made fifty *very* promising contacts!"

Callahan nodded. "I didn't make a single sale all day either."

Michael Gorkin, owner of Unique Women's Wear, was said to be the most ingenious salesman in Los Angeles. He was prone to say to a woman shopper, "Madam, that garment looks as if it was made by the finest designer in Paris—just for you. I tell you, even your closest friend wouldn't recognize you in this gorgeous garment. Why not go out of the shop—into the daylight—examine it there, every feature . . ."

The customer would usually follow the suggestion. And when she reentered Unique Women's Wear, Michael Gorkin would greet her, "Come in, madam. First time here, eh? What can I show you?"

In a small midwestern town, posters appeared:

AMAZING! DEFIES DEATH!
CROSSES FEARFUL CHASM

on June 14

There will appear at the Bannister Landing of our River

The Great

CHESTER GREYSTONE

World famous Trapeze Artist, who will walk across the Desplaines River on a tightrope!

COME ONE! COME ALL!!

25¢ each spectator of the Death-Defying walk

Virtually the whole town turned out. Each eager viewer placed a quarter in a bowl in front of a striped tent.

They beheld a rope tied to a tree, stretched tight fifty feet across the river and anchored to a tree on the other side.

From the striped tent there appeared The Great Greystone—but in a shabby costume and frayed shoes. He climbed up the tree, set one foot cautiously on the tightrope, and turned to make this heartfelt speech to the audience: "Ladies and gentlemen, good folk, Baptists, Methodists, church-goers of every sort: I, too, am a God-fearing man. I have a confession to make. I am not a trapeze artist. I'm just a poor man trying to earn enough to eat regularly. If I should attempt anything as crazy as starting across the river on this rope, I'll fall fifty feet—right in front of your eyes, break my neck, *drown* in those waters! . . . And so to prevent that tragedy, and your innocent, unwilling complicity in it, I am going to take a vote. For a miserable twenty-five cents each, should a poor, hungry man take an awful chance like that? How many of you kind Americans want me to go on?"

Carey Bushnell was a clever sharpshooter and a master of deceit. He had just moved into a new office, on the door of which he had a painter place these words:

BUSHNELL WORLDWIDE INVESTMENT SERVICES
INVESTMENT ANALYSIS AND FINANCIAL ADVICE
C. H. BUSHNELL, PRES.

Carey was sitting in his desk chair, wondering what to do next, when the door opened.

At once he lifted his phone, saying, "No, I don't think the price of gold will bother us." He signaled the man in the doorway to enter and sit down. . . . "I'd buy a hundred thousand shares." Covering the telephone speaker with his palm, Carey whispered to his visitor, "Tokyo calling. Be with you in a moment." Into the phone he said, "Michio, I bought you ten thousand Fynborn warrants. Right. . . . Cotton futures? Not at this time. . . . I've got a call in to Frankfurt to sell your Deutschmarks. . . . Thanks for calling. Sayonara." He put the phone down briskly and addressed his visitor, smiling: "Well, sir. What can I do for you?"

The visitor said, "I just came to hook up your phone, Mr. Bushnell."

Scene: Armenian-American Sports Arcade

Mr. Karkorian watched his new salesman, Georgi, expounding to a particularly glum customer, "An' o'course you need line. *Line:* new, strong line, to fish."

"Okay," sighed the customer.

"Also, with you got line, musta have reel, eh? Nice *reel?*"

"Ah—supposa."

"Also, beeg boots? Up to here—look. Boots? Is no water come in!"

"Yeah, yeah."

"Maybee—aha!—fish *vest,* also! Becouse today—special price . . ."

"Suppose."

Georgi wrapped the whole pile of gear and pumped the gloomy customer's hand. "Goot lock, 'svedanyia."

The customer departed, sighing.

Mr. Karkorian came over to the salesman. "Georgi, fordy year I be in thees *lafka*—and *never* I see salesman lika you! Customer come—ask fishhook. One lousy *hook.* An'a you talkin'm in line, rill, boot, vast—"

"Na, na, na," Georgi interrupted. "*No* come in f'hook. Come in for aspirin'."

"Asprin? Wha' for *a*sprin?"

"He think we drugstore. Say to me, 'Aspirin. For wife. Wife she—you know, time month . . .' So I tell 'm, 'Ah, so while she outa commish, why you no go fish?' "

"Hey, Nat, what a day I had yesterday," said Morty Lazar. "From the Lamston chain! I got an order for six thousand dollars!"

"Sure, sure," said Nat dryly.

"You don't believe me?"

"No."

"Okay, I'll prove it!" exclaimed Lazar. "I'll show you the cancellation!"

The old optometrist was breaking in a new assistant: "—And after you have fitted the new glasses, the customer usually asks, 'How much is this?' and you say, 'Ten dollars.' You wait an instant—and if the customer says nothing you add—'for the frames. The *lenses* are ten dollars more.' Again you hesitate . . . If the customer says nothing, you add, 'Each' . . ."

See also **Business, Ingenuity, Just Jokes, Stratagems**

Sarcasm

In the Golden Grand Hotel, in Atlantic City, the phone rang, early one morning, in Room Service. The manager picked up the receiver. "Room Service. Can I help you?"

"I soitinly hope so," a voice quavered. "I want you should—"

"What is your name, sir?"

"Belkin. Jacob Bel—"

"And your room number?"

"My room is Number four-one-two."

"Now, what can I send up?"

"Breakfast," said Mr. Belkin. "I vant a glass orange juice, it should be very bitter. . . . Then, two pieces toast, they should be boined black. Then the coffee, it should be absolutely cold—"

"*Mis*ter Belkin," protested the manager. "I can't fill an order like that!"

"Vhy not?" asked Mr. Belkin. "You did yesterday. . . ."

A flustered bridge player asked his partner, "How would *you* have played that hand?"

"Under an assumed name."

An English columnist, noted for the sharpness of his pen and the penetration of his wit, one day wrote:

> —the eminently sensible bill was defeated in the House of Commons. One wonders how much longer the people of Britain can have faith in a body half of whose members are idiots.

Several days later, the columnist printed this memorable retraction:

> A spate of angry mail from readers has denounced the author of this column for saying that half the members of the House of Commons are idiots. I have been urged to apologize for so harsh and incorrect a statement. Herewith, my apology. I am happy to correct my observation: half the members of the House of Commons are not idiots.

Never had Macready had so finicky a customer. He showed her strapped shoes, pumps, slip-ons, shoes in suede, in crocodile, in satin—all to no avail. Finally, sunk in a sea of shoes and boxes and tissue paper, Macready wiped his neck. "Mum, do ye mind if Ay rest a wee while?"

"Why? Is anything wrong?"

"T' be pairfectly honest, mum: y'r fate are killing me!"

An actress shaped like Raquel Welch stepped out of the shower, in her suite at a fine New York hotel, dried off, and, stark naked, stepped into the bedroom.

There she saw a window washer, admiring her through the glass.

The actress was so startled that she froze, standing there, speechless, nude. Her trance was broken by the window washer: "What's the matter, sweetheart? Never seen a window washer before?"

Sign over automatic washing machine in Chelsea (London) laundromat

To Our Esteemed Patrons
Should every method you may employ,
to start the operation of one of
these machines, fail to achieve the
desired goal—*do*, please,
read the instructions.

The bus was jam-packed at rush hour. A very large, very fat woman got in and as the bus started up, gazed about angrily. Michael Killigan, a tiny man, hiding behind his newspaper, slunk lower . . .

In a loud, grating voice the woman declared, "Isn't there one polite man here who will offer me his place?!"

Killigan sighed, lowered his paper, and rose. "Well now, madam, I guess I'll make a small contribution . . ."

Rodney Luft, dining at Shimmel Goldfarb's Elite, tasted his thinly sliced salmon, swallowed it, savored it, thought about it—then signaled to the owner.

"Yes, sir?" said Mr. Goldfarb.

"Tell me about this salmon," said Luft.

"What would you like to know?"

"What can did it come out of?"

" 'Can'? You said 'can'? Mister, my salmon doesn't come out of any *can*! It comes—absolutely fresh—from the finest, coldest waters of Nova Scotia!"

"Nova Scotia . . ." repeated Rodney Luft. "Was this particular salmon imported or deported?!"

The diner stared at the waiter who was placing the soup before him. "Are you the same waiter who took my order?"

"Yeah."

"Are you *sure?*"

"Sure I'm sure," huffed the waiter. "Why do you ask such a question?"

"Because by now, I expected a much older man. . . ."

"Mr. Gilhooley," said the country doctor, "that is a bit o' a nasty cough y've got there."

"Ay. Fairly tears out me longs," complained Gilhooley.

"And what are ye takin' for it?"

Gilhooley, a sarcastic soul if ever there was one, said, "Doc, I'll listen to any decent offer."

Our rabbi prayed to the Lord that the rich give more to the poor—and God has answered half that prayer: the poor have agreed to accept.

The waiter lifted his pencil and his notepad. "So what would you like to eat tonight, sir?"

"Waiter," frowned the diner, "I gave my order at least half an hour ago!"

The waiter nodded. "Well, *that* waiter can't serve you. I—"

"Tell me," scowled the customer, "did he leave much of a family?"

Zack Williams was on the banks of Mole Head Creek, in the Ozarks, fishing.

A battered old jalopy pulled up.

Zack continued fishing.

A man in overalls got out of the jalopy and watched Zack for a bit.

Zack glanced at him and nodded.

The stranger nodded. "Fishin'?"

Zack took the match out of the corner of his mouth, "Nope."

"*Not* fishin'?"

"Nope."

"Hope y' don't mind m' sayin' so, friend—"

"Don't mind ef'n y' do."

"—but if y' ain't fishin', then why you standin' there at the edge of the water n'all, with a fishin' pole in your hands?!"

Zack spat a wad of tobacco juice on the ground. "Gess y' could say I hanker t' drown worms."

As old Muldoon, clay pipe and all, entered the elevator of the posh London store, the ex–Coldstream Guard at the controls closed the scissors gate with force and in an insolent tone asked, "Well now, paddy, what floor would *you* want to get off on?"

"Noomber three," grinned Muldoon, "*if* Oy'm not takin' Your Lordship out of your way."

The morning after the Boilermakers baseball team had lost its seventh game in a row, it met in the clubroom for "skull practice." The coach stepped to the center of the locker room and, in his most acidulous manner, said, "Now, girls . . . this"—he held up a ball—"is called a baseball. And this" he—held up a bat—"is called a bat."

"Coach," a voice cut in, "do you mind not going so fast?"

The new arrival at the summer resort sat down in a beach chair. "I got up at dawn," he boasted, "to see the sunrise."

"You soitinly picked the right time," said his neighbor.

"Hey, Carraci. How you *operazione* go?"

"*Buono.* Joosta *buono.* But-a one-a thing I no like. The *dottore* he leave in me one-a sponge!"

"Hey, Carraci. Isa terrible! Isa hurt?"

"*Niente.* . . . But-a, oh boy, alla time—am I-a t'irsty!"

See also **Chutzpa, Groucho, Put-downs, Repartée, Restaurants, Retorts, Shnorrers, Squelches, Waiters**

Scoundrels

A lovely but destitute girl from Sicily, lonely and miserable in New York, walking along the East River, suddenly decided to end it all. She was poised on the planking of the pier when an American sailor shouted, "No! No! Miss! *Don't!*" He ran up to her and pulled her to safety. "How can you even *think* of doing such a terrible thing?"

Weeping, the girl told him of her plight. "I want to go home . . . to Palermo."

The sailor thought for a moment. "My boat is a freighter. We make many stops—but Sicily is our final port. . . . Suppose I hide you in one of the lifeboats? I'll bring you food and water. . . ."

In the pitch of the moonless darkness that night, the sailor smuggled the girl aboard and hid her under the tarpaulin of a lifeboat. And soon he brought her food. And after that he began to share his meals with her. And after four nights, the sailor and his stowaway made love. . . . For three weeks, they made love.

One morning, the captain of the vessel discovered the girl in the lifeboat. She told him her story. "Sicily?" frowned the captain. "What low-down sailor—"

"How can you *talk* that way?" cried the girl. "He is kind and good and—"

"And you," said the captain, "are on the Staten Island Ferry."

One of my favorite childhood memories involves a men's clothing store in our neighborhood, which was owned by a pair of partners who, rumor had it, sent eight children through college simply by pretending to be deaf. The ingenious haberdashers' deaf caper is unmatched, I think, for simplicity, duplicity, and punishment to the greedy. Here is how it worked:

One partner would wait on a customer, extolling the excellence of the wool, the styling, the needlework of this or that suit. Often the customer would, naturally, ask, "How much is this suit?"

"What?" asked the salesman, cupping his ear.

"How—much—does—it—cost?" the customer repeated more loudly.

"Hanh?"

"*How much is the suit?*" the customer would shout.

"Ah, the *price!* I'll ask the boss." Whereupon the "clerk" would turn and shout toward the back of the store: "*How much is the beautiful navy-blue, double-breasted suit?*"

The "boss" would shout back: *"Forty dollars!"*

The "deaf" clerk would tell the customer: "The boss says, 'Twenty dollars.' "

Need I describe how swiftly many otherwise righteous men, young and old, plunked down their twenty dollars and hastened out of the store, chortling?

from my *Passions and Prejudices*

❧

Mr. Bradshaw was walking briskly to his house, down the dark street from the railway station, when a thin, woebegone stranger suddenly came out of a parking lot and stepped in front of him. "Pardon me, sir. Could you help a man who's really down on his luck? So help me God, sir, all I have to my name is this gun."

❧

"Hey, Sheldon. What's wrong?"

"Wrong?"

"Yeah. You look pretty darn miserable."

"I'm miserable because I had a sore toe, so I went to a doctor. He examined me and said, 'It's not too bad. I'll have you walking by tomorrow morning.' "

"And did he?"

"You bet he did. He stole my car."

❧

DEAD MEN TELL NO TALES

Dead men practically turn blabbermouth once a competent coroner cases the corpse. It doesn't matter whether the victim was strangled, poisoned, or sped to Valhalla via forced feedings of halvah: dead men tell the truth, the whole truth, and nothing but the truth—to anyone who knows how to decipher it.

Professional gunmen, keenly aware of this, used to toss their murderees into cement mixers, simultaneously destroying a telltale body and humanizing our highways.

One imaginative ganglord won my admiration by devising an exquisite way of disposing of his enemies: he secretly bought a fine old funeral parlor. From time to time, my hero simply placed a defunct mobster in a coffin *underneath* the body of a blameless client who was about to be returned to the good earth. This double-decker ploy remains a high-watermark in the history of problem-solving.

from my *The Power of Positive Nonsense*

❧

Years ago, old Mr. Lyle carried a milk bottle, filled to the brim with yellow fluid, to the Ballantrae Polyclinic and Health Center. He went into the clinic and handed the bottle carefully to a nurse. "Here it is, Nurse Cameron. The urine specimen. Name of Fergus Lyle . . ."

"Aye. Coom back in three days for the analysis."

In three days, Mr. Lyle returned. He was taken to see Dr. Howard, a young doctor. The doctor glanced down a report and said, "Well, Mr. Lyle. The laboratory report they gie ye is—all fine. Complete bill o'health. No diseases."

Mr. Lyle went home with great speed and scarcely contained delight. Before he was through the door of his house he cried, "Kathy, lass, Kathy! It's great news I am bringin'!"

His wife hurried in from the kitchen. "Aye?"

"Hoot, Kathy, it's fine I am in all respects! And so are ye, and so is y'r old dad, an' y'r brother Nairn, and bonnie cousin Molly, and also me brother Clyde, an' his woman, an' my old friend Douglas, an' th' charwoman . . ."

W. C. Fields once leered, "You can't cheat an honest man." That moralism has become the Eleventh Commandment in American folk thought: but it is not true.

Consider the many victims of a master of skulduggery in Watchung, New Jersey. One Saturday night, just before Labor Day, this scoundrel placed a night-deposit box outside the entrance to a bank in a large shopping center on Route 22. He set his beautifully made night-deposit box, which was a fake, right next to the bank's night-deposit box. Since banks are closed on Sundays and Labor Day, one of the busiest weekends of the year, storekeepers were tickled pink to deposit their cash, and checks made out to "cash," in the night-depository boxes.

Early Tuesday morning, the wizard picked up his receptacle. The illicit contents came to over $26,000 in cash and $3,500 in checks, which provided our *gonif* with much exultation and professional pride.

The police force of Watchung, New Jersey, refused to tell the Associated Press exactly what the fake depository box looked like. This was quite correct of them in my opinion. Excessive verisimilitude in reporting criminal artifacts is pretty certain to: (a) instruct and (b) encourage imitators. Only a fool would publicly provide a good working description of a fake night-deposit box.

As for the name Watchung, I marvel at the esthetic satisfaction that nomenclature can provide.

from my *Passions and Prejudices*

Said Mr. Firkis to the rector of St. Bartholomew's, "Ay, 'tis enough t' tear at th' hardest heart. . . . The widow MacBain, a foyne woman in the eyes of the Lord, with a wee bairn—she is owin' fourteen-pound-ten in rent, and unless she pays, before this very Sabbath night, *evicted* she will be!"

"Och, Mr. Firkis, ay, 'tis terrible t' hear. Oy'll make an appeal at morning service Soonday, Oy will. And here, mon, here is two pounds of me own."

"Thank ye, rector. Thank ye for the widow MacBain."

"And *she* should be thankin' *ye*, Mr. Firkis, for your kind heart an' efforts in her behalf. Might ye be kin to th' widow?"

"Nae, nae."

"Then what was it made ye so heartfelt interested in her sad case?"

"I am her landlord, rector."

Robert and Flora Bascombe received, in the mail, two tickets to the biggest hit on Broadway, a show for which tickets had been sold out for three months. Whoever had sent the tickets had forgotten to include a note with the donor's name. The tickets were for the following night.

The Bascombes went to the show, which they enjoyed hugely. When they returned to their apartment, their bedroom was turned upside down: the woman's furs and jewels were gone, the man's fine cuff links were gone. And on a pillow was this note:

Now you know.

SILKY PINCUS DESCRIBES
THE CASE OF HOKEY SLOCUM

"Hokey" (Hobart) Slocum was one of the most artistic check-hikers in the greater Manhattan area. He really *milked* the bank account of Mrs. Gwendolyn Blair, who was forty-six and loaded. Her hubby is a V.P. at Continental Parachutes, Inc. Hokey nets hisself like twelve grand, with no overhead except pen and ink, before Mrs. Blair finds out she is overdrawn—plenty. She gets very mad on her bank when they can't explain things to her satisfaction. So she decides to hire a P.I.—to find the unknown forger. I take her on as a client and pass the word around our snitch circuit. Soon I get a tip that the penmanship kite has to be the work of Hokey Slocum. . . . I turn that over to Headquarters. . . . Inside fourteen hours the forgery boys collar Hokey. . . . He would of taken a sure 1–5 fall—except for one thing. . . .

Mrs. Blair had to confront Hokey in the station house, to tell the cops if she knows him or ever seen him before. Mrs. Blair is negative. But Hokey puts on such a cornball act, exclaiming he don't know the difference between right and wrong on account of the brain surgery he had to have for his Korea war wound in the service of our country, that Mrs. Blair, who did not know Korea from anemia, gets all choked up. She informs me that if Hokey will return the boodle and promise never to do such a naughty thing again, she will drop all charges. . . .

So I get a smart lawyer, Lester Plosher, and tell him I have come to love Hokey, as who don't, and can he help that true artist out in his moment of need? . . . The mouthpiece lays on a deal with an assistant D.A. he knows and despises, a clown named Hamilcar Strable who happens to be very religious, so he is jumping to save a soul, plus gain a contributor to his forthcoming primary campaign for councilman from Staten Island. To Mrs. Blair, Hokey antes up three grand—and he signs a promissory note that he will cough up the balance in monthly installments. . . . So Justice was done and a trial avoided to save the taxpayers' money, plus our overcrowded prisons don't have to cram another sardine into the can.

Well, Hokey makes his monthly payments—the first of each month, on the dot. He borrows the dough from Chomski and Gell, who are actually bondsmen, but they have a sensitive nose for any type buck, and they charge like 19 percent. . . . The kicker is, that brainy Hokey insists on making his monthly payments to Mrs. Blair in person.

Hokey is a nifty dresser and a talker so smooth you could use his words for eyeglasses. And when, in the fifth month of fulfilling his legal obligation, he cannot go on the cuff for more scratch, from even the firm of Chomski and Gell, Hokey tells Mrs. Blair he is considering hari-kari, even though he never set a foot in Japan. In fact, Hokey cries, "Madam, I throw myself on your mercy!"—and he throws hisself on her *zaftig* body as well.

One thing Hokey always could spot a mile away in the smog is a middle-age dame who is hungry for love, on account of her hubby is not giving her enough of it. Next thing we hear is Mrs. Gwendolyn Blair is filing for divorce. . . . Hokey, who can give lessons in savvy, abets the split by finding the chick in the steno pool at Continental Parachutes from who Mr. Blair has been getting nookey.

So Mr. Blair don't contest the divorce. Gwendolyn flies to Old Mexico. Inside two hours of getting her decree of freedom, she becomes Mrs. Hobart Slocum III. That "III" did not refer to Hokey's pedigree, as your society columnists assumed, but to the number of nuptials he has committed. . . . So in one shrewd play, admired by all students of the con, Hokey has wiped out his debt, avoided the slammer, and is now residing in the spacious Blair spread in Bucks County. . . .

There's a P.S. Hokey is now raising Holsteins or some other type animal. I never in a million years would of cast him as a dairyman—except for one thing: Hokey always had a thing for oversize boobies. And Gwendolyn sure had them!

from my *Silky!*

A classmate of mine at college (let's call him Theobald Prysock) grew so disgusted by the silly hazings he had to endure as a freshman "pledge" to a certain fraternity that he decided to quit. But moral outrage so burned within the soul of Theobald Prysock that he could not simply return his pledge pin. Theobald spent days on end seeking an act of reprisal that would properly express his feelings for the fraternity "brothers" he was disowning. What he finally did was masterful:

One night, after his peers were all snoring away, Theobald tiptoed down the stairs of the fraternity house to the fraternity library. He closed the door, removed a book, turned to the flyleaf, and inscribed therein:

GIFT
OF
THEOBALD PRYSOCK

He put the book back on the shelf and proceeded to the next. . . .

It took my pal Theobald a good four hours, I believe, to donate the entire library of Phi Gimmel Epsilon—to itself.

Can you imagine a happier soul than Theo, his lavish philanthropy completed, as he carried his suitcase into the night?

I feel privileged to have known such a rogue.

from my *Passions and Prejudices*

See also **Aplomb, Chutzpa, Ingenuity, Salesmen, Stratagems, True Tales**

Sex

It could be that there are some things in life that are better than sex, and some things are certainly worse. But no man or woman on earth ever found anything just like it.

W. C. FIELDS

❧

Chastity: The most peculiar of all sexual aberrations.

REMY DE GOURMONT

❧

Christianity has done sex an enormous service by making it a sin.

ANATOLE FRANCE

❧

Sex: The most fun you can have without laughing.

❧

The ability to make love frivolously is the chief characteristic which distinguishes human beings from animals.

HEYWOOD BROUN

❧

The turtle lives 'twixt plated decks
Which carefully conceal its sex.
I think it clever of the turtle,
In such a fix to be so fertile.

A gloss on OGDEN NASH

❧

"Why, Jess Farnow!" cried Mrs. Blair. "I hear you had triplets! Is that so?"

"Oh, yes."

"Well, gracious me! Congratulations! What a rare, rare blessing. How rarely does one hear of —"

"My doctor said triplets happen only once in two million times!" said Jess.

Mrs. Blair blanched. "Good God, Jess! When did you have time to do the housework?"

❧

"Oh, my dear, *dear* Violet," Hensor-Atley murmured, "I—I —I love you most awfully!"

Violet Penfield-Sym sighed, "How true . . . how terribly true."

When they awakened from their night of love, the lovesick girl murmured, "Darling, truthfully—am I the first girl you ever took to bed?"

"It's possible. . . . Were you at Disneyland in 1973?"

"Listen, doc," sighed old Mr. Krantz, "you been my doctor already forty years. You know I am seventy-eight years old—and naturally, things are a little run down."

"For instance?"

"Well, most important, of course, is sex. My, what a man I used to be between the sheets! Now—well, making love once a month is already something to be glad about. But my friend, Nate Eckel, he is at least eighty-three, eighty-four—and yesterday he told me that he makes love to his wife two-three times a week!"

The doctor studied Mr. Krantz. "So?"

"So?" Krantz echoed. "Is that all you have to say? '*So?*' I am dying of *envy!* Doc, isn't there something I can *do?*"

"Sure," said the doctor. "Tell Eckel the same thing."

The marines have perfected survival techniques—that is, ingenious methods of survival if lost on a desert, in a jungle, in a rowboat, on mountains, in forests. . . . In one lecture, the men were being taught about food to be found in any wood: termites, slugs, grubworms. "And grasshoppers," said the instructor, "are a tasty, nutritious food. In fact, King Solomon used to feed grasshoppers to his thousand wives."

A voice cut in: "The hell with what he gave the women. What did *he* eat?"

"Mama," said Lena Levine, "there's a special meeting tonight at the Community Center. Professor Stolman of Vassar is going to talk. She's a wonderful speaker. I want you to come with me."

"What," asked mama, "is her subject?"

"Sex and marriage."

"Thanks, Lena. But I already gave."

"François," said Marcel to his partner, "I must ask—*pardonez-moi*—a very personal question. I hope you do not take offense . . ."

"I? Offense? With you, *cher ami?* Never!"

"*Alors*. François, are you—making sex with Melissa, our beautiful new receptionist?"

"Marcel, I admit this. In her apartment last night. And *mon dieu!* Marcel, this girl . . . why compared to Melissa, my wife has the sex appeal of lettuce!"

A month later, François came into Marcel's office and carefully closed the door. "Marcel, my dear friend, I have been wondering. . . . I cannot help noticing certain things . . . do not think me presumptuous . . ."

"What *is* it, François. Speak up."

"Well, then, Marcel: Have you been sexing with Melissa, our beautiful receptionist?"

Marcel beamed. "*Oui. Certainement.* And François, my friend, you were positively correct! Compared with Melissa, your wife has as much sex appeal as an artichoke."

In the clubhouse of the Westchester Retirement Colony, Mrs. Pasternak, chairman of the Entertainment Committee, greeted the newcomer. "Mrs. Isenberg, welcome to our Ladies' Club."

"Thank you."

"This is your first visit here?"

"That's right."

"Then allow me to acquaint you with a few of our unwritten rules. These rules will make life a good deal happier for all concerned."

"Oh, good."

"First, in card games—gin, bridge, any card game—we *never* tell anyone how she should have played a hand. Second, we never boast about our children or grandchildren. (And if you must show the latest snapshots, do it in your own home, not the clubhouse.) Third, we do not discuss husbands—present, divorced, or deceased. . . . And finally, Mrs. Isenberg, we never discuss S-E-X. Our unanimous opinion is: 'What was, was.' "

I wonder what fool it was who first invented kissing.

JONATHAN SWIFT

One of the medical staff of British Overseas Air, a psychiatrist, was giving a pilot the customary six-month checkup. "And about how much alcohol do you consume a week, captain?"

"Oh, perhaps five or six beers. No whiskey."

"And drugs—drugs of any sort?"

"None, doctor. None at all."

"Cigarettes per day?"

"I do not smoke cigarettes."

"Cigars?"

"Perhaps one a month."

"How do you sleep, captain?"

"Extremely well. Go off a moment or so after my head touches the pillow."

"Do you ever get severe headaches?"

"No, sir."

"Are you likely to develop emotional tension—during, say, an altercation?"

"On the contrary, doctor. I *rarely* get into an argument. And I don't believe I have been involved in an altercation since I was ten."

The psychiatrist nodded, scanned his checklist, and said, "Finally, about sexual adjustment, captain. When was the last time you slept with a woman?"

The captain deliberated. "1958 . . ."

"1958?!" The psychiatrist gasped. "Good lord, captain! That long ago?"

The pilot seemed puzzled. "But, doctor"—he glanced at his watch—"it's only 22:10 now."

Pretty Maureen Feeny, sleeping next to her husband, was having a marvelous dream. A handsome stranger was making passionate love to her. In her sleep, Mrs. Feeny sighed and moaned in ecstasy, then blurted: "Oh . . . good God! I hear footsteps. . . . Go! Fast! It's my husband!"

Mr. Feeny jumped out of the window.

HOW TO TELL YOUR CHILD ABOUT S-E-X

Herman P. Klitcher
201 Placebo Park
Placebo Park, Ill.

Dear Leo:

I just have to write you about something that just happened. A big argument bust out at a party at "Frenchy" Lastfogel's abode last Sat.—on the subject of what is the best way to answer a kid when he or she asks "Where do babies come from?"

Leo, the ideas some of those dummies expressed on this subject were just *disgusting!* Some of the married went "all out" for telling a child the naked "Facts of Life"—

which goes against my grains. Other persons opined that you have to "dress up" the ugly facts on account they can so mix up a sensitive kid that he or she will be a sitting duck for a head-shrinker by the time they hit twenty-one.

Like for instance, our son Alvin. He is sixteen going on seventeen at the present time. Well, Alvin has begun to drop hints to his mother and I about The Subject—and says he wants to get the dope "right from the horse's mouth." That means me, natch—although I am not a horse, and Flo says that the way I drink on festive occassions I have a mouth more like a fish (ha, ha!)!

Anyway, after the party Flo and me are in the private aroma of our bedroom, talking things over. And we decide "before we damage Alvin's entire future outlook on girls (or even on *boys,* the way things are these days) should we consult our doctor, who is a jerk, or should we read up on the best modern straight-from-the-shoulder books about Sex?"

Then Flo has a real inspiration! Exclaiming "Hey, why do we not ask your old hi-school pal Leo?!" So heres our question, Alfred Einstein: "How is the best way to answer your kid when he comes right out and asks you "Where do babies come from"?!"

I hope you will not give us that old jazz about the Birds and the Bees, Leo. We already *told* Alvin about the Birds and the Bees, but he said he can't understand how his own Mother laid eggs, and asks me "Where do you get your pollen from, Dad?" !X#&%!

Or should we maybe put the whole blame on the Stork? (That is pretty hard to put over on a kid with a bass voice going on seventeen!)

Please answer fast, chum, because from one or two little things I have observed lately, Alvin is in a hurry!

> Your old pal,
> Herman ("Herm") Klitcher

Leo Rosten
Sex Counsellor
606 Wassermann Drive
Cocksackie, N.Y.

Dear "Herm":

"What is the best way to tell your kid about where babies come from?" Herm, that question has plagued mankind down the centuries. Last year alone, 9.7 percent of the federal budget was spent on research by psychiatrists for the U.S. Navy who are studying the least harmful way of telling American sailors "the facts of life," in case they are shipwrecked and don't know where to begin.

You have no idea how many nice American boys are confused about the very question that is bothering your son Alvin. (What are the names of your other sons?)

I happen to know *exactly* how one should answer a kid who asks: "Where do babies come from?" Let me tell you how I told "the facts of life" to my own children.

Case 1

My son, Philo. Philo was a gentle, sensitive lad, who was popular with insects. He was constantly being bitten by hornets, yellow jackets, and bees. I think you will agree, Herm, that in his case it would have been *disastrous* to mention "the birds and bees," because he might have ended up thinking that if you bite a girl, the way he did all through nursery school, you make her pregnant.

How well I remember the day Philo first asked me about Sex. It was a Tuesday.

"Dad," he blurted, "where do babies come from?"

At once I replied, "Son, how old are you?"

He counted on his fingers. "Twenty-three."

"Twenty—*three!*" I echoed. "My, my, where does the time go? It seems like only yesterday you were twenty—two."

"Yesterday I *was* twenty—two," said Philo. "Today is my birthday."

"Happy birthday, son."

"Quit stalling," he sneered. "*Where did I come from?*"

Well, Herm, at that point I could not fake a heart attack, as I had been planning to do for years, so I told him the simple truth: that he had been left on our doorstep by someone I certainly would like to get my hands on.

Herm, I have never regretted my candor.

Case 2

My daughter, Madrilene. Madrilene was a sweet girl with an inordinate number of teeth in need of straightening because our dentist was building a ballroom over his garage.

One day, right out of the blue, Madrilene asked me, "Daddy, where does a baby come from?"

Without a moment's hesitation, I answered, "Whose baby?"

"Any baby."

"*Any* baby?" I retorted. "That's a pretty sloppy way to ask a question! Just suppose I talked that way, Maddy. Suppose I asked you: 'Where do Popsicles come from?' You'd answer 'Which Popsicle?' wouldn't you?"

"I would not," said Madrilene, "since the only place in town that sells Popsicles is Schermerhorn's."

"That's true," I said, studying my palms. "Now be a good girl and go play with your Lucrezia Borgia doll."

"Stop stalling, Dad: Where—do—babies—come—from?"

"Very well," I said firmly. I took a deep breath and declaimed, "I happen to have made a careful study of Doctor Spock, and every pamphlet published by the Child Study Association. The truth, dear, is—*I just don't believe their version of how it is done!* Don't get me wrong, darling. I know where babies come *from* (and so do you, judging from the grin on your puss); what I don't understand frankly, is how they *get* there!"

Herm, I have never had reason to regret my frankness.

Case 3

My third child, Peggoty. Peg was an innocent, trusting child who majored in dangling participles. She was busy finger-painting the wallpaper in her room, one night, when I came in looking for my pipe cleaners. (She uses them as hair curlers.) I was greeted by this question: "Father, what about Sex?!"

"What do you mean, 'What about Sex'?"

"You know what I mean!"

"That is true."

"Well?"

"Well what?"

"What—about—Sex?"

Herm, I was right up against the moment every American father dreads. But I knew exactly what to say. After all, I had gone through this identical crisis twice before and had learned a thing or two. So I took my little girl's hands in my own and gently said: "Listen carefully, Peg, because I don't want you to believe the silly things you may hear from other children. I want to talk to you like a modern father—"

"I'll be late for my karate class," she said.

"I'll come right to the point," I assured her. "When a Papa Bee gathers nectar from the rose, he picks up pollen on his back legs, which he rubs off—"

"Oh, *God,*" she moaned. "When I asked you 'What about Sex?' all I meant is what do I write in here?" And she held before my eyes this printed form:

```
NAME:  Peggoty Rosten
DATE OF BIRTH July 4, 1957
SEX:
```

"Write in 'F,'" I said firmly, "that
stands for 'Female.' By George, Peggoty,
you are old enough to know: You—are a girl!"
Herm, I have never regretted my candor.
Your old pal,
Leo

As the groom embraced the bride, holding her in a long, fervent kiss, the whisper of a child in the front row of the chapel was clearly heard: "Daddy, is he spreading his pollen on her now?"

Young Simpkins wrote a long letter to his mother, a week after his arrival at Annapolis, to tell her of his exciting new life, his friends, his courses. "And next week they are going to teach me how to use a sextant."

Mrs. Simpkins telephoned her minister. "Reverend Dean, do you *know* what the navy is teaching our young men?!"

"Say, laddie, an' have y' seen Casey O'Hare in recent days?"

"Nay."

"He's in hospital, with many a broken bone."

"Is he now? What happened?"

"Well, laddie, Casey always said sex on the TV is pretty awful. An' it is, me boy, it is. Casey fell off."

Deep in the night, Brecher shook his wife. "Lena . . . Lena . . ."

She mumbled, "Mmh. . . . what?"

"Darling, I got you two aspirins and a glass water."

Lena sat up. "What's with you, Nat?"

"For your headache, Lena."

"Who has a headache?"

"You don't have a headache?"

"No."

"Great. Let's make love."

See also **Bachelors, Hanky-panky, Love, Marriage**

Shadchens

Note: Jewish marriages were customarily arranged by the heads of families. In Eastern Europe, the professional matchmaker, or *shadchen*, performed a very important social function. Not only did he travel from village to village, to scour communities for available boys and nubile girls; he was a purveyor of news, gossip, rumors; he gathered information about eligible mates, weighing their family backgrounds, noting individual qualities, matching personality factors in an undertaking that is today assigned to computer-dating services.

L. R.

"I can't believe it!" exclaimed Shlissel the Shadchen. "A young man like you—intelligent, attractive, making a good living . . . such a good Jewish boy isn't *married?!*"

"True, true," sighed the young man. "And don't think I wouldn't like to get married. . . ."

"So think of all the nice girls I awready brought to your attention!"

"I know. But the truth, Shlissel, is this: Whenever I meet a girl who would make a good wife—take care of me, share my joys and sorrows, even cook like my mother . . . she *looks* like my father."

Sigmond Shlossberg, having patiently borne with Feivel the Shadchen's hyperbole, said, "But in all the wonderful things you told me about the girl, you left out one important thing!"

"Me? Feivel? Never! . . . What did I leave out?"

"She—limps!"

"Only when she *walks!*" protested the *shadchen*.

In a certain town, there was a grievous shortage of marriageable young men. One of them, Beryl Chodovitch, quite ugly and equally conceited, came to Baruch the Shadchen and said, "I am finally considering getting married. But I warn you—I'll accept nothing but a very *special* match. And the dowry has to be plenty!"

Baruch studied young Chodovitch, then said, "Fortunately, I have just the girl for you! Her father is rich, and she is beautiful, well educated—"

"Wait a minute," said Chodovitch. "Why isn't such a girl married?"

The *shadchen* raised his hand. "You want to know why such a girl is not married? I want you to know—that's why her rich father may accept someone who is not—excuse me, Beryl—the most attractive young man in the world. I will be perfectly frank. This beautiful, educated, charming girl has one affliction: once a year, she goes crazy."

"She goes *crazy?*"

"Yes. Sad, but true. But that doesn't have to bother you, Beryl! She doesn't make any trouble—she just goes quietly *meshugge*—for only one day. Then she's absolutely charming and normal for another year. . . . And her *dow*ry!"

Beryl Chodovitch smiled. "Let's go see her right now."

"Not yet," said Baruch. "This match must wait."

"Until when?"

"Until the day she goes out of her mind again."

Muttel Metchnik, a marriage broker, having sung the praises of a female client, brought his excited young man to see her.

The prospect took one look at the damsel, paled, said, "Glad to meet you," and signaled to Metchnik.

"What's the matter?" asked the *shadchen*.

The young man whispered, "You said she was young, and she's almost forty! You said she was attractive, and she looks like a chicken! You said she was—"

"You don't need to whisper," said Muttel. "She's hard of hearing, too."

Pincus Ofek, an extremely resourceful *shadchen*, was impressing his young prospect, Hi Winkel, with the boundless virtues and charms of the unmarried Ruchel Bernitz, ending, "And to look at, that alone—my boy, Ruchel Bernitz is like a painting!"

Hi Winkel could hardly wait for his blind date. . . .

When Pincus Ofek came to the young man's flat the next morning, he beheld a frosty Winkel.

"You didn't fall head-over-heels with Ruchel?" the *shadchen* inquired.

"*Fall* for her?! Why, her eyes are crossed; and her nose is crooked, and when she laughs, one side of her mouth—"

"Stop!" Pincus Ofek presented an open palm. "Why didn't you tell me you don't like Picasso?!"

Ezra Karper confronted the *shadchen*, scowling, "You lied to me!"

"Me? Lie? *Never!*" retorted the *shadchen*. "Isn't she pretty? Well educated? Loves music?"

"Yes, yes," said Ezra, "but you also told me she comes from a famous family! You said her father is dead—and I just learned *he's in jail*—"

Sneered the *shadchen*, *"That* you call living?"

"Listen, Mr. Greenblatt," the *shadchen* complained, "I'll be glad to look through my files—and even make a special trip to certain places—to find a suitable husband for your Etta."

"If only that could come true!" sighed Mr. Greenblatt.

"But frankly—I have to tell you, your daughter looks like she's forty years old!"

"Looks, looks," scoffed Greenblatt. *"Who* goes by looks? Some teenagers look like mature matrons and some middle-agers—"

"Wait." The *shadchen* raised a minatory palm. "You specifically told me that your daughter is only twenty-nine years old!"

Mr. Greenblatt gazed into the distance.

"Mr. Greenblatt—*twenty-nine* years old? . . . Is that true?"

Greenblatt replied, "Partly."

Asa Schwartz was twenty-nine, attractive, well spoken, well off—and leading a bachelor's dream life.

For such a marriageable young man to remain single (nay, to persist in refusing to consider marriage) struck Shimen the Shadchen as an offense in the eyes of the Lord. "Who ever heard a nice Jewish boy of twenty-nine, shouldn't at least be going steady?!" the astounded *shadchen* asked Asa.

"I," said Asa, "don't go steady, because *I* don't want to get married."

"Why not?" demanded Shimen. "Give me awready one good reason! Just one!"

"Because I'm having the time of my life," smiled Asa. "No ball-and-chain around my neck. No nagging. No whining. No fancy clothes to pay for. And I come when I want, I go where and when I want, I can date a different girl every night of the week! . . . Tell me, *shadchen*, what in the world can be better than that?"

"I'll tell you what in the world can be better than that!" exclaimed Shimen. "The life of a happily married man can be better than that! A man with a loving, giving, devoted wife—like I have. How can you know what joys are in a home? Look, Asa. Think about this. Every single night when I come home—tired out, hungry, even depressed from the long day's work—my dear partner in life, my darling Rosaleh, gives me such a warm hello, a hug, a little kiss, takes off quick my coat, makes me sit right away in the big chair, takes off my shoes, puts on my feet comfortable slippers, brings me the paper, a little glass wine. . . . Then she serves me a dinner—ai, ai, ai! Fit for Count Potofsky! For a *king*, even. . . . And after we eat, we maybe go take a walk, maybe see friends, maybe take in a movie. . . . And then we come home—to a nice, warm bed. And we lie there, under the clean sheets, close together, man and wife—so contented, and my Rosaleh tells me what happened to her all day—the shopping, the cleaning woman, the sink needs fixing, the dropping in by her sister, the call on her mother. . . . She talks, I listen, the house is cozy. I feel my eyes getting heavy. . . . And my Rosaleh talks some more—and talks, and talks, and talks until one day—so help me God!—that woman is going to drive me right out of my aching *mind!*"

Salo Shimshom, a veteran *shadchen*, highly regarded in the orthodox community, was touting the charms of a Malka Janine to Josiah Zetan, a confirmed bachelor.

"Malka?" asked Josiah. "The blondie?"

"The same."

"You must be cuckoo, *shadchen*. She's almost blind!"

"That you call a failing?" cried Shimshom. "That's a blessing—because she won't see, half the time, what you're doing."

"She also stutters!"

"Lucky you," sighed the *shadchen*. "A woman who stutters doesn't dare talk too much, so she'll let you live in peace."

"But she's deaf!" complained Josiah.

"*I* should have such luck! To a deaf wife you can shout, you can bawl her out—"

"She's at least twenty years older than I am!"

"Ah," sighed the *shadchen*, "I thought you were a man of vision. *I* bring you a marvel, a woman you can spend a lifetime with, and you pick on one little fault!"

An eager *shadchen* brought Shlomo Kantrovich, his young male prospect, to the Vishner home to meet unmarried Lena Vishner and her parents.

On their walk back, the *shadchen* said, "Well, Shlomo, did I exaggerate? Isn't that Lena some girl? And think what a big *dowry* she'll bring you! Did you see the furniture in that house? The silverware? The rugs . . ."

Said the young man uneasily, "But her father seemed so *eager* . . ."

"Don't let that fool you!" exclaimed the *shadchen*. "That Lena has two dozen boyfriends!"

"And her mother," said Shlomo, "kept pushing . . ."

"That's only your imagination!"

"Look, for all I know, they *borrowed* the fine rugs and all that silver just to impress me!"

"*Borrowed* it?" echoed the *shadchen*. "Shlomo, are you out of your mind? Who would lend a *nickel* to such deadbeats?"

See also **Aplomb, Bachelors, Chutzpa, Ingenuity, Love, Marriage**

Shaggy Dogs

Dr. Henri Thermond, the celebrated French obstetrician, came home at 5:45 A.M., wearily sank into his easy chair, and said to his wife, *"Ma chère, please—a little cognac. . ."*

"Of course, Henri. . . . I have not often seen you to be so weary. Was the delivery long?"

"Long, long, and with many difficulties. Ah, thank you, Paulette . . ." Dr. Thermond sipped the cognac slowly. "But, *ma chère*, this delivery was indeed worth it. . . . Do you know who it was I this night did deliver? Charles de Gaulle!"

Harlan and Evans were at the bar, where they had been for two hours, paralyzing their gray cells. Finally Harlan hiccuped. "Bob, do you know what time it is?"

Evans yawned. "Yes, I do."

"That's good," said Harlan.

Rinaldo the Great, magician *extraordinaire,* came to the office of the manager of a vaudeville circuit. "Sir, I have perfected a new act that will be an absolute sensation. I saw a woman in half!"

The manager eyed Rinaldo with disdain. "You call that *new?* My God, man, where have you been? Magicians have been sawing women in half for three hundred years!"

"Lengthwise?"

Jacopo Valdarez was visiting his old friend Enrico on the Upper West Side, because Enrico's wife had just died. "Enrico, my old friend," said Jacopo earnestly, "I, too, am without a *sposa.* I, too, have not one boy or girl to be a comfort to me. Enrico, my friend, most important thing for you—as was for me—is to have—hobby. Nice, time-taking-up hobby."

Enrico nodded gloomily, *"Si*, Jacopo. *Grazie*. I have hobby."

"You do? What is hobby?"

"Bees."

"Bees? What kind bees?"

"Kind fly, bzz—bite—bzz-bzz-bzz."

Jacopo looked out of the window, "So where is hive?"

"I no use hive. I keep in bedroom."

"In *bed*room? Don't bees *sting* you?"

"How? I keep them in closet."

"In—*carramba*, Enrico, when you open closet, don't bees whoosh out—?"

"They no can. I keep them in box."

"In box? . . . I suppose you put many holes in box?"

"What for should I put holes in box?"

"For air. The oxygen. If they no get air, bees die!"

"So?"

" 'So?' What's matter with you, Enrico? Don't you care if all bees die?"

Cried Enrico, "It's only a hobby!"

"That turtle certainly is nearsighted!"

"A turtle *near*sighted? How on earth can you tell?"

"He fell in love with an army helmet."

The tall, bronzed man in the safari jacket walked into Malachy's Bar— with a magnificent parrot perched on his shoulder.

"Saints alive!" exclaimed Malachy. "That is a magnificent bird if ever I did see one. Where in the world did you then get it?"

"Brazil," yawned the parrot.

"Oh, man, did *I* have a dream last night!" said Peter Joyce. "I was in Atlantic City, at Caesar's Palace, and everytime I rolled the dice I hit a seven. Every number I bet at roulette came up. Every time I dropped a quarter in a slot machine—bang! Jackpot!"

"Hey-hey!" exclaimed Terence McPhail. "Did *I* have a dream last night! But frustrating! I dreamed two of the most beautiful models in the world walked into my apartment and without a word began to take off their clothes. *Two* of them. What could I *do?* It was the most frustrating—"

"Wait a *min*ute, pal. Why the hell didn't you phone me to come right over?!"

"I *did*, Peter, but you were in Atlantic City."

Simon Hassenfeld, a widower, lavished all his love on his new dog, Hinteleh. He taught Hinteleh to stand on his hind legs, his front paws folded across his breast, for as long as half an hour. Then he taught Hinteleh to wear a *yarmulka* and sway back and forth, as if in prayer. Then old Hassenfeld got a small prayer shawl and taught Hinteleh not to shrug it off his shoulders.

Came the High Holy Days. Hassenfeld hastened to the synagogue with Hinteleh, whom he sat on the bench between himself and his customary neighbor, Svetlow.

At the right time, Hinteleh rose to pray, along with the entire congregation. He swayed back and forth, made grunting, grumbling noises—until Mr. Svetlow cried out, "Hassenfeld! Am I going crazy, or is this dog *pray*ing?!"

"He's praying," said Hassenfeld.

Svetlow gasped, gulped, stared at Hinteleh, then exclaimed, "Hassenfeld, I tell you, with this little dog you can make a million dollars on television!"

"You're telling me? But try and tell that to him. *He* wants to be an accountant!"

The bartender at P. R. Fogarty's Bar and Grill shoved a large lobster in front of Emmet Clancy. "For you, Emmet, me lad. Compliments of the house for your bein' the most regular client of Fogarty's all this year!"

"That's wonderful," said Emmet. "The perfect thing for dinner!"

"Naw," grimaced Fogarty. "He just had his dinner. Why don't you take him to a movie?"

Three fat pigs were wallowing in the cool mud of the barnyard on a hot summer day. The first pig went, "Oink. Oink."

The second pig chuckled, "Oink, oink, oink."

The third pig went, "Mooooo."

The first and second pigs sat up. *"What* did you say?"

"I said 'Mooooo.' "

"Are you crazy?" asked the first pig.

"Pigs don't say, 'Mooo'!" snapped the second.

The third pig said, "I know. I'm trying to learn a second language."

WAITRESS:	Any dessert?
CUSTOMER:	Just coffee.
WAITRESS:	With or without cream?
CUSTOMER:	No cream.
	(waitress goes away; returns)
WAITRESS:	I'm sorry, sir; we're fresh out of cream.
CUSTOMER:	Do you have any milk?
WAITRESS:	Sure.
CUSTOMER:	Okay. Then I'll take my coffee without milk.

The phone rang on the desk of the president of the Algonat bank. He picked it up. "Yes?"

"This," growled a man's voice, "is a stickup!"

"What kind of a joke is this?" snorted the president.

"It's no joke! Mail me fifty thousand dollars or I'll blow your brains out!"

Ike Bushkin often ate at Garber and Gulovitz's Tasty, a self-service restaurant on West Seventy-second Street that specialized in delicacies from the counter marked APPETIZING.

One night, Mr. Bushkin chose a fine, plump "chubb" whitefish, picked up two bagels, a slab of cream cheese, and a bottle of Dr. Brown's Celery Tonic. He sat down at a table for two, cut a bagel in half, smeared each side with cream cheese, lifted his fork to insert under the skin of the smoked fish and lift it off, when he noticed the glazed eye of the whitefish staring at him in a bitter, accusatory manner. This completely unnerved Ike Bushkin. . . . He looked out of the Tasty's window for a moment, observing the stream of passersby. Then he lifted his knife, and with his fork, returned to the task of skinning the whitefish. And again he *felt* the accusatory stab of that cold, unwavering, uncondoning eye.

Ike Bushkin was now so unnerved that he put down his knife and fork and left Garber and Gulovitz's.

Ten days later, Ike returned to the Tasty, again chose a fine, fat whitefish, and again, as he began to lift the skin, the reproving glare from the plate drove all hunger from Ike Bushkin's mind. He left the fish unskinned, uncut, uneaten—and departed.

More than a month later, Ike found himself on the Lower East Side. He went into "Kasha" Kipnin's Lone-Star. To the waiter he said, "A couple of your best bagels—plain bagels, no sesame seeds or onions on them; a good portion your own cream cheese—not Philadelphia; a bottle Dr. Brown's Celery Tonic; and a nice, plump, juicy—make sure it's not dried out— smoked fish."

The waiter assembled these items and deposited them on the table before Ike Bushkin.

Ike cut the bagels in half, smeared cream cheese on them, poured some Celery Tonic into the glass, lifted his knife and fork—and stopped, paralyzed by the icy glare of the fish's eye. Before Ike could even lower his implements, he heard the whitefish sneer: "What's the matter, mister? You don't eat at Garber and Gulovitz anymore?"

Angus Donaldson, traveling from Aberdeen to Blackpool, could not believe that the conductor, collecting fares, was telling him the right amount of the fare to Blackpool. The two men argued with heightening emotion— until the conductor yelled, "There's nae use arguing with a stooborn, jug-headed mon like ye!" picked up Donaldson's suitcase, lowered the window, and, as the train was crossing a bridge, threw the suitcase out of the window. "And ye can get off next stop, too!"

"Ye lyin', no-good Welshman!" cried Donaldson. "Firrst y' try to rob me iv' the price of a ticket—and now y've gone an' drowned m' only son!"

Henkell bought a mousetrap for his kitchen, then discovered there was not a drop of cheese in the apartment. "You know," he told his wife, "mice are pretty smart. Instead of real cheese, I'll cut one of those wonderful color pictures of cheese out of *Good Housekeeping* and put it in the trap as bait. That mouse will have to come very close before it realizes it's not real cheese but a fantastic picture. . . ."

"Marvelous!" said his wife.

The stratagem worked, in a way. Next morning, when Henkell came to the trap, he found, firmly pinned to the bottom—a real-life picture of a mouse.

"Big Mac" McGonigle, the newest prisoner, walked into the exercise yard. He saw a group of men sitting in a circle. . . . Suddenly one convict said, "Thirty-nine!" and the circle broke into laughter.

A second prisoner said, "One hundred and nine." Everyone in the circle laughed.

A third man cried, "Eighty-five!" and a wave of laughter swept across the ranks.

"What in hell's goin' on?" asked McGonigle.

"Well," a prisoner explained, "we been here so long, and tell the same jokes over and over—so we all know them so good, now we just call out the numbers. Go ahead . . . try one."

McGonigle said, "Forty-six."

No one laughed.

"Sixty-two!" cried McGonigle.

Grimaces, shrugs.

"One hundred eighty!"

A few groans, a few grunts.

"What the hell's wrong?" asked McGonigle. "Ain't them jokes funny enough f'r ye?!"

"Oh, sure, those are funny jokes. But, man, the way you *told* them . . ."

Rabbi Rossman, visiting the widow Glatzer, was surprised to see her talking to a beautiful parrot. "How long have you had a parrot?" he asked.

"Ever since my Morty passed away. And I tell you, rabbi, this little bird has been a godsend to me. He understands my sorrow, and, although he doesn't talk much, what he says is honest, direct, and very comforting. . . ."

"Thank you," said the parrot.

"And the cute little tricks I have taught him! Rabbi, just tug his right leg. . . . Go ahead."

Rabbi Rossman tugged the parrot's right leg. "*Sholem aleichem!*" croaked the parrot.

"Amazing," said the rabbi.

"Now tug his left leg. . . ."

The rabbi tugged the left leg.

"*Mazel tov!*" rasped the parrot.

"Amazing!" said the rabbi. "Mrs. Glatzer, what will he do if I pull both legs?"

"*Both* legs?" croaked the parrot. "I'll fall right on my tush, you idiot!"

See also **Dummies, Hillbillies, Just Jokes, Shlemiels, Tall Tales**

Shlemiels

Note: Shlemiel is a priceless word because it embraces such a mélange of simpletons, luckless souls, misfits, patsies, pigeons, pipsqueaks, suckers, born losers, milquetoasts, *et alia.* I know no better way to pinpoint the characterization than by these classic definitions:

A shlemiel falls on his back and breaks his nose.

A shlemiel takes a bath, and forgets to wash his face.

A shlemiel is always knocking things off tables—and a *nebech* always picks them up.

A shlemiel rushes to throw a drowning man a rope—both ends.

If it rained soup, a shlemiel would have only a fork.

A shlemiel has accidents that start out to happen to someone else.

A shlemiel doesn't know how to find a notch in a saw.

YIDDISH SAYINGS

Shlemiels are usually regarded with pity, not scorn: they cannot be blamed for the infirmities of their judgment, the folly of their choices, or the naïveté that governs their hapless course through life.

L. R.

Jack Benny, a grand master at portraying the shlemiel, upon receiving a cherished national award, accepted the honor with these memorable words: "I don't really deserve this beautiful award. But I have arthritis, and I don't deserve that either."

"Doc, doc!" Merkin cried into the phone. "It's my Dotty! She's startin' them labor pains! Just like you said!"

"Now calm down, Mr. Merkin. Get yourself together."

"Sure, doc, sure. What should I do?"

"First," the doctor said, "tell me: How far apart are the pains coming?"

"Uh—they're all in the same place, doc!"

"Does a slice of bread," asked Max, "fall with the buttered side up or down?"

Jacob said, "With the buttered side down!"

Max said, "With the buttered side *up!*"

So they made a bet.

Jacob buttered a slice of bread, raised it, and let it drop. It fell—buttered side up.

"I win!" cried Max.

"Only because I made a mistake," protested Jacob.

"What mistake?"

"I buttered the wrong side."

Three shlemiels were in a bed, trying to sleep, but it was so crowded none could doze off. Finally one man said, "I've got an idea. It's so crowded in here, I'll get out."

He got out and stretched on the floor.

In a moment, one of the men in the bed said, "Listen, Moishe. I think you can come back to bed: there's plenty of room now."

Two shlemiels were at the rail of the great ocean liner, staring at the vast, limitless sea.

"Just look at all that *water!*" exclaimed the first shlemiel.

"You bet," said the second. "And don't forget—that's only the *top.*"

Two shlemiels were drinking tea. In time, one looked up and announced portentously: "Life! What is it? Life—life is like a fountain!"

The other pondered a few minutes, than asked, "Why?"

The first shlemiel thought, scratched his chin, then shrugged, "Okay, so life *isn't* like a fountain."

(*Note:* Shlemiels certainly do not have to be Jewish.)

Scene: St. Wilby's Club, London

"Rupert, old man. I must take you into my confidence. . . ."

"Of course, Ellsworth."

"Well, last night, after a very late directors' meeting, I went home. I crept up the stairway so as not to awaken Sheila, stole into our bedroom—and there, by God, in *bed* with her, naked as a frog, was Leonard Saville!"

"Good Lord!" gasped Rupert. "What did you do, old man?"

"I stared coldly at Saville for a good two minutes, then, without a word, I turned on my heel and walked out, down to the kitchen, and made myself a proper pot of tea!"

Rupert nodded gravely; after a long moment, he said, "I *say.* . . . But—what about Saville?"

"Humph!" huffed Ellsworth. "I thought to myself, By God, let the bounder get his own tea!"

"The best way to keep from getting constipation," said Dr. Hockner, "is to drink warm water an hour before dinner every night."

"I'll certainly do that," said Mr. Erd.

The next time he saw Dr. Hockner, the doctor asked, "Well, how are you feeling now?"

"Terrible."

"Do you drink warm water an hour before dinner every night?"

"Doctor, I tried!" Erd's sigh came from the depth of his being. "But who can keep drinking for more than ten minutes at a time?"

Henry Graver, an indubitable shlemiel, came home early one afternoon to find his wife and his best friend in bed. "Omi*god!*" cried Henry. "What are you two doing?"

His wife turned to her bed partner: "See, didn't I tell you he is a dummy?"

The foreman at the Steuben Glass Factory came over to the new hand. "Nice day's work you've done, Lenski. Did you stencil the important '*This Side Up*' on the top of each crate?"

"Oh, yes," said Lenski. "And to protect them double good, I put the notice on the bottom, too."

See also **Dummies, Hillbillies, Jews, Just Jokes, Nebechs, Shaggy Dogs**

Shnorrers

Note: Every Jewish community once had at least one shnorrer, and often a platoon. The shnorrer was no run-of-the-mill mendicant. He was not apologetic; he did not fawn or whine. He regarded himself as professional. He did not so much ask for alms as *claim* them.

For shnorrers considered they had a license from the Lord: after all, they were *helping* Jews discharge solemn obligations to the poor and the unfortunate. Through these noble acts, a good Jew could accumulate *mitzvas!* Shnorrers seemed to know that they were both exploiting and assuaging one of the most powerful psychological forces in the psyche of Jews: guilt.

The shnorrer "recoiled from demeaning himself . . . from sheer arrogance and vanity. Since he was obliged to live by his wits," writes Nathan Ausubel, "he developed all the facile improvisations of an adventurer. . . . He would terrorize his prey by the sheer daring of his importunities, leaving him both speechless and wilted."*

On the part of the Jewish community, shnorrers were regarded as performing some sort of social function. Exactly what this function was, I could never fathom as a child; but everyone seemed to take it for granted—and took it for granted that no explanation was necessary. (Maybe shnorrers served this purpose: often excellent *raconteurs,* they circulated stories, jokes, gossip.)

In Chicago, walking with my parents, Izzy, "our shnorrer" (as my parents thought of him), would come up to us, extend his palm, receive his nickel or dime, and proceed to his next "clients." Not a word was exchanged: no greeting, no *"Shalom"* or *"Sholem aleichem,"* merely a nod from the mendicant, a sigh from my father, a smile from my mother.

One Sunday, the shnorrer was nowhere to be seen. After we walked the length of the shnorrer's usual territory without encountering Izzy, my mother said, "I wonder what's happened to our shnorrer? I hope he's not sick."

"Sick?" My father snorted. "He's as healthy as a horse."

"Then why isn't he on the street?"

"He's probably in Florida," said my father, "taking his vacation."

L. R.

*Treasury of Jewish Folklore, pp. 267–68.

The blind man stood on the corner in Whitechapel, jiggling his tin cup. A woman stopped and dropped a shilling into the cup.

The blind man said, "May the good Lord shine His face on ye, ma'am. I knew ye had a kind heart the minute I seed y' comin' down th' road."

A shnorrer came to the back door of the Winkel house on his biweekly rounds. "I haven't a penny in the house," apologized Mrs. Winkel. "Come back tomorrow."

"Tomorrow?" The mendicant studied her sharply. "Lady, I hope you don't let this happen again. A man can lose a *fortune*, extending credit."

A beggar stood each morning in front of the World Trade Center, with a box of cheap pencils. "Pencils . . . only ten cents a pencil . . ." the beggar chanted.

One wealthy Wall Streeter each morning dropped a dime into the beggar's box, saying, "Good morning," without ever taking a pencil.

One day the rich man dropped his dime with his usual "Good morning," started to enter the building, but felt a tap on his shoulder.

"Mister," said the beggar. "I've had to raise my prices. Inflation. A pencil now costs a quarter."

See also **Chutzpa, Jews, Retorts, Sarcasm**

Signs

In a student's dormitory in Sweden

Italians are not allowed to sing after midnight.

Germans are not permitted to get up before 5:00 A.M.

In a Kowloon tailor shop

CUSTOMERS GIVING ORDERS
WILL BE
SWIFTLY EXECUTED

On a boarded excavation site in New York

DANGER!

COMPLIMENTS OF

VITIELLO BLASTING MAT CO.

First prize: Sign pinned to dress of pregnant woman at masquerade ball

I SHOULD HAVE DANCED ALL NIGHT

On a roofer's truck in Manhattan

FIEDLER ON THE ROOF.

Menu

TODAY'S SPECIAL
Barely Soup

Sign in deli

> ### Try Our Special Swiss Cheese:
> ### 24% less cavities

In cafeteria

> Swift, courteous self-service

∽

In fancy food store

We sell the finest
homemade imported caviar

∽

Above a bin containing flyswatters, in a hardware store

> **The hand is quicker**
> **Than the eye is**

Beneath this, a cynical customer had printed:

> **But often slower**
> **Than the fly is.**

∽

Sign on bench

> ### WHET PAYNT

PASSERBY: You spelled "wet" wrong.
PAINTER: I know: but when I spell it right no one pays attention.

∽

Sign in Rome

> ### SPECIALIST IN WOMEN
> ### AND OTHER DISEASES.

∽

Sign over dormitory bathtub

> DON'T FORGET YOUR RING!

∽

On house painter's truck

LOVE THY NEIGHBOR! PAINT THY HOUSE.

In an elevator in a Belgrade hotel

> To move the cabin, push but-
> ton for wishing floor. If the cabin
> should enter more persons, each one
> should press number of wishing floor.
> Driving is then going alphabetically
> by national order.

thanks to DONALD CARROLL

Chalked on a post-no-bills wall

DOWN WITH GRAFFITI!

Sign on car bumper

BAN BUMPER STICKERS

On door

PLEASE DO NOT READ THIS

Label on package

> Please notify us at once if this
> label fell off in transit

On a menu

Ice cream	70¢
Pie (like Mother made)	50¢
Pie (like Mother wished she could make)	$1.50

Sign in butcher shop

THIS WEEK ONLY
T-BONE—$1.00

Pedestrians had to step much closer to read the type underneath:

With meat: $6.00

∿

In Austrian hotel

IN CASE OF FIRE
PLEASE DO UTMOST
TO ALARM HALL PORTER

∿

On door to hospital ward

VISITORS:
HUSBANDS ONLY.
ONE PER BED.

∿

Sign I saw in Tokyo (in English)

COMING SOON
HOTEL AND OFFICES
BIGGEST ERECTION IN TOKYO!

On entrance door to State Tax Bureau

WATCH YOUR STEP

On exit door

WATCH YOUR LANGUAGE

∿

On awning manufacturer's factory

JUST A SHADE BETTER

∿

On Sunnyvale Sanitarium

NOBODY LEAVES HERE MAD.

Over author's study

WRITER'S CRAMP

On doctor's house

BEDSIDE MANOR

On retired admiral's house

ALL ABODE

On midget's summer house

TOO LODGE

On ornithologist's house

HOME TWEET HOME

Mrs. James Morse Thirkall
is pleased to announce
the arrival of
Mary Nelly—6 pounds 8 ounces
and
the loss of twenty pounds

Tag on parka

Material
Wool	20%
Unknown	70%
Other	10%

Notice in window of Jurgenson's Skin-Diving Equipment Store

We carry a complete
line of under ware

Boxed note on menu

> *Try Our Famous*
> CAESAR SALAD
> CHEF
>   (Tino Brutus)

Sign in Dade County realtor window

GET LOTS WHILE YOUNG

Sign on tree at roadside of N.Y. Highway 104

KITTENS! KITTENS!
FREE MARTINI WITH
EACH KITTEN TAKEN AWAY

On mathematics professor's house

AFTER MATH

On newlyweds' car

FROM HERE TO MATERNITY.

On chicken incubator

CHEEPERS BY THE DOZEN

Over bed in guest room

Be it ever so humble,
There's no place like home.

At Arizona roadside

IF YOU DRIVE LIKE HELL,
YOU'RE SURE TO GET THERE.

See also **Advice, Graffiti, How's That Again?, Typos**

Snafus

Mrs. Blitzstein dialed her daughter's number and sang out, "Hello, darling. This is your mama. So, how's everything?"

"Everything is just *awful,* mama. The children are acting crazy, the house is a mess, I have a bad back—and we are having three couples for dinner!"

"Stop! Your worries are over! I'm coming right over," said Mrs. Blitzstein. "I'll calm down the children, I'll clean up your place so every corner shines, and I'll cook a dinner for you and six guests no one will never forget!"

"Oh, mama, you angel! That's just marvelous of you! . . . How's Papa?"

"What? Papa? . . . Darling, have you gone mad? Your papa—may his soul rest in peace—died seven years ago!"

A pause fell upon the line. "Er—what number are you calling?"

"Alton-six, four, four, nine, one," said Mrs. Blitzstein.

"This is Alton-six, four, four, nine, *four!*"

"Omigod! I dialed a wrong number!"

"Wait! *Please!*" the voice wailed. "Does that mean you're not coming over?!"

A seventh-grader was so late coming home from his suburban school that his mother was frantic.

"What happened to you?" she cried.

"I was made traffic guard today, mama, and all the kids have to wait for my signal, after I stop a car, before they can cross the street!"

"But you were due home two *hours* ago!"

"Mama, do you know how long I had to wait before a car came along I could stop?!"

Mr. Feibleman called Sanchez and Battista ("Awnings, Shades, Venetian Blinds—Reasonable Prices, Expert Work"). "Listen, do you fix blinds?"

"*Sí.*"

"I mean, just fix. I don't need a new one."

"*Sí.*"

"So come to Forty-six Forley—"

"You no can bring in?"

"Who could bring in such a big, clumsy thing?" Mr. Feibleman gave the man his address. "How soon can you come?"

"*Martes*, Tuesday. I pick up."

"Not sooner?"

"*Señor*, am very, very busy."

The following Tuesday, while Mr. Feibleman was at work, Sanchez came to the Feibleman apartment. He rang the bell.

Mrs. Feibleman, whom her husband had totally forgotten to tell of the repairman's visit, opened the door. "Hello," she said.

"I am Sanchez."

"So?"

"Lady, I come collect—venetian blind."

"Aha." Mrs. Feibleman opened her purse and gave the man a dollar. "May God help your good work. Goodbye."

TRUE

When I learned that three English friends had been trying to reach us at our London hotel, leaving their numbers (we had received not a single message, nor one phone call), my wife said, "Go down to the lobby. Pick up a house phone. Ask for Leo Rosten. . . . I'll bet they don't know we're registered!"

I did as instructed. "Leo Rosten, please."

"*Would* you mind repeating the name?" a duchess crooned.

I repeated my name.

Pause. "How is that spelled?"

I spelled my name.

Fifty-three moments later, I heard: "Awfully sorry, sir, but no one of that name is registered."

"I *know* he's registered!"

A sniff skewered my self-esteem. "Are you certain?"

"I am *quite* certain. I happen to be Mr. Rosten."

The phone went dead. It stayed dead. . . .

I stepped to the next house phone. "Mr. Rosten, please. Leo Rosten."

A Caribbean refugee replied, "Could you please spell thot?"

I did.

"One *moment* please. . . . Sir, I must inform you thot name does not appear on our guest register."

I accosted an assistant manager. "I'm afraid your operators don't understand my American accent. Would you mind phoning the room of Mr. Leo Rosten? . . ."

"Are you *shaw* your party is in the hotel?"

"Absolutely *shaw*," I said. "In fact, you are looking at him."

He flinched. "Do you mean you are trying to ring *your*self, sir?"

"I am trying to get my wife, who is waiting in our room."

The man's face burst into ecstasy: "Ah, then you know your room number."

I showed him my key: 416.

He lifted the phone. "Room *faw*-one-six, please." He handed me the receiver.

"Hullo-o-o," came a hoarse African bass.

"Is this room four-sixteen?" I asked.

"No! Thees room is foh-foh-seven."

I replaced the phone. The assistant manager had evaporated. . . . I lifted the phone yet once more. "Would you take an important message, from the Foreign Office—for room four-one-six? For Leo Rosten. . . . Just tell him that Prince Peregrine Hapsburg of Albania telephoned."

And that night, for the first time, a chit from the Telephone Message Center was slipped under our door. It read:

> Foreign Office phoned Mr. Leo from Boston. He should call Prince Barry Green Hamburg in Rumania.

from my *The 3:10 to Anywhere*

Slocum Barnes was frightened of his own shadow. When he moved to a new town, the first thing he did was build a big storm cellar. He put in two kerosene lamps, a week's supply of drinking water, canned soups, vegetables, etc.

A week after the storm cellar was completed, a terrific wind came up, the sky darkened, and Slocum ran into the storm haven, slamming down the overhead door and the steel bars.

They found Slocum, a day later, buried in the rubble of the earthquake.

See also **Can You Believe It?, Dummies, Embarrassing Moments, True Tales, Typos**

Spelling Spree

Two brave, fearless young beaux,
Were held up and robbed of all cleaux,
While the weather is hot
They won't mind a lot
But what will they do when it sneaux?

An Indian beauty, a Sioux,
As sweet as fresh honeydioux
Liked to flash her knees
As she passed the tepees
And made the bucks holler, "Wioux! Wioux!"

She felt chilled through,
Her lips turned blough;
And yet although
There was no snough,
She sure did cough
And cough her fool head ough!

L. R.

See also **Doggerel, The English Language, Limericks**

Squelches

Shortly after the Nazis came to power, a restaurant in Berlin put this sign on its door:

HORST WESSEL RESTAURANT
ARYAN CLIENTS ONLY

One day, a distinguished-looking man entered the restaurant. The owner bowed and scraped, the cloakroom girl helped the man off with his fine coat and hat, and the headwaiter led him to a table.

As the man sat down, the headwaiter noticed he was wearing—*Gott in himmel!*—a *yarmulka*. The *maître d'* turned pale and signaled to the owner, who hurried over. The headwaiter pointed to the skullcap.

"Sir!" the owner thundered. "We do not serve Jews!"

"That's good," said the customer. "I don't eat them."

"All right, Victor, I know I'm not the perfect wife for you. I'm just outspoken."

"By whom, dear?"

During complex naval maneuvers, a small ship, hit by a wave, scraped against a huge battleship. Very soon the captain of the small ship received this radio message from the commander of the big one:

IF YOU TOUCH ME THERE AGAIN
I'LL SCREAM

Mrs. Robert Carlton was sitting in her husband's office, waiting for him to return from lunch, when a ravishing blonde sashayed in.

"I," said Mrs. Carlton, "am Mrs. Carlton."

"Pleased to meet you," said the blonde. "I'm Mr. Carlton's secretary."

"Oh, were you?"

The proud proprietor of Smolinsky's Superb, a restaurant on lower Broadway, was making his rounds among the tables full of diners. "Hello. . . . Glad to see you. . . . Everything okay?" At one table, occupied by a lone, sour-faced customer, Smolinsky said, "Are you enjoying?"

"Enjoying what?" asked the stranger.

"My food," said Smolinsky.

The customer stared at the proprietor. "Mr. Owner, frankly: I could get more nourishment biting my lips!"

"A lot of men," she said, "are going to be *miserable* when I marry!"

"How many," he asked, "are you going to marry?"

The young rabbi finally summoned up enough courage to say to Mr. Benenson, one of the elders of the community: "I trust you won't mind my mentioning it, but I can't help noticing that—you always fall asleep when I'm preaching."

Replied Benenson, "Would I sleep if I didn't trust you?"

"Well now, Mrs. Driscoll, 'tis *showin'* y'are, if me eyes do not deceive me. Are ye then goin' to have a wee one?"

"No, Mrs. Connor," said Mrs. Driscoll tartly. "I am jist carryin' it for a friend."

Scene: A Narrow Dirt Road in Vermont

A car pulls up in front of a man leaning on a fence:

DRIVER: Sir . . . can you help me?
LOCAL: Can't tell yit.
DRIVER: Which way do I go to reach Ely?
LOCAL: Don't know.
DRIVER: Does this road lead to the main highway?
LOCAL: Can't say.
DRIVER: Look—you don't know much, do you?!
LOCAL: Mebbe; but *I* ain't lost.

At a meeting in China's capital between the Greek premier and the Chinese Communist leader Mao Tse-tung, the latter asked how many people there are in Greece.

"Eight million!" the premier proudly replied.

"Really," said Chairman Mao. "And what hotel are they staying at?"

"Beggin' your pardon, madam," the Piccadilly panhandler whined, "but I'm fair faintin' from lack o' nourishment."

The dowager inspected the man from head to toe through her lorgnette. "I *beg* your pardon?"

"Madame, I've not had a drop to eat in—in three days!"

The dowager tapped the man on the shoulder with her lorgnette. "You must *force* yourself, my good man. Yes, indeed. *Force* yourself!"

Paddy McLarnin (old cap, clay pipe, and all) was on a train platform, next to a veddy English Englishman, at whose feet stretched a large, exotic dog.

"Will ye look now?" said Paddy cheerfully. "What a foine dog ye have there. An' what breed might he be?"

"Mmmh—he's a cross between an ape and an Irishman."

"Bless me soul!" said Paddy. "Related to both of us."

"Freddy," said Mrs. Wainwright, "we're giving a small party to celebrate my husband's birthday. I'm anxious for you to come."

"Fine, Maggie. When is it?"

"On the eighteenth. Seven o'—"

"The eighteenth?" said Freddy. "Do you mean this month or last month?"

"This month."

"Maggie, darling, today is the nineteenth. The eighteenth was yesterday."

"I know," said Mrs. Wainwright. "And where the hell were you?"

A man with a roving eye and a permanent leer got into a crowded hotel elevator operated by a very pretty, very shapely girl.

After they deposited people at several floors, the Don Juan was the only passenger left. He said to the operator, "Sweetheart, I imagine you must be pretty tired after a day of all these stops and starts."

"The stops and starts," she replied, "don't bother me. What I can't stand is the jerks."

The traffic on Twenty-eighth Street was bumper to bumper. The cross-streets were clogged. Cars and trucks inched ahead, stopped, waited, inched on. . . . The passengers in the taxi leaned forward and called to the driver, "For God's sake, isn't there some way you can go *faster?!*"

"Yep," said the driver, "but I'm not allowed to leave the cab."

The *maître d'* of a very posh French restaurant in New Orleans beheld, to his horror, a tourist at one of the tables tucking his napkin into the collar of his shirt. After taking thought, the *maître d'* went over to the customer and, with the utmost politeness, asked, "Do you want a shave or a haircut, sir?"

The fortune-teller said, "I'll read your palm for fifty dollars. And that entitles you to ask three questions."

"Questions about what?" asked the client.

"About anything."

"Isn't fifty dollars an awful lot to charge for that?"

"Maybe. . . . What's your last question?"

In Hernando's Estrella Bar in Miami Beach, José Vitali, watching television's lottery, leaped to his feet, shouting, "*Numero* t'ree-forty-seex! I ween! I ween! Ten t'ousan' doellar!"

The others sang out their congratulations. But one sourpuss called, "Hey you, Vitali! How you peek soch a *numero?* T'ree-forty-seex?"

"From *ensueño* [dream]!" laughed José. "I am by horse race. Horses ron. Wins a *numero* one hondred. Second, comms *numero* twanty. Next, is ninaty-four."

The sour-faced man closed one eye. "One hondred, twanty, ninaty-four?"

"*Sí, sí!*"

"These *numeros* no add op t'ree-forty-seex!! They make two hundred forateen!"

José ruminated and then shrugged. "I choose t'ree-forty-seex, *amigo. You* be da *mathematico!*"

An earnest first-term congressman sent out a long questionnaire to his constituents, asking for their opinions on the economy, military expenditures, school prayer, etc. The final question was: "In the light of all the complex problems that face our nation, what do you suggest Congress do?"

Several answers read: "Adjourn."

A rogue I know likes to discombobulate barbers who never stop yakking. When they finish their ministrations and hold the mirror behind his head for approval, he studies the reflected image, then says, "N-no. A little longer in back, please."

ACCOUNTING OFFICE

TO:　　George Strand
FROM:　Comptroller

We cannot approve your latest expense account.
R. Jackson

P.S. How much would you take for the fiction rights?

Whenever Zvi Meyer rose to speak in the Knesset, even the members of his own party groaned. Meyer gave the dullest, most soporific speeches in the assembly. But one day, he rose and delivered an absolutely brilliant— indeed, a scintillating—oration. So astounded were the members of the assembly that, the moment Meyer finished, they rose as one, applauding furiously.

When their fervor had run its course, and the members sat down, a sardonic voice from the gallery called: "Author! Author!"

Israel Ortov
28 Broadway
New York, N.Y.

Dear Israel:

Knowing of your interest in the work of our committee, I am putting your name down for a pledge of $1,000 in our current drive for funds.
Yours,
Les Alderman

Les Alderman
806 Fourth Ave.
New York, N.Y.

Dear Les:

Thanks for advising me that you put me down for a pledge of $1,000 in your current drive for funds.

I am interested in the work of another fund. So I am putting you down for a $1,000 pledge there. In this way, Les, no money has to pass between us.
Yours,
Israel

At a very exclusive London club, a lord of the realm kept complaining to his waiter about the uncommonly slow service. His complaints did not help. In exasperation, the lord exclaimed, "My God, man, do you have any idea at all of who I am?!"

The waiter responded, "No, sir. I have not been employed here very long. But I shall inquire at the desk, sir, and inform you without delay."

❧

"Ignatius, me boy," said Offaly, "have y' heerd the new joke about the Irishman and the rabbi? Stop me if you heerd it—"

"How?"

❧

Scene: Kumpelmeyer's Bakery

MRS. WEISHAUPT:	Listen, Mr. Kumpelmeyer, every roll I bought in here yesterday vas so stale I couldn't eat vun of zem!
KUMPELMEYER:	Mrs. Weishaupt, I sink you are crazy! Zere's abzolutely nossing wrong wiz mine r-rolls. Vhy, sixty years ago, during ze Depression, people vould have go down on zeir knees and sanked ze *lieber Gott* for r-rolls like zese!
MRS. WEISHAUPT:	Sixty years ago, I vould, also. Zese rolls vere frash zen.

See also **Groucho, Repartée, Retorts, Sarcasm, Waiters, Wit**

Stock Market

AN AMERICAN TRAGEDY

ACT I

BENDER

Hello, Mr. Morley? I think you ought to buy a thousand shares of Latham Optics. That stock is going to go up to the sky!

MORLEY

What's it selling at?

BENDER

Two and a half.

MORLEY

Okay. Buy me a thousand shares.

ACT II

BENDER

Hello, Mr. Morley. Latham Optics is up to seven dollars a share! Maybe you should sell . . .

MORLEY

Nope. Buy me two thousand more shares.

BENDER

Okay.

ACT III

MORLEY

Hello, Bender? I just saw that Latham Optics is up to fourteen dollars a share! Sell all my shares!

BENDER
(after a pause)

To who?

The day after the stock market plummeted to a new low, two brokers were sharing a taxi from Wall Street to Penn Station. "Oh, Lord, what a day!" groaned Wilmott. "And there's not a sign of relief in sight. All the indices are terrible: unemployment, loan demand, interest rates—Charley, to tell you the truth, I can't remember when I last had one good night's sleep!"

"Really?" said Brakaw. "*I*, for one, sleep like a baby."

"*What?* Do you mean that?"

"Absolutely," said Charley. "Every night, I get up every two hours—and cry."

See also **Business, Stratagems**

Stratagems

A mother in Montana simply could not get her ten-year-old to tuck in his shirttails—until, one night, as he was sleeping, she sewed a lace edge on the bottom of each of his shirts.

"Hello. Is this the Rectory of Saint Matthew the Evangelist?"

"That it is."

"May I speak to Father Shannon?"

"I am Father Shannon."

"Well, father, my name is Homer Swaith. I am the assistant deputy director of the Manhattan branch of the Internal Revenue Service. I'm calling, confidentially, about the tax returns of Aloysius Byrne, a member of your parish. . . ."

"Y-yes?"

"Mr. Byrne has claimed a ten-thousand-dollar tax deduction for a contribution he says he made, in *cash*, to your sodality. . . . In strict confidence, Father Shannon, do you remember receiving such a sum from Mr. Byrne?"

There was a moment's silence. Then Father Shannon said, "Well, now, Mr. Swaith, if you will call me tomorrow—just about this time—I *assure* you, the answer to your question will be—yes."

Hans Schwebel, in West Berlin, said to his wife, "I think those Communists are opening every letter I send to our Brunhilde, working as she is for the German embassy in Moscow. I have a plan to fool them. In my next letter I will say: 'I have put in a tiny hair—so if a censor opens this envelope, the hair will fall out.' "

Two weeks later a letter from Brunhilde arrived. Frau Schwebel opened it and read aloud: " 'Dear Papa, stop such foolish worries about the Russians opening your mail. Your hair was still in the envelope when I opened it!' . . . Ah, Hans, see how wrong you were!"

Schwebel chuckled so that his whole body shook. " 'Foolish worries?' 'How wrong I was!'? *Liebchen*, my fears are true!"

"What are you talking about?"

"I didn't put a hair in the letter to Brunhilde."

"Well now," said Ferguson to the American visitor to Glasgow, "coom around siven, if that's convenient for ye—"

"Fine. And where do you live?"

"I'll gie ye m'card. . . . Now, ye push th' button with y'r elbow, an' when—"

"My elbow? Why can't I press the button with my finger?"

"Och mon!" snorted Ferguson. "Ye're not plannin' t' coom empty-handed, are ye?"

William Collier opened a play, *The Patriot*, on December 30. On January 2 a full-page ad blared:

SECOND YEAR ON BROADWAY!

Jock Higgins, a traveling salesman, could not stop gambling. Worse, he could not stop losing. His losses grew so great that his wife, Nelly, warned Jock that if once more—just once more!—he fell to gambling, she would leave him forever.

Jock's sales route included Dublin, where a famous secret game of poker went on, every night, in the room above the pub called The Turk and Harp. For three nights did Jock Higgins play in that game. And he lost not only every penny he had with him, but his gold watch and gold ring as well. . . .

Early next morning, driving back home with a heavy, heavy heart, Jock Higgins pondered hard and long: What could he tell his wife? . . . When he reached his town, he hastened into a notions shop and bought a large red kerchief. . . .

He parked his car, hurried up the stairs to his flat, tied the red kerchief around his nose, put the key in his lock, and entered, with unsteady gait and strangling sobs: "Nelly . . . me own darlin' Nelly . . ."

She came into the room and screamed. "Jock! Oh! Jock! What hap—"

"Waylaid I was, me darlin'. On the dark road. A mad dog he was, Nell. Put a *knife* to me throat, he did! And said if I didn't give him me watch an' ring an' every single penny on me person—me blood runs cold just to think of it!—he would cut off me nose!!"

Nelly fainted.

Jock got some cold water and a towel, and he cooed over his Nelly and cooled her brow and cheeks, and soon he brought his Nelly to.

"Oh, may the saints prisairve you, darlin' Jock," she moaned. "Without—a *nose*! T' go through this vale o' tears—without a nose! Oh Jocko, Jocko, me love, *why* did ye no give that mad dog all y'r money?!"

Jock whipped off the kerchief. "I *did*, Nell! I did."

Why do I throw a lot of weight with politicians? Because I don't put any election stickers on my bumpers until the day *after* we go to the polls.

"Hello, dear. How was your day?"

"The usual. What happened at home?"

"We-ell, George, let's see, how can I break this to you? . . . How many children do we have, dear?"

"What is this, Joan? A joke?"

"No, George. I want to be—diplomatic. How many children do you and I have?"

"Four, for God's sake. So—"

"S-so, sweetheart, *three* of them did not fall out of the tree and break a leg! Isn't that *nice?!*"

A woebegone panhandler, unshaved and bleary, accosted Ned Harrigan and mumbled, "Can y' spare a good Irishman a quarter for a cup of java?"

Harrigan surveyed the derelict with care. "Mac, if you answer me truthfully I might give you five bucks."

"Hey, *man,*" gulped the bum. "Shoot."

"Do you drink?"

"Never touch a tot of the filthy stuff!" cried the panhandler.

"Do you smoke?"

"Not one cigarette since me blessed father died of the filthy weed!"

"Do you gamble?"

"Gamble? May the Lord strike me blind if it ain't ten years since I rolled a pair of dice!"

"Do you spend one night a week with men friends?"

"None of my friends wants to spend ten *minutes* with me!"

Harrigan chortled. "Come with me."

The two men hastened to Harrigan's flat around the corner. Just before Harrigan unlocked the door, he gave the bum a five-dollar bill, flung open the door, and the panhandler stepped in.

Harrigan's wife called, "Hello, dear," and gave a shriek.

"Don't be alarmed, darlin'," beamed Harrigan. "I just want you to see what happens to a man who gives up drinking, smoking, gambling, and going out with the boys one measly night a week!"

TRUE

The lady with a child in her arms, another holding her left hand, another holding her skirt, raised her free hand, shouting: "Taxi! Taxi!"

The Yellow Cab pulled up to the curb beside her.

The lady opened the back door and put one child after another inside, closed the door, and said, "Pull your meter. I'll be back in a jiffy. Forgot my purse." She hurried back in the house.

It was a good eight minutes before the lady returned, smiling broadly. She opened the back door but instead of getting in, she proceeded to take her three offspring out. "How much do I owe you, driver?"

The driver said, "A dollar forty. . . . But I don't get it, lady! Did you change your mind—?"

"Oh, no." The lady gave him two dollars. "You see, I had to make an important call to a lawyer, long distance, and these three have been driving me crazy!"

See Also **Business, Ingenuity, Rabbis, Revenge, Salesmanship, Tact**

Street Scenes

I was strolling down Lexington Avenue. A loving couple approached me, talking a blue streak, exchanging intimacies in that unabashed non-privacy with which New Yorkers enrich the lives of all within earshot.

The man was wearing a Hawaiian shirt, on which efflorescent paint celebrated a hula-hula dancer wriggling under the palms of Waikiki. The woman wore a peekaboo blouse and a miniskirt, with brains to match.

The couple stopped before a surgical appliance store, from whose windows plastic legs and elastic trusses offered comfort to the maimed, and embraced.

"You're the most, doll-face."

"Mmh!" She smacked a smooching kiss on his cheek.

As the love-drenched pair parted, to attend to separate errands, they shouted these adieus:

MINISKIRT

So you won't be long, honey?

HAWAIIAN SHIRT

Naw, faw-fiminutes.

MINISKIRT

So okay. Hurry. The door will be open.

HAWAIIAN SHIRT

Seeya in a jiff.

MINISKIRT
(yelling after him)

And don'figgit my aphr'disiac!

I could end right here; but that would be a disservice to truth, because Miniskirt's next words were: "The cologne, Harry, not the poifume!"

from my *The 3:10 to Anywhere*

One night, strolling down Sixth Avenue, I saw a straw hat glistening in the gutter—and a woman, wearing the hat, in the same locale. I bent down. She reeked of strong waters.

"Are you all right?" I asked.

"My name's not (hic) Albright!"

"Do you live near here?"

"In these surroundings?" she sneered.

"I'll get you a taxi."

"Sure, Sir Gladahad—get me a (hiccup) cab."

I stepped into the street and, by masterful signaling, succeeded in getting a dozen taxis to speed past me. The moment a driver spied the woman in the gutter, he gunned away, trailing uncomplimentary opinions: though quite erect, I was called a creep; sober as a cleric, I was denounced as a lush; anxious to complete a mission of mercy, I was told to get lost.

A taxi finally came to a halt. "Okay, Mac," sighed the old driver, "pour her in. She could be someone's mother."

I got my hands under the lady's arms. "Here we go. Ups-a-daisy."

"Daisy?" she sang. "Who is Daisy?"

I plopped her through the door. "Where shall I tell the driver to go?"

"How d'I know where you want to go?"

"What—is—your—ad-dress?" I asked.

"I (hiccup) bought it in Macy's."

"Listen. Do—you—know—where you live?"

"Shertainly I know where I live! I *live* there, don' I?" and she passed out.

As I closed the cab door, the driver nodded sagely, "So you ain't goin' with her, huh?"

"I don't even *know* her!" I protested. "I just saw her lying there."

His smile was more withering than contemptuous. "You're from out of town, huh?" and away he drove.

from my *The 3:10 to Anywhere*

See also **Taxi Rides**

Tact

Adolph Zukor, the long-lived head of Paramount Pictures, was reputed to be the most courteous producer in the world. He would with the utmost regret suspend the services of an employee. His notices were famous:

> Dear Charley:
>
> You're fired.
> Warmest regards,
> ADOLPH ZUKOR

"Now, Mr. Harkness," asked Mrs. Walton coquettishly, "how old do you think I *am*?"

"Mrs. Walton," replied Harkness, "you certainly don't look it."

Phineas Fitzgerald was a compulsive gambler. Again and again he drove his devoted wife to despair with his losses. One night, as Phineas was about to leave for a poker game, his wife, Katherine, said, "Me darlin', this is y'r last poker game w' the boys. Ye will never gamble again an' remain Katy Shaw's husband!"

That night, Phineas played like a genius. So great was his luck that he won pot after pot. On the last play, he held four queens—and he put his entire stake, winnings and all, on his final bet. His opponent, Donald Casey, met the bet. Phineas, chortling, laid down his four queens. Casey placed his cards face up. He had four aces.

Phineas rose, turned purple—and dropped dead.

Now the other players debated who should go to Phineas Fitzgerald's house and inform his wife, Katy. "What about you, Charley Croly?"

"No, no, not him!" exclaimed another player. "Last time this happened to Jimmy Rafferty, may his soul rest in peace—you, Charley Croly, knocked on th' poor woman's door and asked, 'Do I have the pleasure of addressin' the widow Rafferty?' She fainted. . . . Not you."

"How about Muldoon here?"

"Not on y'r life!" blustered Muldoon. "I could not bear to glance upon poor Phineas's bereaved woman."

"McManus! You, Ryan McManus! Nerves of iron y' have, man, and a steadfast purpose . . ."

And the words were true. So it was Ryan McManus who strode to the Fitzgerald's flat on Eighty-third Street, walked up the stairs, knocked on the door.

Katy Fitzgerald opened the door, "So, Phineas—" Her jaw was set, her arms akimbo, but when she saw McManus, she said, "Ryan McManus, is it? What brings y' at such an hour?"

"Katy Fitzgerald, I have to tell y' somethin' most unusual. Suppose I should tell y' that in the last pot tonight, your good husband held four queens—*four queens*, mind you, bet the whole works, fixin' to win a *lot* of money—an' it turns out that that stumble-bum Donny Casey had four *aces*! Can you imagine that, Katy Fitzgerald! Supposin' this happened. What would y' say?"

"I would say," the indignant woman said, drawing herself to her full height, "may the good Lord teach that Phineas of mine a final lesson! May that man o' mine drop dead!"

"He did, Katy," said McManus. "Goodnight."

The same story is told about a Jewish gambler, Label Trupin, who lost his all playing blackjack—and dropped dead. His friends consulted and agreed that Morty Somech was the best man to break the news to Alma, Label's wife, whom he had never met.

Morty Somech took a taxi to the Trupin apartment house, walked up two flights of stairs, and knocked on the door. A comely woman opened it.

"Do I have the pleasure and privilege," asked Morty, "of addressing the *almoonah* [widow] Trupin?"

"Absolutely not!" said Alma.

"I'll betcha," said Morty.

Norton Plasset, a judge of considerable experience and faultless judgment, has achieved fame in his circuit by the following feat of tact: Whenever a female takes the stand, Judge Plasset announces, in a firm but pleasant voice, "The witness will please state her age"— a winning smile — "after which the clerk will swear you in. . . ."

Elsa Maxwell, the celebrated party-giver, once revealed her formula for making her guests feel good: "When they arrive, I say, 'At last!' And when they start to leave, I say, 'Must you—already?' "

See also **Aplomb, Diplomacy/Diplomats, Rabbis, Salesmen, Stratagems**

Tailors

In Strunsky's Fine Tailor Shop, Oliver Parsons said in dismay: "Man, just look at this sleeve! *Inches* too long!"

Mr. Strunsky nodded, "So—eh, stick out the elbow . . . and bend a little your arm—see, now the sleeve is just right."

"The collar!" exclaimed Mr. Parsons. "That brings the collar halfway up my head!"

Mr. Strunsky pondered. "So you raise your head up and *back*—see, the whole collar goes down!"

"But now the left shoulder!" complained Parsons. "It's wider than the right!"

Mr. Strunsky appraised the situation. "So you *bend*, this way, and it evens out!"

Somewhat dazed, Mr. Parsons left the tailor in this fantastic posture: right elbow stuck out, head far up and back, left shoulder tilted.

A stranger accosted him with a cry. "Sir! Excuse me. But would you mind giving me the name of your tailor?"

"My tailor?" Parsons moaned. "Are you mad? Why would anyone want my tailor?"

The stranger drew erect. "Sir, any man who can fit a deformed figure like yours must be an absolute genius!"

See also **Chutzpa, Jews**

Tall Tales

Chief Mighty Thunder was on a mountaintop with his ten finest warriors, sending smoke signals to another tribe for a forthcoming powwow. The mountain overlooked Alamagordo—where a colossal explosion rocked the earth and a pillar of fire turned into a tremendous funnel of black smoke that became a mushroom-topped phantasmagoria. The ten fierce warriors gaped and gawked—but Chief Mighty Thunder sighed, "Gosh, I wish I'd said that!"

THE MAN WHO GOT A CAMEL

(*Warning:* Finicky readers should
skip this outrageous tale.)

Yonkel Bulbaman, fifty-seven years old, recently widowed, with not a child or relative in the world, hopefully went to Miami Beach. He checked into the Slotnick Astoria, where he had a pleasant room with a little balcony overlooking the pool.

For several weeks, Mr. Bulbaman led a sad, lonely life. He could not seem to make friends. He struck up no rapport with anyone, male or female. He stood behind the pinochle players, watching their interminable games, but he was never invited to sit in and take a hand. He took the sun on a lounge chair, but no one talked to him. In the dining room, no one ever asked him to join their table—or came to his. Poor Mr. Bulbaman was quite miserable.

His next-door neighbor, Louey Tischkin, a debonair bachelor, was the most popular man in the Slotnick Astoria. He was never without at least two companions. People forever gravitated to him, extending invitations to lunch, cocktails, dinner, a walk on the beach, a night on the town.

Day after day, night after night, Mr. Bulbaman noticed this; and finally he screwed up enough courage to ask, "Listen, Tischkin. Who can't see how popular you are? The men, the ladies—everyone likes you. I have to ask you a favor. I'm—I'm not happy here. I can't make friends! . . . You can maybe advise me? Give me some tips? . . ."

Louey Tischkin irritably surveyed the short, unprepossessing Bulbaman—his old-fashioned sun visor, his potbelly, his flappy bathing trunks, the absurd socks he was wearing—and leaned over and whispered, "Get a camel."

"A *camel?*"

"You heard me—a camel."

"But what can I—"

Tischkin waggled a finger. "Come closer. I don't want anyone to hear. You ride the camel up and down Collins Avenue! Every day. In the late afternoon. Day after day. And I promise you, it won't be long before everyone in Miami will be asking 'Who *is* that man?!' And before you know it, you'll get so many invitations you won't have enough time for half of them! . . ." Tischkin paused. "Okay? Now do *me* a favor. Never bother me again with such a cockamamy question!"

Yonkel Bulbaman bought a newspaper and looked through the ads. By good fortune he read of a circus, stranded in nearby Coral Gables, that needed money. Bulbaman telephoned the circus owner and within half an hour had rented a camel for five hundred dollars a week, to be delivered next day to the Slotnick Astoria.

The next afternoon, Bulbaman, wearing khaki shorts, a safari shirt, and a pith helmet, mounted his camel and set forth on Collins Avenue. Need I tell you that *everywhere* people stopped, gawked, buzzed, pointed, hollered, "A camel! Look! A camel!"

Every day for a week, Yonkel Bulbaman rode the trusty creature up and back on Collins Avenue. One morning, just as he was dressing, the telephone rang. "Mr. Bulbaman! This is the parking lot! Your camel—it's gone! Disappeared! Maybe stolen!"

At once, dismayed Bulbaman telephoned the police. A desk sergeant, Connors, answered: "*What?* . . . Can you speak more slowly, sir? It sounded as though you said someone had stolen—your camel."

"That's right!"

"You—where was it stolen from?

"Where I keep it. The parking lot of the Slotnick Astoria!"

Sergeant Connors scratched his scalp. "Er—I'll fill out a form. . . . How tall was the animal?"

"From the sidewalk to his back, a good seven feet."

"What color was it?"

"What color?" echoed Bulbaman. "Camel color! A plain, camel-colored camel."

"Male or a female?"

"*Hanh?*"

"Was the animal male or female?"

"How am I supposed to know about the sex of a *camel?*" exclaimed Mr. Bulbaman. "Does it—wait! Aha! It was a male!"

"Are you sure?" asked Sergeant Connors.

"Absolutely!"

"But, Mr. Bulbaman, just a moment ago you—"

"I'm *positive,* officer! I just remembered that every time I was riding on Collins Avenue I could hear the people hollering, 'Hey! Look! Look at the *schmuck* on that camel!' "

This is said to be a true story:

A writer with a long-festering grievance marched into his producer's office, carrying a large rubber object.

"What's that?" asked the producer.

"An inflatable lifeboat," said the writer. "It can hold eight full-grown men."

"Now what the hell do you need a thing like that for?" asked the producer.

"I'll show you." The writer pulled the rope that opened the compressed-air cylinder and backed out of the office. The fire department had to be called to rescue the producer.

See also **Chutzpa, Hillbillies, Scoundrels, Shaggy Dogs, Texans**

Taxi Rides

I

The driver is no comedian, for a change, but a very tired "Al Navodny," it says on the placard. Pictures of his hideous grandchildren are pasted on the dashboard.

"Mott Street," I say.

"Mott Street in *China*town?" he amazes.

"You know any other?"

He pulls down his flag. "I been driving a hack thirty-two years and in all that time not once does a fare ask for Mott Street!"

"This is your lucky day."

He reaches to kiss the crucifix dangling from his rearview mirror. "Buckle your seat belt. Here we go."

I will not say Mr. Navodny was a bad driver. He just drove like he had to make Venezuela before 7.

"Ain't you gonna take the F.D.R. south?" I dare to inquire.

He looks at me like I'm from out of town. "One conked motor ahead of us and we're a turtle."

He makes it down and around the truck convoys on 2nd and takes a couple of shortcuts I don't know, including a sidewalk. . . . Speed is in this Hunky's blood. So is "Emergency Entrance."

At last, Canal and Mott come up on my Tarot cards. I give the hot-rod ace 6 simoleons.

"My pleasure," he says.

I do not groan. "Those your kids?"

"Where?"

"On your dashboard."

"Naw." Navodny blows his nose. "They're my partner's."

"Tell them they won't live long, driving with you."

"God forbid they *should* live long!" he hollers. "Vlata—that's the big one—ran away with a Spic who robs churches—only Protestant churches, him being religious. And Anton—the punk with the broccoli ears—is number nine on the FBI's Most Wanted—"

I raise both my hands in apology. "Forget it, Al. Excuse me!"

No wonder they call it Fun City.

from my Silky!

II

I tell the cabbie, who looks like the punk *gunzel* in *The Maltese Falcon,* "The Hailsham."

His blobby eyes turn to soggy pancakes. "Hey, man. The Hailsham *Tower?"*

"Yeh."

The jockey almost busts the arm off the fare-lever and tools away. The name on his license is "Floyd Pitchett." He looks it. He has sloppy hair and a sweatshirt which has enough splattered paint to bring 100 grand as a Jackson Polack. "That place makes the St. Regis look like crud. You know, their switchboard *never puts through a call!* Not even from the White House! Every goddam tenant has his own phone! And only one pad to a whole floor! You know who lives there? Texans! Movie biggos! That King of Monte Carlo! I ain't battin' my gums, man!"

"Floyd, how come you know so much?" I pretend.

"I *read,* that's how come I know so much. The *News,* the *Post.* . . . Y' lousy New York *Times* don't give the masses inside stuff like that! They're nothin' but fuggin' stooges for Wall Street! . . . I was in the Big Apple only 2 weeks when I found *that* out. . . . This town got too many Hebes. . . . I'm from Pittsburgh. It stinks. How about you?"

"Never. I wash all over."

He snorts, "I mean, where you from?"

"Out-of-town."

"Where?"

"Ever heard of *Gayindrerd?"* I ask.

"What?"

"Gay-in-drerd."

"Where's that?"

"Idaho."

"*Idaho*?!" Floyd shakes his whole head in astonishment. "I never in my whole fuggin' life met anyone from *Idaho!*"

"That's because you fug too much," I observe. "How old are you, Floyd?"

"26."

"Well, if you live to 27, which I doubt, you will of met at least 1½ persons from that fascinating state."

"You know who's *crazy* to buy the Hailsham?" my jockey is hollering. "An Ayrab! Offered 75 million. Cash. And you know why? So's he can kick out the American tenants and put in his own fuggin' family! 7 brothers, their 38 wifes, plus a barbecue pit on each floor—for roastin' goats. *Goats,* for Chrissake! And you wanna know how I know *that?*" He almost sideswipes a Volkswagen for the pleasure of turning to glare at me. "I know because 2 of them jokers, wearin' round gauze hats and nightgowns, got in this cab last night and discussed the whole fuggin' deal! *That's* how I know." He blinks in the rearview mirror. "What's with you, man? Your tongue cut off?"

"Not recently. Did one of them jokers have a mustache and spade beard?"

"Yeah!" cries the creep. "How'd you know?"

"He's my uncle." (Every Arab big shot wears a mustache and spade beard, for God's sake.)

"*Huh?*"

"My Uncle Sol . . . Solomon Sallah Halvah. We are here on a buying jag. This morning we picked up the Gulf and Western building."

"The *enor*mous G-plus-W, near Columbus Circle?"

"Right. Next week we buy the Gulf Stream."

Floyd, who is already spaced-out by the story he will tell his disgusting pals, erupts: "I'll be a son-of-a-*bitch!*"

"Why wait?"

He don't get it. "Hey, Dad, you puttin' me on?"

"Floyd!" I look hurt. "Why would I—a royal prince of Araby—want to do a crummy thing like that?"

"Quit the crap, man. You look 100 percent American!"

"That's because my mother was born in Babylon."

Brief pause for nation identification. "Then she ain't American!"

"Babylon, Long Island," I zap him.

Floyd is now frowning like a monkey in a cage with 2,000 bananas and his hands glued behind his back. "How come you don't wear a night-gown?!"

"Because I am a master of disguise."

"You talk like a goddam New Yorker!"

"That's because my tutors were imported."

"*Hold* it!" he cries. "You said you came from Idaho!"

"I did. Yesterday."

Suspicion don't die easy in Floyd Pitchett. "Where was you *raised?*"

"In Sholom Aleichem, the far-famed spa of sheiks, in Pakistan, right near the Bolivian border."

All this mental exercise has practically wiped out the jerk, who is as glassy as he is frustrated.

"Whadaya know, Floyd boy? Here's the Hailsham."

The jerk tries to recover his smart-ass personality by sneering at the marquee. Then he does the clench-fist bit that might please Moscow but would flunk Hygiene. "Capitalist Israeli pigs!"

That tears it. "Comrade," I whisper. "Tonight. 7:30. Broadway and 34th."

"What's up?" he hoarses.

"P.L.O. meeting. We're gonna bomb a Sunday School." The tab is $1.95. I get out and take 2 singles and toss them—in the gutter. "Bend for it, you bastard. Then buy some Ban. Roll-on, not liquid. You stink."

He stares at the 2 bucks in the gutter. "You cock—"

I grab his shirt collar and twist it, my fist going against his Adam's apple, and I squeeze and squeeze until his eyes pop and he is gagging and claws at my hand, making sounds like "*ghf*" and "*wfd*"—so I have to end my patient lesson.

I slam the punk's head back against the door post. "So long, slob. Heil Shitler!"

from my *King Silky!*

See also **Traffic**

Telegrams

Two Frenchmen, Raoul Spero and Maurice Vauté, old enemies, had such a violent falling-out that Spero challenged Vauté to a duel.

Promptly at six thirty the next morning, Spero and his second appeared at the designated place in the Bois de Boulogne. Maurice Vauté had not appeared.

At six forty, Vauté's second, Jacques Seligson, came out of a taxi, carrying the pistol case.

By seven, Vauté had still not appeared.

"The man has stained his honor!" scowled Raoul Spero.

"No, wait. Look!" cried Seligson.

The men saw a bicycle swiftly pedaling toward them. But the figure on the bicycle turned out to be not Maurice Vauté but a messenger with a telegram—for Spero.

He ripped open the envelope.

> SORRY. DELAYED. HATE TO
> DISAPPOINT YOU. WAIT NO LONGER.
> SHOOT.
>
> VAUTÉ

JAMISON AND KENNY
14 WAYNE ST.
SECAUCUS, N.J.
   YOU ARE NOW THREE MONTHS LATE IN DELIVERING
OUR MERCHANDISE. CANCEL ORDER AT ONCE.

HANSON BLAIR
TOLEDO.

HANSON BLAIR
709 WENTWORTH
TOLEDO, OHIO
   CANNOT CANCEL ORDER AT ONCE. YOU HAVE TO WAIT
FOR YOUR TURN.

JAMISON AND KENNY

N. SIMMONS
PRESIDENT
ANCOLA CORPORATION
    COMPLETELY SNOWED IN. ALL FLIGHTS CANCELED.
NO CHANGE IN WEATHER PREDICTED. PLEASE ADVISE.
                    TOM GROBAN
                    HOTEL MANSFIELD
                    BUTTE, MONTANA

TOM GROBAN
HOTEL MANSFIELD
BUTTE, MONTANA
    START SUMMER VACATION AT ONCE.
                    N. SIMMONS

Father of newborn boy to wife

MRS. STELLA MARCH
PASSEVANT HOSPITAL

EVERYONE TELLS ME YOU HAD A BOY IN
YOUR ROOM LAST NIGHT.

See also **Graffiti, Ingenuity, Signs**

Texans

"You say you've lived in Dallas all your life?"

"Yep. I was born here. So was m' pappy."

"You must own a lot of cattle."

"Nope."

"Well, I imagine you have a few gushing oil wells?"

"Nope."

"Uh—do you own some land?"

"Land? Yep."

"A lot?"

"We-ll, three and a half acres."

"That's *all?*"

"That's all."

"Three and a half acres—that isn't much of a ranch for a Texan. Tell me, what do you call it?"

"Downtown."

At a dinner table in Houston, one guest said to the diners, "Now you take Miss Barbie Simmons there. Ain't it true, Barbie, I knew you when you didn't have more than one pair of shoes to your name?"

"Sure is, Luke." Barbie turned to the others. "And he asked me what they were."

One November, a Texan and his wife walked into a fine art gallery on Madison Avenue in New York. "How much is that picture in the window?" asked the woman.

"That, madam, is a Dufy—one of his early works—"

"Sure, sure," the Texan cut in. "How much *ez* it?"

"Twenty-two thousand dollars."

"We'll take it."

"Yes, *sir!* If you'll come this way—"

"Wait. How much ez this paintin' on the wall?"

"That, sir, is a Vlaminck—"

"Yeah, yeah. How much *ez* it?"

"The Vlaminck is forty-three thousand—"

"Good," said the woman. "And that picture *thair?*"

So it went, until almost every painting on the walls had been bought by the debonair Texans. "Now, how many pictures does that make in all?" asked the woman.

"Let me see . . . nine . . . ten . . . *twelve* works of art, madam."

"That's fine, honey," said the Texan. "That takes care of the Christmas cards. Now we can start buyin' the presents."

A jeepload of GIs in Iowa approached a very small horse, tethered to a fence. The jeep stopped. "My God," said the first GI. "That's the smallest damn horse I ever seen."

"It looks more like a big dog—"

"Must be the smallest horse in the world—a breed all its own."

"Maybe it's a small Shetland pony."

Along came a farmer.

"Are you the owner of this goldurn animal?"

"Sure am."

"Well, what is it—a pony, a dog, or a horse?"

"It's a horse, all right. No doubt about it. I've got papers back in the farmhouse authenticatin' that this is the smallest true horse in the world!"

"Aw, shucks," drawled a soldier. "Why, back home in Texas we got horses that's as small as two of that one put together."

"Why did Marya turn down that Texas billionaire?"

"He's senile, dear."

"So?"

"She couldn't bear the thought of old age creeping over her."

Caspar Olansky was boasting about the extravagant accommodations and décor at Fort Worth's newest hotel extravaganza. "—And every single room has wall-to-wall carpeting!"

"So? Most every hotel in New York has that!"

Olansky's eyes narrowed. "On the *ceilings?*"

See also **Boasts, Can You Believe It?, Just Jokes, Tall Tales**

Traffic

Sign at school crossing

GIVE OUR KIDS A BRAKE!

❧

An out-of-town woman, in a hurry, took a cab in midtown New York. After a few blocks, the taxi was stuck, immobile, in a fierce traffic jam. The cab sat, absolutely still, then crawled for a few feet, then stopped again.

"Driver," called the out-of-towner, "is it always this bad?"

"Nope."

"I see by my watch—it's almost ten o'clock."

"Yep."

"I suppose I should be grateful that I didn't get caught in the nine o'clock jam!"

"Lady, this *is* the nine o'clock jam."

❧

Sign at bottom of steep incline in Colorado

RESUME BREATHING

❧

On a city bus

TAKE TWICE A DAY—TO RELIEVE CONGESTION.

❧

Traffic lights: Clever devices that safely get pedestrians halfway across a street.

❧

Cry a bit
For Buck Le Mott.
He was lit,
His lights were not.

See also **Taxi Rides**

Travel

The Frankfurt-am-Rhein Travel Society was going by bus through the countryside of England. Being Germans, they appeared punctually each morning, returned to their bus on the minute after visiting a castle or ruin, and chafed if the tour guide ever fell a minute behind schedule.

Now, as the bus pulled up to the meadow at Runnymede, the guide announced through the loudspeaker, *"Meine Herren und Damen,* there is no need to get off here. It is enough to see the meadow and that historic oak tree—for under that tree was signed the historic document from which comes all the freedoms Englishmen today enjoy: the Magna Carta!"

"Ven did zat hoppen?" one Frau asked.

"1215."

The president of the Travel Society glanced at his watch and in a reprimanding tone told the guide, "You missed it by twenty-four minutes!"

Radio travel program in Iowa: . . . I shall never forget the beauties of Rome, that glorious city of fallen arches.

See also **Geography Revised**

True Tales

TRUE

The late great pianist Leopold Godowsky loved to tell friends of the time he was having a formal swallowtail suit made for a forthcoming world tour. To spare the impresario's time and energy, the tailor would come to Godowsky's apartment on Central Park West. This tailor (whose name is, alas, not preserved for history) was a superb, meticulous craftsman, a master of cut and needlework, and a perfectionist of the highest order. And Leopold Godowsky was notoriously impatient.

Week after week, the tailor appeared in Godowsky's apartment, fitting, draping, pinning, marking. Each time Godowsky would fret and scold. "*Another* fitting? Good God, tailor, when will you be *done?!*"

At the sixth such session, Leopold Godowsky lost his temper. "Tailor, in the name of heaven!" he cried. "You have already taken six *weeks*—"

"So?" the tailor responded.

" 'So?' '*So?*' Six weeks for one suit?" Godowsky fumed. "Listen, man. It took God only six *days* to create the entire *world!*"

The tailor nodded. "*Nu?* Look at it. . . ."

From *London Telegraph*

Overheard in the foyer of one of our grandest hotels:

Young lady to old lady seated on a shooting stick: "But, Granny, why not sit in one of the large, soft chairs?"

Old lady: "One *never* sits on a hotel chair, my dear. One never knows who has been sitting there before."

Scene: London

My wife dialed 192. A male operator answered.

WIFE

Is this Information?

OPERATOR

Well, madam, we call it "Enquiries." Never you mind. May I help you?

WIFE

I'm trying to find the number for a pub on Beauchamp Place—

OPERATOR

(wincing)

I believe you mean "*Bee*cham" Place. Silly, isn't it, the way we pronounce "Bochamp"? Upsets our French visitors terribly. And what is the name of the pub, madam?

WIFE

It's a "Mister Benson"—or "Benton"—

OPERATOR

(startled)

"*Mist*er?" For a *pub?!*

WIFE

Yes.

OPERATOR

(stiffly)

I have never heard of it.

WIFE

Don't tell me you know the names of all the pubs in London?!

OPERATOR

I like to think I know *most* of them, madam. That's why I questioned the "Mister" with some confidence. . . . Would you happen to remember the *number* on Beecham Place?

WIFE

No. But it's only a block long—so couldn't you just run down the addresses—

OPERATOR

Of all the pubs in London?! That would require con*sid*erable effort, madam. There are over six thousand—

WIFE

My God!

OPERATOR

I don't think He arranged the number.

WIFE

But this is a new pub—so couldn't you just scan New Listings?

OPERATOR
(sighing)
You shall have to be patient.
(under breath)
"Mast and Yardarm" . . . "Mews and Falcon" . . . well, *well*,
you *are* in luck, madam! It's "Mister *Ben*tley." Fancy that, for a
pub. *Quite* unusual.

WIFE
That's why I remembered it.

OPERATOR
I should have thought he would have chosen something more
traditional: "The Golden Horn" or "Lord Nelson's Arm." By
the way, have you ever been to The Prospect of Whitby? On
the river—

WIFE
Yes. Adored it.

OPERATOR
I really should pop down there one day. . . . Would you care to
jot down Bentley's number?

WIFE
My pen is practically panting over my pad.

OPERATOR
We must take it out of its misery. The number for *Mis*ter
Bentley's Pub is—(gives number).

WIFE
I knew you would find it!

OPERATOR
I never could have done so without your moral support.

WIFE
Thank you.

OPERATOR
Not at all. We're not such a bad lot after all, are we?

WIFE
(laughing)
No. 'Bye now.

OPERATOR
Ba-bye, ducks.

᠅

Some years ago, Leopold Godowsky, star pianist and irrepressible wit, was being pressed by a friend. "You mean to say you would rather take a train for three nights and four days to get to California—instead of taking an airplane that gets you there in ten hours?"

"I would," said Godowsky.

"Are you that afraid of crashing?" asked the friend.

"I don't like airplanes, I don't trust airplanes, I don't *need* airplanes!"

"But, Leopold, I have gone over the cold, hard facts about flying: the actual statistics! Do you realize you are safer in an airplane than in a bathtub? Or riding in an automobile! Or riding on a train—"

"Enough with facts," said Godowsky. "You can do anything with statistics!"

The friend paused. "Well, perhaps you are right, Leopold. After all, every one of us has something of the mystic in him—"

"Mystic? Why 'mystic'?"

"I mean, deep down, I guess, we all feel that when all is said and done, wherever you are, when it's your time . . . It's all a matter of when God calls you!"

"Right, my friend. Right."

"Well, there you are, so you may as well fly. . . ."

"One minute. Not me."

"But you agreed that it's all a matter of when God calls you!"

"Absolutely," said Godowsky. "So why should I be twenty thousand feet in the air when God calls the pilot?!"

A well-run bloomer factory in Central America had forty women employees. One day they stopped coming to work. The boss was puzzled, the foreman frowned, the women were sought out—but they did not care to return to work. They said they had saved enough money for a month or two: why not enjoy it, instead of continuing the daily grind?

The boss was in despair. One day he told an American traveling salesman of his problem. The American laughed. "José, the answer is easy as pie. Here's what you do. . . ."

The boss sent away to the Chicago headquarters of Sears, Roebuck and Company. He asked for fifty mail-order catalogues. When the catalogues arrived in Puerto del Bizyoiness (or whatever the hell the name of the town was), the owner of the factory distributed them—one catalogue to each of his forty vacationing derelicts and ten to younger, unemployed girls.

Before the sun rose next morning, the forty bloomer makers were at the factory gates and so were ten eager job seekers.

See also **Can You Believe It?, Embarrassing Moments, Shaggy Dogs, Snafus**

Typos

Note: I have for years collected typographical errors. Considering the billions of words printed each year in newspapers, magazines, leaflets, weeklies, house organs, it is quite remarkable, in sheer statistical terms, that "typos" are so infrequent.

I am overjoyed whenever my eye falls upon a serendipitous misprint. To list the sources (Elgin, Illinois, *Courier*, Chicago *Herald-Examiner*, Owensburg, Kansas, *Observer*) would simply encumber the text without increasing the pleasure. All of the following are true quotations. Trust me.

L. R.

Cab drivers in Washington get a kick out of taking visitors to the White House. When a woman gave one driver the White House address, he even cut his feet in half.

∽

To curry good luck, he always carried a rabbi's foot.

∽

The proprietor said he would allow no woman in the bra without a man.

∽

WANTED: Lawyer is searching for accomplished, well-recommended deceptionist.

∽

Miss O'Hayer has been raising birds for many years and is credited with having the largest parateets in the state.

∽

Lola Carlisle, a budding author, said she had circulated her navel among various Hollywood producers.

∽

. . . Sergeant Alfred Blaine is a twenty-year veteran defective on the police force.

(next day)

Correction: . . . Sergeant Blaine is a twenty-year veteran detective on the police farce.

❧

He is a student in the Episcopal Seminary at Cambridge, which is afflicted with Harvard University.

❧

He heard himself assailed as a self-centered financial executive who buttered his own beard.

❧

The major was overtired because of his many official cuties.

❧

He got up, dressed, took a shower, and . . .

❧

He clung to the sill by his fingerprints.

❧

The new bride is twenty feet wide and forty feet long.

❧

The bride was upset when one of her flower girls stepped on her brain and made a big tear in it.

❧

Could you possibly print an exercise in your column which will develop my things to make them larger?

❧

At the reception following the wedding, the captivating bride in her low-cut wedding gown was easily the belly of the ball.

❧

Dorothea: I've learned my lesson. Please come home. It was just a passing fanny. Love . . .

Harold

❧

Picking up his hammer, nails, and two broads, he went back into the cabin.

❧

There are millions of desirable women who are unattacked and hungry for love.

❧

In college catalogue

English 406: Three plays by Shakespeare. Intensive analysis of *Hamlet, Macbeth, Anatomy and Cleopatra.*

∽

In bakery window: Cakes iced in white, brown, pink, and glue.

∽

Menu: Dreaded Veal Cutlet

∽

To remove a fresh grease spot on a rug, cover the spot with blotting paper, then press with a hot flatiron. Cover the spot with magnesia, let it remain for 24 years, then brush off.

∽

Correction: It was "Whistler's Mother," not "Hitler's Mother" (as reported in yesterday's *Courier*), that Professor Bixly lectured on.

Nothing is to be gained in trying to explain how the error occurred.

See also **Bloopers, Boo-boos, Definitions (by Children), Geography Revised, Headlines That Haunt Me, History Revised (by Children), Malaprops, News Items That Haunt Me, Signs**

Waiters

When you go to a restaurant, be sure to choose a table near a waiter.

Epitaph on a waiter's tombstone

> Here lies Ephraim Teshler
> WAITER
> "God finally caught his eye."

Waiter: A man who thinks money grows on trays.

In a delicatessen on Fourteenth Street, Abe Tamkin called his waiter over. "Listen, waiter. What is this sandwich I am eating?"

"Just what you ordered: a pastrami on rye."

"Look, I'm half through already—and I haven't hit even one tiny piece of pastrami!"

"So take another bite," said the waiter.

Mr. Tamkin took a bite, chewed, swallowed, and declaimed, "Still no pastrami!"

"You went right past it!" cried the waiter.

Nothing in New York is as unique as its waiters. They are independent, thin-skinned, cynical, and incorrigibly sardonic. After prolonged research, I have come to the following unkind conclusions:

1. A New York waiter hates to tell anyone the correct time. Once, I asked a passing menial, "Can you please tell me what time it is?"

He answered, "You're not my table."

2. When taking your order, the New York waiter grunts or growls; this makes it impossible for you to know whether he really understood you—which is part of the pledge he took during his initiation into the Society for the Dissemination of Ulcers.

3. He hands you the menu upside down. This is done in order to exercise the customer's wrist, toning up your muscles for tipping.

4. He asks you exactly how you like your meat done, so he can tell the misanthropes in the kitchen how long to overcook it.

5. He writes your order down in a secret code. In this way, he can give you the wrong check, which is always larger than it ought to be. You would think that *once,* at least, a wrong check would be smaller than your rightful one, but this never happens. Economists explain this as the Law of Irreversible Gain.

from my *The 3:10 to Anywhere*

"Waiter!" called Mrs. Dodie. "This corned beef you served me—"
"Yeah?"
"The bread tastes like it's left over from yesterday!"
"So?" The waiter shrugged. "Wasn't yesterday a good day?"

Zevi Grossman, an old waiter at a restaurant famous for the independence (not to say insolence) of its waiters, died. And some of his friends decided to hold a séance with a professional medium whose business cards read:

Penelope Schlumberger
Seer-Oracle
Spiritual Intermediary

Now, eight of Zevi Grossman's friends sat around the table, under a shaded lamp, as Penelope Schlumberger went into a trance, intoning, "Zevi. . . Zevi . . . Here, waiting, are eight dear friends . . . eager to hear from you . . . So Zevi . . . are you happy? . . . I am going to rap this table three times, then you should answer . . ." And she rapped—slowly, solemnly—three times.
The friends sat hushed. . . .
"Zevi, Zevi," crooned the oracle, "pay attention! Are you in heaven? United with your dear mama and papa. . . . Now I will knock *four* times— then you give a holler!" And four times—loudly, spaced carefully apart— did Mme. Schlumberger rap on the board. . . .
But the room stayed silent as the grave. . . .
"Zevi! Zevi Grossman! What's the *matter* by you?!" And now the seeress firmly knocked five times—in vain. "Zevi!" cried the oracle. "Stop pretending you are deaf!! I *know* you're there! *Why don't you at least* give a signal? One little word, an answer."
At last came the disembodied voice of Zevi the waiter. "Because . . . you're . . . not . . . my . . . table. . . ."

Scene: Schmaulhausen's Vienna Woods Hofbrau Restaurant

"*Herr ober!*" called Mrs. Grätschel.
"*Ja, gnädige Frau?*"

"Waiter—zis pot roast. You call zis *meat?*"

"Vhat's wrong wiz it, lady?"

"Vhat's *wrong* wiz it?" echoed Mrs. Grätschel. "It—plain and zimple—tastes funny!"

"Zo laugh," said the waiter.

✁

Mr. and Mrs. Jorge Camoza, from Madrid, visiting New York for the first time, entered the Diego Café and Brasserie and sank wearily into a booth near the entrance.

A waiter came over and handed each of the Camozas a menu. Señora Camoza sighed, "Jorge, my feet they are killing on me."

"I also," said her husband. "*Camerero*—'scusa. I do speak Sponish."

"*Señor, yo comprendo,*" said the waiter.

"Ah! *Maravilloso!*" beamed Señora Camoza.

"Waiter," said Señor Camoza, "we are both exhaust. New York is so noisy, so busy, so impolite . . ." He glanced at the menu. "I'll have soup with—what is that?"

Said the waiter, "Dumplings, stuffed with meat."

"I, too," said Señora Camoza. "And waiter, with the soup—*por favor,*" she smiled, "just one kind word to a tired tourist!"

Soon the waiter returned with two bowls of soup. He placed them before the Camozas.

As he started to leave, Señor Camoza sighed, "*Camerero.* Did you not forget something?"

"Eh? What?"

"The kind word," smiled Señora Camoza.

"Ah, *sí, sí,* señora." The waiter bent down, and into her ear whispered, "Don't eat the dumplings."

✁

Mr. Danker started to lift his spoon to his mouth when, to his dismay, he saw a fly thrashing about in the soup. He lowered the spoon and called, "Waiter! *Wai*ter!"

Swiftly, a waiter glided to his table.

"Waiter, *look!*"

"I," said the waiter, "am looking."

"So? Do you see anything?"

The waiter said, "Yeah. I see—a fly."

"Is that all you can say? You see a *fly*—?"

"You asked me if I saw—"

"What is that fly doing in my soup?!" thundered Mr. Danker.

The waiter bent closer to the plate. "To me, it looks like the breaststroke."

✁

Scene: Nolan's Queen of the Sea Restaurant

The snazzy couple in evening clothes were giving their waiter, Vincent, a hard time of it.

MAN:	I want eight oysters, to start with, and my wife wants— Darling?
WOMAN:	Six. And waiter, make sure they are not old.
MAN:	Make sure they're *plump*, waiter.
WOMAN:	Not stringy.
MAN:	Not dried out. Plenty of their own juice!
WOMAN:	And very cold.
MAN:	Freshly shucked!
WOMAN:	Waiter, have you been paying attention?
VINCENT:	Yes, ma'am. I have just one little question, beggin' y'r pardon.
MAN:	What is it?
VINCENT:	D'ye want y'r oysters with or without pearls?!

Scene: Pattashik's 5-Star Restaurant

"Waiter!" called a customer. "*Waiter!*"

A waiter ambled over to the table. "What," he yawned, "can I do for you?"

"For me, you can make like a waiter! Ten minutes I've been sitting here, calling for a waiter. The service in this place is absolutely terrible!"

"How do you know?" said the waiter, blinking. "You haven't had any."

At the great Café Royale on Second Avenue in New York, I first heard this ever-green classic:

Scene: Restaurant

WAITER:	So, gentlemen, what will you have to drink?
FIRST CUSTOMER:	I'll have tea.
SECOND CUSTOMER:	I'll have tea, too. But waiter, be sure the glass is clean!
	(*Waiter exits, returns*)
WAITER:	Two teas. . . . Which one of you asked for the clean glass?

My interest in the New York Waiter began when I was seventeen and visited Manhattan for the first time. My uncle, who had survived four years on Devil's Island, took me to his favorite restaurant.

As we entered, the waiter, spying my uncle, promptly smote himself on the forehead and cried, "He's back!"

UNCLE

"Back?" You eat here once, who has the strength to go anyplace else?

WAITER

There are ten thousand waiters, at *least*, in New York. Why does God have to pick on me?

UNCLE

Maybe He's trying to teach you a lesson—to be polite, once, to a customer.

WAITER

That's not a lesson, that's a jail sentence. Besides, I am an atheist.

UNCLE

(to me)

In this restaurant, they give you ulcers *before* you eat.

(to waiter)

For the sake of my nephew here—a boy with a future, with a right to live—tell me honestly: How is the chopped liver?

WAITER

The chopped liver is no worse than the pickled herring.

UNCLE

I don't like pickled herring.

WAITER

Let me be the first to congratulate you.

UNCLE

Is the gefilte fish, through some oversight on the part of the management, fresh?

WAITER

To my enemies, I wouldn't recommend it.

UNCLE

(to me)

That means, that to his *friends*, it's delicious. . . . I'll take it. And, assuming that we survive, do you recommend the pea, vegetable, or chicken soup?

WAITER

Mister, are you ordering a meal or voting in an election?

UNCLE

I'm hoping, fool that I am, to get a *hint* about the food.

WAITER

For that, ask a chemist; I'm only a waiter.

UNCLE

You hide it beautifully. . . . Let me ask you, man to man: If you were in my place, what would you eat?

WAITER

If I was in your place, I'd kill myself.

UNCLE

That, I'll do on my way *out*. . . . I'll have the chicken soup.

WAITER

Better take the barley. . . . Mr. Nephew, what do you want?

I

I'll have the borscht, please.

WAITER

Don't be a fool; take the vegetable.
(*The waiter brought us our fish, then the barley soup for my uncle and the vegetable for me.*)

UNCLE

That vegetable soup smells delicious! . . . Waiter, why didn't you recommend it to me?

WAITER

You didn't ask for the borscht!

L. R.

Scene: Hirschfeld's 3-Star Restaurant

DINER:	Waiter! Waiter!
WAITER:	I'm here.
DINER:	I asked for two soft-boiled eggs—
WAITER:	Softer, yours can't be.
DINER:	But these eggs aren't *fresh*. They smell. On the menu, it says—(*tapping menu*) that all your eggs come from the country!
WAITER:	Right.
DINER:	Which country did these come from?
WAITER:	The old country.

Scene: Tobin's Romanian Restaurant

"Waiter! Waiter!"

"Here I am."

"Waiter, I can't eat this steak. It's tougher than a leather belt. Get Mr. Tobin."

"Mister, don't waste your time. Mr. Tobin wouldn't touch that steak either."

See also **Can You Believe It?, Chutzpa, Conversations I Cannot Forget, Restaurants, Retorts, Sarcasm, Squelches**

Weather Reports

On London TV I heard a meteorologist (pointing to a radar map):
I was absolutely *shocked* to learn that snow flurries have descended on parts of Scotland!

London Weather (dial *246-8091*)
Scattered showers . . . Rahther cloudy . . . but I *do* believe the clouds will disperse by dusk . . .

And now, the weather. It's zero outside now; no temperature at all.

MINNEAPOLIS RADIO ANNOUNCER

The weather forecast: Snow, followed by little boys with sleds.

And here is the weather forecast: rain and slow, followed by sneet.

Weirdos

MY FRIEND WILBUR

I first began to wonder whether Wilbur was some kind of nut when we were in high school. We were walking along one afternoon when Wilbur, without warning, announced: "Schatzski's Ring is a constriction of the lower esophagus."

I stopped. "Is anything wrong with your esophagus?"

"No."

"Then why did you tell me that?"

"What?"

"About Schatzski's Ring."

"I don't know," said Wilbur. He blinked, "I thought it would interest you."

Or take the time our gang was hanging around the corner, discussing you-know-what and Wilbur suddenly declared: "A conger eel can lay fifteen million eggs a season!"

"Willy," said Zack Pinchik, in a voice that dripped disgust, "you are the type who one-a-these days they are gonna throw a net over his head so's you will spend the rest of your life playing 'Chopsticks' for doctors in white coats . . . Eels," he echoed. "'F' cryin' out loud, why *eels?*"

Wilbur flushed. "I—thought it would interest you. . . ."

Or take the time Wilbur went into a fit, shouting: "Yes, sir! Yes, siree! Carpathian peasants trim their bunions only under a new moon! How about *that?* Huh? Wow!" (I checked the source Wilbur gave me and he was absolutely right: Peasants in Carpathia simply shun podiatry unless a full moon is shining.)

I often wondered what quirk in Wilbur's nature made him store up such weird odds-and-ends. After long contemplation I came to the conclusion that Wilbur must have discovered, early in life, that ideas confused him—so he began to collect information. There's nothing wrong in that, mind you: some boys collect stamps, others coins, grownups gather matchbook covers. Well, Wilbur collected trivia. In that way, he was able to substitute facts for conversation. Wilbur's brain was not deep, but it *was* retentive. He desperately wanted to be liked, and he gave you the only treasures he possessed. He was so eager to make friends, and so clumsy in the ways he went about it, that he reminded me of the old Chinese proverb: "He is like a man in a barrel of rice with his lips sewed up." Come to think of it, I heard that from Wilbur.

I think God had chosen Wilbur to be one of his *shlemiels*—well meaning, generous, and hopelessly inept. When you took a walk with him, for instance, you found yourself bumping into him, even though you were both in the normal, side-by-side arrangement for walking. And when you introduced Wilbur to someone, he would pump the other person's hand as if there was a water shortage.

After high school, Wilbur went to work in the basement of a department store, selling curtain rods. Inside of a month, his sterling character, zeal, and erudition gave the basement manager a nervous breakdown.

Now, Wilbur started door-to-door selling. He swiftly progressed from touting ironing-board covers to extolling cemetery plots. He neither shone or starved in his new profession, since he took plenty of time "breaking the ice," he told me, employing smiles, chuckles, and friendly small talk—about things like the origin of the word "bloomer" or the mischievous tributaries of the Tallahassee River.

One day I lunched with Wilbur at a vegetarian restaurant. (The sight of red meat made him faint.) We had no sooner sat down than Wilbur beamed, "I recently had geographic tongue!"

"What?"

"Geographic tongue," said Wilbur. "That's when your tongue has entire areas of blotches that differ in color like a map."

"How did you get it?" I asked.

"I don't know," said Wilbur. He plopped sour cream into his borscht. "That's one of the most interesting things about it. *No* one knows what causes it or what makes it disappear! Look." He stuck his tongue out. I had never realized what a long tongue Wilbur had, but it looked perfectly normal: pink, moist, and in no way like a map.

"Your tongue looks perfectly normal," I said, "pink, moist, and in no way like a map."

"That's because it disappeared," said Wilbur.

"What was the treatment?" I asked.

"What treatment?" asked Wilbur.

"The treatment for geographic tongue."

"Oh . . . None. It just went away. That's because it was a benign, migratory *glossitis!*"

I ate my blintzes thoughtfully.

"Thank God it wasn't the *rhomboid type!*" Wilbur blurted. "How about you? Have *you* had any unusual ailments since we last met?"

I felt a genuine twinge of regret. "I'm afraid not, Wil."

Among other nuggets of data with which Wilbur dowered me were these:

> In Borneo, they call 1.36 pounds of anything a Catty.
> The sawfly is often wingless.

The zip code of Yum Yum, Tennessee, is 38390.
In Blowing Rock, North Carolina, *snow falls upside down!**

I often wondered if Wilbur would ever get married. His cousin Oscar once fixed Wilbur up with a blind date. Wilbur was to pick the girl up at her apartment at seven o'clock. At 7:19 the girl phoned Oscar and said, "I am going to break every bone in your body!"

You can imagine how astonished I was when I spied Wilbur, one Saturday afternoon, on a bench in Central Park with a girl. He leaped to his feet and hopped up and down in delirium as he introduced me. "Hey! Say! Listen! This in N-Naomi Spredforth!" She was a thin, pleasant waif of a girl, slightly bucktoothed. Her eyes were navy blue. "Naomi comes from Comfort, Texas!" boomed Wilbur, who had never been good at keeping a secret.

"You don't have a Texan accent, Miss Spredforth," I said.

"That," said she, "is because I was only born in Comfort; financial reverses compelled my father to take us to live with his sister Mineola, who lives in Cos Cob, which is a tiny community five miles from Stamford, Connecticut. . . . Do you mind if I tat?" She opened her tote and removed a tiny hand shuttle with a needle stuck in some embryonic lace.

Wilbur suddenly blurted, "Did you know that in Burma, girls born on a Sunday are supposed to marry only boys who were born on a Tuesday?!"

Naomi's mouth stayed open wider than is customary. A knowing expression crept into her eyes. "The Greeks," she lilted, "think Tuesday, not Friday, is the unlucky day of the week."

"*Really?*" gasped Wilbur. "The Burmese drive bamboo stakes into the ground so that their spirits will have a place to sit!"

Naomi laughed as her fingers deftly tatted. "Did you know that there is a tree in Florida called the Gumbo tree—and it can reach a height of *sixty-three* feet?"

They were married three weeks later. And I don't have to see Wilbur anymore.

from my *People I Have Loved, Known or Admired*

See also **Baseball, Heroes of Mine, Scoundrels**

---

*Because a wind sweeps up through the rocky flume below, in the immense cliff that overhangs a gorge in the Blue Ridge Mountains, making a very powerful updraft.

Wills

All the relatives and staff of Gunnar Thorgelsen, the immensely wealthy, eccentric iron magnate, were assembled in the library of the Thorgelsen mansion as Sven Johannes, lawyer, read the Thorgelsen will. "To my dear wife I leave . . . To my beloved daughter I leave . . . To my brother, I bequeath . . . To my faithful housekeeper . . ."

On and on Johannes droned.

"And finally . . ." The lawyer cleared his throat. "To my only nephew, Arvid . . ."

The elegantly dressed wastrel in the back row, trying to conceal his excitement, sat up.

". . . who was so attentive to me during my final illness, who said he considered himself the son I never had, who was always curious about what I would put in my will, and once subtly reminded me not to forget to mention him . . ."

The young man in the back row held his breath.

"Hello there, Arvid."

Old Hamish Currie was on his deathbed in Aberdeen. "Now, Jamie Cameron," he addressed his lawyer, "take out your pencil, mon, and make the followin' changes in the last will an' testament, be it, of Hamish Currie, born and died in Aberdeen. . . . I be buried in the parish yard, nixt to my true beloved wife o' fifty years. . . . T' my oldest boy, David, should go the soom of twenty thousand pounds sterling. To my darlin' daughter Margaret, should go the soom of fifteen thousand pounds sterling. To each o' the twins, Michael and Douglas, should go ten thou—"

"Hold on, Hamish!" interrupted the lawyer. "Are ye hallucinatin' then, mon? Th' entire estate ye be leavin in this worrld cooms to a wee two hundred seven pound. How, by the ghost of Saint Andrew, can ye leave yer loved ones twenty thousand, fifteen thousand, ten—"

" 'Leave' them?" croaked old Currie, propping himself on his elbows. "Nae. Read my words! . . . I want the lazy blighters t' work thair hands to the bone for every ha-penny, the way I did!"

See also **Lawyers**

Wit

No man ever forgets where he buried the hatchet.
"KIN" HUBBARD

Although he was not a good fielder, he was not a good hitter, either.
RING LARDNER

Wagner's music is not as bad as it sounds.
MARK TWAIN

When it comes to giving, some people stop at nothing.
GEORGE JESSEL

"Shut up," he explained.
RING LARDNER

Keeping a secret from his wife is like trying to sneak the dawn past a rooster.

He was so skinny he looked like he'd been pulled through a keyhole.
FRED ALLEN

He looks like a dishonest Abe Lincoln.
WOLCOTT GIBBS (of Harold Ross)

You certainly have a ready wit. Tell me when it's ready.
HENNY YOUNGMAN

Never slap a man in the face if he's chewing tobacco.
ABE MARTIN

There usually is an answer to any problem: simple, clear, and wrong.

H. L. MENCKEN

❧

Sleep faster, we need the pillows.

Out of snow, you can't make cheesecake.

How is it possible that the clod who wasn't good enough to marry your daughter is the father of the smartest grandchild in the world?

The man who marries for money will earn it.

When two divorced people get married, four get into bed.

The longest road in the world is the one that leads from the pocket.

Don't call a man honest just because he never had a chance to steal.

YIDDISH SAYINGS

❧

When Mark Twain started to register in a hotel in Canada, he placed his signature under the entry above it, which read:

Sir Edmund Lee and valet
Mark Twain and valise.

❧

I would rather go to bed with Lillian Russell stark naked than with Ulysses S. Grant in full military regalia!

MARK TWAIN

❧

Statisticians

Men who know that if you put a man's head in a sauna and his feet in a deep freeze, he will feel pretty good—on the average.

❧

The higher a monkey climbs, the more you see of his ass.

GENERAL JOSEPH STILLWELL

Diogenes, 'tis said, went around the known world, holding his bright lamp in his noble quest to find an honest man. When he got to Romania, someone stole the lamp.

Cleanliness is almost as bad as godliness.

SAMUEL BUTLER

When a man brings his wife a gift for no reason, there's a reason.

MOLLY MCGEE

He's a real wolf; he can take one look at a girl and tell what kind of past she's going to have.

Partner, I suppose that you learned how to play bridge only yesterday. But may I ask: what *time* yesterday?"

GEORGE S. KAUFMAN

George Moore, Irish author, was asked on his eightieth birthday what accounted for his long and exceptionally healthy life. "I have thought a good deal about that," said Moore, "and I am convinced that both my age and my health are to be explained by an obvious fact: I never touched a cigarette, a drink, or a girl until I was almost ten years old."

Cornelia Otis Skinner opened in a New York revival of Bernard Shaw's *Candida*. The next morning she received this cable:

EXCELLENT! GREATEST!
SHAW

Bowled over by such superlatives from a notoriously acidulous critic, the actress cabled back:

A MILLION THANKS. BUT UNDESERVING SUCH PRAISE.
CORNELIA OTIS SKINNER

Within two hours came this reply:

> I MEANT THE PLAY.
>   SHAW

To which the incomparable actress responded:

> SO DID I.
>   SKINNER

The massed sunbathers in the chaise-longues area around the pool of the Emerald Isle Hotel in Miami Beach were annoyed by a heated argument from a nearby cabana. One of the sun loungers groaned, "What's all that argument about?"

"*Who* knows? It's like that every single day. The daily battle of wits."

"Wits? *Here?*"

"Certainly. Linkowits, Bronkawitz, Lefkowitz, and Shlumewits."

The difference between truth and fiction is that fiction has to make sense.

MARK TWAIN

See also Cynics' Dictionary, Definitions to Cherish, Graffiti, Groucho, Old Saws Sharpened, Repartée, Retorts, Reviews of Note, Signs, Typos

Women's Lib

At the Amazon Garage, Ms. Maude Crawford, an ardent women's-rights advocate, comes up to a customer's car at a gasoline pump, asking, "Fill him up?"

W. C. Fields, who was a misanthrope no less than a misogynist, was once asked by a matron to address her garden club. As Fields hemmed and hawed, the matron said, "I am *sure* that a man of your wide experience favors clubs for women."

"Indubitably, madam, indubitably," declaimed Fields. "But only if every other form of persuasion fails."

See also **Applications, Birth Control, Hanky-panky, Love, Marriage, Sex**

Wordplay

HAZEL (*reading paper*): What do you think of a man—a father—of seventy-eight getting married again?!

ALICE: I think it's absolutely disgusting! How many children does he expect to have in one lifetime?

❧

When the chambermaid came into the Dublin hotel room, disheveled and carrying a slop bucket, the American tourist said, "Hey, you're pretty dirty!"

"Oh, thank y', sir," replied the maiden. "And I'm aven prettier when I'm clean."

❧

JOHNSON: How's your wife?

SMITH: Compared to what?

❧

BROWN: Is it true that life begins at forty?

WHITE: Begins to what?

❧

Postcard from Jackson Hole, Wyoming

Dear Phil:

We both miss you as much as if you were right here.

❧

On her first trip to London, Mrs. Crowley could hardly wait to go shopping at Yardley's, the world-famous soap emporium. The salesgirl asked, "Madam, do you want it scented or unscented?"

"I'll—uh—take it with me."

❧

An American, riding in the first-class section of the British Railway train, found himself in a compartment with an elderly, tweedy Englishman, and a Welshman who, judging from his large ear trumpet, was very deaf.

The American, to make conversation, said, "I—uh—think we just passed Wembley."

The Englishman shook his head. "Think not, sir. This is Thursday."

"So am I," said the Welshman, pulling a flask out of his pocket. "Let's have a drink."

A panhandler accosted a visitor to New York, a first-time visitor from Missouri.

"Hey, Mac," said the panhandler. "Will you give me a quarter for a sandwich?"

The Missourian studied the panhandler. "Depends."

"Depends?" the panhandler frowned. "Depends on what?"

"First lemme see the sandwich."

The very vain actress shook the latest photograph in the face of the photographer furiously. "This picture is a disgrace, a caricature, a— Leslie, tell me the truth. Do you really think this godawful photograph bears any resemblance to me?"

"Darling," replied Leslie, "the answer is in the negative."

Scene: Atheneum Club, London

"Terrible mess, our young," said Lord Stonehurst.

"Ghastly, my dear Stonehurst, simply ghastly!" said Lord Chadwyn.

"No standards. No morals. Pop into bed with anyone. *I* didn't sleep with my wife until we were married. What about you?"

Lord Chadwyn pondered for a moment, downed some whiskey, then sighed, "Can't remember, old chap. What was her maiden name?"

Scene: Trafalgar Square

"I sy, guv," said the panhandler, "d' ye 'appen t' 'av a bob for a cup o' java?"

"No, I don't. But you need not worry about me. I'll manage, I will. I'll manage."

NOTICE TO ALL EDITORS

From: Bernard Kilgore, chairman.

If I see the word "upcoming" in the *Wall Street Journal* once more, I shall be downcoming, and some copy-checker will be outgoing.

NOTICE TO WRITERS

From: Harold Ross, editor, *The New Yorker*

I am damn annoyed by the careless, cozy way "pretty" and "little" are beginning to pop up all over the magazine!

In the next issue appeared a column by James Thurber, containing:

". . . observers agree that the building is pretty ugly and a little big for its surroundings."

The young couple stood in front of the finest jewelry store in Dublin. Teresa greedily studied the window and snuggled up to Liam. "Oh, Liam, luv, do ye not see that little bracelet?"

"Ay."

Teresa pressed his arm harder. "I would *love* a bracelet like that, I would."

Liam was silent.

"Liam, luv," said Teresa. "Did ye not hear me? I said I would greatly love a bracelet like that . . ."

"I heerd you, darlin'," said Liam. "But I was considerin' my reply. For it is incumbent on me to elucidate that exigencies of a recondite nature militate against the acquisition of such an exorbitant artifact."

"Liam, me luv, I don't get it!"

"Exactly," smiled Liam.

Little Lila Griffiths was lost in her homework, when her grandfather said, "An' what be ye readin', me darlin'?"

"It's about how the South changed, grampa, after a man named Whitney invented the cotton gin."

"The *what?!*" astounded grampa asked.

"The cotton gin."

"Faith, an' can ye believe somethin' like that, me girl? That them southerners actually drink *cot*ton?!"

See also **Cynics' Dictionary, Definitions to Cherish, Geography Revised, Groucho, How's That Again?, Repartée, Retorts, Sarcasm, Waiters, Wit**

Yiddish

Yiddish is the Robin Hood of languages. It steals from the linguistically rich to give to the fledgling poor. It shows not the slightest hesitations in taking in houseguests—to whom it gives free room and board regardless of genealogy, faith, or exoticism.

Never in history has Yiddish been so influential—among Gentiles. (Among Jews, alas, the tongue is running dry.) We are clearly witnessing a revolution in values when a Pentagon officer, describing air-bombardment patterns, informs the press: "You might call it the bagel strategy." Or when the London *Economist* captions a fuss over mortgage rates: *Home Loan Hooha.* Or when the *Wall Street Journal* headlines a feature on student movements: *"Revolution, Shmevolution."* Or when England's illustrious *Times Literary Supplement,* discussing the modern novel, interjects this startling sentence: "Should, schmould, shouldn't, schmouldn't."

My earliest awareness of the marvelous resilience of my mother tongue came when I was quite young. An old woman, bowed under the weight of shopping bags, stopped me:

"Yinger mon, ir farshteyt Yiddish?" ("Young man, do you understand Yiddish?")

"Yaw," I answered.

"Vat time is it?"

Words and phrases are not the chief "invasionary" forces Yiddish has sent into the hallowed terrain of English. Much more significant, I think, is the adoption by English of Yiddish linguistic *devices:*

1. Blithe dismissal via repetition with an *sh* play-on-the-first-sound: "Fat-shmat, as long as she's happy."
2. Mordant syntax: "Smart, he isn't."
3. Sarcasm via innocuous diction: "He only tried to shoot himself."
4. Scorn through reversed word order: "Already you're discouraged?"
5. Contempt via affirmation: "My *son*-in-law he wants to be."
6. Fearful curses sanctioned by nominal cancellation: "A fire should burn in his heart, God forbid!"
7. Politeness expedited by truncated verbs and eliminated prepositions: "You want a cup coffee?"
8. Derisive dismissal disguised as innocent interrogation: "I should *pay* him for such devoted service?"
9. The use of a question to answer a question to which the answer is so self-evident that the use of the first question (by you) constitutes an

affront (to me) best erased either by (a) repeating the original question or (b) retorting with a question of comparably asinine self-answeringness.

Or consider the Ashkenazic panoply in which insult and innuendo may be arrayed. Problem: Whether to attend a concert to be given by a neighbor, niece, or friend of your wife. The same sentence may be put through maneuvers of matchless versatility:

1. "*Two* tickets for her concert I should buy?" (Meaning: "I'm having enough trouble deciding if it's worth one.")
2. "Two *tickets* for her concert I should buy?" ("You mean to say she isn't distributing free passes? The hall will be empty!")
3. "Two tickets for *her* concert I should buy?" ("Did she buy tickets to *my* daughter's recital?")
4. "Two tickets for her *concert* I should buy?" ("You mean to say they call her screeching a 'concert'?!")
5. "Two tickets for her concert *I* should buy?" ("After what she did to me?")
6. "Two tickets for her concert I *should* buy?" ("Are you giving me lessons in ethics?")
7. "Two tickets for her concert I should *buy?*" ("I wouldn't go even if she gave me a complimentary!")

Who has not heard or used phrases such as the following, which are literal translations from the Yiddish:

Get lost.	He's a regular genius.
You should live so long.	Go hit your head against the wall.
My son, the physicist.	You want it should sing, too?
I need it like a hole in the head.	Plain talk: He's crazy.
Who *needs* it?	Excuse the expression.
So why do you?	With sense, he's loaded.
Al*right* already.	Go fight City Hall.
It shouldn't happen to a dog.	I should have such luck.
O.K. by me.	It's a *nothing* of a dress.
He knows from nothing.	You should live to a hundred and twenty.
From that he makes a *living*?	On *him* it looks good.
How come only five?	It's time, it's time.
Do him something.	Wear it in good health.
This I need yet?	Listen, *bubele* . . .?
A person could bust.	

What other language is fraught with such exuberant fraughtage?

from my *Joys of Yiddish*

See also **Accents, The English Language, Israel, Jews, Yinglish**

Yinglish

Accusing someone of asininity by echoing a question
The true *maven* of Yinglish knows the sweet uses of scorn:

Q. Don't you want to meet a wonderful boy, get married, and have a fine family?

A. No, I don't want to meet a wonderful boy, get married, and have a fine family. (Meaning: "How stupid can you be to ask such an idiotic question?")

Accusing someone of idiocy by denying the obvious
This deadpan ploy is typical of Jewish sarcasm:

Q. How would you like an all-expense-paid trip to Hawaii?

A. I prefer to spend the winter in a foxhole in the Bronx. (Meaning: "How can you even *ask* such a stupid question?")

Affirming indignation by repeating a question in the form in which it was asked, with varying intonational emphasis
This is a favored ploy in Yiddish, and a major contribution to the scornful persiflage of Yinglish. Note the dramatic effect achieved by the shift of stress, *seriatim:*

1.
Q. Did you send your mother flowers on her birthday?

A. *Did* I send my mother flowers on her birthday? (Meaning: "Are you implying that I could forget an important occasion like that?")

2.
Q. Did you send your mother flowers on her birthday?

A. Did *I* send my mother flowers on her birthday? (Meaning: "What kind of monster do you think I am—not to send my mother flowers on her birthday?")

3.

Q. *Did you send your mother flowers on her birthday?*

A. Did I *send* my mother flowers on her birthday? (Meaning: "And suppose I didn't send them? Suppose I brought them in person? Is that a crime?")

4.

Q. *Did you send your mother flowers on her birthday?*

A. Did I send *my* mother flowers on her birthday? (Meaning: "Have you forgotten that I sent *your* mother flowers on her birthday? If I sent flowers to your mother would I forget to send flowers to mine?")

5.

Q. *Did you send your mother flowers on her birthday?*

A. Did I send my *mother* flowers on her birthday? (Meaning: "You know that I always send flowers on their birthdays to my wife, my sister, my aunt, my cousins in New Jersey, so are you implying that I am the kind of *paskudnyak* who would send flowers to them and not to my own *mother?*")

6.

Q. *Did you send your mother flowers on her birthday?*

A. Did I send my mother *flowers* on her birthday? (Meaning: "Flowers were just the *beginning* of what I gave my mother on her birthday!" which suggests anything from a round-trip ticket to Israel to a condominium in West Palm Beach.)

7.

Q. *Did you send your mother flowers on her birthday?*

A. Did I send my mother flowers on *her* birthday? (Meaning: "If I always send my mother flowers on *my* birthday, what kind of *grubyan* would I be not to send her flowers on hers?")

8.

Q. *Did you send your mother flowers on her birthday?*

A. Did I send my mother flowers on her *birthday?* (Meaning: "Flowers you don't have to send your mother on New Year's or the Fourth of July—but on her *birthday?!*")

᠎

Alright already

From Yiddish: *genug shoyn*
1. Enough!
2. Say no more, for God's sake!
3. Will you please shut up?
4. I can't *stand* any more!

"Alright already," a thriving export from the Bronx, is, to be exact, a version of "Enough already!" And in that context "Alright already!" signifies exasperated agreement:

5. Okay, okay, just stop nagging me!
6. You win: save your voice.
7. I give up: you shut up.

Big deal!

> This withering dismissal comes right from Yiddish: *A groyser kunst!* ("Some big art!") or the sarcastic *Khokhma!* with the accent on the *ma* ("Stroke of genius!").

I can hear the auditorium ring with objections: " 'Big deal' is English!" and "What is Jewish about 'Big deal'?" So I'll tell you what's Jewish about "Big deal." The phrase is sarcastic. The mood is derisive. The phrase is not descriptive, but deflative. It is uttered with emphasis on the "big," in a dry, disenchanted tone.

In such usage (as against, say, "He signed a big deal today"), the exclamation was launched in the 1940s (see Wentworth and Flexner, *The Dictionary of American Slang*). It swiftly gained popularity as a blasé retort among the young, especially on our high school and college campuses:

"He made the Ping-Pong team!"
"Big deal."

Cockamamy

1. Confused, mixed up.
2. Implausible, ludicrous.
3. Farfetched, offensive to credulity.
4. Imitation; fraudulent.
5. Cheap, not worth much.
6. (As an epithet) Silly! Absurd!

The number of definitions suggests the utility of this admirable concoction, a linguistic gem from the Lower East Side, cherished in Brooklyn, pampered in the Bronx, and now indispensable to the argot of urban life. I, for one, have found no pejorative synonym so pungent.

7. Decalcomanias: dye pictures transferred to the back of the hand, after wetting, rubbing, and peeling off the paper.

The slang coinage seems inevitable: How many children on Broome Street or Flatbush Avenue could pronounce, much less spell, the forbidding "decalcomania"? True, the word became shortened to "decal," but can "decal" hold a candle to *cockamamy?* Never.

Contempt via reiteration, plus the scathing "sh—" gambit

"Who says she's not clean? Clean-shmean, let her shave off her mustache."

"Honest-shmonest, he sings like a frog."

"Nice-shmice, did they give a penny to charity?"

Could be

From Yiddish: *Es ken zayn*, pronounced *'s ken zyn*.

1. It may be; it may come to pass.
2. But maybe not.
3. Time will tell.
4. Anything is possible.
5. Wait and see.
6. *Who* knows?

The following illustrate the denotations numbered in the definition above.

1.

A: Darwin said that man is descended from animals.
B: Could be.

2.

A: Do you think Pfaumbach is telling the truth?
B: Could be.
A: You don't sound confident.
B: I'm not.

3.

A: I wonder if Schultz will pay that bill.
B: Could be. . . . How long do you expect to live?

4.

A: Will Dora really marry a man forty years older?
B: Could be.
A: It's hard to believe.
B: With *Dora?*

5.

A: I don't think Mishkin will have the *nerve* to show up. What do you think?
B: Could be.
A: Could be what: Yes or no?
B: Neither.

6.

A: You think *she* was the one who tipped off the police?
B: Could be.

A: Or do you think *he* did?
B: Also, could be.
A: You certainly like to straddle the fence!
B: I know how to say, *Who* knows?

Don't ask!

From Yiddish: *Freg nit* (or *nisht*). "Don't ask *me*" is English; "Don't ask" (or "Dun't esk!") is Yinglish.

1. Things are bad.
2. The answer would be so disheartening I prefer not to give it to you.
3. The answer is obvious.
4. Absolutely!

This laconic imperative contains a symphony of signals:

"Don't ask me to tell you (whatever it was you asked me) because I would rather not even *mouth* the answer."

Or: "Were I to answer your question instead of putting you off with a 'Don't ask!,' it would depress you so much you'd be sorry you inquired!"

Or: "Take a hint: do me a favor; desist."

"How's your wife?"
"Don't ask." (She's in bad shape.)

"It will be the best party of the year! Are you coming?"
"Don't ask." (Absolutely!)

"You look terrible, Joe. How's business?"
"Don't ask!"
"Ah . . . Listen, for this time of year, that's not so bad."

"*Shalom*, Teddy. How's your wife?"
"Still sick."
"And your children?"
"*They*, thank God, are fine."
"And your *gesheft*?"
"I can't complain. Excuse me, Henry, I have to go—"
"Wait a minute. Has it ever occurred to you, Teddy, that in all the years we've known each other, it's always *I* who asks the questions—never you. Have you even *once* asked how I am, how's my Shirley, my job?"
"Migod, Henry, you're right. How thoughtless have I been! From today on—Henry! How are things with you?"
Sighed Henry: "Don't ask."

Fancy-schmancy

100 percent pure Yinglish.

1. Overly ornate.
   "Did you ever see such a fancy-schmancy reception?"
2. Pretentious, affected.
   "That fancy-schmancy Maurice Vermont. I knew him when he was Morris Greenberg."
3. Attempt at style that fails, hence is vulgar.
   "Their decorator is classy, but their furniture is fancy-schmancy."

The employment of the sardonic *schm* must have been among the earliest reduplications adopted by Lower East Side Jews. "Fancy-schmancy" came to the attention of cosmopolitan New York when it appeared in the very popular vaudeville sketches of Potash and Perlmutter, Smith and Dale, *et alia*.

. . . give!

Yinglish.

Slang imperative for:
1. Talk!
2. Tell!
3. Open up!

This colloquial command is familiar to any moviegoer:
   "Who paid you, Lefty? C'mon, *give.*"
   "Who killed her, pal? . . . *Give!*"

Go know . . .

Yinglish. From Yiddish: *Gey vays.*

1. How could I know?
2. How could you *expect* me to know?
3. How could *anyone* know?

This vivid disclaimer shifts blame from one's self to the universe; it is matchless as a stratagem of self-exculpation: "Go know my line was tapped."

Hoo-ha

1. An exclamatory flourish that accentuates sentiments ranging from aspirated admiration to hoarse scorn.
2. A big to-do; confusion, complexity.
   "That was some *hoo-ha* in Times Square!"
   "What was I supposed to do in the middle of such a *hoo-ha?!*"

3. A fuss, "stink," a stir, an issue magnified.
   "Did she make a *hoo-ha* about the service!"
   "I'll give them a *hoo-ha* they'll never forget!"

As an expletive, this immensely versatile declamation serves to express:

1. Admiration: "His new wife? *Hoo-ha!*"
2. Envy: "Is he well off? *Hoo-ha.*"
3. Deflation: "That you call an actor? *Hoo-ha.*"
4. Skepticism: "It's a foolproof deal? *Hoo-ha.*"
5. Astonishment: "He joined the Navy? *Hoo-ha!*"
6. Scorn: "Does she gossip? *Hoo-ha.*"

Do not for a moment think that this sextet exhausts the affective possibilities of this hyphenate. Facial and vocal counterpoint will register other sentiments with distinctive piquancy or dubiety:

7. You can't mean it! ("You'll leave home? *Hoo-ha!*")
8. Imagine! ("He moved to Japan? *Hoo-ha.*")
9. Wow! ("The party? *Hoo-ha!*")
10. Like hell. ("I should donate to his campaign? *Hoo-ha.*")
11. Who do you think you're fooling? ("Do I believe you? Every syllable, *hoo-ha.*")
12. Well, I'll be damned! ("In the chapel, in the middle of the eulogy, she just stood up—*hoo-ha*—and walked out!")
13. I'd like to live long enough to see that! ("He's going to win the Kentucky Derby? *Hoo-ha.*")

DISCIPLE: Master, do you believe that money isn't everything?
SAGE: *Hoo-ha.* It isn't even enough.

. . . know from nothing . . .

From Yiddish: *fun gornisht (gornit)*

> In Yiddish, double negatives are both proper and common: e.g., *Zie hot nit keyn mon* (She has not no man). What I find even more piquant is that in Yiddish one can use a *triple* negative: *Keyner hot nit keyn vort gezugt* (No one had not no word uttered)—which in English would be "No one uttered a word."

"He don't know from nothing" emphasizes meaning by mocking English grammar triply: 1) in using "don't" instead of "doesn't"; 2) in adding the unnecessary "from"; 3) in doubling the negatives.

Look who's talking

Yinglish: analogue of the Yiddish *Kuk nor ver s'ret!* ("Just take a look at who's talking.")

This imperative is not intended to make you direct your eyes to the speaker. It is intended to announce to the world that the speaker is:

1. Utterly unqualified to make the statement.
2. Incompetent, even if qualified.
3. Shamelessly biased in the matter.
4. A well-known liar, not to be trusted in *any* matter.
5. Off his/her rocker.
6. The very person who loused everything up in the first place.
7. The pot calling the kettle black.

DOLLY PARTON: Look at the *bust* on that girl!
ANYONE: Look who's talking.

Nu

nu(?!)
nu-nu

> Rhymes with "do." From Russian: well; so; and German *nu* and *nun.* Cognates of *nu* are common in Indo-European tongues; but in which is *nu* put through such prodigious acrobatics as glorify it in Yiddish?

> A huffy/whimsical emphasizer, qualifier, interjection, sigh, aside, lament, expletive, or comment.

Nu and *oy* are quintessential Yiddish and sturdy Yinglish. These versatile utterances are the sonic equivalents of a moan, a groan, a nod, a sob, a grin, a grunt, a sneer, a complaint. . . . Consider the nuances of this two-lettered arsenal:

1. *"Nu?"* (How are things? What's new?)
2. "Should we go? *Nu?"* (What do *you* say?)
3. *"Nu,* what could I do?" (Well . . .)
4. "I saw her leave your apartment at three A.M. *Nu* . . . ?" (So—o—o? Explain.)
5. "—he ran out! *Nu?"* (Can you beat that?)
6. "Listen, I want the money. *Nu?"* (Will you or won't you pay?)
7. A.: "I'm going to a funeral."
   B.: *"Nu?"* (So what's the hurry?)
8. "They raised the rent again! *Nu."* (Nothing can be done.)
9. "They liked the book. I—*nu?"* (I did not, but I leave it to you to guess why.)
10. "— so buy the damn thing. *Nu?"* (Put an end to the shilly-shallying.)

When used in tandem, *nu* becomes a sentence:

"Can you imagine how I felt? *Nu-nu."* (I know you can, so I'll skip an elaborate description.)

"They argued, they fought—*nu-nu.*" (Why go on?)

"She says you're an animal! *Nu-nu?*" (You've got to respond to that.)

I should warn the unwary that to ask a Jew "*Nu?*" invites the frustrating, even infuriating, reply: "*Nu-nu?*"

Other uses:

1.

"Would you like a Danish?"

"*Nu-nu?*" (Of *course* I want a Danish.)

2.

"Listen, Jerry. The whole building knows . . ."

"*Nu?*" (So what?)

"Don't give me with the '*Nu?*' Jerry! *Nu-nu?*" (Open up. Talk.)

3.

"Hector, are you Jewish?"

"*Nu?* (What else?) Are you, Claude?"

"*Nu-nu?*" (Of course I am.)

Labedz wrote out this wire to Kuznets:

> HOW ABOUT PAYING ME BACK? I LENT
> YOU 200 DOLLARS. ALREADY FOURTEEN
> MONTHS.
>
>   LABEDZ

Labedz reread the message, then struck out the first line, then the second. Then, after scratching his chin, the third. Instead of the whole kit-and-caboodle of words, he wired Kuznets:

> NU?
>
>   LABEDZ

That afternoon he received this reply:

> NU-NU?
>
>   KUZNETS

Oy

Oy is not a word; it is a vocabulary. It is used to express:

1. Simple surprise. "When she saw me, she said, '*Oy*, I didn't expect you!' "
2. Startledness. "She heard a noise and exclaimed, '*Oy!* Who's there?' "
3. Small fear. "*Oy!* It could be a mouse!"
4. Minor sadness (sighed). "When I think of what she went through, all I can say is *o-oy.*" (Note the *oy* prolonged, to indicate how sensitive one is to the troubles of others.)

5. Contentment. "*Oy*, was that a delicious dinner!"
6. Joy. "*Oy*, what a party!"
7. Euphoria. "Was I *happy? Oy!* I was dancing on air!"
8. Relief; reassurance. "*Oy*, now I can sleep."
9. Uncertainty. "What should I do? *Oy*, I wish I knew."
10. Apprehension. "Maybe he's sick? *Oy!*"
11. Awe. "He came back alive yet? *Oy!*"
12. Astonishment. "*Oy gevalt*, how he had changed."
13. Indignation. "Take it away from me. *Oy!*"
14. Irritation. "*Oy*, is that some *metsieh!*"
15. Irony. "*Oy*, have you got the wrong party!"
16. Pain (moderate). "*Oy*, it hurts."
17. Pain (serious). "*Oy, Gottenyu!*"
18. Revulsion. "*Feh!* Who could eat that? *O-oy!*"
19. Anguish. "I beg you, *tell* me! *Oy!*"
20. Dismay. "*Oy*, I gained ten pounds!"
21. Despair. "It's hopeless, I tell you! *Oy!*"
22. Regret. "*Him* we have to invite? *Oy!*"
23. Lamentation. "*Oy*, we cried our eyes out."
24. Shock. "What? Her? Here? *Oy!*"
25. Outrage. "That man will never set foot in this house so long as I live. *Oy!*"
26. Horror. "—married a dwarf? *Oy gevalt!*"
27. Stupefaction. "My own partner . . . *o-o-oy*."
28. Flabbergastation. "Who ever *heard* such a thing? *Oy!* I could *plotz!*"
29. At-the-end-of-one's-wittedness, or I-can't-*stand*-anymore. "Get out! Leave me alone! *O-O-O-o-o-oy!*"

Mrs. Fishbein's phone rang.

"Hul-lo," a cultivated voice intoned, "I'm telephoning to ask whether you and your husband can come to a tea for Lady Windermere—"

"*Oy*," cut in Mrs. Fishbein, "have *you* got a wrong number!"

Repetition—to escape the obvious and maximize persuasiveness

"I'm going, I'm going."
"I know, I know." (Usually "I know, I *know*.")
"You'll like it, you'll *like* it."

This kind of repetition is a staple of Jewish communication and illustrates the propensity of Yiddish to employ irony for the banishment of the banal. The difference between "You'll like it" and "You'll like it, you'll *like* it" is as monumental as the difference between "I don't know," which is bloodlessly phatic, and "I don't know, I don't *know!*" which is a defiant assertion of ignorance.

Sarcasm via the use of innocent adjectives/adverbs in malefic contexts

"She wasn't depressed: she merely tried to hang herself."

"He knocked out only four of my teeth."

"I doubt that he ate more than fifteen sandwiches."

"Was that much to ask: ten million dollars?"

Shmegegge

Rhymes with "the Peggy." Derivation: unknown (alas).

1. A drip, a *shlepper*, a jerk.
2. A clumsy *klutz*.
3. A sycophant.

This admirable, disdainful neologism, an epithet for a class of human nerds, is a gem in the coronet of Yinglish. It won my heart when I first heard it in New York. I had never heard *shmegegge* in the Jewish enclaves of Chicago, Washington, or Los Angeles. I have never been able to find so much as a hint of a spoor of its origin.

There's no one here to talk to

Hyperbole from Yiddish: *Nito tsu vemen tsu reydn!*

1. It's useless for me to talk; you refuse to listen.
2. You are not *capable* of understanding!
3. You are too stubborn, too prejudiced to listen, so why waste my breath trying to reason with you?

The words are English and the syntax ordinary: What then makes the content Yinglish? The rhetorical murder of everyone except the aggrieved speaker.

What's with . . .?

From Yiddish: *Vos iz mit . . .?*

1. What's wrong with . . .?
2. Please explain that.
3. Why are you (he, she) acting this way?

The proper English phrasing would be "What's the matter with . . .?" or "What's wrong with . . .?" or "What's bothering . . .?" The syntax of "What's with . . .?" is distinctly Yiddish; its popularity in American and British slang has made it Yinglish.

Who knows?

From Yiddish: *Ver veyst?*

1.   I don't know.
2.   Maybe someone, somewhere, knows the answer, but I doubt it.
3.   You may search the whole world for an answer to that queston but—believe me!—there is none.

Any language contains the neutral interrogation "Who knows?" But as rendered in Yinglish (*"Who* knows?" or, with umbrage, "Who *knows?"*), the phrase is not interrogatory; it is declarative. It is also accusatory ("Why do you ask me for an answer to a question that is clearly unanswerable?"), or sarcastic ("What a dope you are to think I can answer something like that!"), or philosophical ("Beware the surface innocence of the question; to answer is to risk entrapment in epistemology").

The ironic ploy of "Who knows?" may be transferred to any number of pseudointerrogative asseverations: "Who *cares?"* "Who could?" "Who should?"

4.   It's Greek to me.

. . . you should excuse (the expression; me; my frankness)

From Yiddish: *Zolst mir antshuldigen:* You should excuse me. Please excuse . . .

This genteelism, long a feature of New Yorkese, takes on a satirical note in conversation among the sophisticated:

"He is a Good Humor (you should excuse the expression) salesman."

Intramural aspersions are more easily expressed in this barbarism than in naked disdain:

"Professor Montzer is a (excuse the expression) Keynesian."

"Professor Tunkel is a (pardon the expression) monetarist."

"He wants to play rock-and-roll (excuse the expression) music."

from my *Hooray for Yiddish*

See also Accents, The English Language, Israel, Jews, Yiddish

Postscript
How Not to Tell a Joke

A friend has asked me if I can teach "the ordinary reader" how to tell a joke. It is much easier to tell a reader what *not* to do.

1. Don't begin by saying, "I may botch this up" or "I'm not good at telling jokes." A prefatory warning of incompetence invites your listeners to be on the alert as to exactly how and where you will fulfill your prophecy.

2. Don't begin with "Do you want to hear the funniest, most *hilarious* joke I've ever heard in my whole life?!" or "This is going to have you rolling in the aisles!" or even "I thought I would *die* laughing!" Such hyperbole challenges disagreement, framed in such unspoken retorts as "The hell it is" or "Like hell I will."

3. Never start with "This man," "This nurse," or even "This undertaker." Since "this" requires prior identification, you may be well into your joke while your audience is still preoccupied with wondering "*Which* man?" or "Why an undertaker?" They will surely miss part of your narration while groping for a clue or an answer.

4. As you talk, look directly into your listener's/listeners' eyes—not at your napkin, his/her ear, or the birdcage in the corner.

5. Act as if you *enjoy* telling the joke, which suggests you know how to do it.

6. Smile, grin, chuckle (in moderation); this cues your audience into doing likewise.

7. Don't hem, haw, clear your throat or honk your sinuses—unless it is to mimic the conduct of a character in your joke. Mimicry is marvelously effective, if you have a talent for it; if not, don't try it. Poor mimicry induces wincing.

8. The same is true of dialect. It is superb, if delivered with mastery. But such skill is rare—even among professional comedians. Do not use dialect unless you have a faultless ear, an acute larynx, and a sensitive sense of the tremulous line between the affectionate and the derisive. You would be surprised by how many Jews are sensitive to "Yid" accents, how many Italians resent imitations of the superabundant vowels that attend their presumptive solecisms, how many Poles, Greeks, or Germans ("Chermans") think it condescending for anyone to imitate their particular articulations.

9. Do not digress. Stick to the central narrative thrust. Focus full attention on the story. Intrusions such as "Incidentally, my husband and I visited that part of Louisiana five—maybe six—years ago and we *loved* it!" or "That reminds me, be sure to ask me for the name of a great restaurant we discovered in Acapulco last year."

10. Do not introduce irrelevant details. If the breed of dog is not essential to the joke, do not give it. If the height, weight, posture, or pockmarks of a character do not tie directly into the crucial "payoff," do not introduce such distractions.

11. Be very careful of your choice of verbs. It raises the hackles of your audience to be told " 'Certainly!' he demurred." Or " 'It's a mile farther,' she told." Or even " 'Drop that child or I'll blow your brains out!' the parson hinted."

12. When what is spoken is plain, do not deploy the overly energetic: " 'I'm not at all certain that the doctor meant me to tell you this,' he shouted at the top of his lungs."

13. Conversely, when vigorous action is described, do not undermine it with coy attempts at subtlety: "He kicked the wrestler in the face and then in the groin, explaining, 'And those are for Aunt Matilda.' " Or, " 'I will not stand by and see an old lady tied up, strapped to a wheel, and tortured!' the sheriff admitted."

14. If you are unsure of your command of an audience, choose brevity over length. Patience is never exhausted by swift narration. The shorter the yarn, the less opportunity for irritating padding or unintended boo-boos. A sparse wit is better than a fat bore.

15. At all costs, deliver the final, climactic line without a smidgeon of uncertainty—no fumbling or floundering or lame self-correction. The wording of a punch line (which includes its rhythm, pace, pauses, emphasis) is the final and decisive factor in inducing laughter.

Let me illustrate these points (themselves worth the price of this volume) with a *miserably* executed joke:

God, Jack! I heard the most hil*ario*us joke last week—no, it was the week before—at the party Joe and Sue Nifkin (you know Joe, don't you?) gave to celebrate their tenth wedding anniversary. What a *bash* that was! At least forty, maybe fifty people—and did we get loaded! . . . Anyway, here goes—and I hope I get it right, because telling jokes is not exactly my dish. . . . Anyway, there was this big, big husky man—he could maybe be a Wall Street banker or the chairman of IBM, which is the largest and most profitable corporation in the world, comes out of a fancy hotel—like, say, the Ritz in Paris. (There isn't a Ritz in New York, is there? No.) Let's see, where was I? Oh, yes, this big, husky man comes out of a fancy hotel, let's say the Regency in New York, or—yes!—Claridge's in London!

Well, the doorman, who is Irish to the core, naturally tips his hat—I mean, touches the visor, you know the cap of his uniform, politely—and asks, "Begorrah, mon, an' kin I be helpin' ye?"

The big, husky man, who is a German or Austrian from Berlin, I guess, replies,"*Ach*, I belief you *can* help me, doorman."

"How, sir? Jist ye say the worrd and it's as good as doon."

So the big, husky man (he's not wearing a hat, by the way) says, "Vell, yust call me a taxi."

So the Irish doorman does a "take," I guess they call it in movie lingo—you know, he looks like he ate a green apple and is wondering about the consequences—so, as I was saying, the doorman says, "Okey-dokey, gov-'nor." Then he straightens up—like this, see, bracing his shoulders—and hollers, "You are a taxi!"

> (*Reluctant note:* The entire joke should go:
> "Doorman, call me a cab."
> "Yes, sir. You're a cab.")

Bye now.

ABOUT THE AUTHOR

LEO ROSTEN is a writer of extraordinary versatility and range. Evelyn Waugh once said, "He has as true and inventive an ear as there is in the English-speaking world."

When the University of Chicago honored him with its Alumni Distinguished Achievement Award, the citation read: "Leo Rosten has made an uncommon impact on our times. His *Hollywood* and *The Washington Correspondents* are classics of social science. His creation H*Y*M*A*N K*A*P*L*A*N gave a new dimension to American humor. . . . *Captain Newman, M. D.* and *The Joys of Yiddish* will stand among the best books of our generation. . . . His career exemplifies a keen appreciation of intellectual life, a passion for scholarship, and a rare gift for writing with humor, elegance, and substance."

Mr. Rosten is a Ph.D. from the University of Chicago, an Honorary Fellow of the London School of Economics and Political Science, and has received honorary degrees from the University of Rochester and Hebrew Union College. His name has often appeared on the movie screen.

The Giant Book of Laughter is his thirty-third book.